Rediscovering Aesthetics

Rediscovering Aesthetics

Transdisciplinary Voices from Art History,
Philosophy, and Art Practice

Edited by Francis Halsall, Julia Jansen,
and Tony O'Connor

Stanford University Press
Stanford, California

Stanford University Press
Stanford, California

"The Future of Aesthetics" © 2007 by Arthur Danto. Reprinted with permission by Georges Borchardt, Inc., for the author.

"Intuition and Concrete Particularity in Kant's Transcendental Aesthetic" by Adrian Piper is published with permission of the author.

"The Stones of Solace" by Michael Ann Holly was first published in *The Coral Mind*, ed. Stephen Bann © 2007 by the Pennsylvania State University Press.

Publication assistance for this volume was provided by the College of Arts, Celtic Studies, and Social Sciences at University College Cork.

Printed in the United States of America on acid-free, archival-quality paper.

Library of Congress Cataloging-in-Publication Data

Rediscovering aesthetics : transdisciplinary voices from art history, philosophy, and art practice / edited by Francis Halsall, Julia Jansen, and Tony O'Connor.
    p. cm.
    Includes bibliographical references and index.
    ISBN 978-0-8047-5990-8 (cloth : alk. paper)—ISBN 978-0-8047-5991-5 (pbk. : alk. paper)
    1. Aesthetics.   2. Art—Philosophy.   3. Art, Modern.   I. Halsall, Francis.   II. Jansen, Julia (Julia Alejandra), 1973–   III. O'Connor, Tony, 1943–
    N66.R44 2009
    111'.85—dc22   2008025758

Typeset by Westchester Book Group in 11/13.5 Adobe Garmond regular

Contents

Contributors

CLAIRE BISHOP is Associate Professor at CUNY Graduate Center, New York, and Visiting Professor at the Royal College of Art, London. She is a regular contributor to *Artforum* and is the author of *Installation Art: A Critical History* (2005) and *Participation* (2006). She is currently writing a book on the politics of spectatorship in socially engaged art.

DIARMUID COSTELLO is Associate Professor of Philosophy at the University of Warwick and Co-Director of a three-year AHRC research project on "Aesthetics after Photography." He has published widely on the aesthetics and art theory of Kant, Wittgenstein, Benjamin, Heidegger, Cavell, Greenberg, Fried, de Duve, Danto, and Lyotard in *Critical Inquiry, The British Journal of Aesthetics, Journal of Aesthetics* and *Art Criticism, Rivista di Estetica and Angelaki*, among others. He is the co-editor of *Art: Key Contemporary Thinkers* and *The Life and Death of Images: Ethics and Aesthetics*.

PAUL CROWTHER is Professor of Art and Philosophy at the International University Bremen. His major publications include *Philosophy after Postmodernism: Civilized Values and the Scope of Knowledge* (2003), *The Transhistorical Image: Philosophizing Art and Its History* (2002), *The Language of Twentieth-Century Art: A Conceptual History* (1997), *Art and Embodiment: From Aesthetics to Self-Consciousness* (1993), and *Critical Aesthetics and Postmodernism* (1993).

ARTHUR C. DANTO is Emeritus Professor of Philosophy at Columbia University and an art critic for the *Nation*. His books include *Nietzsche as Philosopher* (2005), *The Abuse of Beauty* (2003), *Mysticism and Morality*

(1972), *The Transfiguration of the Commonplace* (1981), *Narration and Knowledge* (1985), *Connections to the World: The Basic Concepts of Philosophy* (1989), and *Encounters and Reflections: Art in the Historical Present* (1990).

NICHOLAS DAVEY is Professor of Philosophy at the University of Dundee and President of the British Society for Phenomenology. His principle teaching and research interests are in aesthetics and hermeneutics. He has published widely in the fields of continental philosophy, aesthetics, and hermeneutic theory. His most recent book is *Unquiet Understanding: Reflections of Gadamer's Hermeneutics* (2006). He is also completing *Seeing Otherwise: Gadamer, Aesthetics, and Hermeneutics* (forthcoming).

THIERRY DE DUVE is Professor of Art History at the University of Lille 3. His books include *Pictorial Nominalism: On Marcel Duchamp's Passage from Painting to the Readymade* (1991) and *Kant After Duchamp* (1996). He curated *Voici—100 Ans d'art contemporain* at the Brussels Palais de Beaux-Arts in 2000 (in English as *Look! One Hundred Years of Contemporary Art*, 2001) and the Belgian pavilion at the 2003 Venice Biennale. At the moment he is preparing a book titled *Archéologie du Modernisme en Peinture* and a collection of essays on aesthetics.

JAMES ELKINS holds the E. C. Chadbourne Chair in the School of the Art Institute of Chicago. His recent books include *Visual Studies: A Skeptical Introduction* (2003), *On The Strange Place of Religion in Contemporary Art* (2004), and *What Happened to Art Criticism* (2003). He has edited a number of collections in art history and theory, such as *Visual Literacy* (2007), *Is Art History Global?* (2006), and *Master Narratives and Their Discontents* (2005).

FRANCIS HALSALL is Lecturer in history and theory of modern and contemporary art at the National College of Art and Design, Dublin. His monograph, *Systems of Art* (2008), focuses on systems-theoretical approaches (such as Niklas Luhmann's) to art. Recent articles include "No Medium—Just a Shell: How Works of Art Configure Their Mediums" (2006), "Art History versus Aesthetics?" (2005), "What Does Visual Culture Studies Want?" (2006), "Niklas Luhmann" (2007), and "Chaos and Fractals and the Pedagogical Challenge of Jackson Pollock's 'All Over' Paintings" (2008).

MICHAEL ANN HOLLY is Director of Research and Academic Programs at the Clark Art Institute. A cofounder of the Visual and Cultural Studies Graduate Program at the University of Rochester, she was also chair of the Art History Department there for thirteen years. She has also been codirector of two National Endowment for the Humanities and two Getty summer seminars on similar subjects for humanities faculty. Her books include *Art History, Aesthetics, Visual Studies* ed. with Keith Moxey (2002), *The Subjects of Art History: Historical Objects in Contemporary Perspective* ed. with Mark Cheetham and Keith Moxey (1998), *Past Looking: Historical Imagination and the Rhetoric of the Image* (1996), *Visual Theory: Painting and Interpretation* ed. with Norman Bryson and Keith Moxey (1990), *Visual Culture: Images and Interpretations* ed. with Norman Bryson and Keith Moxey (1994), and *Panofsky and the Foundations of Art History* (1984).

JULIA JANSEN lectures in philosophy at University College Cork, Ireland. Her current research explores the intersections of Kant's theoretical philosophy, Husserlian phenomenology, aesthetics, and cognitive science. Her recent publications include "Imagination in Phenomenology and Interdisciplinary Research" (2008), "Schnittstelle und Brennpunkt: Das ästhetische Erlebnis" (2006), and "Husserl's First Philosophy of Phantasy" (2005). Currently she is finishing a monograph on imagination and transcendental philosophy in Kant and Husserl.

MICHAEL KELLY is Chair of the Philosophy Department at the University of North Carolina at Charlotte. Former Executive Director of the American Philosophical Association and managing editor of the *Journal of Philosophy* (Columbia University), he is the author of *Iconoclasm in Aesthetics* (2003) and editor of the *Encyclopaedia of Aesthetics* (1998). Before moving to Charlotte in 2005, he also taught philosophy and art history at the University of Delaware. His current work is on art and aesthetics in the 1960s.

ROBERT MORRIS has been said to be the leading voice of his generation. In the early 1960s he was a central figure in experimental dance theater in New York and made a conceptual series of works influenced by Marcel Duchamp. In the mid- to late 1960s he was a leading exponent of minimalist sculpture. He was included in the following exhibitions: *Documenta 4, 6,* and *8* at Kassel (1968, 1977, 1987), *Information* at the Museum of Modern Art, New York (1970), and the Venice Biennale (1980). Solo shows include Green Gallery, New York (1963), Tate Gallery, London (1971), and Solomon R. Guggenheim Museum, New York (1994).

TONY O'CONNOR lectures in philosophy at University College Cork, Ireland. His current research interests lie in the connections among philosophy, politics, culture, and the arts. His recent publications include

"Rereading Merleau-Ponty" (with D. Davis, 2007), "Post-Politics: Contingency and Genealogy" (2004), and "Human Agency and Social Sciences: From Contextual Phenomenology to Genealogy" (2002).

PETER OSBORNE is Professor of Modern European Philosophy and Director of the Centre for Research in Modern European Philosophy, Middlesex University, London. He is an editor of the journal *Radical Philosophy* and author of *The Politics of Time: Modernity and Avant-Garde* (1995), *Philosophy in Cultural Theory* (2000), *Conceptual Art* (2002), and *How to Read Marx* (2005). He has edited several collections, including *Rethinking Art: Beyond Traditional Aesthetics* (coeditor, 1991), *From an Aesthetic Point of View: Art, Philosophy and the Senses* (2001), and *Walter Benjamin: Critical Evaluations in Cultural Theory* (2005). He has contributed to numerous journals, including *Art History, October,* and *Oxford Art Journal.*

ADRIAN PIPER is a Professor of Philosophy at Wellesley College, where she teaches courses in modern philosophy and contemporary ethical and political theory. She is also a conceptual artist whose work, in a variety of media, has focused on racism, racial stereotyping, and xenophobia for nearly three decades. Trained at the School of Visual Arts in New York City, she is the recipient of Guggenheim, Awards in the Visual Arts, Personal Chronology, and numerous National Endowment for the Arts fellowships and of the Skowhegan Medal for Sculptural Installation. She has exhibited at the Museum of Modern Art, the Hirshhorn Museum, the Gallery of New South Wales in Sydney, Australia, the Musee d'Art Moderne de Ville de Paris, the Fukyui Fine Arts Museum in Japan, the Museum of Contemporary Art at the Finnish National Gallery in Helsinki, Finland, the John Weber Gallery in New York, Galleria Emi Fontana in Milan, and the Thomas Erben Gallery in New York. She was recently elected as a Distinguished Scholar at the Getty Research Institute for Art History and the Humanities. Since 2001 several major retrospectives of her work were shown in the United States and Europe. Her principle publications are in metaethics, Kant, and the history of ethics. A completed two-volume work, *Rationality and the Structure of the Self,* is forthcoming.

DAVID RASKIN is Associate Professor in the Department of Art History, Theory, and Criticism at the School of the Art Institute of Chicago. His publications include "Flat" (2005), "Spare Me" (2005), "Donald Judd's Moral Art" (2004), and "Specific Opposition: Judd's Art and Politics" (2001).

CAROLEE SCHNEEMANN is a multidisciplinary artist who transformed the artistic discourse on the body, sexuality, and gender. Her painting, photography, performance art, and installation works have been shown at the Los Angeles Museum of Contemporary Art, Whitney Museum of American Art, Museum of Modern Art, New York, Centre Georges Pompidou, Paris, and most recently in a retrospective at the New Museum of Contemporary Art in New York entitled "Up To And Including Her Limits." Film and video retrospectives have been shown at the Centre Georges Pompidou, Paris, Museum of Modern Art, New York, National Film Theatre, London, Whitney Museum, New York, San Francisco Cinematheque, and Anthology Film Archives, New York. Her books include *Cezanne, She Was A Great Painter* (1976), *Early and Recent Work* (1983), and *More Than Meat Joy: Performance Works and Selected Writings* (1979, 1997). Forthcoming publications include *Imaging Her Erotics.* A selection of her letters, edited by Kristine Stiles, is also forthcoming.

RICHARD SHIFF holds the Effie Marie Cain Regents Chair in Art and directs the Center for the Study of Modernism at the University of Texas at Austin. His scholarly interests range broadly across the field of modern art from the early nineteenth century to the present, with emphasis on French painting and postwar American and European art. He has been particularly involved with theory and criticism. His publications include *Cezanne and the End of Impressionism* (1984), *Critical Terms for Art History* (1996, 2003), *Barnett Newman: A Catalogue Raisonné* (2004), and numerous studies of critical and methodological issues. Recent essays have focused on Georges Seurat, Pablo Picasso, Robert Mangold, Donald Judd, Chuck Close, Bridget Riley, Georg Baselitz, and Terry Winters, among others. He is now at work on three book projects: an interpretive account of Willem de Kooning, a study of the tension between practicing art and practicing criticism, and a collection of his earlier essays.

WOLFGANG WELSCH is Professor for Philosophy at the Friedrich Schiller Universität Jena, Germany. He has been a visiting professor at Stanford University, Emory University, and Humboldt Universität Berlin. In 1992 he received the highly acclaimed Max Planck Research Prize. He has published widely in the areas of aesthetics, Hegel, Aristotle, and epistemology, with particular consideration of theories of reason and rationality beyond anthropocentrism. Among his many books are *Undoing Aesthetics (1997)*, Grenzgänge der Ästhetik *(1996)*, Vernunft. Die zeitgenössische Vernunftkritik und das Konzept der transversalen Vernunft

(1995, 2000), *La terra e l'opera d'arte. Heidegger e il Crepusculo di Mi-chelangelo* (1991), *Ästhetisches Denken* (1990, 2003), *and* Aisthesis. *Grundzüge und Perspektiven der Aristotelischen Sinneslehre* (1987).

RICHARD WOODFIELD is Emeritus School Research Professor in Art and Design at Nottingham Trent University, and the first Vice President of the International Association of Aesthetics. He was previously the head of art history and cultural studies in the School of Art and Design and his most recent teaching focused on the history and theory of the photographic image. He has been the editor of *Point*, the research journal for art and design in higher education, and the *Journal of Visual Art Practice*, which focuses on fine art in higher education. He is currently the guardian of the *International Association of Aesthetics Yearbook*. He has edited Gombrich's *Reflections on the History of Art* (1987), *The Essential Gombrich* (1996), and *Ernst Gombrich, Dal mio tempo: Città, maestri, incontri* (1999). He has published *Art History as Cultural History: Warburg's Projects* and *Framing Formalism: Riegl's Work,* both in the series *Critical Voices* (2000). He is currently working on the Vienna school of art history in the context of its contemporary philosophy and psychology.

(Re)Discovering Aesthetics
An Introduction

Francis Halsall, Julia Jansen, and Tony O'Connor

TWENTY-FIRST CENTURY DISCOURSES in art history, philosophy of art, and art practice have inherited a long tradition of aesthetics, as well as of the many important challenges that have been brought against this tradition. Increasingly, however, contemporary art historians, philosophers, artists, and curators acknowledge the limitations of traditional aesthetics while renegotiating the continuing and fundamental importance of aesthetic questions. Their work is not just a continuation of traditional aesthetics but, in effect, a "rediscovery" of aesthetics. With this rediscovery comes a growing awareness of the cross-disciplinary[1] nature of aesthetics and, therefore, of the interconnectedness of art history, philosophy, and art practice. This book brings together important international voices from these three fields that rearticulate traditional aesthetical positions with a view to developing an aesthetics that can respond to contemporary issues and circumstances.

This book shows that recognition of pernicious theoretical and practical limitations of traditional aesthetics does not necessitate the elimination of aesthetics tout court. Instead it brings about its "rediscovery" in a way that breaks sharply with older models. This rediscovery of aesthetics drives a complex but dynamic and valuable set of discourses and debates exploring the material character, theoretical influences, and, increasingly, political contexts of artworks and their explanations.

In this regard, many of the essays in this volume are reactive: against formalism, against the sovereignty and autonomy of the traditional view of aesthetic judgment, and against context-free universalist approaches to

1

questions of validity and truth in aesthetics. They are not, however, only reactive, because many of them actively seek to determine the conditions and implications of aesthetic identifications and explanations of artworks and of their public and private reception. From these discussions emerge diverse and powerful contestations of traditional aesthetics that open a wide field of possibilities for future aesthetics.

"Rediscovering Aesthetics" thus promises a renewal of interpretation and debate within and across the various disciplines that work to undermine and replace traditional models of theoretical explanation.

The focus on cross-disciplinary approaches is one of the most important aspects of recent aesthetics. It underscores the fact that aesthetics has no single definition or subject matter. It is taken to mean simply "philosophy of art";[2] following Immanuel Kant's lead, it also invokes general questions of beauty and taste[3] (an approach that has come under attack for its alleged reliance on the sociopolitically problematic notion of "pure" aesthetic judgments[4]); and it also refers to various types of "sensuous" experiences and effects more generally, such as experiences of the ugly, the disgusting, and so on.[5] In an even broader context, one also hears of an "aesthetization" of entire cultural domains, such as religion or politics. Due to its polysemy, aesthetics can appear like an arbitrary placeholder for a wide range of incommensurable issues. Aesthetics' seeming lack of "substance," combined with stereotypical ideas about its preoccupation with subjective taste and ineffable emotions, to some suggest nonrigorous reflection and uncritical value judgment. This nurtures the two perhaps most serious concerns to which any rediscovery of aesthetics must respond: It involves withdrawal either from critical and rigorous thinking or from social action and life.[6] The key issue is how to maintain a role for critical thought in aesthetic discourse that ensures that aesthetics is not relativized to the point where it dissolves into a mere matter of taste. One possible way is to provide open but discursively negotiated spaces in which different approaches and explanations can be debated and criticized without the presumption or expectation of agreement. We hope that this volume offers such a space.

In the first part of this introduction we outline recent rediscoveries of aesthetics in art history and art theory, philosophy, and art practice. It is written keeping in mind readers who are either new to aesthetics or new to the ways in which aesthetics has been taken up in areas other than their own. Those who are well familiar with aesthetic discourses across the various fields might want to jump to the second part. There we highlight three themes that we consider crucial for maintaining a critical position on any rediscovery of aesthetics: the issue of validity (motivated by inquiries into the peculiar validity of aesthetic judgments), the issue of subjectivity (motivated by the stipulated "special link" between aesthetics and the human subject), and the issue of the political dimension of aesthetics (highlighted by the political implications of pluralist approaches to aesthetics, such as the need for negotiation and appeal).

Recent (Re)Discoveries

Art History/Theory

In art history and art theory, aesthetic considerations have only recently been rehabilitated as the analysis of experiential or perceptual qualities of historically reconstructed artworks. Thereby "rediscovered" aesthetics is freed from concerns with beauty and taste, which historians tend to treat with great suspicion.

This suspicion seems justified, at least initially. Until recently art history, in many respects, relied upon its distance from aesthetic reflection to ensure its autonomy and credibility as a distinct discipline. Art history, it seemed, did not need aesthetics to achieve good results. Indeed, aesthetics might remove art history from what properly concerns it, namely, the concrete and changing historical circumstances of the emergence and development of particular artworks and styles. Aesthetics, understood as little more than connoisseurship, is thus taken to compromise the historically rigorous or "scientific" study of art in the Germanic tradition of *Kunstwissenschaft*.[7] In short, at the heart of the art historical suspicion lies the legitimate concern that attention to specific art objects, styles, periods, and so on (and to their historical, sociological, anthropological, and other contexts) could be replaced with personal taste.

Another art historical suspicion identifies aesthetics with attempts to provide general ontologies of artworks, definitions of art "as such," or analyses of isolated aspects (depiction, make-believe, artistic or moral value, etc.). Art historians often consider these philosophical issues far removed from the art historical "business as usual"[8] as they appear directly opposed to art historical concerns with material and historical specificities.

One important source for renewed interest in aesthetics is the historiographic turn of art history following the publication of major texts on the history of the discipline.[9] This "archaeology" has uncovered an uneasy relationship with art history's immediate neighbors: philosophical aesthetics and visual culture studies. In the view of many art historians, both philosophers and researchers of visual culture neglect the rigorous and systematic study of particular artworks in their specific historical contexts for the sake of establishing universal accounts of either art and aesthetic experience (philosophy) or images in general (visual culture studies). The disciplines thus make an uneasy ménage à trois, which, as W.J.T. Mitchell put it, catches them in an unresolved "triangulation."[10]

However, if art history is distinct from one of its immediate neighbors—visual culture studies—then this is precisely by virtue of its relationship with the other—philosophical aesthetics. After all, art history is the study not of images or the visual in general but of very particular objects—works of art—that, at the same time, have been the paradigmatic objects of aesthetic judgment. This suggests that art historians might have to acknowledge that aesthetic considerations and processes have formed part of the conditions under which that work has been understood historically. This is true also for "an-aesthetic" and "anti-aesthetic" practices of twentieth century and contemporary art because they too (perhaps most of all) are dialectically related to aesthetics.

For these reasons any wholesale rejection of aesthetics by art historians (both traditional and "new"[11]) appears not only somewhat disingenuous but also neglects some potentially important implications of aesthetics for art historical practice.[12]

Philosophy

In philosophy, the claim of a "rediscovery" of aesthetics is perhaps most contentious. However, while philosophers working, for example, within phenomenological, hermeneutical, or post-structuralist frameworks have continuously granted aesthetics a central role in their overall thought, the status of aesthetics within philosophy as a whole has been a troubled one. Often considered less serious or less important than "core" disciplines of philosophy such as ontology, epistemology, and ethics, aesthetics has also suffered, especially in the Anglophone tradition, from a considered "dreariness" that John Passmore had already identified in the 1950s.[13] In 2003 Richard Rorty still described Anglo-American aesthetics as "the most isolated and least respected branch of what one calls 'philosophy'"[14] and even on the current official Web site of the American Society of Aesthetics, Mary Devereaux observes:

> there is little room for disagreement: philosophers widely regard aesthetics as a marginal field . . . not only in the relatively benign sense that it lies at the edge, or border, of the discipline, but also in the additional, more troubling, sense that it is deemed philosophically unimportant.[15]

Devereaux suggests that this marginalization "is relatively recent, largely an artifact of the rise of analytic philosophy itself," whose emphasis on linguistic philosophy, logic, and conceptual analysis most likely pushed aesthetics away from the central position it had enjoyed until the days of British Idealism (in opposition to which analytic philosophy was conceived). Consequently, aesthetics became associated with so-called continental philosophy and a more literary style of thought. Moreover, since the 1960s, aesthetics has been under attack for its traditional foundationalism, elitism, and bourgeois values. The identification of aesthetics with the institutional perpetuation of capitalist ideology has cast serious doubts on its legitimacy.[16]

That aesthetics recently has received much attention, especially in analytic aesthetics,[17] despite these serious concerns is perhaps due to the fact that, as conceptual artist Joseph Kossuth said, art theory, and art itself, have become "more philosophical"[18] and self-reflexive. A more likely explanation, however, is that recent philosophical aesthetics has been paying more attention to art. Less inclined to follow the stereotypical philosophical impulse to ignore material and historical particularities and to concentrate on conceptual or ideal universals, aesthetics has gained new vigor and, above all, has added new, "undreary" substance to the debate. As Anita Silvers has said, "Happily, . . . we have begun to get aesthetics right, for philosophy now turns to art, rather than art to philosophy, for illumination."[19] According to Peter Osborne and Andrew Benjamin this also means that philosophical aesthetics needs to cross its institutional boundaries: "Philosophy and criticism become inextricably intertwined, and both become bound to art history."[20]

The Art World

Contemporary art criticism, curatorial practice, and art practice have also seen a significant reevaluation of aesthetics. Mark Wilsher, commenting in *Art Monthly* on the ongoing debate about aesthetics and artistic practice in the journal, observes that aesthetics is returning in a "surreptitious rather than overt form" as renewed reflections on "the idea of beauty."[21] Celebrated examples include the installation artist Olafur Eliasson who creates spectacular (and extremely popular) artworks, which are, above all, sensuously pleasing. Other examples include the unapologetically sensuous films and installations of Bill Viola and Matthew Barney's astonishing *Gesamtkunstwerk* [total work of art], the *"Cremaster* film series.

There are specific historical reasons for the art world's regained "aesthetic appetite." They include, for example, the desire, inherited from the modernist avant-garde, to differentiate oneself from preceding artistic generations and paradigms. Currently, this plays out in a move away from the postmodern era (itself a problematic concept), which, in order to borrow Hal Foster's term, was "anti-aesthetic"[22] at least insofar as its rejection of modernism implied a rejection of modernist aesthetics.

A renewed interest in art of the 1960s and early 1970s has also been central to the current reevaluation of aesthetics.[23] First, this occurred because aesthetics gained prominence in art of the 1960s as the target of resistance and opposition. When the work of Marcel Duchamp was rediscovered by Fluxus artists as well as Robert Rauschenberg and later by Bruce Nauman and Robert Morris, it was appropriated as a means to criticize a modernist doctrine enforced by Clement Greenberg. Subsequently, in rejecting Greenberg's limited version of formalist (Kantian) aesthetics, these artists anticipated a link between antimodernism and anti-aesthetics that became characteristic of postmodern discourse and art practice. Thus artists of the 1960s explicitly engaged with aesthetic questions and paradigms even if only to reject them.

Second, art practice after modernism challenged the traditional distinctions that had long supported the (self)recognition of aesthetics as a unitary discourse. It radically challenged the notion of an ontologically stable work of art by exploring what Lucy Lippard famously called the "dematerialised" art object.[24] Further, when the distinction between art and nonart was blurred (which led Arthur Danto to his famous reflections on the "end of art"[25]), the loss both of the art object's identity and of the distinction between "art and life" resulted in a corresponding loss of certainty about what the rightful object of aesthetics actually was. Just as art was "up-for-grabs," so was aesthetics.

Third, the recent resurgence of interest in art of the 1960s has motivated a general reassessment of its own aesthetic dimension. For example, minimalism has proved receptive to theoretical accounts couched in phenomenological, bodily, sensuous, and aesthetic terms, which is not surprising given the influence that artists and critics at the time (such as Robert Morris and Rosalind Krauss) drew from phenomenologists such as Maurice Merleau-Ponty.[26]

However, aesthetics remains problematic for art practice. It has been argued that a return to narrowly aesthetic and stylistic issues anachronistically divorces artworks from their original volatile economic, political, social, and historical contexts. The critical edge of radical art practice from the late 1960s and early 1970s may thus be blunted by the focus on effect, spectacle, and falsely constructed notions of communality and spirituality.

These objections have catalyzed curatorial defenses of a new aesthetics. For example, the French curator Nicolas Bourriaud has criticized traditional, less "spectacular" art practice for falsely asserting "an independent and private symbolic space." In opposition, he announces aesthetics' necessary move into "the realm of human interactions and its social context."[27] However, the "aesthetic turn" as a curatorial strategy is also contentious because it is feared to prioritize aesthetic (i.e., sensuous, playful, or pleasurable) effects over critical social and political dimensions of contemporary art practice.

Such objections, however, apply not only to the practical business of making, curating, and writing about art. They should inform all debates about aesthetics and about the implications of its recent rediscoveries.

Themes of (Re)Discoveries

In this second part of the introduction we will briefly discuss three core themes that are meant to indicate important general issues for critical cross-disciplinary debate: the issue of validity, the issue of subjectivity, and the political dimension of aesthetics.

It is important to acknowledge that discussing these themes in relation to aesthetics does precisely not mean newly to "discover" aesthetics, as if one could ignore its rich and problematic history, or nostalgically to "rediscover" it, as if one could go back behind "*an*-aesthetic," "anti-aesthetic," or "in-aesthetic" critiques.[28] Rather, it is precisely attentiveness to the complex history and problematic nature of aesthetics that makes possible a more historically and politically sensitive view of both its inescapability and its potential.[29]

In art history, philosophy, and artistic practice, structures of justification and legitimation obviously involve institutions and consensual efforts. But even though beliefs in transcontextual universal ideas of value and truth have been destabilized, the need to identify or establish standards, if only as situational agreements, remains. In the light of our everyday practices of making claims, of judging and of being judged, the outright denial of the possibility of such standards is both ethically dubious and theoretically unconvincing.

The notion of aesthetic judgment helps to understand how standards of truth and value, now understood in terms of *validity,* can be maintained despite their contextual nature. The critical point here is that validity claims about artworks are paradigmatic insofar as they are framed by contextual factors, which acknowledge positions within conventional, historical, and thus social and political situations. At the same time, however, humans are both free in making aesthetic judgments (they typically do not refer to "objective" cognitive or moral, normative demands) *and* are open to question the limits and frames of reference of these judgments. (Humans instead appeal to their sense of "communal values" and are thus left to negotiate disagreement and dissent).[30] Accordingly, validity claims in general must be recognized as phenomena that, like artworks, evoke multiple interpretations, not universal, once-and-for-all explanations. They are not based on abstract, extra-worldly principles but are features of the complex everyday disciplines and practices we use to understand and explain them. Thus, aesthetic judgments show how we expect discourse to function in general—not in a neutral and absolute way but as interlocutory, argumentative, and open to debate.

The position outlined here can be appreciated more fully in light of a philosophical tradition that has, at least since Alexander Gottlieb Baumgarten and Kant, anchored aesthetics in the experience, creativity, taste, and judgment of human subjects, whose sensual and affective characteristics are regarded as irreducible to cognitive capacities or objective principles. In contemporary discourse, this is often investigated in terms of not transcendental but concrete (i.e., embodied and situated) subjects who experience the contingency and particularity of their sociohistorical situations. Consequently, because individual subjects always already find themselves within an intersubjective context, there is no single perspective available for them from which they could make absolute judgments. This also means that our judgments do not always get assent from everyone and that there is no single way to enforce assent. Others are always free to dissent or ignore our claims, so that, for example, Barnett Newman might well be right to say that aesthetics is for many artists "like ornithology must be for the birds."[31]

As a consequence of the social character of human identity, aesthetic judgments (or experiences) are never politically neutral, but they are utterly implicated in structures of social power and division, without however—and this is important—being reduced to narrowly political or social concerns. As Andrew Bowie has shown, one of the most important lessons we learn from aesthetics is that "it is a mistake for philosophy to relegate subjectivity to being merely a function of something else, such as language, ideology, history, or the unconscious."[32] On the contrary, aesthetics reminds us of the irreducibility of human subjectivity.[33] At the same time, it teaches us to attend to how we live through and negotiate our own autonomous (yet embedded) subjectivity in order to form and defend our individual (yet socially committed) and relative (yet by no means merely private) positions on grounds of personal and social experiences. Aesthetics is thereby inextricably connected with issues of subjectivity, validity, and politics.

Understood in this way, aesthetics effectively takes on board the criticisms Hal Foster described as "anti-aesthetic" and thus becomes "a practice, cross-disciplinary in nature, that is sensitive to cultural forms engaged in a politic . . . or rooted in a vernacular."[34] Such aesthetics, as Paul Mattick pointed out, "is actually quite unlike ornithology." Artists themselves participate and intervene in aesthetics because they, "unlike birds in the wild, are engaged in a cultural and therefore historically evolving activity."[35] The role of aesthetics in this activity as well as in the construction of communities of shared values and "truths," and hence the complex relationship between aesthetics and politics, are thus of critical importance.

At the heart of this debate lies the question of the autonomy of aesthetics. Simply put, the question is: If there is an autonomous "aesthetic realm," does this mean that it is separate from social (and thus political) realms, or does its very autonomy provide the opportunity for resistance, dissent, and freedom, in short the opportunity for political action? The early Greenberg, for example, argued polemically that the avant-garde's antipathy to kitsch placed it in a dialectical and politically charged relationship with capitalism. Thus, whilst radical art was tied to the bourgeoisie by an "umbilical cord of gold" it also offered an alternative value system to, *and thus critique of,* capitalism.[36]

The question of aesthetic and artistic autonomy in the arena of political action receives a considered articulation in critical theory. Max Horkheimer, Theodor Adorno, and Herbert Marcuse, for example, argued that aesthetics has an important function in the project of freeing practical reason from the dominance of "instrumental rationality." This position resurfaces in Adorno's polemical call for art's autonomy. In distinction from an art for the masses that promises radical democracy, he posits a "committed art" that proves its commitment by continually struggling to liberate itself from "the real," that is, by continually reasserting its autonomy from the political and social status quo as well as from its inescapable materiality.[37] Clearly, then, exploring the possibilities aesthetics affords for politics does not imply a single position or approach but allows for different and even diverging views.

However, it can also be argued that art gains a political agency by giving up its independence from sociopolitical values. According to this view art is political precisely because it is deeply embedded in society and can change peoples' opinions. The highly charged works of Joseph Beuys and Hans Haacke, for example, take political action as their driving force. They bring to mind Benjamin's call for an "activist art" for which the artist puts "an end to his autonomy" and uses his artistic activities in the service of the political goals he supports.[38]

In conclusion, we propose that rediscoveries of aesthetics need not merely reflect earlier dilemmas but can bypass or even transcend them. For example, many of the contributions to this volume show that the opposition between modernist aesthetics and postmodern anti-aesthetics is already being surpassed by contemporary aesthetics (in philosophy as well as art history) and by contemporary art practice. This opens up an entire realm of questions that had been closed during much of the second half of the twentieth century, when it seemed almost impossible to conceive of aesthetics in terms of anything but the opposition between modernism and postmodernism. Now there are also political reasons for getting beyond that deadlock. As Isobel Armstrong warns us in *Radical Aesthetics,* by neglecting aesthetic questions, these "questions are implicitly left to the

reactionaries—an assumption that makes it more rather than less important to remake aesthetic discourse."[39] For the issue of aesthetics—far from
being a matter of mere connoisseurship or apolitical enjoyment of beauty
and pleasure—is relevant to the preservation of the possibility of criticism
and debate in a pluralist world.

Synopsis

The contributors to this volume do not adopt a single, coherent, and
agreed line. This is to be expected since they come from different theoretical and practical backgrounds whose presuppositions and practices are being reshaped in significant ways as interpretation and debate emerges. This
has important implications for aesthetics under construction. The essays in
this volume—under the influence of critical theory, feminism, hermeneutics, phenomenology, pragmatism, and other paradigms—often show, rather
than explicitly say, what is at stake here: That henceforth aesthetics must
strive to escape from the limitations of abstraction and disinterestedness in
favor of a more historically and politically sensitive view that recognizes
both the inescapability and positive potential of aesthetics.

The book is divided into three sections. The first section focuses on
a rediscovery of aesthetics in art history, the second section contains
philosophical reflections on the status of aesthetics in contemporary discourse and on the future of aesthetics, and the third section emphasizes
the complex relation between specific art practices and aesthetics.

I. Aesthetics in Art History and Art Theory

Richard Woodfield gives a historical account of the ambiguous relationship between aesthetics and the discipline of art history. He points
out that the first rediscovery of aesthetics occurred at the beginning of the
twentieth century when academic philosophical aesthetics was rejected in
favor of a new aesthetics that drew from the materials of art history. It was
called *Kunstwissenschaft* by Ernst Gombrich and others. Woodfield concludes that contemporary art historians stand at "the end" of art history.
Thus, they are free to escape the straightjacket imposed by the Enlightenment concept of art and its modernist consequences.

James Elkins conducts a discussion on why any rediscovery of aesthetics by scientific discourse is problematic. Art and science, he suggests,

are very different because they have different value systems and thus different criteria of success. For example, few artists have been decisively influenced by science (although many have been influenced by technology) and virtually no scientists have required art in their work (although many have used it). Moreover, Elkins argues that science and art put different values on such terms as "beauty," "aesthetics," "elegance," and so on. He concludes that the two cultures really are substantially separate, resulting in different accounts of image production and interpretation.

Michael Ann Holly discusses the art historical writings of British art historian and critic Adrian Stokes. She uses Stokes's *Stones of Rimini* to reveal a new model of writing about art that blends scientific and poetic moments. It is concerned with both art historical facts *and* aesthetic judgments. She further explores how art history is an essentially melancholic activity as one mourns and attempts to reconstruct the "lost" objects of historical and aesthetic reflection. In turn, this opens up a discussion on the nature of art historical discourse and on the role that aesthetic judgment plays in art historical method.

David Raskin argues that art had never forgotten aesthetics; rather, it was trapped in an orthodoxy from the 1960s when "nothing short of conviction mattered at all." Through a discussion of positions advanced by Rosalind Krauss, Michael Fried, and T. J. Clark, Raskin questions how modern and postmodern art challenge us precisely to separate facts from values.

Richard Shiff explores the disconnection between experiences of artworks and the language used to describe those experiences. He argues that a model of aesthetic experience can be used to reappraise art from the 1960s (late and postmodernist art). He examines how works by Newman, Bridget Riley, Donald Judd, and Richard Serra produce relevant perceptual effects that need to be accounted for in terms of the phenomenological experiences they engender.

Thierry de Duve engages in aesthetic terms with Robert Morris's work from the late 1960s. He thus shows that anti-aesthetic art remains part of modernist aesthetic discourse. He returns to Kant's account of aesthetic experience in the *Critique of Judgment* and applies it to minimal and conceptual art. In particular, de Duve demonstrates empirically that Morris's work illustrates how Kantian "free play" remains relevant to art hitherto characterized as antiformalist and anti-aesthetic.

II. Aesthetics in Philosophy

Arthur Danto thinks that aesthetics will be an inescapable feature of experiencing art as long as "there are visible differences in how things look." He claims that the concrete future of aesthetics will be conditioned by the overall differences between the disciplines of art history and philosophy. He holds that the rediscovery of aesthetics involves a rethinking of the role played by aesthetic qualities in the visual presentation of meanings. Danto's argument thus implies a major turn from ontological questions (which he had previously made central) to aesthetic questions.

Diarmuid Costello argues that aesthetics became marginalized in postmodern art largely due to the dominance of art critic and theorist Clement Greenberg. Costello discusses how Greenberg's coupling of medium specificity with aesthetic quality, and his grounding of this in a limited reading of Kant, overdetermined subsequent art world conceptions of aesthetics. Thus, when Greenberg's theories were rejected by artists and writers, so too was a particular understanding of aesthetics. Costello investigates the historical conditions of this rejection and suggests how Kant's theory of art might be used to retrieve aesthetics for contemporary debate.

Paul Crowther criticizes the ways in which art has become a primarily managerial phenomenon. He claims that in late modern and postmodern times, art is often reduced to a position of "use." What artworks mean is determined by critical, historical, curatorial, and administrative interests, which are "parasitic" upon art practice. In this guise, he argues, art has no significant future. To secure a post-managerial future for art he proposes a rediscovery of aesthetics as the rediscovery of the intrinsic value of art and of aesthetic judgments for evaluating the merits or demerits of particular artworks.

Nicholas Davey argues for a rediscovery of hermeneutical aesthetics that examines how meaning shows itself in special ways in our encounters with artworks. He, with Hans-Georg Gadamer, shows how the hermeneutic nature of aesthetic experience highlights the dialectic between "the disclosed" and "the withheld" characteristic of all attempts at understanding and interpreting.

Peter Osborne holds that the recent revival of aesthetics heralds a new openness to some problems posed by twentieth-century art but a foreclosure of others. In particular, he finds a return to Kantian modernism problematic. He argues instead for a return to a different conception of modernism, one concerned with negation and mediation. Such modernism structures the entire field of contemporary art understood as a field of historically critical practices.

Wolfgang Welsch argues for an "aesthetics beyond aesthetics" because in its institutional form, often universalist or formalist in character, aesthetics has been incapable of doing justice to the singularity of artworks. Invoking Ludwig Wittgenstein's notion of "family resemblances," he claims that there is no essence of art. He advocates the opening of aesthetics to transdisciplinary issues beyond art. Art is still the main interest here, but its analysis now requires the introduction of transdisciplinary perspectives.

Adrian Piper uses contemporary art practice to question philosophical aesthetics. In an unusual move, she juxtaposes Kant's *Critique of Pure Reason* with contemporary art practice. She tests the soundness of Kant's theory against the processes of art production and objects to his claim that intuitive awareness of an object or process does not constitute a form of knowledge.

III. Aesthetics in Artistic and Curatorial Practice

Carolee Schneemann surveys her radical artistic practice from the last forty years to explore complex interconnections between aesthetics, performance, politics, pornography, and censorship. She poses two questions to her own work: To what extent does its erotic content subvert its formal properties? Can its feminist base lend new meaning to existing aesthetic issues? She argues that performance art reconfigures the experience of aesthetic reflection by expanding the boundaries of art beyond the surfaces and frames of modernism. She also reveals how throughout her career censorship has attempted to subject her work to aesthetic constraints with specifically political consequences.

Robert Morris poses a series of questions about the supposed innate nature of aesthetics. Through various authorial voices he interrogates the meaning and truth of aesthetics and brings several deflationary notions of aesthetics into play. In order to open a new adventure of thinking the possible he invokes Analytic Cubism, the readymades of Duchamp, and the work of Jasper Johns and Simone Foti. He holds that rethinking commodity capitalism can lead to a new visual democracy by undercutting the elitism of "high art" in favor of democratic folk art.

Claire Bishop, from a curatorial perspective, explores contemporary art practices under the names of "experimental communities" and "socially engaged," "community-based," "dialogic," "littoral," "participatory," "interventionist," "research-based," or "collaborative" art. She explores how such practices are linked by a belief in the empowering creativity of collective action and shared ideas. Using examples from the work of Superflex and Jeremy Deller, she discusses how such practices engage in a redeployment of aesthetics in social spheres. She concludes that the best recent collaborative art makes both art and collectivity more complex.

Michael Kelly conducts a detailed analysis of Gerhard Richter's Baader-Meinhof series. He takes Richter's paintings as pictorial statements about matters of (political, artistic, personal) life and death—matters that anti-aesthetic theorists typically consider beyond the "representational substance" of today's art. Kelly investigates Richter's resistance to anti-aesthetic interpretations of his work and explores it as a site of regeneration of aesthetics as a theoretical practice that can explain and support the substantial accomplishments of artistic practice.

Part I   Aesthetics in Art History and Art Theory

1

Kunstwissenschaft versus *Ästhetik*
The Historians' Revolt Against Aesthetics

Richard Woodfield

IF AESTHETICS IS BEING rediscovered by art historians, it will be the second time. The first was around the year 1900. It was based on a rejection of academic philosophical aesthetics and the creation of a new aesthetics out of the materials of art history. It called itself *Kunstwissenschaft*.

At the time, academic aesthetics was too remote from the concerns of art history, which did not become an academic discipline in England until the mid-1930s. When it did, Herbert Read, who had been in contact with German aestheticians, wrote:

After Kant the world . . . swarmed with aestheticians. I have never been able to believe the idealistic conception of art, developed on the basis of Kant's aesthetic by writers like Fichte and Schelling, and given a more popular romantic expression by poets like Richter and Novalis, is worth the time that would be involved in mastering its mysteries. It consists mainly of a discussion of abstract categories like imagination and fancy, form and idea, and these are rarely, if ever, related to objective works of art.[1]

He went on to declare that "science is prior to philosophy, and a science of art must establish its facts before a philosophy of art can make use of them."

By the time Max Dessoir published *Ästhetik und Allgemeine Kunstwissenschaft*[2] in 1906, philosophy had ceased to be the master science and had given birth to the disciplines of anthropology, ethnology, psychology, and sociology, which laid claim to specialist and scientific (*wissenschaftliche*) approaches to their subjects. Professional psychologists asserted their authority in the institutional world of academia by insisting on the rigorous standards of the physical sciences, involving hypotheses, experiments, and the arrival at laws. In aesthetics, Gustav Fechner's *Vorschule der Ästhetik* (1876) set an example for later work, and Wilhelm Dilthey's hermeneutic approach was given scientific support by the new theory of empathy (*Einfühlung*).[3] Independently from each other, the painter Conrad Fiedler and the sculptor Adolf Hildebrand approached figurative images on a perceptualist basis, concerning themselves with the mental activities of artists.[4]

Heinrich Wölfflin had started his art historical career by applying the principles of psychology to architecture. He began his book, *Die klassische Kunst* (1899), which was popular well into the 1960s, by saying:

The reader no longer expects an art-historical book to give mere biographical anecdotes or a description of the circumstances of the time; he wants to be told something of those things which constitute the value and essence of a work of art, and he reaches out eagerly for new concepts—for the old words will no longer serve—and once again, he is beginning to pay attention to aesthetics, which had entirely been shelved. A book like Adolf Hildebrand's "Problem der Form" fell like a refreshing shower upon parched earth: at last there was a new method of approach to art, a point of view which was not only expanded in breadth by new material, but which also made a deep study of detail.[5]

Wölfflin's books, including *The Principles of Art History*[6] offered an aura of objective analysis that would strengthen art history in the academic curriculum. It would fend off accusations of subjectivity associated with connoisseurship and offer a target for other art historians also concerned with the *scientific* footing of their discipline.

Art history had been established in Vienna as an auxiliary study at the Institute for Austro-Hungarian History. Under the leadership of Franz Wickhoff and Alois Riegl it assumed an independent role in the university but now had to justify its existence as an academic discipline. Thus Riegl put connoisseurship behind him and instead adopted a combination of visual philology (evident in *De Stil*) and psychology (in *Spätrömische Kunstindustrie*) to work on a wide range of material including decorative arts from Egypt to Byzantium and the plastic and industrial arts from Egypt through the Middle Ages to the modern period.

The entire field of art history had expanded in the nineteenth century. By 1906 there was a greater appreciation of non-Western art, including the "developed" art of China, Japan, India, and Persia as well as the "primitive" art of Australia, New Zealand, Africa, and the Americas, not to mention smaller groupings. Tradesmen, colonial explorers, and ethnographers brought home exotic art from all over the world. Moreover, the public had grown used to displays of objets d'art in the various Universal Expositions and state-sponsored fine arts exhibitions.[7] Finally the traditional set of academic values that had underpinned art school education and had been celebrated in the official salons was undermined by the growth of realism and impressionism and then, with the invention of photography, by alternative pictorial practices that culminated in fauvism and cubism. Japanese art, in particular, made a major impact and led to the rejection of the normative standing of the classical ideal. By the end of the nineteenth century, museum officials felt obliged to give their non-Western material the same kind of consideration and scholarly attention as they gave their Renaissance collections. Riegl was acutely self-conscious of his historical position as an art historian. He wrote that "in spite of its seemingly independent objectivity, scholarship takes its direction in the last analysis from the contemporary intellectual atmosphere and the art historian cannot significantly exceed the character of the *Kunstbegehren* of his contemporaries."[8]

The Viennese art historians were not just responsible for training Austria-Hungary's future museum officials; they participated actively in its cultural life and were sensitive to a wider responsibility for promoting cultural values. Aesthetics, Riegl declared, had been the master builder of the history of art.[9] Unfortunately it had not been up to its job: The histories of painting, sculpture, architecture, and, later, industrial arts had progressed independently and unsystematically. The result gave Riegl "the impression of a ruin."[10] Aesthetics "has long been dead, and any effect that she possesses resides in the scattered auditoriums of academic philosophy." There was, though, an "heiress" who "recognizes that her very right to exist lies rooted in the history of art."[11]

Riegl offered such a new aesthetics, a *Kunstwissenschaft*. He described it with a formula he subsequently applied in *Spätrömische Kunstindustrie*: The purely artistic character of artworks is their "treatment of the motive [*sic*] as shape and color on the plane and in space."[12] According to Riegl, art develops inexorably from a concern with a haptic (tactile) response to an optic response to objects in space, both in terms of their perception and their depiction. This has implications for the way in which the motif is treated on the plane and in space. Any moment of historical development has its own *Kunstwollen*, driven by the *Weltanschauung* of its host race. In hindsight it can be seen that Riegl's approach was strongly affected by his work as a museum curator. He attempted to identify a sequence of largely anonymous objects across historical time and classify them into national groupings. With Morellian method as an example of scientific work he was concerned to legitimate his own approach in terms of the new sciences of perceptual psychology and *Volkpsychologie*, itself legitimated through the publications of Wilhelm Wundt. He also held on to a transcendental concept of art developed by the neoidealists in which art was the expression of cultural psyche offering direct access to its spiritual realm. This was subsequently promoted by his successor in the Vienna School, Max Dvořák, as *Kunstgeschichte als Geistesgeschichte* and shared by his critic, Erwin Panofsky, in his iconological approach to the history of art.

While Riegl had a great many admirers he did not, immediately, have any followers. It wasn't until the 1920s that, with the encouragement of Julius von Schlosser, art historians in Vienna republished and significantly revised Riegl's ideas. While Riegl wanted to understand the reasons for change in stylistic development (leaving aside matters of artistic value) by reinventing aesthetics from within art history, Schlosser wanted to make judgments of aesthetic value, which he equated with artistic value, by separating the history of style from the history of visual language.

Schlosser—who was quite a remarkable character, an interesting and innovative art historian, and a close friend of the Italian aesthetician Benedetto Croce—described his early experiences of aesthetics as having been "gloomingly touched" by the spirit of Schelling, "who was then quite despised."[13] He remembered studying "with feverish enthusiasm those large weighty tomes of the German aestheticians like Lipps, Volkelt, Dessoir and so on but was unable to derive the slightest benefit from them although they were adequately enough adorned with the rags and patches of art historical learning, much less with observation: today they have long been consigned to one of the darkest corners of my library."[14]

For Croce, and thus for Schlosser, the work of art was pure lyrical expression: It was a linguistic utterance. The idea of art as language had already been established by Fiedler and Wölfflin and it was one that Riegl took very seriously himself:

We have long been accustomed to using the metaphor "artistic language." We say that each work of art speaks its own particular artistic language, even though the elements of visual art are naturally different from those of verbal language. But if there is such a thing as artistic language, there also exists a historical grammar of that language. This, too, is of course metaphoric; but if the one metaphor is justifiable, surely the other must be accepted as well.[15]

Following Croce, Schlosser argued that what is called "the stylistic history of art" is, in fact, a history of the language of the means of art. Art proper is the "sole object of aesthetic knowledge [and] is the first and fundamental category of the theoretical, contemplating sphere of the spirit prior to and next to the logical one, corresponding to the two others of the practical, active sphere, the economic and the ethical."[16] The only artists who possess "'style' are those who 'demonstrate pure lyrical intuition which has become expression, both things indissolubly and indivisibly fused with each other; any attempt to separate them leads irretrievably to dualism and all its consequences whether in the aesthetics of "content" of Romanticism or in the aesthetics of "form" as embodied most impressively and effectively by Herbert."[17]

In consequence, the only valid stylistic history is that of the "insular creative monad," not the empirical artist in his culture but the artistic personality as exemplified by his work. The "genuine great artist is as an artist sufficient unto himself, himself 'audience,' and neither requires nor thinks of any other."[18] The work of art is pure expression. Any notion that it is communication mistakes the perfection of the work with its effect on the outside world and the "past history" of the monad, its "schooling," is basically just as little part of its inner nature, its true "history," as its "later history," its effect on others, its "influence" and its (often so changeable) "posthumous reputation."[19]

Schlosser contrasted the "true history of the artistic monad with the falsely causal connection with other individuals . . . which leaves the field of expression and goes into that of impression, of social communication, in short of language. [It] moves from the centre to the periphery and ceases to be autonomous."[20] Philosophical-historical criticism, on the contrary, will have nothing to do with context. Wölfflin's book on Dürer was "a peak towering in isolation" that was "wholly tailored to the artistic essence, the 'style-historical' in the most elevated sense, refraining in wise restraint from the merely biographical as from all wanting-to-explain, in the manner of history of ideas." Schlosser thus was critical of "that hermaphroditic creature, so called 'sociology' [that] sticks out its ass's ears here: the schematisation of facts, which are always concrete and individual, in types and norms of an utterly abstract 'event,' in 'laws' which in the end have always proved to be commonplaces."[21] The true history of art rejects dissolution of the individual into the universal: "Rembrandt does not appear 'as art,' but 'art as Rembrandt' ".[22]

Invoking the history of ideas renders the individual work of art inexpressive because it has stripped away the individual. Artists concern themselves with previous artists' problems only insofar as they make them their own. The artist's "historical inheritance are 'suspended' (*aufheben*) within him, i.e. are overcome and recast in accordance with his purpose and his mission."[23] Art is language and language is art. The linguistic heritage is at first creative and expressive but then it sinks and is carried into general circulation, becoming a common language. The creation of the individual "blends into the total body of the nationally determined language or of its 'dialects,' as the collective nature of the medieval stonemason's lodge blends into the *Gesamtkunstwerk* of the Gothic Cathedral."[24] The art of late antiquity was "an area which comes almost completely under the history of language."[25]

At the end of his review of Riegl's work, Schlosser mentioned that the problem of the inner linguistic form was now being addressed, "with some youthful impetuousness,"[26] by one of his students, Hans Sedlmayr, using Ehrenfels' techniques of Gestalt psychology.

Sedlmayr, following Croce and Schlosser, allowed room for a description of works of art "*without understanding the product as an artistic product.*"[27] This is his "first" study of art, which focuses on themes, formal opportunities, and external style. At this first level, he argued, it was possible to engage in attribution and the traditional art historical techniques of stylistic criticism. The "second" study of art involved a direct understanding of its objects, working not with empirical groups but with Croce's "aesthetic personages."[28] This led to the central question, "Can criteria for rigorous decidability be established from within the second study of art?"[29] While the first study of art did have such rigorous criteria of decidability, the second study was in a state of flux. The way out of this would be establishing relevant methods. And at this point Sedlmayr invoked the new discoveries of gestalt analysis. It is in this light that one should understand his formulation: "This thing only possesses artistic properties when it is approached with an 'artistic' attitude, and it only possesses specific artistic properties when it is seen in accordance with a specific attitude."[30]

Rejecting the rather dated ideas of associationist psychology, he acknowledged the role of global perception in responding to artworks: They are greater than the sum of their parts. They were "repeatedly re-created and formed anew by viewing subjects."[31] Thus ensued the problem of adequacy: Re-creation was not a matter of simple spectator response but the appropriateness of response to the intended artistic object. If determining the original attitude was contestable, the probability of correctness would be enhanced by its level of explicability. The best explanation was the one that did greatest justice to the greater whole (i.e., the wider historical and cultural context):

This rests on the idea that a culture, like a sum of events, is a unified organic whole with a determinable structure and organization. The correct attitude toward a work of art not only must "fit into" this structure but also must serve a specific function within the overall organization of this whole. (A specifically European attitude toward an African sculpture is spurious and incorrect because it is incompatible with other established knowledge about the primitive mentality.) In this case one must step outside the realm of artistic phenomena in order to determine whether an attitude is correct: this is *one* good reason for the slogan "art history as the history of the spirit."[32]

Another way to state this is to suggest that the cultural gestalt is a legitimate factor in determining the specific gestalt of the artwork. Sedlmayr called this the "physiognomic character of the work," which "in most if not all cases is the attitude *demanded* when considering works of art."[33] He did make the qualification, however, that considering artworks as expressions of personality, national spirit, or zeitgeist was legitimate only insofar as the autonomous consideration of a work of art *as a work of art* was maintained. His essay concluded with a call for a "new appreciation of methodological self-consciousness."[34] Enter the young Ernst Gombrich.

Gombrich had written his "school-leaving essay" on the history of art appreciation from Winckelmann to his own day.[35] He had clearly fallen under the spell of Dvořák and believed that the study of art history

offered an exciting point of entry into the mind of the past. His essay
ended with the conclusion that:

> Just as all developments in man's intellectual life seem rather confused and confus-
> ing at first glance, and yet are governed by an inherent order, in the same way I
> would discern a similar pattern in the appreciation of art; as haphazardly as the vari-
> ous trends fizzle out, as irreconcilable as the opinions which stand alongside one an-
> other seem to be, they do follow a certain law of development, which I will venture
> to sketch experimentally. After a period which favours an exclusively intellectual ap-
> proach there will follow as a reaction a new emphasis on those things which appeal
> purely to the senses. In the struggle between these two fundamental views a synthe-
> sis will form, in which, beside the scrutiny of reason, usually most concerned with
> the subject, there will also be room for the senses, which seek colour and beauty of
> form, until the next trend, under the pressure of a longing for greater spiritual depth
> gains a victory for an approach more rooted in emotion. This pattern seems to have
> repeated itself twice, on different levels, in the period since Winckelmann, and with
> a growing historical consciousness each style in the development opened the way to
> new and uncharted territory in our artistic heritage. Even if one cannot rely on the
> laws of intellectual history to be as constant as the laws of nature, nevertheless one
> can quite safely predict that a new approach will arise in the study of art, one based
> on reason, a "new objectivity" (*einer "neuen Sachlichkeit"*). This will of course not
> dispense with the gains made thus far, to which after all we owe our widened hori-
> zons, and for the serious representative of this new movement a work of art will be
> what it has always been to the powers of reason and to the emotions, to the eye and
> to the heart: experience (*Erlebnis*).[36]

I quote this concluding passage from Gombrich's *Hausarbeit* at
length because the problem of changes in art appreciation was going to
preoccupy him throughout his professional career. It certainly shaped his
views on what he was taught at university. One of the Viennese profes-
sors cited in Gombrich's essay was Hans Tietze, who had made the following observation: "We have experienced in recent years the daily
discovery of new worlds and undergone an hourly revaluation of all our
values. We now stand in a more direct relationship to Antiquity and to
the Gothic and Baroque ages than ever before, and in the art of the ori-
ental and black peoples we meet with a humanity which is profoundly
startling."[37]

Gombrich was fully aware of the "revaluation of all values" and the problems that it would create for an objective approach to the study of the history of art. When he enrolled in the university he discovered that he would have to choose between Schlosser's 2nd Institute of Art History and Strzygowski's 1st Institute. He chose Schlosser.

But Gombrich had no time at all for Croce's aesthetics. He witnessed Schlosser's difficulties in trying to describe the significant features of individual works of art, those qualities that made them what they were: "How could the historian get hold of that elusive insularity of the work of art if he found it embedded in the artistic idiom? To hear him meditate about these perplexities in front of a lantern slide of the Arch of Constantine was not always an entertainment, but I hope it was an education."[38]

Gombrich had no difficulty in seeing through Schlosser's problem. It was the old one of trying to capture the individual by means of using universals: Language was limited in the extent to which it could grasp the world as it is based on general categories. Gombrich believed that Schlosser could come to terms with his problems if he took a more linguistically informed approach to the study of his subject. Vienna's linguistics expert was Karl Bühler, and Gombrich made a point of familiarizing himself with his work (which also gave Gombrich the intellectual equipment to critique Hans Sedlmayr's *Structuranalyse*).

Gombrich attended Bühler's lectures on the psychology of expression[39] and studied Bühler's work in the area of linguistics.[40] Bühler took the view that if utterances were simply made for the sake of expression, man would remain at the level of animals. In his *Theory of Language: the Representational Function of Speech*, he argued that humans shared features of expression (*Ausdruck*) and appeal (*Appell*) with the animal world but that human language was marked off from animal cries and calls by its function as representation (*Darstellung*). Criticizing Hermann Paul, Ferdinand de Saussure, and Edmund Husserl, he maintained it was a mistake to separate thought and utterance, sense and speech. He developed an *Organonmodell der Sprache* based on the triadic relationship of symbol, symptom, and signal, and he addressed the topic of symbolic fields in nonlinguistic representative implements.[41] All of this was grist to Gombrich's mill.

Gombrich would later develop these ideas in *Art and Illusion* but the immediate effect of Bühler's work lead to Gombrich's conception of visual configurations as information-bearing stimuli that could be processed for meaning. The specific information conveyed by an image emerges from its representational field. A visual image is a structure bearing features with communicative significance. However, only some of the object's features are communicatively significant. The problem is, as Gombrich wrote in a later text:

No sign or symbol can refer to itself and tell us how much it is intended to signify. All signs have the characteristic which Karl Buehler called "abstractive relevance." The letters of the alphabet signify through certain distinctive features but in normal contexts their meaning is not affected by their size, colour or font. The same is true of the images which interest the iconographer, be they coats of arms, emblems or personifications traditionally marked by certain attributes. In every one of these cases there are features which are strictly speaking without a translatable meaning, and only a few which we are intended to read and translate.[42]

Thus the question of pictorial meaning was, again, one of context. For any moment of historical time one had to reconstruct the range of significant features as well as their referential, expressive, and appellative functions.

From an experiment on reading facial expression in photographs organized by Bühler's student Ruth Weiss, Gombrich "learned to appreciate how many different interpretations one can read into such photographs as soon as one lacks the key to the action and context."[43] If the detection of facial expression in a photograph were simply a matter of intuitive recognition then there should be a high level of consensus in interpretation. The fact that instead consensus was established through the verbal addition of context spoke against the validity of such an intuitive view. This significantly undermined Sedlmayr's theory of an unproblematic aesthetic response to works of art. Now it seemed an aesthetic response to works of art could simply be the product of verbalization.[44]

In two early contributions to *Kritische Berichte*,[45] Gombrich directly applied Bühler's theories to the ideas of Riegl and Sedlmayr. In the first essay he used the phenomenon of the gold ground in late antique art to conduct an experiment in analyzing its characteristics as *Kunstsprache*, explicitly disavowing any concern with aesthetics. Passing on from a consideration of its optical function in the mosaics at the Basilica di Santa Maria Maggiore, Gombrich began to use Bühler's observation that "such a surface—similar to freshly fallen snow in sunlight—is not really perceived as the boundary to a space, so that it swims beyond it."⁴⁶ His analysis undermined Riegl and Panofsky's attempts to describe the image as representing space. For Gombrich, the mosaic was a colorful material object that functioned as a pictogram. The form analysis of the use of the gold ground established its presence not as a representation of a physical object, say a road or sand, so much as a space in the image replacing the traditional middle ground. Such a space was not discontinuous within an overall spatial continuum, as Panofsky had suggested, but a purely pictorial device, an unrepresentable "between-space." In Santa Maria Maggiore, the mosaic of the *Crossing of the Red Sea* was divided into three fields for the sake of pictorial legibility.

Fifty-four years later, Gombrich redescribed the mosaic in English:

The new purpose which [Christian Medieval] art had to serve is too well known for me to dwell on it. The sacred story had to be conveyed with optimal clarity. No wonder we can observe an element of regression towards the symbolic or pictographic mode which is already manifest in that great landmark of Early Christian art, the mosaics of *Santa Maria Maggiore* of the fourth century. Take the scene of that cycle of the passage of the Jews through the Red Sea, where it is the Pharaoh with his army who suffers the defeat at the hands of the Lord. No doubt there are many residues here of the methods of Hellenistic illusionism, the individual treatment of bodies, movement and draperies, but there is now no spatial framework, but rather a map-like treatment of the event to allow us to have a full view of the scene with the drowning victims of the miracle, while the towering figure of Moses dominates the representation in a manner which recalls the earlier pictographic approach.⁴⁷

The central difference between classical and late antique art was the former's dependency on illusion and the latter's dependence on the symbol, each requiring what Gombrich would later call a different "mental set."

Riegl had suggested that the driving force behind the changed spatial conventions of late antique art was a *Kunstwollen* forcing a switch from haptic to optic modes of perception. This had been paralleled by *geistesgeschichtliche* changes: "One has to think of a pre-stabilised harmony of autonomous streams, not of the interactions of cogs in a machine," said Gombrich. Against Dvořák, who explained the style as an expression of its epoch (namely the supra individual unity of early Christianity), Gombrich complained:

The unity of the art concept (*Kunstbegriff*), of the spiritual and social function of art within different spiritual and cultural circles and constellations is unreflectively assumed. Art is always understood in the first place as *"Kundgabe"* (statement or manifesto) in Bühler's sense, and in essence thoroughly unhistorical aestheticism, which can transmit experiences but scarcely knowledge. A similar error occurs when we try to interpret physiognomic characteristics pathognomically; that is, when we try to evaluate the whole structure of the expressive apparatus in an expressive sense.[48]

Instead Gombrich wanted to explain changes in formal structure between the images of classical and late antiquity by the specific demands placed on visual imagery within the respective cultural environments. He adopted a functionalist approach, which he would later articulate as an ecological theory of the image.

The second contribution to *Kritische Berichte* pursued two fallacies: First, the assumption that the medieval artist's thought processes and working practices were identical to the modern artist's, in other words that there was one state of mind in which the work of art was created; and second, that an artistic style itself was to be treated as the expression of a state of mind (Gombrich termed this the "physiognomic fallacy"). Significantly, he attributed the latter to the very success of "art history today":

A scientific appraisal of expression . . . can be concerned only with judgments based upon the understanding of the language and the discrimination and elucidation of the individual expressive features within it. Certainly the kind of language a people possesses is not a matter of mere accident. The style employed by the artists of a period is no accident either. But to see it as a super-work of art made by a super-artist is the residue of a romantic philosophy of history, and one should only subscribe to this if one knows what one is doing. To insist upon this is to forego a source of strong and subjectively very genuine enjoyment. The social success of art history today, its receptivity to the art of all times and all peoples, rests all too often upon just such a view of the art of the past. It is not the individual work of art which is enjoyed; rather, it is the language in which it is formulated, which is treated as if it were itself a work of art.[49]

Sedlmayr's projection of aesthetic values into an image or object was precisely that. Consequently, Gombrich distanced himself from aesthetics while remaining committed to working within the tradition of *Kunstwissenschaft*. This does not mean that he denied aesthetic responses to artworks, but he felt that they were bound to be subjective. If aesthetic expression occurs within a language in the context of a range of possibilities it has to be acknowledged that those possibilities change over the course of time. As T. S. Eliot wrote in "Tradition and the Individual Talent" (1919):

The existing monuments form an ideal order among themselves, which is modified by the introduction of the new (the really new) work of art among them. The existing order is complete before the new work arrives; for order to persist after the supervention of novelty, the *whole* existing order must be, if ever so slightly, altered; and so the relations, proportions, values of each work of art toward the whole are readjusted; and this is conformity between the old and the new. Whoever has approved this idea of order . . . will not find it preposterous that the past should be altered by the present as much as the present is directed by the past. And the poet who is aware of this will be aware of great difficulties and responsibilities.[50]

The poet may be aware of the difficulties but less so the un-self-critical spectator. Looking at a Raphael can never be the same after looking at a Caravaggio, and looking at a Caravaggio can never be the same after looking at a Burne-Jones. The global perception of the history of art is bound to work back on the experience of its constituent parts. That is both the fact and the problem of the experience of gestalt.

In the introduction to *The Story of Art,* Gombrich talked about liking a statue or a picture. It is natural, he argued, to like a picture for the appeal of what it depicts but "this bias for the pretty and engaging subject is apt to become a stumbling block if it leads us to reject works which represent a less appealing subject."[51] That less appealing subject may be down to the varying standards of beauty. Memling's angel is more awkward than Melozzo da Forli's: "It may take a little longer to discover the intrinsic beauty of Memling's angel, but once we are no longer disturbed by his faint awkwardness we may find him infinitely loveable."[52] What is true of beauty, Gombrich argues, is also true of expression: The expressive effect of Picasso's cockerel is decidedly different from his hen. Artists, themselves, don't talk about "beauty,"[53] they talk about getting their pictures "right." Getting a picture right is like arranging a bunch of flowers. At this point he follows traditional lines: "Anyone who has ever tried to arrange a bunch of flowers, to shuffle and shift the colours, to add a little here and take away there, has experienced this strange sensation of balancing forms and colours without being able to tell exactly what kind of harmony it is he is trying to achieve."[54] But, we might observe that if it were Duc Jean Floressas des Esseintes doing the flower arranging[55] the results would be rather different from Ilse Gombrich's: "Here, there were plants like the Bosphorus giving the illusion of starched calico spotted with crimson and myrtle green; there, others such as the Aurora Borealis flaunted leaves the colour of raw meat, with dark-red ribs and purplish fibrils, puffy leaves that seemed to be sweating blood and wine. Between them, the Albane and Aurora Borealis represented the two temperamental extremes, apoplexy and chlorosis, in this particular family of plants."[56]

Gombrich's homely example of flower arrangement makes it clear that the term "beauty" does little justice to the range of effects that artists have achieved in their work through and across cultures. Furthermore Lady Gombrich and des Esseintes were both captivated by the perfumes of their bouquets—the latter, no doubt, in relation to a whole range of exquisite liqueurs. Take the painting out of the museum and a whole range of further aesthetic possibilities opens out: It becomes part of a larger environment including other paintings, as in the case of a triptych; or for sounds, as in the case of Rubens' *Adoration of the Magi* on Christmas Eve when the Kings College Chapel choir performed the service of "Nine Lessons and Carols."

Any art historian pondering the rediscovery of aesthetics at the moment would do well to follow Riegl's advice and contemplate "the *Kunstbegehren* of his contemporaries." While the artist of the early twentieth century prototypically exhibited paintings and sculptures in a gallery or salon for purchase in home or museum, the artist of the twenty-first century may work in a variety of media where divisions are no longer stable. The concept of the work of art has extended to include land art, performance, installation, sound, multimedia, and photography, film, television, and other yet-emerging media. For museum curators and private collectors the individual painting is a prime object of financial and intellectual investment, but the art historian would have a duty to restore it to its past as a complex aesthetic object functioning within a past material and spiritual culture. The two terms "material" and "spiritual" refer to different aspects of the same object.

As Bernard Berenson observed in *The Arch of Constantine*: "If we agree that the plastic monuments of late Antiquity were painted and gilded, the talk of the Riegls and Wickhoffs about deliberately thought-out preference for the play of light and shade and emancipation from background with the consequent abstraction of space, attributed by the first to the artists of late Antiquity and for the 'impressionism' and 'illusionism,' ascribed to them by the other, would turn out to be ill-founded."[57] Many contemporary late antique texts referred to the luxuriance both of the works of art and their decorative ambiences, not to mention the rich apparel of the presiding bishop. We have to think as well of the effects of candlelight and the smell and sounds of worship to truly appreciate the works as aesthetic objects. Think also of the solitary white classical statues mounted on their plinths in luxurious modern galleries. At home in their original sites they would have been part of a multicolored "traffic jam"[58] bearing a close relationship to a sight in Disneyland.

The *Kunstbegehren* of 2007 is rather different from that of 1948, when Gombrich wrote *The Story of Art*. If we stand at the end of the history of art, we become free to engage in unconstrained aesthetic enjoyment of all art. While the art historian can do nothing to re-create past aesthetic experience as "that way is barred by the angel with a flaming sword,"[59] it should be possible to escape the straightjacket imposed by the Enlightenment concept of art and its modernist consequences. Before becoming a secular religion in the Enlightenment, the creation of art was imbricated within material culture: Its aesthetics were part of the material world.

2

Aesthetics and the Two Cultures
Why Art and Science Should Be Allowed to Go Their Separate Ways

James Elkins

I HAVE NEVER BEEN convinced that science has much to do with painting—or with art in general. This makes its relationship to aesthetics problematic insofar as people in the arts can have a very different sense of aesthetics from those working in scientific disciplines. From this point of view, any claim that there is an aesthetic understanding shared by art and science—a dimension that might be "rediscovered"—becomes especially problematic.

Several times I have started and abandoned a book project with the title *The Drunken Conversation of Science and Painting*. The title is meant to conjure a comedy of errors and misunderstandings, and the drunkenness is to imply that the two sides have some infatuation with one another, which compels them to keep talking without really connecting or making too much sense.

If there is any rediscovery of aesthetics in the discourses of science or art, it doesn't seem to be enacted in recognizable ways. There is, in fact, an intermittent conversation about aesthetics going on between art and science—it takes the form of colloquia, sessions in conferences, scattered scholarly papers, and occasional books—but I would claim it's a "drunken conversation" involving more or less drastic mutual misunderstandings of basic terms. I have elaborated this at length in an essay reprinted in *Art History versus Aesthetics*, so I won't repeat it here.[1] What I am aiming at here is a heuristic introduction to the *possibility* that art and science are disconnected because they do not share some crucial common terms, especially regarding aesthetics.

There is what I will call a *standard art–science narrative* about the points of intersection between science and art. That narrative stresses the empiricism of the early Renaissance, the geometrization of vision in the fifteenth century, the nineteenth-century infatuation with color theories, and the twentieth-century exploration of computer-assisted painting. If science is taken in a more capacious sense, then painting can be said to have come close to science many times. There have been full histories written around the standard narrative, from Ernst Gombrich's surveys of naturalism to John Gage's studies of color theory and Martin Kemp's books and his columns in *Nature*.

But there are reasons to say that the standard narrative is not wholly convincing. The first argument in the *Drunken Conversation of Science and Art* was to have been that even though the main points of the standard narrative are true, they capture very little of what makes art significant for the majority of viewers. A second argument would be that the standard narrative overestimates the scientific content of the links that it finds.

Art history's disenchantment with science is inversely proportionate to the enchantment of some scientists with what they perceive as deep consonances between art and science. Those arguments should take place within aesthetics, because they turn on the idea that science and art share central values such as simplicity, elegance, harmony, and beauty. That argument, which I think should be called the *aesthetic argument about science,* can be found for example in Subrahmanyan Chandrasekhar's book *Truth and Beauty: Aesthetics and Motivations in Science,* and in various popular treatments of the "art of science."[2]

I'd like to register my dissatisfaction with the standard art-science narrative and the aesthetic argument about science. The bulk of this essay is a review of three case studies: art historical writing about linear perspective, the "science" in Georges Seurat's *La Grande Jatte;* and the appearance of fractal geometry in some contemporary art. In each case I argue that science doesn't appear in the art, or in the art history, and that by implication an aesthetic discourse can't bridge them.

I end with some comments on the curious fact that few art historians care very much about science. It is fair to say that interest in the theme of science and art is small within art history. Conversely, scientists who write about the science of art are sometimes happily oblivious of the low quality of the art they investigate. When I suggested to Sidney Perkowitz, author of an article called "Science and Art Are Closer Than You Think," that most interesting art has little to do with science, he pointed me to his book *Empire of Light: A History of Discovery in Science and Art*—but few of the artists in it are taken seriously by critics, museums, or art historians. (He cites, for example, Kelly Houle, Mark Dagley, and Dale Eldred.[3]) I would like to come to a better understanding of why my colleagues who are interested in art-science connections and technologically informed art tend to be avoided by the plurality of the discipline and why digital painting and graphical (as opposed to political or contextual) Internet art is still an anathema to the serious art world. Of course the unpopularity of a subject has no bearing on its truth, but the lack of talk between the sides is significant for the intellectual life of the university as a whole.

Reasons to Be Skeptical of the Aesthetic Argument About Science

There is an enormous uncollected literature of the uses of terms like "beauty," "elegance," "concision," "harmony," and "balance" among scientists. It is uncollected, probably, because it is usually nearly contextless. For example, the photographer Felice Frankel, interviewed the astrophysicist Jeff Hester about the famous Hubble image of the Eagle Nebula, which he helped produce. In the course of the interview Hester says, in passing, "interestingly, the beauty of the image is not happenstance. When people talk about 'beauty,' they are talking about the presence of pattern in the midst of complexity." Frankel, the interviewer, doesn't question this, and I think it is a common enough definition among scientists. But I have never heard it among art theorists, critics, or historians, except when the subject is Rudolf Arnheim (who had theories of pictorial symmetry that lend themselves to such conclusions).[4]

Concerning the aesthetic argument for an art-science link, Leo Steinberg's attack on scientists' uses of aesthetic terms in his essay "Art and Science: Should They Be Yoked?" is exemplary. He reports on his experience at a conference of scientists. They were congratulating one another on sharing crucial concepts with art, especially an "involvement with the specific materiality of things," "the emotion of delight," and "elegance in composition."[5] Steinberg says that art's relation to materiality has lately grown somewhat intractable because of conceptual art, and he suggests that the new art demands philosophical thinking, like Arthur Danto's. He doubts that artists are interested mainly in elegance or delight, and to prove it he cites incidents of attacks on paintings and sculpture that had recently been documented by David Freedberg, in *Power of Images*. Essentially Steinberg asks if throwing acid on a painting, or striking a sculpture with a hammer, are evidence of delight. It is a brilliant move, using Freedberg's sources in such an outlandish way, and it is devastating to the sanguine and abstract notion that art is essentially "elegant."

Words from aesthetic discourse such as "beauty," "elegance," simplicity," "harmony," "delight," and "pleasure" often recur in scientists' writings about the supposed common ground with art. The terms have different histories: "Pleasure" in this sense certainly comes from Immanuel Kant, while "harmony" and "delight" could be traced back to Renaissance humanists such as Alberti, Leonardo, Filarete, and Pomponius Gauricus. But as they are deployed by contemporary scientists, I think words like "beauty" and "delight" owe more to notions of art that were current at the fin de siècle: They have the hazy idealistic feel of art criticism at the time of the symbolists, Wilde, Pater, and Stokes. Steinberg's criticisms could be sharpened by demonstrating that scientists are applying a late romantic, premodern aesthetic to art in general and that Steinberg and Freedberg's interests in distinctly non-Kantian reactions are more in tune with modern and postmodern art.

Steinberg ends on an indecisive note, wondering if the whole issue might be argued the other way. I am less undecided than him. I don't often see the work that is done by calling an equation "elegant": it is more an acknowledgment of its succinctness or its fruitfulness, or the way it compresses notations, than it is a *purpose* or even a quantifiable property. On the other hand—and here I completely agree with Steinberg—I seldom hear artists talking about how elegant, fruitful, or even beautiful their work is. Certainly those words would sound strange, or insufficient, in an art critic's mouth.

I don't think that aesthetic concepts like beauty, delight, and elegance really are the workable bridges between art and science. Those words are too unfocused, too vague and ethereal, too well intentioned, emotionally pallid, sentimentally idealistic, formal, and slippery to yoke anything I recognize as science to anything I think of as art.

Arguments Against the Standard Art-Science Narrative

I'll consider four possible arguments, in no particular order.

1. Saying, as I did, that the standard art-science narrative does not link science to *much* of art—that it hits the high points but leaves the vast majority of art untouched—does not amount to an argument that the standard narrative is wrong. But it means it can only explain part of art even in the centuries and cultures it includes. From a scientific viewpoint it does not matter if a theory explains only a little of a given subject, except that it will be abandoned if a different theory explains more of the subject—and that has not happened with the standard narrative.

2. It is the case that artists prominent in the standard narrative tend to be minor in art historical accounts. There is the seventeenth-century painter Ludovico Cigoli, who knew Galilei Galileo and painted the mountains of the moon; or the French painter Henri Valenciennes, who studied clouds with great accuracy; or the Dutch painter Gerard Ter Borch, known since his revival as a master of silks and satins; or the contemporary artist Vija Celmins, who paints stars and galaxies in the style of painterly abstraction. If you were to read only introductory chemistry and crystallography texts, it would seem that the minor artist M. C. Escher is one of the century's most important innovators, but he remains absent from art historical textbooks. The canon of scientifically interesting artists is a strange one, a fact that should be bothersome because the values that make the art worth studying to begin with are at odds with the values that proceed from inquiries that search for scientific content.

3. It's also true that in the twentieth century in particular, artists have been more interested in the applications of science in technology, new media, and engineering than in science itself. The conceptual apparatus of hypothesis and experiment hardly figures in art, while the technological apparatus of machinery, engineering, architecture, and scientific schemata have been ubiquitous since the "machine aesthetic" first came to the attention of the surrealists in the 1920s.

4. What appears as science in modern art in particular is actually popularized science. Pablo Picasso learned a little about relativity from a high school teacher. Cubism cannot be explained well in terms of

relativity, and Picasso himself didn't care: He used the bit of relativity he knew in a wilfully eccentric fashion. Popular science was a source for Odilon Redon, Max Ernst, René Magritte, Francis Picabia, and many others: But which artists made use of unpopularized science? The really exemplary scholarship of Linda Dalrymple Henderson shows this over and over: There is an intricate dialogue between modernism and science, but what appears as science is almost always popular science—or at least misunderstood, or reimagined science.

The science in art, especially in the past two centuries, is simplified, misunderstood, or otherwise modified, and after a point it becomes counterintuitive to think of it as science at all. I take it as a starting point in this subject that science per se will not appear in art, because without the art it would *only* be science. The scientific content will therefore be embedded in a new matrix, one that will necessarily work against the scientific content as much as it enriches or otherwise alters it. At some point this should be troubling to people who study appearances of science in art, because it seems that what is being counted as scientific content is nothing more than remnants of scientific forms stripped of their content. Intentionally nonsensical uses of science are an exception, as in Marcel Duchamp's inversions of scientific—but mainly technological—ideas. Many more artists take bits and pieces of science and put them together collage-fashion without attending to their original meanings.

In sum: Western art has not obtained much of its meaning from science. To paraphrase T. J. Clark, science dines very poorly on the leavings of art.[6] (He said it the other way around, but both are true.)

The Refraction of Perspective in Art History

I now turn to the less scientific and empirical aspects of this subject, and try to explain why art historians care so little for science, and I turn to the aesthetic argument. There are some large explanations available here, having to do with different educations, with the "two cultures," as C. P. Snow defined them, and with the histories of disciplines. Some headway can be made by taking specific examples. I'll consider two: the first has to do with the way that the mathematical discourse of linear perspective is deformed when it is imported into art history.

Art historical texts that deal with perspective normally adopt one of two ways of working. Either they tend to be nontechnical and stress unquantitative qualities of the artworks or else they present themselves as technical papers, of interest to specialists in the history of perspective. Each subgenre has a typical methodology adapted to its public.

In the first type, mathematical argument is avoided in favor of heuristic approaches couched in nontechnical language, normally peppered with perspective terms. Recent texts have taken perspective and its chief concepts in metaphoric and poetic senses, in part on the authority of the roots of perspective in ancient rhetoric; scholars have read symbolic, rhetorical, and expressive significance into mathematical terms such as "picture plane" and "axonometry." There have been Lacanian and Husserlian readings of perspective and claims that epistemology itself is optimally modeled and to some extent prefigured in perspective. Perspective has been taken as a model of capitalism, of subjectivity, of the Kantian experience of space, and of the self-alienation of the philosophic subject.

In the second type of writing, perspective's terms are confined to nonallegorical meanings and the flow of the text itself may be interrupted by diagrams and formulas. The grafting of geometry onto humanist narrative can give such texts a consistent unresolved tension.

In *The Poetics of Perspective* I conclude that perspective is an instance of the refraction between art history and a rigorous discourse it admires. Technical terms, dropped into what the classicist Wesley Trimpi calls "literary" writing (as opposed to "geometric" writing), have an unpolished, inharmonious relation to their surroundings.[7] That contextlessness propels the terms, and the narratives that embed them, toward ever more unified, holistic connotations, and in extended texts individual terms such as "picture plane" can even become referents for "rigorous perspective" *as a whole.*

Perspective thus enters art history not only as a loose, partly inconsistent collection of rhetorical redefinitions (as in Svetlana Alpers's work) or as an ahistorical presence borrowed from mathematics, but also as a thing signified as a whole: Its individual meanings, proofs, injunctions, applications, technical procedures, specific history, and so forth—the range of its original meanings and uses—collapse into the flow of nontechnical, "literary" prose. When perspective terms act as an aggregate, they can buttress the persuasiveness of the text as a whole and create a certain scientific tone that can be used to underwrite broader conclusions—

even if those conclusions aren't really supported by the dazzling imported technical terms. The distance point, ground point, plane of projection, standpoint, measuring points, sociography, inverse perspective, reverse perspective, curvilinear perspectives, and the many rules for ellipses, ellipsoids, hyperbolae, and other exotic forms in perspective comprise a kind of homeless language that drifts, without adjudication, in the pages of art historical texts.

The complexities of these transformations can give art historical texts on perspective a quality not often encountered in their perspectival originals: They can be effectively free of the possibility of clear refutation or confirmation. This is so because the technical glosses necessary to prepare their arguments for refutation or confirmation would be unwieldy. I cannot argue this fully here, because a demonstration would involve close readings of selected texts (e.g., Peter De Bolla's Foucauldian analysis of the introductions to English perspective texts or Hubert Damisch's Lacanian and Husserlian analysis of the *città ideali* paintings). What *can* be shown is that perspective *in* or *as* art history is disconnected from its geometric, mathematical, deductive original: It becomes, for better or worse, something new. Perspective is excerpted, the mathematics are removed, the actual constructions are deleted. "Perspective" in art history becomes incommensurate with its original.

The *Grande Jatte* Problem: What Is Science When It Is Immersed in Art?

Masaccio's *Trinità*, as every textbook proclaims, is the first surviving painting in linear perspective. Does that mean, to draw the standard implication, that mathematics and painting were allied at that moment? Seurat's *La Grande Jatte* was made with color theory in mind: But does that mean late nineteenth-century color theory and postimpressionism were linked? These aren't straightforward questions, because on one level the answer is yes to both, but in another sense some violence is done to both color science and mathematics when they are said to be present in the paintings. It's a longer argument than can be accommodated here; my example will be *La Grande Jatte*.

Even after more than one hundred years, *La Grande Jatte* resists those who claim to see everything in it. The painting puts up formidable obstacles to any interpretation. To begin with, it is not always easy to know what Seurat knew: The most frequently cited sources for Seurat's scientism are near-contemporaries Félix Fénéon and Paul Signac, and Seurat is not on record unambiguously agreeing with either one.[8] In addition, Seurat was an uneven reader of science—some things he studied hard; others, offhandedly, and there are examples of willful misunderstanding and selective reading. It is clear that he misunderstood a great deal, and some of the theorists he misunderstood were themselves mistaken.[9] Assessing that kind of error involves studying twentieth-century color theory, which is itself a difficult subject. And aside from each of these problems, the painting itself seems unreliable, since its colors have faded unmeasurably and unevenly over time.

Even so, these are only preliminary obstacles. They allow us to say—and this is the emerging consensus in recent scholarship—that Seurat was a poor scientist, confused even in comparison to the popular science writers of his day, so that *La Grande Jatte* is not, in this respect, "a definitive formulation of the technique, method, and theory of Neo-Impressionism."[10] It may be true that Seurat's "earnest convictions . . . provided both the justification and motivation for artistic projects more ambitious than he might otherwise have undertaken," but that does not explain what the projects were.[11] If pseudoscience was a catalyst to Seurat's creation, what did it allow him to get on with?

It needs to be said clearly that Seurat had no reason to paint any of the color effects he had been studying, because if they were accurate records of our subjective experience, they would be produced for us by any painting or natural scene. There is no reason to paint the world in dots in order to simulate the surfaces of the world, and there is no reason to paint simultaneous contrast, halos, iridescence or Mach bands, chiaroscuro, gradation, or any of the other phenomena since they would be reproduced in the act of perception. That is the fundamental stumbling block to calling Seurat "scientific," and it is striking that Seurat himself copied a warning to this effect directly from Michel Eugène Chevreul.[12] Seurat read Chevreul fairly loosely, and it is at least possible that his interest in depicting simultaneous contrast was sparked by the fact that Chevreul had a large color illustration of it printed in his book.[13] On the other hand Hermann von Helmholtz's essay on painting and science, which Seurat apparently did not read, would have given him a reason to reproduce certain effects. When pigments cannot match the intensities of outdoor lighting, Helmholtz says, then painters might resort to subjective phenomena in order to remind viewers of the original conditions. But even if Seurat had seen that essay, it would not have any bearing on his project in *La Grande Jatte*, because the phenomena he studied are also effects of less intense illumination.[14]

Seurat's "science" mixes empiricism and idealism in a manner that is at once specific and opaque to any single explanation: To adapt a phrase of Martin Kemp's, it is neither science, pseudoscience, nonscience, nor non-sense. It is not entirely "specious in its theoretical formulation . . . applied with an indifference to any critical appraisal," but neither is it "a definitive formulation of the technique, method, and theory of Neo-Impressionism."[15] The problem is initially a matter of finding out how Seurat conceived science, empiricism, logic, and self-consistency; but ultimately, the difficulty is finding *any way* to construct a responsible account of the picture. No matter which scientific theories we may decide to accept and which rules of application or irrelevancy we may adopt, the painting refuses to play along. *La Grande Jatte* is not an example of *any* theory, mistaken or otherwise.

As we know from Seurat's writings and from his friends, theory is what got his pictures started: He imagined theories as their underpinnings, their raisons d'être, and their necessary and sufficient explanations. But his imagining was flawed. Science and painting do not get along in *La Grande Jatte*—they do not speak for one another, and they do not exemplify or signify one another. Their mutual disregard is uneven and sometimes—as in the "dots" that Joris-Karl Huysmans so brilliantly called "running fleas"—destructive.

John Gage concluded that Seurat was indeed "scientific," because of his "experimentalism,"[16] and years before Robert Herbert had said the same thing. To Herbert, Seurat was scientific because he studied ephemeral phenomena of vision.[17] "Science" in Herbert's and Gage's texts is an activity involving hypothesis, experiment, and falsification, and those are efficient and common characterizations of the scientific project. But two things stand in the way of enlisting Seurat's painting as science, as thus defined. First it would have to be shown how *La Grande Jatte* is an instance of any experiment, or a consistent application of some coherent hypothesis. But then, even if *La Grande Jatte* embodies an experiment, it would have to be shown that the experiment had relevance to contemporary color science. To say his work is "experimentalist" is to say it borrows the *idea* of experiment from science, not that it is an example of a scientific experiment. It engages popular notions of science and translates them, unscientifically, into paint.

There's a certain anxiety here regarding painting's inability to contain science. Why else should Seurat want to claim that his method demanded no manual skill? What else did he mean by saying his painting showed "the strictest application of scientific principles seen through a personality"? Why else might he have said that "they see poetry in what I have done. No, I apply my method and that is all there is to it"?[18] To *insist* on the absence of affect is to protest too strongly and therefore to reveal an unease about the supposedly affectless "method." "Painting" has to be done indirectly, by thinking only about "science," but at the same time—and this is the "failure" of the painting and ultimately what makes it so interesting—science is ruined by painting, it cannot exist in painting, it dies in painting.

Herbert supposes that this might have provided a kind of rationalist crutch—that the theory was a poorly built bridge from art to science. The painters wanted pure colors, Herbert proposes, and their theory helped them along with a bit of rationalism. It also helped the viewers, who could begin to read the canvases with the help of a theory.[19] Alan Lee has echoed this in saying that the neo-impressionist movement needed to see itself as scientific in order to get under way.[20] But there is more here than science, or theory, as springboard for invention: The science is woven into the work itself and into our experience of it. Science is stuck in *La Grande Jatte* like an insect in amber, preserved as the "flaw" that completes the work.

I draw two conclusions from these examples. First, after a point—one that I think can hardly be defined—it ceases to make sense to refer to what happens in some artworks as science. The "science" becomes something weird, a dream or nightmare or collage or garbled mistranslation of science, but it isn't science. The best way to understand what happens in a work like *La Grande Jatte* is to let the science go and think of its traces in the work as a kind of necessary fiction. Second, this is where art history comes in, because what matters is how Seurat and his contemporaries thought of what they were doing—how they came to believe that what they were doing was scientific or that it had "method." It is profoundly unscientific to think in terms of groups of people, discourses, and conventions that lead people to believe certain things are true: But it is the only way to make contact with the reasons that *La Grande Jatte* or the *Trinità* are still central to what we think of as painting or art. Let me call this the

Grande Jatte problem: To get at the science in art it is necessary to leave the science behind.

Chaos Theory and Painting

An analogous argument can be made about fractal geometry and chaos theory, kinds of physics and mathematics that are strongly visual. The swirling, "paisley" patterns and "biomorphs" that are familiar on calendars, postcards, and computer screens are drawn by the computer in the same way that a parabola or a circle is drawn by a geometry student— except that the calculations necessary for detailed fractal forms are beyond human capacity. Most of the attention in the technical literature is focused on the properties of the equations or on their applications. But neither the scientists nor the mathematicians are free of artistic purpose, and they alter and enhance the bare mathematics in order to make their printouts into aesthetically pleasing pictures. That artistic overlay is significant for a number of reasons: The scientists who create the images tend to have an unsteady grounding in the history of art, and they draw on nascent and uncognized aesthetics to choose and arrange their images. Writers in the humanities therefore experience the new geometry at a double remove, because they see the forms without their mathematical meanings and with an overlay of colors and compositions that are not dictated by the equations.

Despite the growing literature, neither side sees the other very clearly. There are two "strange attractors" (a fractal geometry expression) involved in this conversation: One, the seductive world of art, aligned, as it seems to those outside it, with culture, meaning, and a host of ghostly values including elegance and beauty. The other, the forbidding world of mathematical physics, empowered so it seems to those outside it, with a wondrous new way of understanding the world. As in the two cases of perspective and nineteenth-century color theory, science and art are enamored of one another, and, like lovers in a comedy, they imagine the object of their attention somewhat unrealistically.

Within mathematics, there is no question of the importance of the new discoveries. The "new geometry" knows itself to be fundamental: "Euclid," Benoit Mandelbrot announces in *The Fractal Geometry of Nature,* will be "used in this work to denote all of standard geometry."[21] Interestingly this new geometry also knows itself to be beautiful and thus deliberately invokes an aesthetic reflection upon its products as if they were art (though the nature and extent of that knowledge are open to question). Mandelbrot quotes an article in *Science* that makes a parallel between cubism, atonal music, and modern mathematics beginning with "Cantor's set theory and Peano's space-filling curves." He sees a rococo phase in mathematics before the modern era, followed by a visual austerity.[22] When it comes to art, he makes a poorly articulated and unconvincing historical and aesthetic reading of his own fractal inventions, according to which the extravagant, ebullient forms he has visualized are "minimalist art"—a most unlikely identification.[23] There is also an unwillingness on Mandelbrot's part to mix art and science: When computer printouts are to be judged aesthetically, he gives them self-parodistic titles such as the "Computer Bug as Artist, Opus 1," thereby publishing aesthetic results as mistakes, "bugs" in programs. Part of the meaning of such titles resides in Mandelbrot's mimicry of contemporary painting styles; "Opus 2" is like an angular Clifford Still or Franz Kline. He also thinks his polychromic computer printouts are "austere."[24] The reason is they have simple mathematics behind them, and so his misidentification with minimalism is an example of nonvisual thinking—what a mathematician would call "analytic" rather than "synthetic" reasoning.[25]

Meanwhile, mathematicians such as Hans-Otto Peitgen "wrap" fractal images around spheres, so their computers can generate "moons" and fantasy spacescapes that are less like the tongue-in-cheek graffiti of Kenny Scharf than they are like the serious kitsch of the fin de siècle. Computer palettes continue to be set in psychedelic, hokey, holographic, iridescent, heavy metal combinations. (Colors are not part of the mathematical properties of fractals. They are chosen at will by the programmers.) The aesthetic values of the mathematicians are circumscribed by the domain of fantasy, especially medieval revival and late-twentieth-century primitivism, and their formal strategies devolve from unacknowledged sources in German romanticism. They are anything but postmodern, though the artists that admire the new geometry often are.[26]

The art world certainly has not done much better in understanding what the mathematicians are saying. Discourse is marked by misuse of mathematical terminology, a love of catchwords, and the construction of more or less tenuous metaphorical bridges between the concerns of the humanities and the claims of the new geometry. The lexicon of this *scienza nuova* rhymes with terms already given us by post-structuralism:

chaos theory, chaotic dynamics, fractal, fractoid, fractal dimension, rupture, elementary catastrophe, laminar flow, turbulence, irregularity, imbalance, iteration, self-similarity, spikes, dwell bands, connected sets, and a host of eponymous attractors (Rössler's, Lorenz's, Ueda's), all resonate with figures already at use in contemporary visual theory and literary criticism.

For example, Slavoj Žižek's *Looking Awry* describes a swirling, wreathlike strange attractor as an " 'anamorphotically' disfigured circle." This usage takes anamorphosis (as in his title) and the misspelled word "anamorphotically" (the usual form is "anamorphically") from Jacques Lacan's description of the gaze and brings them into a context in which they have no mathematical meaning. Anamorphosis has resonance with other passages in *Looking Awry,* but it is interesting that Žižek does not find it necessary to remark either on the meaning of the new spelling or on the absence of any projection in chaotic dynamics that might give the term mathematical sense. This particular kind of ruptured context is often accompanied by "risky" homologies (the word is Žižşek's), and in this case he draws a parallel between the opposition of normal and strange attractors and "the opposition between the balance toward which the pleasure principle strives and the Freudian Thing embodying enjoyment."[27] Both neologisms and "risky" homologies function by eliding scientific context.

Both the mathematicians and the artists are agreed on one point: Fractal geometry might somehow be applied to painting (or to film or computer graphics) because it models natural forms so well. But even that notion may not be as straightforward as first assumed. On the surface, it is easy to see why some artists and computer graphics experts are intrigued by the potential uses of fractals. It's not just that the new geometry looks like everything in nature from frost ferns to silver trees. It's that it looks so much like older styles of Western and non-Western painting. In one place, its forms are virtual duplicates for rococo frills and swags. Other equations recall rocaille, *Ohrmuschelwerk* (cartouches in the form of ears), arabesques, and even paisley. And there are echoes of the intentional asymmetries of Alexander Cozens and John Constable, and the "leaf beauty" of John Ruskin. The meteorologist E. N. Lorenz, who helped found chaotic dynamics by discovering the first "strange attractor" in a simplified model of atmospheric circulation, has recently become interested in these associations.[28] I visited him once in his lab at MIT, and he showed me printouts of strange attractors (systems of differential equations) in which tangled lines within larger tangles reminded him of a bird in a thorn bush (he labeled his printouts that way)—but such forms also speak of painting and bear an uncanny resemblance to some Chinese painting such as Chu Ta's many versions of *Bird and Rock*.[29] The metaphoric range appears unlimited within the domain of represented and real organic and inorganic growth.

This apparently unlimited applicability may then be contrasted to the near-absence of geometric rules in modern painting. Modern art had long ago "overthrown" linear perspective, which was the traditional theoretical geometric accompaniment of artists' organic improvisations. Postmodernism has long since forgotten that act of forgetting, and for several decades, except in the specialized case of geometric abstraction, painting has been without its traditional geometric foundation. Since chaotic dynamics and fractals are the first theories that purport to account for those nonlinear phenomena that were once taken to be ungeometric and beyond the reach of Euclid, they have the potential to be far more decisive in painting than linear perspective with its patently artificial rules could ever hope to be. Potentially the new geometry could ground every organic, asymmetric, complex form in painting in a way analogous to the way linear perspective stands behind the infinite, the isotropic, the mechanical, and the architectonic. In such a scenario the relation between painters and their geometry would also change: Artists could no longer escape the heritage of geometry by turning to organic forms like landscapes, and, conversely, it would no longer be as clear what would constitute a use or even acceptance of the new geometry, since fractals would presumably remain impractical for drawing (except by computer). There will be no book titled *Elementary Lessons in Fractal Drawing*.

Mark Tansey has done several paintings with fractal themes. In one, surveyors attempt to measure a wild coastline. Their instruments are no match for their subject, especially since it is itself a gigantic version of a Julia set, one of the derivatives of the Mandelbrot set, a fundamental fractal form. The rocks pun into fractal "seahorses," forming a progression of nearly but not perfectly identical forms. The lowest seahorse, the one behind the female surveyor at the right, epitomizes the new mysteriousness by sporting an implacable sphinx's face; and beneath her hand smaller seahorse sphinxes curl away into an undefinable infinity. This is a new way for geometry to be with painting: Instead of being "in perspective" or "in" some other geometry, the painting is "about" geometry. Renaissance painters used perspective, but they didn't draw pictures *of* perspective. The new approach is self-reflexive, but it is also problematic, since it is not an *application* in the sense that fractals seem to promise.

I do not mean to promote sobriety, or to say that there is some ideal form of responsible communication between these scientists and these artists. Instead, I would like to suggest that we consider the meanings and the potential of our writing on the subject rather than continuing as if the new forms could simply be "applied" to the world or "imported" into art, or as if any metallic enhancement of a computer graph would make an acceptable picture. Equally it is hard to know what is inappropriate. The relation of perspective, the outgoing geometric standard, to this new source of geometry is problematic and unresolved. It is possible that the mathematicians' dependence on fantasy art and decadent popular illustration might be close to contemporary art in ways that we do not yet appreciate. Nor does it necessarily make sense to emend the humanists' use of scientific terms for distant rhetorical purposes, since that custom is well attested in the history of Western thought.

The art world imbibes its science with some abandon, and scientists sidle up to art without knowing quite what to say. The various mistranslations may be evidence that the exchange between geometry and painting has not yet run its course. In particular, I would like to read the metaphorization of mathematics by the humanities, and the rewriting of visual history in mathematical terms, as legacies of the unresolved—unresolvable—traditions of linear perspective.

Conclusions

The cognitive scientist Ellen Winner's essay, "Art History Can Trade Insights with the Sciences," is an example of the kind of perplexity with which scientists note art historians' lack of interest in science.[30] Winner says, plausibly, that the only reason the claims advanced by the physicist Charles Falco are known in art history is because he teamed up with David Hockney and was prominent at the N.Y.U. conference in December 2001, at which art history was under "attack." At the beginning of her essay, Winner lists seven reasons why art historians reject Falco's claims about the use of optical aids by Renaissance artists, beginning with "artists did not need to 'cheat' because they were highly trained in drawing from observation," and so forth. She notes that four of the seven do not rule out optical devices. She does not comment on the seventh reason: "the lens hypothesis . . . is of no interest to art historians." Toward the end of the essay, she notes that Falco and Hockney "did not speak of the meaning or beauty of a work, issues that engage humanists. But why didn't art historians think it important to learn *how* an artist created that work?"

No answer appears in her essay. It is a crucial question, however, for the abyssal misunderstandings between art and science. Part of the answer is that few art historians think that it is promising that "neuroscience is moving into the study of the arts," so that magnetic resonance imaging allow scientists "to track how the brain processes works of art."

Another part of the answer is that historians relativize truth to its contexts. For example, Winner shows that if an art historian like David Galenson argues that Picasso's *Women of Avignon* is his best work, that shows he is the product of a certain history of the reception of Picasso, one that he partly orchestrated. Other histories—which are available—would have given Galenson different starting points.[31]

Still another part of the answer is that art historians don't talk in terms of evidence, hypothesis, and conclusions—not always (though certainly often) because they are not "trained" in it. This occurs for a more systemic reason: They belong to a different writing tradition, the one Wesley Trimpi calls "literary." Winner is right to keep calling on art historians to pay attention to science; but she misunderstands the reasons why most art historians will not answer, no matter what their educational background. It does not need to be laid at the door of education, as C. P. Snow did: It depends on a deeper division in Western discourse.

Three insuperable problems and the result is a lurching incoherent conversation: The one we have had for the last hundred years and which shows no signs of sobering up.

3

Stones of Solace

Michael Ann Holly

REDISCOVERING AESTHETICS—or better yet, writing in its service—is a quest that comes in many shapes, in many guises. In this essay I engage in three intertwined meditations on this vexed and vital topic. First, I think about art historical narrative as an essentially melancholic pursuit. In the discipline of art history, we have a loss (the past) without a lost object (the work of art). Second, the concept of *research* in art history often goes so unquestioned as to be almost invisible, and I tentatively call it into visibility. And, third, a recently renewed interest in the writing of a nearly forgotten mid-twentieth-century British aesthete, Adrian Stokes, offers an occasion to explore one of the roads not taken in the evolution of the history of art.

On July 5, 1925, the young Stokes, who was to become an essayist, painter, ballet aficionado, and psychoanalytic soothsayer, visited the rather triste seacoast town of Rimini for the first time and knew on that bright morning "at once of the life, the landscape, the condition of which the Tempio [Malatestiano] is the emblem."[1] Asking himself "why it should be worth my while to transpose into terms of drama what is immediate and objective to the eye," his "excuse" was that "poetry pure and simple" must be leavened by "a good deal of explanation as well."[2] As is forever fated to be the case, the explanation he left us three-quarters of a century ago has become dated and historically questionable, but the "poetry pure and simple" of his prose lingers for those of us who have a taste for the melancholic.

Stoke's text, *The Stones of Rimini*, written in 1934, is a curious, almost oxymoronic, blend of the scientific and poetic. Long passages recounting the geological origins of limestone gracefully transform themselves into an invocation of the deepest sensations of feeling embodied in both the physical act of carving and the metaphysical act of looking. Permeating the work is a sense of loss about time and life gone by. And yet his vivifying rhetoric constitutes a powerful act of reparation. Given his psychoanalytic convictions (Stokes was long a patient of Melanie Klein),[3] this process is not surprising. What is remarkable is Stokes's ability to turn the act of writing itself into a luminous invocation of what is both simultaneously lost and found in the very materiality of images.

It's this edge of melancholy that interests me most: not the iconography of the humor, but rather its translation into a historiographic point of view. The actual physical materiality of objects that have survived the ravages of time in order to exist in the present frequently confounds the art historian who retroactively sets out to turn them back into past ideas, social realities, documents of personality, and, in Stokes's case, even "the action of wind on water." In their obdurate resistance to such an easy mediation between past and present, the still stilled works of art (the silence of stones) sometimes provoke a heuristic despair that is difficult to overcome. According to David Carrier, "Stokes links the stillness of Quattro Cento art to outwardness, to objectivity, and to death. He has a special admiration for stillness in art, for he associates it with the absence of musical rhythm found in purely visual art. Quattro Cento sculpture achieves stillness, which is to say that it is detached, or deathlike. 'Detached thought is near death, is death's instrument, turning life to stone.'"[4]

Yet solace is not far behind. Objects of art, like souvenirs, metonymically express what Susan Stewart has characterized as the "lost presence."[5] Images are so often what we depend upon "in order to take note of what has passed away."[6] The contemplative conundrum that arises from the recognition of an inability to make words connect with images, that is, to write a definitive history of art, was for Stokes, as it was at the same time for Walter Benjamin, that prescient theologian of melancholy—the essential trait of the mournful sensibility.[7]

An allied and idiosyncratic question that *The Stones of Rimini* provokes for me pivots around the role of research in art history. Surely it is not too absurd to wonder why we don't write today as Stokes once did. By way of my fascination with this particular text, I want to "use" him to try and think about contemporary art history. I am a convinced advocate of retroactive readings, in other words, using the commitments of the present to engage ideas from the past, and vice versa.

Here is the main object Stokes is talking about in *The Stones of Rimini*: the Tempio Malatestiano (the Malatesta Temple). In the middle of the fifteenth century, Leon-Battista Alberti was given the commission to enclose the Gothic church of San Francesco with an exterior temple design that became a monument to one of the most erudite but nevertheless one of the most ruthless tyrants of the Renaissance, Sigismondo Malatesta, and his wife, Isotta degli Atti. Sigismondo carries the distinction of having been the only man in history to have been "publicly condemned to Hell while still alive: the ceremony was performed with due solemnity by the humanist pope Pius II in front of St. Peter's."[8]

Neither Alberti's facade nor Sigismondo's follies, however, are what Stokes the aesthete traveled from England to see. Once inside the temple he bowed in reverence to one of the forgotten masters of Renaissance sculpture, Agostino di Duccio, whose reliefs celebrate not only the romance of Sigismondo and Isotta, but the heavens and gods who exerted the celestial influences that intertwined the lovers into eternity.[9] First things first, however. It's the quiet ancient limestone—the actual physical thing itself—with which Stokes himself had become enamored. His fierce and poetic commitment is to the material medium itself, the stone: not what stands behind the work of art (social realities, iconographic programs, religious sentiments, etc.) and certainly not what stands before it (spectators, interpretations, reception theory, etc.), but the actual ancient limestone itself before it comes to life in the carver's hands. So often in the history of art its practitioners pass through the medium as though it had no felt substance, as though it were there merely to support the stories or to lend corporeal embodiment to the artist's skill. The looking glass through which Alice in Wonderland as art historian passes from one side to the other remains invisible in so much aesthetic writing from Kant onward. Yet Stokes refuses to let it be so. A cascade of unconnected sentences and the reliefs to which they randomly refer can show you what I mean.

"I write of stone,"[10] he declares in his first short sentence. Stone, the concretion of time, that which possesses an "aesthetic meaning that corresponds to no conscious aesthetic aim."[11] "Stone the solid, yet the habitat of soft light like the glow of flesh, is the material, so I shall maintain, that inspires all the visual arts."[12] "How intimate and how ancient the association between images of limestone and of water."[13] "Agostino's root preoccupation was with water forms and water movement."[14] "In the Tempio reliefs Mediterranean life has complete expression: there, water is stone."[15] "And what beautiful things water does to stone, just as stone to water."[16] "The Agostino reliefs have the appearance of marble limbs seen in water."[17] "Fish slither and wriggle in Quattro Cento relief and arabesque. The stone is alive with them."[18] "The reliefs are for the most part low, yet their forms possess many values of sculpture in the round: while the quickened mass of a human shape between wind-strewn films of drapery, the delicious torture of hair and clothing by an unseen, evocative wind upon the outer and intermediary surfaces of a relief, give to its body the effect of vitality, of that stone-blossom we prize so high."[19] "The material, earth or stone, exists. Man makes it more significant."[20] "From the stone comes a new fearless energy . . . [the putto] makes the air move. . . . He bursts stone like earth, at Rimini he rides the dolphin, his tempestuous energy kindles a flame that withers tasteful ornamental foliage poor in sap, and heats the luscious growth to a vibrant, tropical bulbosity."[21] "This particular sensitiveness to luminous gradations of marble, Greek or not Greek, is through and through Mediterranean . . . relief . . . [is] a dramatized form of carving. The shape is on the surface, the matrix behind it."[22]

The matrix within which Stokes's particular imagination exists has always been, for me, evocative of a few unforgettable passages about the past in the disparate writings of Aby Warburg, Fernand Braudel, and Martin Heidegger: It is almost as though a conversation is going on among the four of them—which of course it chronologically could not have been—beneath or beyond their manifest subject matter. Where do such correspondences come from, and how else do we write about these resonances except through the melancholic imagination that gathers bits and pieces together to construe another kind of narrative? It is the kind of story that compels Stokes to meditate on ammonites and storms at sea and turn it into a story of Renaissance sculpture. Stokes's recourse to tangled hair and its sensuous flowing patterns, along with his turn to drapery and its revealing pleats and folds—and the ways in which both touch on the most primal of psychic needs—are themes in direct correspondence with Warburg's obsessions throughout his whole life, of which so much has been made of late in the revival of his legend.[23] Stokes's geo-

logical evocation of the "longue durée" of the material world of Mediterranean culture presages Braudel's masterly two-volume study of the same
place and time, in which the annaliste wonders if it might be "possible
somehow to convey simultaneously both that conspicuous history [see
Stokes's reference to the iconography of the reliefs] which holds our attention by its continual and dramatic changes—and that other, submerged,
history, [see Stokes's action of wind and water upon stone] almost silent
and always discreet, virtually unsuspected either by its observers or its
participants, which is little touched by the obstinate erosion of time."[24]

The most striking revelation about the compulsions that drive any
of us to write about the past, however, occurs somewhere in the space that
lies between Stokes and Heidegger. Both of their phenomenological commitments run deep; their turn to Greek temples as a metaphor for the
enduring nature of art is memorable. Here are a couple of lengthy excerpts, with illustrations of the temple of Segesta in Sicily as backdrop,
which Stokes described as set "amid the young, folded hills, a temple
stands commanding the far-flung sea."[25] Stokes first:

[Looking at it there] then we may understand how mere marble men and women
could be works of art and could be deities, why the waters of springs were gathered
deep and clear in marble shrines; why fountains of limestone, colonnades of limestone, baths of pillared hues and crystalline cooling depths, porticoes of deep shadows reverberating like wells, are common in classical art; . . . why . . . in all stonework
typically Mediterranean there is somewhere expressed the identification or mutual
consummation of limestone and water, there is expressed water made solid, permanent, glowing instead of glassy, set in space and brightened by the dripping rains.[26]

[Alas] we can never see Greek temples as they were meant to be seen, quite apart
from the destruction they have suffered of their more transient adornments. In a
more profound sense they want their completeness; their steps; their porticoes want
the flashing gait and the young, garlanded head. They want the slow climbers to
their hills and promontories."[27]

And here is Heidegger, from "The Origin of a Work of Art":

Standing there, the building rests on rocky ground. This resting of the work draws
up out of the rock the mystery of that rock's clumsy yet spontaneous support. Standing there, the building holds its ground against the storm raging above it and so first
makes the storm itself manifest in its violence. The luster and gleam of the stone,
though itself apparently glowing only by the grace of the sun, yet first brings to light

the light of the day, the breadth of the sky, the darkness of the night. The temple's firm towering makes visible the invisible space of air. The steadfastness of the work contrasts with the surge of the surf, and its own repose brings out the raging of the sea. Tree and grass, eagle and bull, snake and cricket first enter into their distinctive shapes and thus come to appear as what they are. The Greeks called this emerging and rising in itself and in all things *phusis*. . . . The temple, in its standing there, first gives to things their look and to men their outlook on themselves.[28]

The raw sentiments behind these poetic passages differ, of course. Stokes imagines himself, like John Keats,[29] back in the world of truth and beauty that bred these garlanded heads, these perfect proportions, this glow of the temple after a soft and dripping rain. Heidegger, on the other hand, like Wallace Stevens, in his poem "The Anecdote of the Jar," sees the work of art, in its eternal steadfastness, as always making visible the storms and seas that surround it, bringing to light the light of the day, resting solemnly in the darkness of the night. The invocation of the temple—the steadfast icon of what is past but nevertheless is also still always there—is what wraps the historian Stokes's words round with melancholy and causes the philosopher Heidegger to dream of "worlding" utopias that have not yet arrived. The objectness of the object of art and the contemplation of the past that can envelop the viewer in its otherness are here serving two very different intellectual and ideological agendas.

Stokes had a word for this process: "incantatory," the overpowering pull of the work of art that may or may not be accompanied by a process of reparation that eventuates in solace—in the boldness of psychoanalytic terms of the thirties (especially those of Melanie Klein, Stokes's own psychoanalyst, and her legacy in object relation theorists) and the restoration of the good mother, whom we feel "ourselves to have damaged in fantasy and that we therefore set about restoring in the activity of art."[30] In more contemporary language, as Christopher Bollas puts it, aesthetic appreciation may consist of a "deep subjective rapport with an object . . . an uncanny fusion . . . of something never cognitively apprehended but existentially known."[31] Perhaps this is the aim of making art, I would argue, but not the result of writing about it, for language inevitably puts distance between the work and the apprehending subject.

The comparison between Stokes and Heidegger brings out just how much the art historian or critic, dedicated to the restitution of a work of art and not its primal "origin," must inevitably suffer from the pangs of melancholy. I once imagined that the two thinkers could embody—in their differing uses and abuses of the past—the Freudian distinction between mourning and melancholia. In mourning, what Freud called "non-pathological," the past is seen as "over"; the recognition that the death (literal or symbolic) of the beloved is not in turn the death of oneself is liberating. In melancholia, the wound continues to bleed, and the griever introjects the death as his own. In mourning, loss is conscious; in melancholia, loss is unconscious, and in this condition pathologically repeats "the absence that death is" over and over again.[32] Yet this distinction won't work for Heidegger, for his invocation of the temple is not about a loss of any kind but only a creation, a bringing to birth, a "worlding." So does it work for Stokes? Does Heidegger's temple throw into relief the "suffering" of Stokes?

In her work on depression, Melanie Klein repeatedly stresses how the rebuilding of the inner world of the psyche after loss is a labor often without end.[33] Of course, it is this impulse toward reparation that leads to the making of art as well as the act of writing about it. Art history lives in a paradox: It writes about loss without lost objects. Its narrative structure is necessarily elegiac, but the materiality of works of art that are its subjects presents a challenge to ever seeing the past as over and gone. Stokes deeply mourns the diminution of the world of the Greek temple by the manufacturing of "plastic" materials that obliterate the beauty of stone from distant geological ages: "Synthetic materials take the place of age-old products in which fantasy is deposited. . . . Mountains and pebbles still exist: but so far as stone loses its use as a constructive material, it loses also power over the imagination."[34] Nevertheless his prose papers over that loss as it works at summoning the felt world of the past, constructing reparations time and again. And of necessity it fails. Maurice Blanchot once said that writing is always a product of dread: "One dies at the thought that any object to which one is attached is lost."[35] Through the construction of "stories of art," we rescue objects from the ravages of time and save ourselves (but not quite) in the process. The best-known disciple of Klein, D. W. Winnicott, has spoken of the "endless memorial search for something in the future that resides in the past."[36] No better summary of Stokes's work could exist.

Writers on art who allow this sentiment to lace through their studies—Walter Pater and John Ruskin come first to mind—are often branded as aesthetes or mere critics and dismissed from the canon of serious art historians. I have often wondered why this is so, and I cannot help but think that it is their reception of the sublime, almost threatening, power of the past that their detractors fear. "Nothing in writing," Stokes claimed, "is easier than to raise the dead."[37] "The tension is all of life: from death is borrowed but its objectivity, its unmitigated petrifaction."[38] Every work of art, accompanied by the writing on it, stages a confrontation between loss and recovery, absence and presence. To Stokes's limpid sensibility:

We are most at home when the bell of a church appears to conspire with balcony, doorstep, and sky. We feel no less strongly that some environments are entirely forlorn, broken, distracted. . . . In our towns today we are largely strangers to stillness, to apparent deliberateness and silence. . . . In the old days, art was a means of organizing the incantatory element that had been felt in the length of land or in the restless sea. . . . [But even in art today there exists a] contemplative purpose, organization, a degree of wholeness. That is why art is no less a *solace* now, and perhaps little less an achievement, than it was in great ages.[39]

In Stokes's words, the reader gradually, soothingly (as if listening to the waves gently lapping at the base of Venetian buildings), comes to understand without being able to say exactly why.

Writing about art: What is it? Why do we do it? "Writing is loss as it comes to exist in another form."[40] As so many of us discover, it is the process of writing, indeed the very language we use as a means of preserving the past, that comes to be implicated in the loss of original meaning.[41] "The explanation," in Stokes's words, can unfortunately overpower the "poetry pure and simple."

Which brings me to my other, no doubt disjointed, major question, one I want to see if Stokes can help me answer: What is research in art history today anyway? Are the research paradigms now any closer to capturing the "truth," the poetry, even the immediacy, of a work of art, or does "research" push them further away? The research impulse is, in its own way, a mimetic impulse: the attempt to make the historical representation and the "real" coincide. Yet the "real" so often refuses to play the game of rationality. When any of us begins a study of a certain problem or period or artist or object in art history, we carve out a territory from the much larger map of the field and keep magnifying it until we see something that no one has seen before. If this activity involves a lot of reading before looking, it is called *research*. Many of us have the pleasure of rooting around in archives or ferreting around the shelves of libraries and then coming upon *something* that explains something else, supposedly a work of visual art. Yet our peculiar disciplinary and mimetic passion—turning images into words and calling it "research"—often goes unremarked.

The dictionary yields several reassuring, though perplexing, definitions such as "to search again anew, a close reading (as for hidden treasure), a studious inquiry, and an exhaustive investigation having for its aim the discovery of new facts and their correct interpretation"—actually a litany of tasks, I realized, all of which Adrian Stokes ignored.[42] These are all protocols implying a certain digging deep, a burrowing in, if one can just find a rabbit hole supple enough, as though the hidden treasure were down there (buried by whom?) waiting to be unearthed by the right researcher with the right tools in search of the correct interpretation. Granted, when the researcher emerges from either the library or the archive, facts have been discovered, connections have been made. But the romance of writing about the past has been squeezed out of our profession, and I think that's why I have turned to Stokes to put some of it back in again.

What troubles me most is that this scurrying about in the name of research is the danger of losing something along the way. Heidegger put it best: "Art-historical study makes the works the objects of a science. . . . in all this busy activity do we encounter the work itself?"[43] The manipulations and maneuvers of any research paradigm can contribute to the process of stripping the work of art of its awe, no doubt the reason art *still* matters in the first place. Where did the wonder in serious writing about the art of the past go? All that is in excess of *research*. The art of art history. The melancholic urge to have the past still matter. The romance of research.

No matter what our chosen genres in art history are—biography, social history, even visual and cultural studies—those of us who write and read about visual images are, of course, fated to a certain incompetence. Michael Baxandall says that there is always "an awkwardness about dealing with a simultaneously available field—which is what a picture is—in a medium as temporally linear as language: for instance, it is difficult to avoid tendentious reordering of the picture simply by mentioning one thing before another. . . . What a description will tend to represent best is thought after seeing a picture."[44]

Those features that belong to the image as image, art as art, are transformed under the discursive mandate to turn impressions into words, to explain rather than to experience, and to turn the simultaneity of vision into ordered chronological syntax. What kinds of insights do we look for in art historical analyses? Why do some histories last and others fade into oblivion? Even if questions such as these don't reveal the art of art history, they surely drive a stake in the heart of dutiful research. How does a study, such as *The Stones of Rimini,* become a classic in the history of art? Stokes offers a partial explanation, even though he is talking about art rather than the writing of its history: "Why always seek for rhythm in visual art, . . . why desire from the concrete an effect of alternation, since the very process of time can be expressed, without intermittence, as the vital steadiness of a world of space, as a rhythm whose parts are laid out as something simultaneous, and which thus ceases to be rhythmical? Rhythm, surely, is not so proper to visual art as immediacy."[45] Rhythm, sequence, alternation are all aspects of one of language's primary means of making meaning: the binary opposition. Without being too structuralist here, Ferdinand de Saussure's insights into the dual nature of the linguistic sign—the necessary combination of signifier and signified as the basis for the production of linguistic meaning[46]—would appear to be that which Stokes seeks to oppose with what he calls "the visual steadiness of a world of space, as a rhythm whose parts are laid out as something simultaneous."

In the penultimate chapter of *The Stones of Rimini,* "The Chapel of the Planets," Stokes comes closest to presenting the results of what today we might call research —even a kind of triumph of Warburgian iconology—or what he calls the "background . . . of 15th-century culture. The revival of Learning was the revival of Pantheism, neo-Platonic, neo-Babylonian, neo-Aristotelian."[47] In particular, the "sidereal considerations" that "exercised the minds of the most thoughtful men for several thousand years. And who shall say they were wrong in the importance they attached to the stars?"[48] The connections he makes, however, are not born of studiousness but of imagination:

The relation between astrological image and fantasies inspired by stone is equally well seen from either side . . . think how the stone was carved to disclose forms that appear as if responding to some influence. In many Quattro Cento reliefs the movement of figures suggest a response to magnetic power. To wind and water are attributed the most flamboyant impulsions. Shells come up from the sea to line a doorjamb; and there they stick encrusted. All Nature is alive, all concrete things show sidereal powers of influence. *Sol Invictus* has a thousand incarnations. Flowers strain their fighting roots to lay open; dolphins plunge in air. These fantasies are solid stone.[49]

"In the Tempio we *see* Influence," he says, "we do not gather it from an accumulation of words."[50] Standing outside the temple, he mused that "science and art, delicacy and strength, were never so close together as in the early Renaissance" imagination,[51] as it blossomed under the influence of the stars that cradled it.

We can use Stokes's evocative approach to the art of the past to compare, even perhaps reimagine, the role of art history in the intellectual culture of the early twentieth century and the role of it today. What is *research* in art history now? Matters might be clearer in scientific study, so I followed Stokes's lead and looked to the stars for answers. The comparison of research paradigms between astronomy and art history, of course, is as old as the memorable one once invoked by Erwin Panofsky.[52]

Astronomers may not look deep into the archives or temples of history, but they do longingly gaze outward into the heavens, where the much, much older past still shines forth. Since visual images are crucial to their endeavors of discovery, I trust that what I am about to invoke is not a totally inept comparison. In 1995, a "stunning picture of the Eagle nebula taken by the Hubble Space Telescope . . . became . . . an [instant] icon of the age of space exploration." According to the *New York Times*, this lone photograph provoked endless speculation and research about the origin of the spectacular "cosmic architecture" (apparently it is seven thousand light-years away, and its pillars of clouds are almost six trillion miles high):

So sublime and stately are the Eagle Nebula's huge cloud columns, so brooding are the dark clouds and the sprinkling of emerging dense globules the size of the solar system, or larger, which appear to be cradles of newborn stars. The majesty of the prospect and intimations of cosmic regeneration [according to one reporter] left even astronomers awestruck. Forsaking the usually dispassionate language of the profession, [the researchers] dubbed this most famous of Hubble pictures the "Pillars of Creation."

Jave Kane, a theoretical astrophysicist at California's Livermore Research Laboratory, explained that in computer simulations of astrophysical phenomena one works backward from the past on through to the beginning. Since the initial conditions for what is being simulated are not known, he said, "You take the results you see and tweak parameters of possible initial conditions to get the results you see."[53]

A comparable research endeavor that comes readily to mind in art history is the early-twentieth-century search for "style," a fascination that engendered a lyricism the discipline has since abandoned. Seduced by the idea of style, meditative art historians imagined their own experiments along similar dreamy lines. "The influence of material upon style," Stokes lamented, "is an aspect of art history that is never sufficiently studied,"[54] so he ventured as far backward as the geological history of the earth. An acknowledgement of style, like astronomical inquiries into the origins of time, could only achieve its legitimacy by connecting the dots in the opposite direction, by performing a kind of diachrony in reverse. Maybe that's why the discussion around the idea of style has tentatively returned today. The topic taps into the poetry of art history. In the aftermath of a pervasive post-structuralist suspicion about the sovereignty of empirical history (a narrative, however dry, that at least functioned on the illusion of moving forward), there is something appealing about dealing with a theme—such as style—that can only be pursued by contrary means. We only know that it was there because of where it ended up, which is to say that we only recognize it when it's all over (the quattrocento, the Renaissance, etc.). We can come to know time, as Kubler persuaded us, only indirectly by what happened in it.

Style is the narrative thread that we have to wind back around the spool. "Tweaking" the products of its presence once upon a time, we read backward to establish, in reverse order, chains of cause and effect and relationships among phenomena that we only in retrospect call "style." "A work of art," Focillon pronounced, "is immersed in the whirlpool of time; and it belongs to eternity."[55] This desire to compare art historical "science" to stargazing, though audacious, is hardly without parallel. Quests after styles in art history may not now parade under the banner of a legitimate research program, but they indeed once summoned their poets. Of course, when I claim that contemporary research in science has more romance to it than that in art history, perhaps I am only talking about journalism versus serious scholarship. But I'm not so sure.

For example, biography as a genre in art history would seem to offer a more traditional and acceptable contrast, which is to say that we might all agree on what constitutes a solid investigation into the life of an artist (e.g., Agostino di Duccio) or a patron (e.g., Sigismondo Malatesto). The task of the biographer is always a daunting one: He or she must put together once again the bits that remain of a life lived over many decades. And once this picture is pasted together, the art historian has to smooth down the rough edges, sort out the chronology, and pretend that the missing pieces aren't really missing, and so on. All in the name of coherence rather than art, "explanation" rather than "poetry." In the wake of post-structuralist theory, it has become increasingly clear that the coherency we seek in biography is only located there by the interpreting biographer or historian. Biography, even for art historians, has come to be accepted as a heuristic tool employed by those in the present rather than something found in the past.

Astrophysicists, who rarely have the luxury of completion, also trade in biographies. Consider the design of an experiment going on in the Brookhaven National Laboratory on Long Island—actually something designed to figure out the life history of the universe. Here every day for the past couple of months physicists are smashing ions together at 99.99% of the speed of light in the hopes of briefly re-creating a bit of the earliest matter of the universe, called the quark-gluon-plasma. They try "to mimic conditions that existed at the start and understand how they affected the universe's first seconds, years and epochs."[56] The big bang theory claims that a grapefruit-sized bit of plasma expanded to give rise to atoms, stars, our tiny solar system, and all the beyond of the cosmos about which we know so little. Cosmologists struggle to reverse the process, melting away boundaries between particles to go backward into the creation of the original soup. All once again to satisfy our need for origins. As Dr. Thomas Kirk, director of nuclear physics at Brookhaven, recently put it: "This universe came from somewhere . . . Was there a beginning and will there be an end? These are the most profound questions you can ask and are the kinds of things we're trying to investigate."[57] This search may be of the same metaphorical nature as the search for "style" or the search for the biography that enables us to fit artist and artistic life together. In the context of research, all evince a search for meaning rather than its resolution.

The philosopher Ernst Cassirer once claimed that to understand culture one has to reduce all human products—such as art—to their *fieri* (the forging process)—to the moment before they took on recognizable shape and substance.[58] In this sense, writing a good art historical biography is more than progressively contextualizing the life and desires of one being. It's about reaching backward into the seething cauldron and extracting a fistful of embers, the stuff of which a life, a work, a universe will subsequently be made—the spiritual, psychosocial, cultural plasma. Of course no biographer could possibly discern all the quarks and ions that resulted in the life of this one artist, this one art, this one age. Biography is not a chronological exercise but rather the demonstration of a metaphysical commitment or a bigger-than-life psychic urge on the part of the biographer, art historian, or astronomer. And this comparison to research in the heavens makes me at least feel as though I am getting closer to understanding the romance of research in art history—or at least the intellectual commitments of Adrian Stokes.

We have come a long way from not only the ancient stones of Rimini but also from Stokes's meditations on the action of wind on water and the influence of the stars upon human action. No doubt there are many ways to explain the deep structure of the discipline of art history, but I want to return to my earlier suggestion. We study and write about the past because we cannot let it go. In other words, we suffer from a case of disciplinary melancholy. It is almost "as if the image launched desire beyond what it permits us to see."[59] The objects from the past stand before us, but the worlds from which they came are long gone.

What should we do with these visual orphans? *Research* is that defense mechanism erected against the recognition that there is very little about them that we can recover other than the immediacy of their being. In *Black Sun,* her essay on melancholy, Julia Kristeva has argued that "the imaginative capability . . . is the ability to transfer meaning to the very place where it was lost in death and/or non-meaning."[60] If this kind of melancholic attitude frames the discipline of art history, what are the institutional and ideological forces that repress it? In short, what is it that forbids art historians to acknowledge the poetry of loss, the romance that motivates *research*?

We know what we should do as art historians, but we do not often meditate on why we do it. Writing about images that are present but whose world is long gone presents more challenges, as Adrian Stokes intuited, than a research protocol devoid of poetry can ever acknowledge. "Knowing the past," Kubler once said, "is as astonishing a performance as knowing the stars. . . . Like the astronomer, the historian is engaged upon the portrayal of time."[61]

It may be a bit supercilious to suggest that *research* in art history is in pursuit of something it can never catch, but that unknowability is also part of its charm. The present observer must struggle to make the objects of the past continue to shine even as she dulls them with the rhetoric of analysis. We can never forget that an individual work of art and the historical constellation of which it is a part, like a light radiating from a distant galaxy, has come from a time and place that still resonates. *Research* may make visible the absence that death is, but it also perpetually resurrects the desire to make meaning where it no longer exists. "A written melancholia," Kristeva claims, "surely has little in common with the institutionalized stupor that bears the same name . . . loss, bereavement, and absence trigger the work of the imagination and nourish it permanently as much as they threaten it and spoil it."[62]

The overheated passions that course through so much of Adrian Stokes's writing—a testimony to empathy, eloquence, or even excess—were provoked, of course, by the northerner's flight—like that of Goethe or Stendhal or Burckhardt or Pater or Ruskin—to the warm and sunny world of the south. Nevertheless, he suffered all his life long from the "malady" of melancholy, and his analyst Klein did not know what to make of his writings on art. This essay has tried to give her an answer. And the solace that Stokes found in studying stars and stones—quattrocento carving cajolingly, gently releases the life compacted in the fossilized stone, resulting in a luminosity as pure as moonlight—has given me a secondary occasion to meditate on the drives and disappointments of my own profession.

4

The Dogma of Conviction

David Raskin

ART HISTORIANS, EVEN THOSE OF US interested in issues and problems of modern art, believe that works of art describe reality in some way or other. On an idealist basis, Michael Fried argued in 1964 (and still believes) that modernist art's self-reflexivity "has taken on more and more of the denseness, structure, and complexity of moral experience—that is, of life itself, but life lived as few are inclined to live it: in a state of continuous intellectual and moral alertness."[1] Rosalind Krauss developed a perspectivist alternative to Fried's perfectionist claims, seeking, as she characterized her project in 1993, to show how modernism's deictic aesthetics hides its social and political ramifications: " 'My' modernism is, of course, another name for a discursive field that, like any other field, is structured. The set of concepts that grids its surface not only organizes the facts within it but determines what, by their lights, will even count as facts."[2] A third conception of our reality, one that develops art's social agency, is exemplified in the following remark from 1982 by T. J. Clark: "For me a strategy of negation and refusal is not an unreasonable response to bourgeois civilization since 1871, and indeed it is the ruthlessness of negation which lies at the root of what I admire—certainly what I feel is still usable—in modern art."[3] Although there are many other voices worth learning from, Krauss's transient contexts make room for nearly all of them, and it seems to me that few would seriously dispute that this eminent trio and their methods for meaning could get to what matters to most of us today, for better or worse.

What I particularly like is that the three have covered the breadth of modernism, antimodernism, and postmodernism, from mimesis to abstraction. Fried championed Frank Stella in 1966, Gustav Courbet in 1990, and photography in 2005; Krauss explained from Auguste Rodin to Michael Heizer in 1977, surrealism in 1993, and installation art in 1999; Clark celebrated Courbet in 1973 and mourned for all of the nineteenth and twentieth centuries in 1999. As everyone who reads their voluminous writings knows, it is hard to argue against any of them, even as they have made it necessary for us to take stands in relation to their achievements. Just try to talk about minimalism without engaging Fried or Krauss. Where would any conversation about Édouard Manet go without Clark or Fried? If push came to shove on the nature of modern art, how could we choose among them? And yet. . . . How did we make our choice? We made it because one of the three fits each of us best, not, I believe, by argument alone, but by the feel of the argument. Their sense of self and world built through art suits ours, not, I venture, because we have the right to believe but because we have the will.[4]

In this investigation I am not especially interested in testing the inner dynamics and particulars of the complex positions Fried, Krauss, and Clark elaborate. I instead would like to focus on the fact that each uses art to postulate a relation between self and world (regardless of whether the art, the self, or the world is seen as contingent). Fried's "life itself" pinpoints the stakes of his conceptions, and so too does Krauss's misuse of the artist Donald Judd's phrase "what the world's like" and Clark's hyperbole: "Call it the Body, the Peasant, the Economy, the Unconscious, the Party, the Plan. Call it Art itself."[5] Each in his or her own way asks art to carry metaphysical weight and serve an epistemic function (even if the lessons art is supposed to teach are ultimately skeptical ones). In every instance, they assign art an exegetical role in our past, present, and future; but as this unexamined privileging has permeated the discipline, it has degenerated into partisan politics, with aesthetics and critique squaring off in an endless stalemate over art's value.

Aesthetics versus critique is, I believe, a paralyzing dichotomy that has captured both today's plurality and our thinking about art over the past few decades, trapping us within a closed system. As recently as 2004, one younger scholar wrote: "Indeed, in the face of the onslaught of catastrophes that have come to define our contemporary moment, it is not entirely surprising that writers who unequivocally reject the validity of critical artistic practices should call instead for a pathos-infused, humanist aesthetics."[6] Others, too, seem caught up within this aesthetic and critique continuum, even as they helpfully search for a solution to its implications. Two of them asked, "In compiling this collection [devoted to the dyad and from which I quoted the above contention], whether discussions of the aesthetic might incorporate, rather than simply negate, a criticality that has traditionally been the terrain of the anti-aesthetic."[7] One proposal (again, from the 2004 collection) is to compromise between the fixed alternatives, suggesting that the Duchamp effect passes beyond the found object in artists like Mary Kelly and Gabriel Orozco, which has in turn generated "an aesthetic beyond the pleasure principle . . . that breaks the self-critical circle and opens itself to wider issues of subjectivity and sociality, loss and memory, love and death."[8]

I also wish to break the circle and want wider issues from art, but when I remind myself what objects and phenomena are, I know that the love and death I project on them are mine alone, that they are an occasion for my memory or loss, my sociality or subjectivity. But when I give in to the promise of art, to the strengths and weaknesses of my own convictions (as I do when I choose among the trio), I remain as trapped within the structure as before, finding exactly what I desire. I am arguing that in placing art between self and the world, whether we are commanding aesthetic experience or critical information or seeking to negotiate these alternatives, we are making two conjoined mistakes that lead to dogma and stagnation. We are dividing values from facts and using art to grasp reality.

Behind aesthetics and critique is the antirealist assumption that the perception and conception of our world requires a representational interface. In 1991 Mieke Bal and Norman Bryson phrased the idea this way: "Human culture is made up of signs, each of which stands for something other than itself, and the people inhabiting culture busy themselves making sense of those signs."[9] Whether antirealism is overt in approaches dedicated to context or tacit in appeals to intuition, we should be aware that it is the residue of seventeenth-century metaphysics and epistemology, which held that a medium of some sort was needed to bridge the gap between the material body or world and the immaterial mind or soul. During the past several centuries, from René Descartes to Daniel Dennett, various names for this go-between have included "impressions," "sensations," "experiences," "sense-data," "phenomena," "stimuli," and "qualia." In dualist accounts, these intermediaries are construed as immaterial mind processes; in monist versions, they are considered identical with the electrical or veridical activity of a physical brain.[10] In either instance, whether we are talking about Cartesian theater or social heterophenomenology, representationalism opposes a type of natural, realist position that our conjunctive conceptions and perceptions are enmeshed in an emerging and material world. (Readers will note that this "natural" realism first introduced by Edwin B. Holt and the "new realists" in 1910 does not entail the old-fashioned metaphysics of direct or "naive" realism with its fantasies of positive fixation.)[11]

In discussions of art we may not favor terms like qualia or stimuli, but sensations, sense-data, phenomena, and experience were favorites in art writing of the 1960s and 1970s and have retained some of their usage; Maurice Merleau-Ponty, an authority for both Fried and Krauss, wrote the singular "quale."[12] That was a period when the problem of the relationship among perception, conception, and art dominated one kind of polemics in the United States. Critics and artists enmeshed in the broader social turmoil unwittingly invoked one version or another of the interface (antirealist) formulation in making judgments of art's ethical values. The best-known instance of antirealist thinking is Clement Greenberg's formalist intuition: "Quality is 'content.'"[13] And for Greenberg's quality, we could substitute Fried's conviction ("Nothing short of *conviction* . . . matters at all"), Krauss's position ("What I must acknowledge is not some idea of the world's perspective but simply my own point of view"), and Clark's opposition ("The medium has appeared most characteristically as the site of negation and estrangement").[14] Here are three differing registers that place art as a medium between ourselves and our world. The buzzwords that signal each metaphysic are never used as systematically as they are in philosophy of mind—I nominate "conviction," "point-of-view," and "negation," respectively, as possibilities—but my point is that we ask these words to *buzz*. But this is all antirealist convention—a truism from Martin Heidegger could serve as a slogan: "Only where there is language, is there world."[15]

Here Clark is right when he objected in 1983 to "metaphysical buzzwords [that] seem to provide the ground on which the more persistent, not to say strident, appeals to 'intuition' rest," though he had only Fried's in mind.[16] I should also note that Clark came close to making my central point about antirealism in contrasting his commitments with Fried's (though it now appears they admire each other's ideas): "The mistake [the priority-of-perception thesis] makes is in its notion of what close reading *is*: the question being whether it is an exclusive and intensive focusing, a bracketing of knowledge, a giving-over of consciousness to its objects [this is Clark's assessment of Fried's transcendent position], or whether successful reading is a mobilization of complex assumptions, commitments, and skills, in which the object is always being seen against (as *part* of) a ground of interest and argument [the view Clark advances]."[17] But while Clark's method is close to a natural, realist one, it is his dualism that belongs to the betweenness of antirealism; Clark's is the position that Hilary Putnam calls "Cartesianism *cum* materialism" in his Dewey Lectures (he is referring to John R. Searle and Daniel Dennett, especially).[18] In short, "against (as *part* of)" is a structure that disguises the rhetorical conjunction by presenting it as a parenthetical insertion, seeking to hide the "and" that belongs to the intermediary "against" by figuring it as identical with the external world "(as *part* of)." It is here that Fried was correct when he observed a mirror of nature in Clark's dialectics: "According to Clark, on the other hand, artistic modernism must be understood as something like a reflection of the incoherence and contradictoriness of modern capitalist society."[19] What Fried also noted, though he did not phrase it this way, is that Clark's principles also contain that old formalist ideal of judgment, that the "work of art could," in Margaret Olin's words, "validate its representation within perception itself."[20] (On this point I should mention that every time I watch the Open University program that records Fried and Clark standing in front of Jackson Pollock's all-over paintings and debating "pictures" and "picturing," I am convinced that they believe that a medium is an intermediate.[21])

Given Fried's overt commitment to traditional metaphysics and Krauss's to their antithesis, it is easy to follow their antirealist trails, which lead to the division of the work from its sensible or cognitive report. But because materialism, even of Clark's dialectical sort, is often conflated with realism and sometimes even with positivism, the distinction turns on the nature of the secure foundation for knowledge of the world. In this sense, I would like to stress that however we tell a work of art to communicate, we are assigning intermediary standing to its physics, construing material in representational terms—as a "mode of cognition" to use Krauss's phrase or in the post-Marx (Althusserian) phrasing of Charles Harrison and Fred Orton, as "mythical rather than rational."[22]

In pressing my natural, realist claims, consider how unremarkable the antirealist alternative has become. Fried, for instance, believed in 1965 (though in 1998, he wrote that he never had a stake in opticality as modernism's defining characteristic), "The materiality of [Pollock's] pigment is rendered sheerly visual, and the result is a new kind of space . . . in which conditions of seeing prevail rather than one in which objects exist."[23] Krauss, for her part, claimed in 1993 that "the liquid gesture was perhaps the most efficient in that in one and the same stroke it canceled and testified, like the graffito mark, like the clue. Twombly had decoded Pollock's gesture one way, Warhol in another. In the late 1960s when Robert Morris was to consider the logic of 'Antiform,' he would decode it yet a third."[24] And Clark, in the most recent of the efforts quoted from here, apropos of the colonization of experience by bourgeois consciousness, argued, "The roundabout character of my descriptions does not derive so much from Pollock's paintings' wild uniqueness as from their ordinary (strictly representative) distance from the world they were part of. Abstract painting intended to set the world aside. And therefore it truly is difficult to think at all of *Number 1, 1948* as belonging to a social body."[25] Here is art writing's linguistic turn in its various manifestations, canonized.

At the risk of belaboring the issue, let me once again say that whether we know it or not, any division we make among our self, art, and world commits us to the position that any beliefs about actuality that we think we have never come directly; they instead always arrive shaped through some sort of intermediary, representation, or picture. In the antirealist mind-set, truth coheres to theoretical propositions. As Arthur Danto explained forty years ago: "Art, in its way, reveals the world in the respect that, between the work of art and the world, there has to be a gap or distance of just the sort which exists between language and the world, or between science and the world."[26]

There is no doubt that antirealism like that of Danto, and that of Fried, Krauss, and Clark, is serious, because it tries to answer the challenge posed by skepticism, the view that we cannot know the world as it is with any sureness; it solves this problem by nominating apperception as reality, and though this is no small achievement, it is a dubious one.[27] There is no reward in this order for what Terry Eagleton called the tough work of "argument, evidence, experiment, investigation," some of the empirical and scientific strategies that acknowledge that there can be no escaping point of view while never making facts a function of "culture," one name we give the signifying system by which we make sense of the world.[28] As was the case with aesthetics versus critique, the only rationale for subscribing to one metaphysic over any other or to none at all is faith alone. (Clark rightly noted with respect to Fried, "The intuition *is* the religion—not a very satisfactory one, I should imagine."[29]) I am arguing that it is the use to which we have put art by positioning it as a medium between ourselves and our world that results in the division of facts from values; this division colors art with creed, and it is our faith in art's special status that stills life's currents.

This stasis is easiest to see in Krauss, since she herself told us that contexts determine facts, but it is perhaps less common to see speculative thinking in all its post-structuralist presentations and on which her perspectivism depends as being in itself a value system designed to construct and deconstruct cultural facts. Here can be nothing but a deferral to propositions.[30] How else, other than by moving from values to facts, would a contextualist commitment attempt to forward any vision of social reality, even if one characterized by displacement? With Krauss it is facts peeled from personal values, or, as she suggested in 1972, "I must acknowledge not some idea of the world's perspective but simply my own point of view."[31] Of course, the idea of a self that her private values authorize is not a pleasant one; the dystopian project has entailed moving from point of view to point of view, promulgating a terrifying mise en abyme that prevents the individual from adhering in experience.

Fried is little different. For him, important art (especially painting) is made by an artist engaged in a particular ontological problem made pressing through his or her historical awareness of and competition with the works of the recent past that matter. Though this heuristic is complex, it plays out in his art criticism from the 1960s in Fried himself judging the rightness of the artist's proffered solutions, and in his writings about art's history, with Fried himself matching contemporary assessments and assertions to those artistic ambitions. In Fried we have Krauss's points of view projected as Fried's autonomy, an anchorite first built in the 1960s whose ultimate security has been the aim of decades of his history writing. (He would offer no objection here, because he has never abandoned his construal of art as an ethical endeavor, as he wrote in 1996: "In any case, Manet's modernism, with respect to the issue of beholding, consists precisely in the doubleness of its relation to the Diderotian tradition: on the one hand, marking the close of that tradition by insisting as never before on the 'truth' about painting that the tradition had come about to deny or forestall; on the other hand, demonstrating by example that there could be no mere laying bare of that 'truth' and therefore no entire extinguishing of that tradition."[32]) Fried's hermeneutics are fully dependent on the force of his persuasiveness, and it is with a sense of his achievements that in 1998 he proudly divided values from facts (inadvertently repeating a quotation that he had translated from French somewhat differently in 1965): "As I realized only recently, preparing to teach in . . . a seminar. 'A man is judged by neither intention nor fact but by his success in making values become facts,' Merleau-Ponty wrote."[33]

Clark again presents a slightly dissimilar case, if only because the ambition of a careful materialist history is to puzzle out the complexities of the world's social particulars, which should entail the interpenetration of facts and values. It is here that I would like to suggest that it is dialectic itself that creates the gap between ourselves and our world. Though its adherents sometimes present it as an empirical endeavor it is in practice a rhetorical one.[34] This status can partially be seen in its loose grammar, which uses the key word "negation" as a logical principle, an antinomy, a description, an agent of development, and an explanation. If dialectics were actually empirical or scientific, the contradictions that are held to produce negations would never be accepted in the first place and would never exist to produce the supposed antithesis and never lead to any transcendent or materialist sublation. Even for a natural realist, contradictions are never overcome; they instead eliminate the working hypothesis from contention precisely because its lack of viability fails to help us survive as best we might. Admitting contradictions in values abandons any pretense to truth and reality, because the logical contradictory itself—the "Some S are not P" that contradicts the "All S are P"—lets us deduce every possible premise whatever. As Karl Popper explained in his criticism of this style of thinking, "We therefore convey with such a contradictory theory—nothing. A theory which involves a contradiction is entirely useless, because it does not convey any sort of information."[35] By conveying nothing that can be refuted, dialectics are one type of historicism, the theoretical elevation of description to explanation and prediction, which establishes values first then facts, as with Fried, as for Krauss, as in the system of aesthetics and critique.[36]

When we take instead the natural, realist view that our conjunctive and disjunctive experiences are the content of a developing material and immaterial life, of the indivisibility of facts and values, we describe a probability that weaves the carpet of "perception, understanding, representation, verification, and truth," in Putnam's circle of life.[37] This social fabric lets us proffer knowledge claims that are accountable to the material "facts" we continue to discover, refine, and reject through the difficult work of empiricism and science while testing the convictions by which we must live our lives.[38] Our only reality is a duration of past, present, and future relentlessly subjected to falsification.

The practical consequences of natural realism in art, in stripping art of its special standing as a medium, are at least threefold. First, we should not be misled by a terminological confusion with stylistically realist art, such as that by Courbet or Manet. Representational ambitions are deeply antirealist in a philosophical sense: When pictures work through beholding, their commitment is to illusionism, to demanding materials are lodged in an abyss of signification. Realism lets art reject an untenable dualism. Second, our commitment can no longer be to aesthetics or critique, since the foundation for reality can never be the ideal or the material. William James with his common sense proposed reality to be a single substance in flux and with his poetry called this unsure foundation for actuality "the stream of my breathing."[39] Third, the most far-reaching consequence is that aesthetic indivisibility is also human indivisibility from other people, trees, streams, and rivers, New Orleans, Darfur, the Middle East, and so on in a relentless list. We have no choice but to act locally and globally for the mutual well-being on which our shared existence depends.[40] In this natural, realist order, the world is behavior, events, and affairs only; it can never be modeled, represented, or known in any abstract manner.[41] Instead, our emerging lives take shape in the process of attempting to build consensus, a mandate for affiliation that guides and reforms all faces of lived existence, from the individual to the collective. Truth and reality correspond and cohere in a universe we have no choice but to build together.

This evolutionary maxim has no place for the self-important topography of modernism, antimodernism, and postmodernism, and it has no time to waste with aesthetics and critique. Yet our open and deflationary works of art can remain rich. "As I have said for several years," Dan Flavin wrote in 1966, "I believe that art is shedding its vaunted mystery for a common sense of keenly realized decoration. Symbolizing is dwindling— becoming slight. We are pressing downward toward no art—a mutual sense of psychologically indifferent decoration— a neutral pleasure of seeing known to everyone."[42]

5

Sensation in the Wild
On Not Naming Newman, Judd, Riley, and Serra

Richard Shiff

That things are simpler than they are is something that theory asks us to imagine:
to imagine, not to believe. And it does this so as to get us to recognize similarities
between things that, so long as we continue to think about them in the fullness of
their empirical detail, will always seem very different.

Richard Wollheim[1]

Unless thought [of a form] becomes physical feeling, it doesn't really work. . . . Ideas
have to become physically specific.

Bridget Riley[2]

CONSIDER THE TWO EPIGRAPHS as if they were but one argument: First, Richard Wollheim's acknowledgment of the divide between
theory (its fantasy of simplicity) and the evidence of art (its experiential
complexity), then Bridget Riley's call to return ideas to concrete experience. Given the gap between art and theory, it may be that works of art
undermine themselves by stimulating viewers to speculate and theorize,
subjecting the viewer's unprocessed sensations to systematic reduction.
With its powers of conceptualization, theory invokes any number of intellectual abstractions, such as classification by style. Speaking as a creative
artist, Riley counters: "Sensation is not a question of style."[3] Evaluation
by style (or by any abstract category) clouds the immediacy of sensation,
even as it clarifies and validates interpretive analysis. Experiential art and
theories of experience are at odds with each other.

Riley's interpretive judgments are pragmatic facts of her experience,
subject to change; for her, the sensation at hand is paramount. She admires

works by Piet Mondrian and Jackson Pollock, regardless of the divergence in style. Systems of classification, standards of picture-making, the self-consciously individualized styles that artists develop to solidify professional identity—considerations of this sort would merely distract Riley from her aesthetic project. She is correct to have sensed a kindred spirit in Mondrian, who remarked: "I don't want pictures. I just want to find things out."[4] To identify a picture by its style, or to develop one's own style, is only to have situated a package of sensory data within a cultural matrix. Like the common names that are ours but also belong to others, artistic styles may be less personal than we first imagine. In culturally coded ways, they *refer* to individuality, opening works to mediated semiotic analysis. Semiosis relates one thing to another by acknowledging differences but then treats difference as if it hardly mattered (as if all things were "simpler than they are," as Wollheim writes). One artist–one style is a formula for recognition, not aesthetic particularity.

Quite possibly, Riley agrees that the cultural formation of identity is as serious a concern as the writing of critics and historians today suggests it is; but she also knows that accepting the terms of identity formation and manipulating them (like many modernists) or exposing the cultural manipulation of identity (like many postmodernists) has never been *her* concern. For her, the recurring points of modernist and postmodernist debate become at most a side issue. She escapes entanglement in them by several means, including the use of assistants to produce the final versions of her paintings. Because her "touch" is absent from the rendering in its exhibited state and even from the more advanced of her preparatory studies, she avoids refining the personality of her execution. Her inventive procedure is nevertheless sufficiently unique to be recognized by anyone familiar with her career. And yet it remains impersonal. With its look of anonymity, the sensation Riley projects can be individual without being coded as personal; nor does it engage in the cultural semiotics of expressiveness and personality.[5] "For quite a long time," she says, "I was embarrassed by using the word 'I,' the first person, in relation to my work."[6]

Just as an artist's sensation need not degenerate into questions of personality, so the medium need not be restricted to a range of technical strategies. Over the years, Riley has maintained a principle she articulated in 1965: "Perception is the medium." She formulated her statement following the reception of her work as shown in The Responsive Eye, an exhibition at The Museum of Modern Art, New York. Reviewers assumed inaccurately that her work pretended to an advanced knowledge of physiological optics. Hence Riley's emphatic correction: "I never studied 'optics.' . . . My work has developed on the basis of empirical analyses and syntheses, and I have always believed that perception is the medium through which states of being are directly experienced. . . . The basis of my paintings is this: that in each of them a particular situation is stated. . . . I want the disturbance or 'event' to arise naturally, in visual terms, out of the inherent energies and characteristics of the elements which I use."[7]

A somewhat later statement suggests what Riley meant by "inherent energies," sensory qualities to be appreciated outside cultural identities and references: "When [visual] elements are *not* asked to do something which is against their nature—not asked to serve concepts or to represent—*then* [they] show their vitality. . . . These energies are, in a proper sense, 'wild.' . . . The medium both carries you and threatens to carry you away."[8] If "perception is the medium," then painting—with its history of references, allusions, and theories—cannot be the "medium" in the same sense (nor can sculpture, video, performance, etc.). The customary categories of visual art medium cannot be the locus of the "wild" sensory event that Riley both directs and is directed by. If her colored surface begins to vibrate, moves into apparent depth, or merely remains as flat as it ever was, the effect should not be explained through theorizing a specific medium with respect to its typology and history. Riley's art is instead a product of concrete action and its physical, sensory consequences— in short, its aesthetics.

Her contemporary Donald Judd shared this understanding and expressed it in the way he responded to another artistic presence as identifiable as his own, Barnett Newman, who, like Riley and Judd as well, avoided equating personality or cultural identity with art. Judd argued that the character of Newman's painting resulted from (merely) "the way the paint was applied." Such a statement has more significance than its obviousness indicates. In interpreting sensory effects, Judd avoided attributing motivating causes that could not be observed firsthand: no underlying personality, no countercultural resistance, no involvement with historical forces, no concept of an avant-garde. Newman's art, he reasoned, "doesn't claim more than [any one person] can know."[9] In lieu of theorizing, people know precisely what they experience, neither more nor less; sensation is their knowledge, even if unformed. (Accordingly, Judd approached politics pragmatically, through actions that were local. He dealt with what he knew.)

From Sensation to Perception to Sensation

Given Riley's or Judd's practice of art, perception is only a shade more organized than sensation. In perceiving, we face an apparent totality, as opposed to the succession of fragments that characterizes raw aesthetic sensation in its temporal flow. We have a "sensation" of yellow, but we "perceive" a yellow chair, the specific object—*this* yellow chair, which we assume is more than a fleeting optical instant. The latter experience parallels a condition established by Riley's art: Each of her paintings, she once said, states "a particular situation."[10] Charles Sanders Peirce reserved a certain declarative immediacy for perceptions, distinguishing them from mediated images, which form a more functional unit of understanding: "An 'image' usually means something intended to represent—virtually professing to represent—something else, [but] the chair I appear to see makes no professions of any kind, does not stand for anything [and] offers no reason, defense, nor excuse for its presence. . . . It silently forces itself upon me."[11] Peirce implied that perception is closer to intuition than to analytical deduction—more like an inescapable feeling than a rational thought. Yet, it can be both, at least in Riley's terms: Her paintings engage the physical side of mental life, the sensory cusp of perception.

Raw, nameless sensation—*wild* is Riley's word for it—has been the inspiration of many artists, but only some have pursued it to its lair. One was Paul Cézanne: "His *petite sensation* [was a] guiding star for him, not only at the beginning but throughout a painting and the measure of the end"—sensation as at once the motivation, the process, and the destination.[12] Riley paints sensation: "I used to try and push the [formal] elements to such a point that they hovered on the brink of sheer sensation"—an example might be *Turn* (1964), in which the configuration appears to resolve itself into two or three relatively compatible progressions. She continues: "Now I try to take sensation as the guiding line and build, *with* the relationships it demands, a plastic fabric which has no other raison d'être except to accommodate the sensation it solicits"—an example here might be *Ease* (1987), in which it is difficult to avoid seeing multiple motifs and countermotifs in rapid succession.[13] In either case, the effect of Riley's art becomes self-intensifying; rather than leading from sensation to a concept or a fully developed theory, it stimulates still more sensation. Recall Mondrian: "I don't want pictures. I just want to find things out."[14]

Richard Serra joins Riley, Judd, and Newman as one of a significant number of late modern artists who seem to share the belief that "ideas have to become physically specific" (as Riley phrased it).[15] In their different ways, Serra and Riley have a concern for the *wall*: They work toward an aesthetic transformation of this fundamental architectural feature. Unlike Riley, Serra vigorously applies his hand throughout the process of bringing a wall-oriented project to completion. Yet, like Riley, he commits himself to anonymity even when making his characteristic, large-scale Paintstik drawings. Paintstik is a dense oil crayon that leaves a mark of intense blackness; as a drawing material, it corresponds to the heaviness of the lead and steel typical of Serra's sculptural practice. When he covers paper or canvas with multiple layers of Paintstik, his individual strokes are repetitive and invariable in color—differentiable only because of nuances of texture, which affect reflectivity. The result of his stroking should be, he says, "as anonymous as possible, so that [the surfaces] don't call attention to themselves."[16] Why avoid distinctive gestures? If only by association with more cultivated forms of drawing and paint handling, a gestural mark is likely to evoke a personality type, rather than hold consciousness attentive to wild sensation.

Serra's reference to anonymity hints at a notion more complicated than avoiding the conventional signs of artistic identity and emotional expression. His "anonymous" manner of drawing inhibits the development of an image (in Peirce's sense), escaping imagery by denying pictorial distinctions of every traditional kind. His marks do not separate according to conceptual abstractions such as darkness and light, proximity and distance, figure and ground, action and reaction, positive and negative, reality and fantasy, sublimation and desublimation. Such dichotomous intellectual constructs of varying degrees of material reference—I have attempted to order them from the most sense-oriented to the least, but this can only be tentative—convert physical sensation into a configured, conceptual image. They tend to fix the range of evaluative possibilities, defining each form as if its conceptualized qualities were to be measured on a scale from perfection (fullness of quality) to chaos (lack of quality). All too quickly, dichotomous constructs refer the viewer's experience to the history of image-making and its prevailing critical dialogue. Marks that can be categorized not only identify the expressive hand of the artist, but they also articulate a surface compositionally, converting it into disembodied, framed space in which a programmed conceptual drama plays itself out. Compositional inflection introduces a self-contained illusionistic "picture" or pictorial field (which does not pre-exist such inflection), a world apart from the physically inhabited, unlimited space of sensation.[17]

Art, for Serra, reflects his "obsession with space, weight, balance, size, scale, placement, density."[18] Like the rhythms and harmonies that we associate with successful visual composition, these physical properties can generate a metaphoric vocabulary of their own, which might be applied as a parallel means of analysis (as when we say that a composition is "weighted" to, or "heavy" at, one side). Yet these same properties either compromise or utterly resist metaphoric appropriation because they belong so fundamentally to the material objects and substances they would describe.[19] We normally experience their quality in relation to the body's physical orientation to things that are apart from it (as in the case of space, size, scale, and placement), or we become aware of these qualities through touch and commonplace instances of gravitational force and bodily resistance (as in the case of weight, balance, and density).[20]

Serra seems determined to escape whatever of himself belongs more to his culture than to his immediate experience. Only in this way does sensory experience break free, becoming wild. It would be reasonable to wonder what, in our time, could possibly be devoid of a restrictive concept of style and personality type. To avoid style and typecasting, art would need to generate sensations appearing to derive from a situation or condition just as it is—sensations resulting from the way the materials themselves work, or how a body, any human body, operates (recall Judd interpreting Newman: "the way the paint was applied"). Even if achieved, such a condition of stylistic anonymity cannot be permanent; it would fall into a collective history of perception. Serra stated in 1992: "I wanted . . . to avoid the histories of existing styles, even my own. I wanted to free myself from my own readymade handwriting. . . . I wanted the Paintstik mark to build up separately from its form-making capacity."[21] By drawing, Serra has taken the radical step of freeing himself *from himself*—at least for the moment. (Automatism, already a historical style, could never have been his option.)

Given his concern for anonymity, Serra feels free to employ assistants to create the deep, thickened blackness of his forms. Yet, for purposes unrelated to the final surface quality, he performs much of the labor himself: "Theoretically, there is no need for me personally to surface my drawings. But in the process of covering a canvas with Paintstik, moving from the inside out, I often find the solution needed in terms of weight and shape of the drawing in relation to the total field of the wall and the total volume of the space. The cutting decisions have to be based on the actual experience of the site of installation."[22]

Serra's double act of drawing extends through time: first stroking the surface to cover it, moving in all directions, then cutting the surface to determine its final dimensions in relation to the wall. These actions situate the artist in the space he temporarily inhabits. By drawing, Serra lives *into* this space, as if he were simultaneously encountering and reflecting the conditions of his situation—free of historical style, also free of whatever preconceptions he may have about himself. His passive observation of his environment becomes something very active (the only experience an individual can "know," as Judd said of Newman). By making a drawing to sense where he is, he alters the nature of this same space. What results is an art object, but its significance has more to do with Serra's process of discovery than with nuances in the appearance of the blackened surface that he leaves for other viewers. He states, "There is no way to make a drawing [as an object]—there is only drawing [as a process]."[23]

In 2003, Serra created *Consequence*, which consists of two large strips of linen covered with Paintstik, each about 18 meters long and over 2 meters high (55 by 7 feet); these are set against walls about 4 meters high (12 feet). Serra positioned one black strip flush with the top of a wall and the other flush with the bottom of an opposing wall. His asymmetrical placement of areas of blackness along an otherwise symmetrical corridor of space creates the feeling not only of compression but also of a twisting or torquing. The fact that one black element rises more than halfway from the floor while the other drops more than halfway from the ceiling accentuates the sense of a twist.[24] It is as if Serra's extended presence, his effort in drawing, were absorbed by the neutral or passive space of the architecture, activating it. A viewer senses that something has happened to the space, that it has in some way been altered or become eccentric so that perception must adjust to it. Neither cultural reference nor theory, but sensation alone, seems needed for the perceptual appreciation of the situation. Serra's space (to invoke words of Peirce) "does not stand for anything . . . It silently forces itself upon me."[25]

"Drawing," Serra has said, "is the most direct, conscious *space* in which I work. I can observe my process from beginning to end, and at

times sustain a continuous concentration." Whereas an act of drawing is
something in itself, leaving its traces, it also becomes an index of the immediate mental state or feeling of the person who draws. The indexed
condition should not be equated with a personality type, which is nothing
more than a generalized abstraction of a set of feelings—not *this* feeling.
Serra regards his process of "drawing" a space as a "way of seeing into your
own nature."[26] He registers his immediate response to adjusting the state
of his momentary environment. This is to draw within a continuous loop
of sensation, without fixing on abstractions of style and personality. Serra
once said of Newman's art, a precedent he acknowledges: "When you reflect upon a Newman, you recall your experience, you don't recall the
picture."[27] An artist's vision is more than spatial; it "unfolds in time."[28]

Art in Space and Time

Just as Judd shared with Serra his appreciation for Newman, he admired Serra among his peers as one of only a few to develop a comprehensive sense of space in art.[29] Judd and Serra might both have taken inspiration
from a favorite of Riley, Maurice Merleau-Ponty: "Only the painter is entitled to look at everything without being obliged to appraise what he [or
she] sees."[30] Judd had a somewhat different way of making this distinction
between looking and appraising, sensing and determining: "What you feel
and what things are aren't the same."[31] In this instance, the phrase "what
things are" refers to what things are supposed to be, that is, what they are
identified as, defined as, or customarily related to, when regarded as elements within the usual dichotomous systems. Authorized identity may or
may not correspond to "what you feel." Identities are multiples, generalizations calculated to fit many cases. "What you feel" is singular and specific.[32] As Judd said with respect to Newman, art derives from what *one*
person knows (that is, *feels*) and not from generalities.

Each of Judd's repeating, multiple-unit "objects" demonstrates this
point, because no two units within a work look or feel the same from any
real position of viewing. They become alike only in ideal, schematic drawings or verbal descriptions—as Wollheim might say: similar in theory,
different in sensation. The situation is complex enough when Judd ar-
ranges a stack of identically fabricated boxes and all the more complex
when the units vary. For *Untitled* (1988, aluminum with blue-over-black
Plexiglas), Judd inserted a single horizontal panel at different positions in

each of six open boxes. Here the play of internal and external illumination alters perceptions of projection and depth as well as the sensation of color. The quality of blue-black within each box differs in relation to the position of the inserted panel, which affects the amount and direction of illumination that the colored Plexiglas receives.

With his bent-aluminum wall constructions of the 1980s and 1990s, such as *Untitled* (1985), Judd often introduced instances of what he called a "two-color monochrome." He used this type of color effect to fuse a sense of integration to a sense of differentiation—a contradiction for critical analysis but not for perception. Rather than rely on traditional harmonies and contrasts, he capitalized on sensory affinities sufficiently flexible to allow judgments of wholeness and polarity to converge in one form. In the case of *Untitled* (1985), four kinds of two-color monochrome provide parallel sensations in no particular order: affinity by chroma (magenta and red), by tonality or value (magenta and black), by complementarity (white and black), and by saturation (white and red, as well as white and black).[33]

Judd's bent-aluminum structures project abruptly from their supporting wall and can be viewed not only from the front but also from above and from the side (some can be viewed from below). The situation activates a felt sense of height and width, which become more than conceptual abstractions of measurement. With analogous effects, Judd's floor-oriented works project upward. *Untitled* (1989), a box of Cor-Ten steel, is one meter high, so a person can see down into it while approaching it. Variation in the level of illumination, a result of the depth and partitioning of this open form, reveals the structure of the box dynamically. Light and shadow become constituent qualities as palpable as the rigidity of the metallic shell, the recession of its planes, and the axial vectoring of its two transversal panels, which distinguish themselves as physically thick and thin, spatially higher and lower. Illumination does more than define the integrated structure of the box; it animates all the differentiable elements as independent tangible features. Like a two-color monochrome, a Judd box is both a perceptual whole and a collection of sensations, each of which is a part of the whole but not subservient to it. Among sensations, there is no hierarchy.

Judd proclaimed that "space is made. . . . [My] smallest, simplest work creates space around it, since there is so much space within."[34] The simplest among Judd's objects draw space in and out of them, if only because of the play of ambient light, neither inside nor outside. It is as if his open forms were breathing. Here I indulge in a metaphor, but this one has a particular pedigree in the history of resistance to the separation of perception and sensation—resistance to the whole and the part, to thought and feeling, and to any number of other dichotomous pairs used to distinguish internalized and externalized experience. Works by Judd, Riley, and Serra, as diverse as they may be, share in counteracting the rigidity of this type of distinction; they serve as examples for theorizing without theory. William James is one of many who might be invoked to represent the related philosophical tradition, for he set abstract thought and felt emotion into a single embodied space: "In myself, the stream of thinking . . . is only a careless name for what, when scrutinized, reveals itself to consist chiefly of the stream of my breathing. . . . Breath moving outwards [is] the essence out of which philosophers have constructed the entity known to them as consciousness."[35]

Judd expressed a similar sentiment: "I've always considered the distinction between thought and feeling as, at the least, exaggerated. . . . Emotion or feeling is simply a quick summation of experience, some of which is thought—necessarily quick so that we can act quickly. . . . You have to [think and feel] all at once."[36] Encountering an object by Judd, we feel that something specific happens to the work—in the work—in the space and time of viewing. We become more conscious of our own space: We *feel* space and time, body and mind, all as sensation.

Just as Judd constructs a space using three-dimensional elements, Riley draws a space using two-dimensional elements. Both spaces encompass the observer. Since 1998, Riley has created five large circle drawings as wall installations at particular sites. She installed *Composition with Circles 4* in Sydney in 2004 and *Composition with Circles 5* in Berlin in 2005. She writes of these works in general: "Different constellations of circles emerge here and there and then sink back again. This activates the depth and gives a feeling of air."[37] Her description suggests breathing. She has also said: "For an artist those fleeting sensations which pass unrecognized by the intellect are just as important as those which become conscious."[38] "Fleeting sensations" are visual breathing. They are also feeling. And they are thinking, even if unconscious with respect to naming and its cultural semiotics.

The architectural setting for *Composition with Circles 4* is a long, narrow wall. The problem, as Riley expressed it, was "to get from one end to the other, eventfully, but without congestion and without fixing [the viewer's] focus unduly."[39] Her solution: "All is concentrated on an easy rise and fall right across the field. It has a movement like breathing, but it is not so even that it is without event. Accumulations and dispersals are still there and so are long running overlaps." This description of *Composition with Circles 4* allows us to sense the breath in *Composition with Circles 5*. The latter work approaches a compact square, but Riley has given it "an open and relaxed movement"—a movement in all directions, including forward, into the airy space of the viewer.[40]

"The Wild" in the Wild

Barnett Newman has been an underlying presence in this account of nominally incompossible aspects of Judd, Riley, and Serra. The three younger artists admired him deeply, especially for his "stance," his attitude toward the situation of art and of artists in the later twentieth century.[41] The metaphor of breath connects to Newman's *The Wild* (1950), which, in its own way, breathes. This painting is about 2½ meters (8 feet) in height but only about 4 centimeters (1⅝ inches) in width. Like the more relaxed of Riley's *Circle* compositions, its linear movement, to invoke her words, is "not so even that it is without event." If we follow the linear path of Newman's application of color along the narrow length of *The Wild*, we see subtle variation but no pattern, nothing to be associated with standards of a personality or a style. What we experience is living sensation, unencumbered with cultural links (at least for the moment); and so, as Newman would wish, we too come alive. Taking it as it is, we breathe along with *The Wild*. Newman said, "I hope that my painting [gives] someone, as it did me, the feeling of his own totality, of his own separateness. . . . I think you can only feel others if you have some sense of your own being." His task was to create a place where a person might know "he's there, so he's aware of himself."[42]

According to Newman, neither culture nor cultivated personality becomes a factor of a person's self-awareness. Sensation alone is needed, embodied sensation—in Riley's words, "physical feeling."[43] In 1950, Newman made six paintings in the unusually narrow format of *The Wild*, though the dimensions of the others are less extreme. *Untitled 3, 1950* has a more irregular internal edge than *The Wild*, but both paintings lack customary indications of expressive characterization; the distribution of color appears neither decidedly composed nor decidedly spontaneous. To trace the movement of the dividing edges, whether by eye or hand, is to perceive no particular rhythm. Nor do the grays and reds of these paintings seem to generate a true harmony. Newman's various combinations of elements have no ready descriptions despite the fact that they often bear names; they are anonymous not only as gesture but also as sign. Most likely, his title *The Wild* alludes to the freedom of birds: free as a bird, a bird in open space, a bird in the wild. He said that his narrow bands of color were "like the cry of a gull in the vastness of the Northern tundra."[44] Like indecipherable cries, Newman's paintings are either utter sensation or something very close to it. By no means did he wish to develop a type, creating "another Newman."[45] His paintings were not "his" but were what they were—each of them total and separate. Each needs now to be seen for how it *feels*.

The art of Newman, Judd, Riley, and Serra is united in offering sensory opportunities for emotional self-awareness.[46] But this is itself an interpretive generalization—a dubious proposal to venture, having encountered sensation in the wild.

6

Kant's "Free-Play" in the Light of Minimal Art

Thierry de Duve

IN §9 OF THE THIRD *CRITIQUE,* Immanuel Kant asks himself "whether in a judgment of taste the feeling of pleasure precedes the judging of the object or the judging precedes the pleasure." He adds that "the solution of this problem"—a sort of transcendental chicken-and-egg problem—"is the key to the critique of taste and hence deserves full attention."[1] Although he seems to offer a clear-cut solution (the judging precedes the pleasure), actually he does not solve the problem at all. He begins by ruling out the idea that the pleasure comes first, because this would betray an interest in the object, thereby ruining the legitimacy of that kind of pleasure's claim to go beyond mere agreeableness in sensation and be grounded in its own universal shareability. And he merely states repeatedly, without clarifying whether this is a requirement of theory or something akin to a moral obligation, that the pleasure in question *must* be of a different kind, one that accompanies the mental state experienced in the free play between imagination and understanding "insofar as they harmonize with each other as required for cognition in general."[2]

I do not intend to undertake here close reading of what may be one of the most obscure and frustrating passages in the third *Critique*. Rather, I wish to draw attention to the ambiguity of the following sentence: "Now this merely subjective (aesthetic) judging of the object . . . precedes the pleasure in the object and is the basis of this pleasure, a pleasure in the harmony of the cognitive powers."[3] This appears to show that the initial chicken-and-egg problem is now transformed into the problem of distinguishing between "the pleasure in the object" and "the pleasure in the harmony of the cognitive powers." It can be argued, empirically, that pleasure is pleasure and that I have no way of telling apart the pleasure that I take from looking at the object and the pleasure that I feel from sensing in myself some harmony or free play between my imagination and my understanding. Obviously, Kant at once conflates and distinguishes them because the solution to the riddle requires that the ground for the aesthetic judgment be universal, and not because he feels in himself two different kinds of pleasure when he judges aesthetically. He does not proceed from his own experience but from his reflective activity as a transcendental philosopher. And yet, as we know, a page or so into the paragraph that supposedly holds the key to the critique of taste, Kant postpones discussion of the transcendental question and, meanwhile, asks an utterly empirical one, "namely, how we become conscious, in a judgment of taste, of a reciprocal subjective harmony between the cognitive powers: is it aesthetically, through mere inner sense and sensation? or is it intellectually, through consciousness of the intentional activity by which we bring these powers into play?" His answer is unequivocal, this time: "Hence that unity in the relation between the cognitive powers in the subject can reveal itself only through sensation."[4]

This chapter attempts to take Kant's unequivocal answer here and to subject it to an empirical test. It tries also to put Kant's aesthetics into a certain context dating from the 1960s, which was precisely the context in which it was declared irrelevant in light of the development of the most advanced art movements of the times, namely minimal and conceptual art. At that time Kantianism seemed to be on the side of the formalist and modernist artists and critics, while the antiformalist, and soon to be called postmodernist, artists and critics upheld a rather vigorous anti-Kantianism. Then an artist like Donald Judd could declare: "A work of art needs only to be interesting,"[5] implying that it doesn't need to yield pleasure and be judged aesthetically in order to be appreciated as art. Alternatively, a critic like Clement Greenberg could say: "I'd rather go into the reasons my own experience offers for agreeing with [Kant]," the better to dismiss Kant's transcendental chicken-and-egg problem as a merely empirical one: "In short: if the judgment of taste precedes the pleasure, it's in order to *give* the pleasure. And the pleasure re-gives the judgment."[6]

To this day, the prevailing or orthodox reading of the critical debates of the 1960s pits the two camps against each other as if each had its own objects as well as theories. Kantian aesthetics would apply to modernist painting, whereas the new anti-aesthetic and postmodern art theory would apply to minimal and conceptual art. Works in the latter camp are simply supposed to have made the kind of experience Kant had in mind, if not impossible, at least irrelevant as far as their evaluation as art is concerned. This remains to be tested. To repeat: According to Kant, we become conscious of the free play of our cognitive powers through sensation, not intellectually: "This sensation . . . is the quickening of . . . imagination and understanding to an activity that is indeterminate but . . . nonetheless accordant: the activity required for cognition in general."[7] Whether we call it pleasure or, perhaps better, excitement (the "quickening," etc.), it is a sensation that finds its occasion in the object and its cause in itself as a bodily experience. It is an inner cause triggered by an outer occasion: my heart starts beating faster and I am all excited; the object I am beholding makes me feel intelligent; it is as if the object increased my knowledge, although I would be at pains trying to say what knowledge; I therefore tend to ascribe "intelligence" to the object itself; and so on. In other words, I get a sense that my intelligence is involved in my pleasure-judgment or in my judgment-pleasure (Greenberg's chicken and egg), even though pleasure is but a subjective feeling, and even though my intelligence does not grasp any concept. This is the kind of experience of "free play" I intend to test at the hand of two examples, one in each camp.

My modernist example is the (perhaps mythical) anecdote of Kandinsky entering his studio around 1910 and discovering, in the dim light of the evening, one of his own figurative canvases on its side. He recalls having had an intense aesthetic experience (one of pleasure but even more so, one of utter excitement) because, not recognizing the work, he was struck by its astonishing abstract beauty. This experience, he said in retrospect, triggered his switch to nonfigurative painting. For a fleeting moment, Kandinsky, stunned by the beauty of the canvas, does not understand that it is one of his own works. He does not recognize the landscape in the canvas standing on its side. What was conceptual and intentional in his work has momentarily vanished, leaving him with a sense of "purposiveness without purpose," or with a cognitiveness from which all cognition or recognition has retreated. He knows that he has painted a landscape, yet this knowledge gets momentarily forgotten in what he now sees as a pure product of his imagination. And the excitement he feels is one of liberation. It is this liberation he will later invoke to justify his switch to abstract art. I believe this example to be paradigmatic of what Kant had in mind when he spoke of the free play of imagination and understanding in aesthetic experience. Disinterestedness is here guaranteed by Kandinsky's surprise and the fact that he approaches his own work as if it were the work of someone else, or even a product of nature. He is unable to subsume one of his own paintings under the concept of painting, yet his feeling is not frustration. It is an intense feeling of beauty triggered by the object, which sets in motion an equally intense cognitive activity. He seems to intuit that his feeling is as universally communicable as is cognition in general, at the very moment when cognition fails him. He suddenly feels freed of the duties of figuration, and in this freedom he will later ground his claim to have invented a new universal language called *Malerei*. A language, and thus a means of communication, whose communicability, however, is not based on concepts but rather on feelings.

My postmodern example, Robert Morris's *Untitled (Three L-Beams)* of 1965, is much more conceptual than anything Kandinsky ever produced. Let us examine whether it invalidates Kantian aesthetics altogether, as postmodernism maintains, or whether it offers another model of how the interplay of imagination and understanding operates, one that forces us to displace, amend, or update Kantian aesthetics and, in so doing, deepen our understanding of its implications. What is very much to the point and may explain the antiformalists' conviction that Kantian aesthetics doesn't apply, is that instead of being retrospective, this model is generative. It has generated the work in the artist's mind as much as it accounts for the viewer's experience. Perhaps it can be said to take the interplay of imagination and understanding as its very subject matter, in a typically late modernist, self-referential way.

Imagination may appear to be an inappropriate term to apply to the early work of Robert Morris, an artist who, like his other fellow minimalists, favored banal, unimaginative geometric shapes—gestalts with a "sense of the whole" as he himself said.[8] But, unlike some of the later conceptual art, Morris's minimalist pieces need to be seen, perceived, experienced in real time and space. They even emphasize the "reality" or literalness of this time and space, presenting, as it were, time as duration and space as a function of gravity. In Kantian terms, imagination is precisely the faculty of presentation. It schematizes and synthesizes raw sense data; it unifies the manifold of empirical experience into a gestalt, which it presents to the understanding. Imagination in this case can be taken to be identical with perception. I shall now describe the experience of Robert

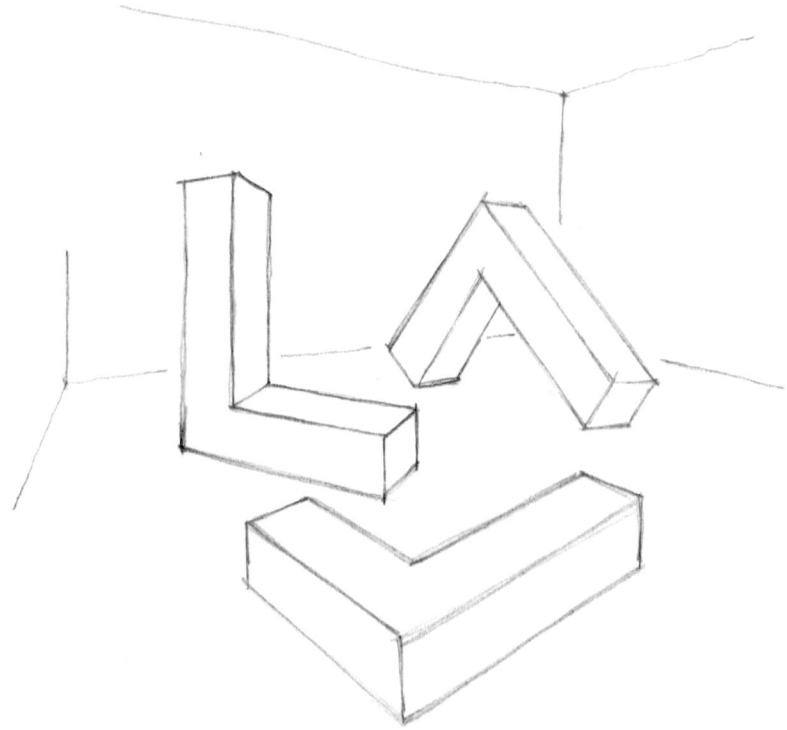

Figure 6.1   The author's rendering of *Three L-Beams*, 1965

Morris's *Three L-Beams* in terms of the Kantian faculties and decompose it for convenience's sake into a number of moments, alternating perception or sensation and conception or interpretation (i.e., imagination and understanding). These moments, it seems to me, are by necessity chronological, and their order may represent a variation on Greenberg's empirical chicken-and-egg problem. I don't pretend at all that it represents a solution to Kant's chicken-and-egg problem, which is transcendental, not empirical, de jure, not de facto.

1. *Perception.* We are looking at the piece, without further ado, taking it in, at a glance. The faculty involved is imagination. What the experience yields is a feeling or a sensation of difference, discontinuity, variety, and dissociation. If it were expressed by way of language (although this is unnecessary), it would be through sentences like the following:

"Oh, it's amazing how these three volumes look and feel different. In the one lying on its side, I feel gravity pulling it downward; in the one standing erect, I feel sculpture's struggle against gravity; in the one poised on its edges, I feel a precarious balance between gravity and the desire to escape its downward pull, as in dance."

2. *Cognition.* We are still looking at the piece, now registering what it is we are actually seeing. The faculty involved is the understanding. What the experience yields is knowledge, the recognition of sameness, identity. It is empirical and conceptual, since it subsumes three different perceptions or images under one and the same concept of "this L-shaped form." It automatically expresses itself through language (although it does not need public expression): "Oh, I realize that these three volumes are identical."

3. *Sensation.* We are not only looking at the piece, we linger on, as if in an effort to rescue moment 1 from moment 2 and make Kandinsky's fleeting loss of recognition last. What is involved is the free play of imagination and understanding—in other words, of my perception and my cognition of the piece. "Free play," really? Why the effort, then? Is it not, rather, contrived by the artist? The sensation I get is not one of excitement and exhilarating freedom, as in Kandinsky's enraptured experience; it is one of contradiction between what I saw and felt in moment 1 and what I know from moment 2. If it were uttered in language (again unnecessary), it would express itself with a sentence such as this one: "Oh, my perception and my cognition of the piece do not coincide. What I see is not what I know, what I know is not what I see." Perception and cognition are at odds with each other. Kant would have to conclude that imagination and understanding are not in harmony. The relation between the two faculties is only felt as "free" inasmuch as the feeling yielded by the perceived images cannot be accounted for by the concept of identical volumes, but it is also felt as forced or contrived, and certainly not as liberating. The feeling received from this free yet contrived interplay is discontent, rather than sheer pleasure.

4. *Judgment.* We are contemplating the piece, the faculty involved is taste, the faculty of aesthetic judgment. Its outcome, as always, takes the form of a linguistic utterance, whether explicit or tacit: "Morris's *Three L-Beams* is a good—or a bad—piece." But taste, according to

Kant, is not a separate and autonomous faculty the way sensibility, understanding, or practical reason are separate faculties. It is a passageway among the faculties and, where beauty is concerned, a bridge between imagination and understanding. Hence the free play. Taste is the faculty of feeling this free play and of reflecting on it so as to conceive of this very feeling as a sign of its own universal shareability. In other words, moment 4 is the ground, or the as-if ground, for moment 3. It precedes or, to stay closer to Kant in §9; it *must* precede moment 3, not temporally but transcendentally. Or so it would if the sensation gained from moment 3 had been free play. But in this case it wasn't. Instead of harmony between the cognitive powers, moment 3 yielded disharmony and conflict. What then with moment 4? There are two, and apparently only two, possibilities at this point. The first is to stay within the confines of a strict application of Kantian aesthetics and to declare Morris's piece bad—meaning ugly—because it doesn't satisfy the so-called criterion of harmony. Such a reason for their negative verdict was often ascribed to the formalist critics (Clement Greenberg and Michael Fried most famous among them) by their adversaries, who embraced the second possibility: to declare Kantian aesthetics irrelevant. Taste simply doesn't apply where the artist has deliberately broken with Kandinsky's modernism, by making the latter's after-the-fact model into a generative one. Aesthetic judgment has lost its grasp on the work where the artist has taken the interplay of imagination and understanding as the self-referential subject matter of his piece. If we insisted on judging it aesthetically, we would have to admit that Morris's piece is at best a parody of Kandinsky's epiphany. Better shunt moment 4 and jump to moment 5.

5. *Interpretation.* We may or may not be looking at the piece. The faculty involved is understanding. What the experience yields is nothing, for this moment is not concerned with the experience any longer. It is concerned with reflecting on the experiences from moments 1 and 2 and their noncoincidence, that is to say, on the sensation or feeling of discontent and contrivance experienced in moment 3. This can be done in the absence of the work; yet, to have experienced the work is a prerequisite. Interpretation must express itself through language (although, again, it doesn't need to do so out

loud). The sentence it would use is the same as in moment 3: "My perception and my cognition of the piece do not coincide." But this sentence would not express a feeling; rather, it would reflect on this feeling, or interpret it self-referentially, so as to conclude: "This is what the work is about." Expressed in terms that emphasize difference, contradiction, and negation, the work's aboutness or subject matter constitutes whatever knowledge of the work we have gained through the whole process (Fig. 6.2).

Moment 5 is equally accessible to a formalist critic as it is to his antiformalist opponent. Both might even come up with the same interpretation of Morris's piece, their divergence in appreciation notwithstanding. What matters for the time being is that the antiformalist bypasses moment 4 (aesthetic judgment) and is interested in developing a discourse on the meaning of the piece that is not at all concerned with aesthetic quality. Appreciation follows implicitly from the discourse's level of interest. But this is not the last word of the formalist-antiformalist quarrel, since

Moment	Perception	Cognition	Sensation	Judgment	Interpretation
Faculty	Imagination	Understanding	Free play of imagination and understanding	Taste	Understanding
Yielding	Feeling of difference	Knowledge of sameness	Feeling of contradiction (between moments 1 and 2)	Contradiction reflected upon (feelingly)	Contradiction reflected upon (intellectually)
Utterance	"Three volumes look and feel different."	"Three volumes look identical."	"Perception and cognition do not coincide."	"This is a good (bad) piece."	"Perception and cognition do not coincide = what the work is about."

Figure 6.2   The Experience of Robert Morris's *Three L-Beams*

part of the difficulty of assessing both positions concerns the fact that it is essential to the antiformalist or postmodernist discourse to include a representation of the discourse of its adversaries, which acts as a foil. Since Greenberg and Fried notoriously rejected minimal art, their critics assume that they could declare Morris's piece bad—meaning ugly—because it doesn't satisfy the so-called criterion of harmony. This or a similar judgment is ascribed to them, moreover, in the order that Kantian aesthetics indeed assumes: from moment 3 to moment 4, at which point they are reproached for not taking into account the meaning of the piece obtained in moment 5 and for missing the point of postmodernism altogether. Whether this is a fair representation of the formalist position remains to be seen. It has probably become clear by now that I myself set out to speak in defense, if not of formalism as such (whatever that means), at least of the continued validity of Kantian aesthetics. The toughest, and therefore the best, place to test this validity is in the interpretive discourse of its detractors. Lest I, too, be accused of constructing a representation of my opponent acting as a foil, I shall have recourse to an actual reading of Robert Morris's *Three L-Beams* by one of the major proponents of the antiformalist or postmodernist discourse.

I am speaking of Rosalind Krauss no less, who, at a particularly crucial moment of her intellectual career, embedded a discussion of Morris's three L-shaped volumes in a text that takes as its explicit subject the cultural change involved in the passage from modernism to postmodernism and the abandonment of a formalist model in favor of a structuralist one. The text in question is an article on the architect Peter Eisenman, dated 1980 (but written in June 1977) and entitled "Death of a Hermeneutic Phantom: Materialization of the Sign in the Work of Peter Eisenman."[9] Basically rehearsing what she wrote on Morris's piece in *Passages on Modern Sculpture*, Krauss makes it stand for an exemplary symbol of the paradigm shift she and the culture are going through.[10] Her reading of the piece, once cast in the five moments I have isolated above, will help us understand some of the implications for Kantian aesthetics of the postmodernists' avowed anti-Kantianism.

First, Krauss presents what she says is the "standard analysis" of this work, to be found in Marcia Tucker's book on Robert Morris: "Given the unlikeness of each of the Ls' positions—one is up-ended, the second is lying on its side, and the third is poised on its two ends—this analysis proposes that the meaning of the work addresses the way the viewer can mentally correlate the three forms, seeing each as a physical instance of a single master idea."[11] Second, Krauss proceeds to contradict this "standard analysis" with her own (which she presents as *the* objective meaning of the piece):

Now it must be said of this work by Morris, that its meaning lies in a direction 180 degrees opposite to the one suggested above. That is, what Morris is calling on us to see is that in our experience those forms are *not the same*. For their placement visually alters each of the forms, thickening the lower element of the up-ended unit, or bowing the sides of the one poised on its ends. Thus no matter how clearly we might *understand* that the three Ls are identical (in structure and dimension), it is impossible to see them as the same. Therefore, Morris seems to be saying, the "facts" of the objects' similarity belong to a logic that exists *prior* to experience; because at the moment of experience, or *in* experience, the Ls defeat this logic and are "different."

Third, Krauss offers her own reading of the contradiction between logic and experience. The text continues: "Their 'sameness' belongs only to an ideal structure—an inner being that we cannot see. Their difference belongs to their exterior—to the point at which they surface into the public world of our experience. This 'difference' is their sculptural meaning." And finally, Krauss theorizes this "difference" as an embodiment of the passage from modernism to postmodernism and aligns the latter with an attack on Kant:

It is because of this fact that one would want to place this work of Morris's within a post-modernism tradition. Because what this sculpture is rejecting is the notion of the perceiver as the privileged subject who confers significance on reality by recourse to a set of ideal meanings of which he is himself the generator. It refuses, that is, to allow the work to appear as the manifestation of a transcendental object in some kind of reciprocal relationship to its viewer/reader, understood as a transcendental ego or subject.

Now, let us recast this text into the five moments that I have outlined above. When Krauss dismisses the "standard analysis" prompted by Marcia Tucker, it is as if she reproached Tucker for staying with moment 2, or conflating moment 2 and moment 5 into a single (and single-minded) interpretive moment. Krauss, by contrast, sees the necessity of a plurality of moments in the experience and interpretation of the piece, and she adequately starts from moment 1. She beautifully describes her experience in phenomenological terms, as an optical illusion of sorts. The surprise effect of the piece, and her own feeling of having been jolted out of her expectations, belong to the subtext of her comments. Then, very symptomatically, she jumps over moment 2, and though it is there by implication, in what appears to be an account of moment 3, she denies its empirical reality: "Thus no matter how clearly we might *understand* that the three Ls are identical, it is impossible to see them as the same." This is a startling assertion, for she must have *seen* that they were the same. Even if the optical illusion generated by the beams had been so strong that she had to measure them in order to verify their sameness, it would still have been through an empirical experience that she would have gained cognitive access to what she calls "a logic that exists *prior* to experience." Her shunning of moment 2 (empirical knowledge) is the pretext she needs for her shunning of moment 4 (aesthetic judgment).

Nowhere does she state an opinion as to whether the piece is good or successful as art. Only by implication do we surmise that, since it gave her so much food for thought, it must be a good piece. As if the appreciation of Morris's *art* exhausted itself in the overtly anti-Kantian meaning she ascribes the piece, she conflates moments 3 and 5. Indeed, she reads moment 3 (Kant's moment of free play between imagination and understanding, or our moment of contrived interplay between perception and cognition) as if it pitted the phenomenological difference sensed *in* experience against "das Ding an sich" (the thing-in-itself)—in her terms: a *transcendental object* on which the *perceiver* as *transcendental ego or subject confers significance by recourse to a set of ideal meanings of which he is himself the generator.* Kant is not mentioned by name, but the buzzwords of pop-Kantianism are there. Krauss's Kant is a caricature of Kant, a Kant who has not gone beyond the *First Critique* and acts as a foil for her own position. Yet Krauss's phrasing, *meanings of which he* [the subject] *is himself the generator,* symptomatically points at a real problem *Three L-Beams* by Robert Morris poses to Kantian aesthetics.

Let us recall Kant's question: "how we become conscious, in a judgment of taste, of a reciprocal subjective harmony between the cognitive powers: is it aesthetically, through mere inner sense and sensation? or is it intellectually, through consciousness of the intentional activity by which we bring these powers into play?" His answer had been, unequivocally: through sensation. In the case of Morris's piece, this spells only half the truth—the truth contained in our sensation from moment 3. The other half, to paraphrase Kant, is that we become conscious of a reciprocal subjective *disharmony* between the cognitive powers through consciousness of the intentional activity by which *the artist brought* these powers into play. Krauss is wrong in claiming that the sameness of the three L-beams "belongs to a logic that exists *prior* to experience," understood as a transcendental logic. She would be right, however, if she had meant "a logic that exists *prior* to *our* experience" as viewers, because our experience was planned by the artist, and it feels. The sense of contrivance attached to the felt conflict of the faculties in moment 3 is the result of Morris's intention. As I said, Morris made Kandinsky's retrospective model into a generative one. Therein, and not in the dismissal of Kantian aesthetics, lies the alleged break with tradition that makes Krauss speak of postmodernism. What minimal art has done to the early modernism of someone like Kandinsky is that it excludes the innocent viewer; it forbids us to judge Morris's piece aesthetically by simply sliding smoothly from moment 3 into moment 4. Krauss has perhaps good reasons to avoid judging aesthetically, for although it is likely that she would gladly admit that the L-beams are a parody of Kandinsky's epiphany, it is less likely that she wouldn't fear to see the parody backfire. Just imagine Kandinsky performing it himself. What kind of "free play" would be experienced if Kandinsky had made an installation piece reproducing the famous liberating canvas three times over and had showed it once upright hanging on the wall, once lying flat on the floor, and once leaning on its side propped between wall and floor?

Clement Greenberg had a word for art that elicits that kind of contrived free play. He called it "concocted art." Minimal art was first on the list, an embarrassing verdict for anyone who has not stopped looking at recent art with an open mind. "Concocted" is a mean word, but that's not what's most embarrassing about it. More embarrassing is that Greenberg applied it as a blanket term to minimal art at large. "Roses in general are beautiful" is not an aesthetic judgment, Kant reminds us, it is a logical judgment based on many aesthetic comparisons. I try not to allow myself such generalizations, least of all when recent art is concerned. But I cannot end this paper without having said what I think of *Three L-Beams* by Robert Morris. My verdict is that it is a very interesting piece—interesting in Donald Judd's sense—and that this is its limit. It is too didactic a work. It has no secret, it explains itself away. In other words, it exhausts itself in moment 5 (interpretation). Moment 4 (judgment) is either redundant or beside the point. The strategy employed by Morris to make three identical volumes feel different is far less elegant and far less effective in its aesthetic outcome than, say, Rodin's strategy in the *Three Shades* topping his *Gates of Hell*, a work that is also composed of three identical sculptures arranged in such a way that they look and feel different; they manage to sustain that feeling, no matter how long you look at them and how well you know that they are actually identical. Facing *Three L-Beams*, by contrast, it is hard to sustain the feeling received from moment 1 once moment 2 is reached, which is why moment 3 is short-lived and quickly gives way to moment 5, which is why the work is didactic and why it doesn't quite succeed as art.

My judgment, I realize, has a formalist ring to it. Michael Fried might have uttered it with virtually the same explanation. It is thus all the more vulnerable to the counterargument of the antiformalists. Now, they might say, aren't you unwittingly playing into the hands of Rosalind Krauss when claiming that moment 4 is either redundant or beside the point? Aren't you admitting that minimal art, and Morris's piece in particular, have made aesthetic judgment in Kant's sense irrelevant? What are you doing, then? Are you mourning the innocent viewer? Are you, like Michael Fried, regretting the *presentness* and *grace* of truly modernist sculpture, and are you not, on this basis, rejecting minimalism wholesale because it forbids you to proceed innocently from moment 3 to moment 4, that is, from the pleasure in the harmony of your cognitive powers to the judgment that presupposes the same harmony in all viewers?[12] How can you be so nostalgic for harmonious, Apollonian art, after all you have said about disharmony, conflict, and contradiction in your account of moment 3? Are you naive or perverse?

Neither. Or both, if you want. How to recover naiveté from perversity is the great challenge of so-called antiformalist or postmodernist art. There are a number of works by Bruce Nauman, which Greenberg would have deemed concocted and which I think are masterpieces of precisely that kind of recovery, just to emphasize that I am not rejecting anything wholesale. And you will agree that Nauman's work elicits just as much, if not more, disharmony, conflict, and contradiction as Morris's. You seem to have missed my point about moment 4 being either redundant or beside the point. Unlike Krauss, I said this as a judgment, not as an interpretation. And I said it as a judgment about an interpretation. Hers, precisely, but not only hers. Mine as well. Or yours, the one that is inevitably imposed on all of us by "what Morris is calling on us to see," as Krauss said.

To wit, the interpretation expressed in moment 5 by the sentence: "My perception and my cognition of the piece do not coincide; this is what the work is about." This "aboutness" or subject matter is expressed in terms that emphasize difference, contradiction, and negation and that constitute whatever knowledge of the work we have gained through the whole process, as I said above. To put things simply: My aesthetic judgment (moment 4) is a protest against the artist's—or the critic's, for that matter—authoritarian manipulation of difference, contradiction, and negation as ultimate meanings (moment 5). It is not at all a denial of the relevance of difference, contradiction, and negation as feelings had from moment 3. It just happens that in the case of Morris's *Three L-Beams*, my feeling disagrees as to how to interpret the meaning of the disharmony among the cognitive powers elicited by the piece. Much remains to be said about this feeling before the disharmony in question gets positively integrated by Kantian aesthetics, which is, I believe, the real challenge art since minimalism poses to theory. Meanwhile, one thing should be clear: The formalist straw man constructed by the antiformalists and postmodernists is a chimera. Aesthetic judgment does not simply proceed from moment 3 to moment 4. Moment 4 includes moment 5 and pertains to it; it drags it along and is posterior to it. Today's sophisticated art lover has learned to deal with a multilayered experience of art where judgment is not the outcome of one single epiphany but rather, alternates feelings about meanings and meanings about feelings, and this as many times as there are layers of self-referentiality in the work. But feeling always has the last word. Such a feeling is aesthetic, which means that it is no more than a feeling, arrived at involuntarily. But also that for this feeling I claim universal validity. I don't have to account for that. Please judge for yourselves.

Part II Aesthetics in Philosophy

7

The Future of Aesthetics

Arthur C. Danto

IN EARLY 2004, the American Society for Aesthetics published two "call for papers" announcements on its Web site, each for a conference on aesthetics as a neglected topic in the treatment of art. They were issued by two disciplines that do not ordinarily share a perspective: art history and philosophy. The organizers of each of the conferences appeared to agree that aesthetics is more central to art than either of their disciplines had recognized. Art historians, according to the first call, having lately addressed art primarily from political and social points of view, are beginning to find merit in approaching it aesthetically. And philosophers of art, said to have almost exclusively focused on how we define a work of art and what role is played by art world institutions in that definition, now ask if they have not lost sight of what is valuable about art. The question that interests me is what the impact will be if aesthetics really is restored to its alleged prior role.

By aesthetics, I shall mean the way things show themselves, together with the reasons for preferring one way of showing itself to another. Here is a nice example. I was president of the American Society for Aesthetics when the organization turned fifty, and I offered to coax the artist, Saul Steinberg, a friend, to design a poster to celebrate the occasion. Saul agreed to take the task on as long as he did not have to work too hard. He was not entirely certain what aesthetics was, but rather than attempting to explain its meaning, I had the *Journal of Æsthetics and Art Criticism* mail him a few issues, to get a sense of what aestheticians think about. That was a lot to ask of someone who did not want to work very hard, but in the end, true to his character, Saul was much more fascinated by the diphthong Æ on the cover of the journal than with anything between the covers—if he even read them. Friendship has its limits. He phoned one day to say he had solved the problem, and I have to say, as an aesthetician, that he got closer to the heart of the matter than anyone who works merely with words could possibly have done. He had borrowed back from the artist Jim Dine a drawing he had done for him, which showed a landscape with a house and a big blocky *E* next to it—the kind you see on the optician's eye chart—dreaming about a cosmetically enhanced and more elegant *E* than its current font allowed. This enhanced letter was displayed in a thought balloon above itself. All Saul did was replace the latter with the journal's diphthong, *Æ*. The blocky *E* dreamt of being a diphthong, the way the puny ninety-pound weakling in the physical culture ad dreams of having the abs and biceps that make girls swoon. That was aesthetics in a nutshell. But of course it could go the other way. The diphthong in its soul of souls might wish that it had the honest modern look of the blocky *E*. It is worth pointing out that so far as how the word sounds is concerned, there is not a scrap of difference. Differences in font are mere coloration, as the logician Gottlob Frege would say. Still, a written letter has to look one way rather than another, and there are always grounds for preferring one look over another. As long as there are visible differences in how things look, aesthetics is inescapable. I had three thousand posters printed, which were put on sale to members of the organization. What I found, not surprisingly, was that aestheticians were not enough interested in art to pay for it, and, so far as I know, the posters are gathering dust while stacked in the organization's storeroom somewhere. My hunch is that art historians would have snapped them up, knowing the value of work by Steinberg, who has since, alas, died.

That brings me to the overall difference between the two disciplines in the present state of things. Philosophy has been almost immune to the impact of what has, since the 1970s, been called "theory": a body of largely deconstructionist strategies that has inflected nearly every other branch of the humanities—anthropology, literature, art history, film studies, and the like—all of which have been refracted through the prisms of attitudes that were scarcely visible before the 1960s and have since flowered into academic disciplines with canons and curricula of their own, beginning with women's studies and black studies in the U.S. university structure and ramifying out into varieties of gender and ethnic studies—queer studies, Chicano studies, and the rest. These, I believe it fair to say, have been driven by various activistic agendas, which in the case of art scholarship, criticism, and practice have endeavored to alter social attitudes, purging them of prejudices and perhaps injustices toward this or that group. Deconstruction, after all, is taken to be a method for demonstrating the way in which society has advanced and reinforced the interests of special groups—white, for example, and male; and, along a different coordinate, Western or North American.

Against this diversified background, it is worth reflecting on what a new focus on aesthetics can mean. Will it simply become grist for these new disciplines—black aesthetics, Latino aesthetics, queer aesthetics—as such popular programs as "Queer Eye for the Straight Guy" suggest, where aesthetics is taken as one of queerdom's defining attributes, and where new gender attitudes are in the offing, as in the recently identified category of the metrosexual—straight guys with aesthetical eyes? Or does it mean an abandonment of the deconstructionist reorganization of knowledge, so that art will be seen less through the activist perspectives of recent decades and instead be addressed "for itself," as something that affords pleasure to eye and ear irrespective of what we might consider the gendered eye, the ethnic eye, the racial eye, and so on? Or is the turn to aesthetics not so much an end to the social and political way of considering art but rather a prolongation of these into what might have been neglected dimensions—namely, female aesthetics, black aesthetics, queer aesthetics, and the like—in which case the turn to aesthetics is not really a change in direction at all?

"Theory" entered academic consciousness in the early 1970s. The earliest of the writings of Jacques Derrida and Michel Foucault that form part of it date from about 1967 and 1968, that year of university uprisings throughout the world. The events and movements that give theory its activist edge in the United States date mainly from the mid- to late 1960s: 1964 was the Summer of Freedom in the United States; radical feminism emerged as a force after 1968; Stonewall, which detonated gay liberation, took place in 1969; and the antiwar movement went on into the next decade. Theory was then to define the attitudes of many who entered academic life by the 1980s, and it became a sort of fulcrum that tended to split departments almost on the basis of age, between traditionalists, who tended to consider art formalistically, and activists, whose interest in art was largely defined through identity politics. I know that aesthetics became politicized in art criticism by the mid-1980s. Conservative art critics insisted on stressing aesthetics as what those they perceived as left-wing critics neglected or overlooked. From the conservative perspective, the turn to aesthetics would mean the return to traditional ways. The fact that there is the call for papers on aesthetics from an art history department could be taken as good news for the conservatives. It would mean, in effect, what was called after World War I in France a *rapel a l'ordre*—a call to order—in which avant-garde artists were enjoined to put aside their experiments and represent the world in ways reassuring to those whose worlds had been torn apart by war. It would be exceedingly disillusioning to those who see things this way, then, if aesthetics itself were just a further way to think of art from the perspective of theory. By the same token, it would hardly be thinkable that art historians whose syllabi, bibliographies, and reputations are based on political approaches to art should all at once turn their back on these and embrace an entirely new approach—one, moreover, that treats art as if gender, ethnicity, and the like no longer mattered. It would mean that they had finally thrown their lot in with the traditionalists. As academic and cultural life is now structured, this would be a tremendous transformation, but hardly one likely to be made.

The situation in philosophy is entirely different. As I have already mentioned, theory had virtually no impact on philosophy as an academic discipline in Anglo-American universities. Young people who went into graduate work in philosophy emerged from the same historical matrices as those who went into art history or cultural studies, but the kinds of concerns that created factions in the other divisions of the liberal arts somehow never did this in philosophy, and philosophy departments were never polarized along the same lines as other departments of *les sciences humaines*. The texts that split the rest of academic life into irreconcilable factions were simply not taken seriously as philosophy by main line philosophers in Anglophone countries. In part, I think, this was because the language in which they were written was perceived as grotesquely at odds with the standards of clarity and consequence to which philosophical writing was expected to conform. These standards were monitored by the editorial boards of the main periodicals for which articles were refereed. And the principles of "publish or perish" Darwinized out papers written in the giddy new idioms. And since no one but other philosophers any longer read philosophy, there were no venues other than the standard journals.

Beyond that, philosophy never really presented itself as a candidate for deconstruction. The reason for this is that most of the main movements in twentieth-century philosophy already consisted of programs for the reform of the discipline. Ludwig Wittgenstein had declared that "most propositions and questions that have been written about philosophical matters, are not false but senseless. We cannot therefore, answer questions of this kind at all, but only state their senselessness."[1] This was an extreme statement of a radical skepticism regarding traditional philosophy, the problem now being to find something philosophers could do instead. Phenomenology sought instead to describe the logical structure of conscious experience. Positivism dedicated itself to the logical clarification of the language of science. "Philosophy recovers itself," the pragmatist John Dewey wrote, "when it ceases to be a device for dealing with the problems of philosophers and becomes a method, cultivated by philosophers, for dealing with the problems of men."[2] Richard Rorty proposed that philosophers engage in conversations with those in disciplines that knew what they were doing. So when Derrida or Foucault came onto the scene, philosophy had survived so many wholesale critiques that it was, for better or worse, virtually immune to their attacks. What remained was a more or less neutral method of analysis that, had anybody been interested, could have been applied to some of the major elements of theory, such as Derrida's famous thesis that there is no *hors du texte* ("outside the text") or Foucault's remarkable idea of *epistemes*,[3] which define historical periods. Feminism in philosophy became a field of analytical philosophy, rather than a radical challenge to philosophy as unacceptably masculinist—and if it is true that there are ways of knowing that are inherently feminine, this might have found its way into the discussion without begging the question of whether there is a way of discussing such a charged position open to men and women alike. Most female philosophers today are feminists, I think, without this entailing that they see a need for deeply altering the nature of the discipline. It is, on the other hand, striking that the standard third person pronoun is "she" or "her" in the standard journals, unless the subject is specified by name.

Except in the great era of German idealism, aesthetics has been viewed as a somewhat marginal subdiscipline in philosophy, and its issues have not been considered sufficiently important to the practice of philosophy that philosophers other than specialists have seen reason to take much interest in them. So a reconsideration of aesthetics would have little if any impact on philosophy as currently practiced, by contrast with the impact it might have on art history. But the premise of the conferences in London and Cork was that, to put it somewhat paradoxically, aesthetics seems to have disappeared from aesthetics. That is, aestheticians, according to the conference's organizers, have made aesthetics so marginal to their analysis of art that they have forgotten, or failed to recognize, how important aesthetics actually is in art and the place of art in human experience. The calls for papers went out in order to rectify this situation. They were a call to bring aesthetics back into the philosophy of art in some more central way than recent practice has acknowledged.

This is where I come into the picture, since I was singled out, along with Marcel Duchamp, as at least in part responsible for the way things have gone. Duchamp had indeed said that "aesthetic delectation is the danger to be avoided,"[4] and part of his intention with the famous readymades of 1913–1917 was to constitute a body of art in connection with which aesthetic considerations did not arise. Duchamp clarified this in a talk given at the Museum of Modern Art in New York in 1961: "A point which I want very much to establish is that the choice of these readymades was never dictated by aesthetic delectation. This choice was based on a reaction of visual indifference with at the same time a total absence of good or bad taste . . . in fact a complete anaesthesis." If all art were readymade, as Salvador Dali once imagined could happen, there would indeed be no room—or at least little room—for aesthetics. But despite Duchamp's somewhat mischievous suggestion that "since the tubes of paint used by the artist are manufactured and ready-made products, we must conclude that all the paintings in the world are readymades aided and also works of assemblage," it was clear that it required some special effort to identify works of art with the null degree of aesthetic interest. It was one thing to make room for art in which the absence of aesthetic interest was the most interesting fact about it, quite another to claim that aesthetics has no role to play in art at all. In his dialogues with Pierre Cabanne, Duchamp makes it plain what his overall objective is, namely to modulate what he regards as the excessive importance given to what he terms "the retinal."[5] In a way, he and the organizers of those conferences were reciprocals of one another. They were insisting that too little attention was being paid to what he felt too much was being paid. He was saying that painting had functions other than providing aesthetic gratification—"it could be religious, philosophical, moral."[6] *They* were saying that he had gone too far. It was not really much of a disagreement.

For me, Duchamp's philosophical discovery was that art could exist, the importance of which was that it had no aesthetic distinction to speak of, at a time when it was widely believed that aesthetic delectation was what art was all about. That, so far as I was concerned, was the merit of his readymades. It cleared the philosophical air to recognize that since anaesthetic art could exist, art is philosophically independent of aesthetics. That is a discovery that means something only to those concerned, as I was, with the philosophical definition of art, namely, what are the necessary and sufficient conditions for something being a work of art.

The problem, as I saw and still see it, arose for me initially with Andy Warhol and his *Brillo Box,* which was perceptually so like the workaday shipping cartons in which Brillo was shipped from factory to warehouse to supermarket, that the question of distinguishing them became acute—and this I took to be the question of distinguishing art from reality. I do not mean distinguish them epistemologically but rather ontologically—sooner or later one would discover that one was made of plywood the other not. The question was whether the difference between art and reality could consist in such discoverable differences. I thought not, but from the beginning my strategy was to find how there could be differences that were not perceptual differences. My thought was that there had to be a theory of art that could explain the difference. A handful of philosophers were on this track in the 1960s. Richard Wollheim phrased it in terms of "minimal criteria," which was a Wittgensteinian approach and really did not meet the question, inasmuch as Wollheim supposed the minimal criteria would be ways of picking art out from nonart, and hence perceptual, which was to beg the question. George Dickie explicitly phrased it as one of definition, at a time when Wittgensteinians and others saw definition in art as impossible and unnecessary. I saluted Dickie for his bravura but faulted his definition, which is institutionalist: Something is an artwork if the art world decrees it so. But how can it consistently decree *Brillo Box* an artwork, but not the cartons in which Brillo comes? My sense was that there had to be reasons for calling *Brillo Box* art—and if being art was grounded in reasons, it no longer could be, or merely be, a matter of decree.

These, I think, were the main positions, and those who drafted the call for papers are clearly right, that aesthetic qualities played no role to speak of in the ensuing discussions. Dickie built into his definition that a work of art is "a candidate for appreciation,"[7] and this could very well be aesthetic appreciation, but Dickie never wanted to be too explicit.

I have said at times that if the indiscernible objects—*Brillo Box* and the Brillo cartons—were perceptually alike, they must be aesthetically alike as well, but I no longer believe this to be true, mainly because of having brought some better philosophy to bear on the issue. But this, as you will see, makes the issue of aesthetics more irrelevant than ever.

Let us attempt to distinguish between artworks and objects—*Brillo Box,* for example, and the particular stenciled plywood box in which any given token of the work consists. There were, perhaps, three hundred such tokens done in 1964, and a hundred or so more in 1970. It somewhat complicates the indiscernible relationship between these tokens and the ordinary Brillo cartons, which happen to be tokens of a different artwork, namely a piece of commercial art. Warhol's boxes were fabricated in the Factory at 231 East 47th Street in Manhattan by Gerard Malanga and various other of Warhol's assistants in 1964, as well as by Warhol himself. Meanwhile, there were many thousands of tokens of the Brillo carton, shaped and printed in various box factories (probably) in the United States over a period of time. Both of the boxes, one fine and the other commercial art, are parts of visual culture, without this in any way blurring the difference between fine and commercial art. We know who the commercial artist was—James Harvey—whose identity is complicated by the fact that he was a fine artist in the abstract expressionist mode, who merely made his living as a freelance package designer. Now Harvey's work was appropriated by Warhol, along with the works of various other package designers in the 1964 exhibition at the Stable Gallery—the Kellogg's cornflake carton, the Del Monte peach half carton, the Heinz tomato juice carton, and so on. But the only box that is generally remembered is *Brillo Box*—it was the star of the show and is almost as much Warhol's attribute as the Campbell's soup label. And this is because of its aesthetic excellence. Its red, white, and blue design was a knockout. As a piece of visual rhetoric, it celebrated its content, namely Brillo, as a household product used for shining aluminum. The box was about Brillo, and the aesthetics of the box was calculated to dispose viewers favorably toward Brillo. Warhol, however, gets no credit for the aesthetics for which Harvey was responsible. That is the aesthetics of the box, but whether or not that aesthetics is part of Warhol's *work* is another question altogether. It is true that Warhol *chose* the Brillo carton for *Brillo Box.* But he chose for *that same show* five other cartons, most of which are aesthetically undistinguished. I think this was part of his deep egalitarianism, that everything is to be treated the same. The truth is, however, that I don't know what aesthetic properties if any belong to Warhol's *Brillo Box* itself. It was, though the term did not exist in 1964, a piece of conceptual art. It was also a piece of appropriation art, though this term was not to come into existence until the 1980s. Warhol's box was a piece of pop art, so called because it was about the images of popular culture. Harvey's box was part of popular culture, but it was not a piece of pop art because it was not about popular culture at all. Harvey created a design that obviously appealed to popular sensibilities. Warhol brought those sensibilities to consciousness. Warhol was a very popular artist because people felt his art was about them. But Harvey's box was not about them. It was about Brillo, which belonged to their world, since shining aluminum belonged to the aesthetics of everyday domestic existence.

An obituary of the brilliant young fashion writer, Amy Spindler, credits her with recognizing that "fashion was as important a cultural indicator as music or art." The question that leaves us with is what marks the difference, if any, between fashion and art? A dress can be a work of art as well as a cultural indicator, but wherein lies the difference, since not all dresses are works of art? Georg Wilhelm Friedrich Hegel drew a distinction between two kinds of what he termed spirit: objective spirit and absolute spirit. Objective spirit consists of all those things and practices in which we find the mind of a culture made objective: its language, its architecture, its books and garments and cuisine, its rituals and laws—all that falls under *les sciences humaines* (sciences of man) or what Hegel's followers called *Geisteswissenschaften* (mental sciences). Absolute spirit is about us, whose spirit is merely present in the things that make up our objective spirit. Harvey's boxes belong to the objective spirit of the United States circa 1960. So, in a way, do Warhol's boxes. But Warhol's boxes, being about objective spirit, are absolute: They bring objective spirit to consciousness of itself. Self-consciousness is the great attribute of absolute spirit, of which, Hegel felt, fine art, philosophy, and religion are the chief and perhaps the only moments. The aesthetics of the Brillo cartons tells us a lot about the objective spirit to which it belongs. But what if anything does it tell us about absolute spirit?

This is enough metaphysics for the moment. I have brought it in to help explain why, until my recent book, *The Abuse of Beauty*,[8] my work has had relatively little to say about aesthetics. The explanation is that my main philosophical concern, prompted by the state of the art world in the 1960s, was the definition of art. In a crude way, my definition had two main components in it: something is a work of art when it has a meaning—is about something—and when that meaning is embodied in the work—which usually means it is embodied in the object in which the work of art materially consists. My theory in brief is that works of art are *embodied meanings.* Because of works like Warhol's *Brillo Box,* I could not claim that aesthetics is part of the definition of art. That is not to deny that aesthetics is part of art! It is definitely a feature of the Brillo cartons as pieces of commercial art. It was because of the aesthetics of popular art that the pop artists were so fascinated by popular imagery—commercial logos, cartoons, kitsch. But that is not to say, though I love popular imagery, that only popular art is aesthetic. That would be crazy and it would be false. But it is also false to say that aesthetics is *the* point of visual art. It is not at all the point of *Brillo Box*! Nor is it the point of most of the world's art. And this, in his dialogues with Pierre Cabanne, is what Duchamp more or less said. Aesthetics got to be part of the point of art with the Renaissance, and then, when aesthetics was really discovered in the eighteenth century, the main players could maintain that the point of art was the provision of visual pleasure. Since art was taken as imitation, its purpose was to bring before the eyes of the viewer what was aesthetically pleasing in the world—pretty people, scenes, objects. In Hans Belting's great book, *Kult und Bild*,[9] he discusses the "point" of devotional images from early Christianity until the Renaissance, in which aesthetics had no role to speak of. Images were prayed to and worshipped for miracles, like the *Vierzehn Heilegen* of the German baroque, which are incidentally aesthetically pleasing. But the cult of the *Vierzehn Heilegen* loved them for helping in difficult births, illnesses, bad fortune. Their unmistakable beauty is merely what was expected of statuary in the eighteenth century, not what the statuary was about. But if aesthetics is not the point of art, what is the point of aesthetics?

This is too swift. I don't want to deny that there may be art the point of which is aesthetic. I'm not sure that I want to furnish examples of this yet, but I can say that most of the art being made today does not have the provision of aesthetic experience as its main goal. And I don't think that was the main goal of most of the art made in the course of art history. On the other hand, there is unmistakably an aesthetic component in much traditional and in some contemporary art. Now it would be a major transformation in artistic practice if artists were to begin making art the point and purpose of which was aesthetic experience. That would really be a revolution. In paying attention to aesthetics, philosophers would be mistaken in believing they were paying attention to the main neglected point of art. But it may be, or rather, I think it is true that when there is an intended aesthetic component in art, it is a *means* to whatever the point of the art may be. And this certainly would be worth paying philosophical attention to, even if aesthetics is not part of the definition of art. And if, again, aesthetics really is an artistic means, then art history, in paying attention to it, is paying attention to how art, considered politically or economically or socially or however, achieves its goals. In brief, the reconsideration of aesthetics, whether in philosophy or in aesthetics, can tell us a great deal worth knowing about art, whatever our approach to it may be, as well as about the social world—or the world as objective spirit.

I want now to move to a rather deeper level, to a concept of aesthetics that almost certainly has some impact on how we think about art philosophically but could have an even more significant impact on how we think about some of the central issues of philosophy itself. This is an approach to aesthetics that, because it is associated with one of the most respected names in modern philosophy, might recommend itself to philosophers inclined to be scornful of aesthetics as a minor discipline, preoccupied by frill and froth. In 1903, William James arranged for the philosophical genius, Charles Sanders Peirce, to give a series of lectures at Harvard University on the meaning of pragmatism. In the lectures, Peirce specified three normative disciplines, logic, ethics, and aesthetics—what is right in thought, in action, and in feeling—of which aesthetics was the most fundamental. Peirce believed that logic is founded on ethics, of which it is a higher development. He then says, surprisingly, in a letter to James in November 1902, that "ethics rests in the same manner on aesthetics—by which, needless to say, I don't mean milk and water and sugar."[10] Peirce, incidentally, was unhappy with the term "aesthetics" and proposed in its stead the clearly unaesthetic word "axiagastics," which is the science that examines that which is worthy of adoration. I want to quote somewhat extensively from a passage in Lecture 5:

I find the task imposed upon me of defining the esthetically good . . . I should say that an object, to be esthetically good, must have a multitude of parts so related to one another as to impart a positive simple immediate quality to their totality; and whatever does this is, in so far, esthetically good, no matter what the particular quality of the total may be. If that quality be such as to nauseate us, to scare us, or otherwise to disturb us to the point of throwing us out of the mood of esthetic enjoyment, out of the mood of simply contemplating the embodiment of the quality,—just for example, as the Alps affected the people of old times, when the state of civilization was such that an impression of great power was inseparably associated with lively apprehension and terror, —then the object remains nonetheless esthetically good, although people in our condition are incapacitated from a calm esthetic contemplation of it.[11]

Peirce derives the consequence that "there is no such thing as positive esthetic badness . . . All there will be will be various esthetic qualities."[12] He wrote to James, jocularly, that "I am inclined in my aesthetic judgments to think as the true Kentuckian about whiskey: *possibly* some may be better than others, but all are aesthetically good."

I am not a Peirce scholar, and have no idea to what extent if any these ideas are developed in any detail elsewhere in his voluminous writings. But I have the sense that what Peirce had in mind by aesthetic qualities must have been close to what Martin Heidegger spoke of in *Time and Being* as *Stimmungen* (moods). Heidegger writes: "A mood makes manifest 'how one is, and how one is faring.'"[13] "To exist as what he calls *Dasein* (being there), is always to be in some mood:[14] The pallid, evenly balanced lack of mood, which is often persistent and which is not to be mistaken for a bad mood, is far from being nothing at all." One of the moods that Heidegger famously explores in his 1929 essay, "Was ist Metaphysik" is boredom. In section 40 of *Sein und Zeit*, he deals with anxiety or angst. The state of mind that Jean-Paul Sartre explores as "nausea" is yet another example. I think terror, as exploited by the Department of Homeland Security, is a *Stimmmung*—a mood in which everything is disclosed as threatening. I think what Kant designates as "Bewunderung and Ehrfurcht" (wonder and awe) before "the starry heavens above"[15] is a mood in which sublimity is felt. There is little doubt that certain works are intended to create moods, sometimes quite powerful moods. The Nuremberg rallies of Nazism are examples of mood manipulation. The aesthetics of music, in some case of architecture, in many cases of movies, are used to put us into moods. Book II of Aristotle's *Rhetoric,* since which, according to Heidegger "scarcely one forward step worthy of mention has been made,"[16] deals with these affects in a systematic way.

What I admire in Peirce and Heidegger is that they have sought to liberate aesthetics from its traditional preoccupation with beauty—and beauty's traditional limitation to calm detachment—and at the same time to situate the beauty as part of the ontology of being human. But this would be the mood we are put into by beautiful days or beautiful settings.

Let me consider a case where the beauty of an artwork is specifically intended to put its viewers into a special mood—Jacques-Louis David's great painting, *Marat assassiné,* of 1793. One has to know something about Marat and the French Revolution to see it as a political painting, but when David painted it, everyone would have known this and would have known the circumstances: That Marat, the fierce polemicist, had been treacherously murdered by a young woman, Charlotte Corday, who had hoped to restore order in France by killing Marat. She was the female suicide bomber of the French Revolution. David did not depict the act of killing but the effect, through what Charles-Pierre Baudelaire describes as a visual poem. The painting looks like a descent from the cross. Marat is holding a pen through which he was to perform an act of kindness for his assassin by signing a petition. A knife is on the floor; blood stains the sheet, which has become his shroud. Marat's body almost glows, as Christ's body glows in the Transfiguration. His wounds are almost ornamental, as are Jesus's wounds in Renaissance descents. Only in the seventeenth century, under the influence of the Council of Trent, did it become important to show Jesus as bloody and torn. That continues in an almost excessive way with Mel Gibson. It depends upon whether we are to see Jesus as human or as divine. In David's painting, one is to see Marat as Jesus, dead but transfigured, and be moved by pity to identify with his cause and his sacrifice. We know the feelings we are intended to have, but we today don't quite have those feelings since we are not part of the reality of the painting's moment. We cannot translate into action the feelings we have, but the actions the painting is intended to arouse are political, as the feelings themselves are, and if *we* can do little more than look at the painting, that does not mean that the feelings and the intentions they enjoin do not belong to the experience. It was meant to arouse, and that power is still felt. As a philosopher, what strikes me is that visual beauty is, in this work, internal to its political effect. The beauty underwrites the metaphor between Christ and Marat, and it validates his suffering. He died for you. So what are you going to do to demonstrate he did not die in vain? *Allons enfants de la patrie!*[17] I don't think we ourselves can be put into the mood of revolutionary indignation that David's audience felt or was intended to feel. We simply recognize and analyze it and note how it contributes to the work's meaning.

Now I think the rediscovery of aesthetics is best understood as the rediscovery of the role that aesthetic qualities play in the use of art to present meanings by visual means. Ontologically, aesthetics is not essential to art—but rhetorically, it is central. The artist uses aesthetics to transform or confirm attitudes. That is not the same as putting us in the mood of calm aesthetic contemplations, which has tended to hijack the concept of aesthetics. I don't say it is unimportant, but it is not the only important role aesthetics plays in art.

Returning to the two calls for papers, I would say that the rediscovery of aesthetics means an enrichment rather than a transformation of current art historical practice. It shows how, in the domain of objective spirit, art has played an important role in society. So far as philosophy is concerned, it is probably a good thing for philosophers to be liberated from the ontological preoccupations that obsessed me and my contemporaries. It is to address art now pragmatically, from the perspective of life.

8

Retrieving Kant's Aesthetics for Art Theory After Greenberg
Some Remarks on Arthur C. Danto and Thierry de Duve

Diarmuid Costello

The Fate of Aesthetics in Contemporary Art Theory

In art theory since the early 1980s the discourse of aesthetics has been notable by its absence. This suggests that the majority of art theorists believe that the historical or conceptual limits of aesthetic theory have been breached by the internal development of art after modernism. But why would art theorists believe this?

In answer to this question I suggest—I take it noncontroversially— that the widespread marginalization of aesthetics in postmodern art theory may be attributed to the success of the art critic and theorist Clement Greenberg. In co-opting the discourse of (particularly Kantian) aesthetics to underwrite *modernist* theory, Greenberg mediated the art world's subsequent rejection of both aesthetics in general and Immanuel Kant's aesthetics in particular. But one need only reflect on the centrality for *post*modern theory of *anti*-aesthetic figures like Marcel Duchamp or of movements (such as surrealism), marginalized in Greenberg's account of "the best modern art," to see that for all their antipathy to Greenberg, many postmodernist art theorists continue to operate within a broadly Greenbergian view of aesthetics—which is *why*, of course, they are forced to reject it. What Greenberg valued is now devalued, but the theoretical framework underwriting those valuations is taken up into postmodern theory largely unremarked.

What I mean by this is not that terms like "medium-specificity" weren't central to such debates—on the contrary—but rather that it was largely taken on trust that such ideas were coherent. Hence, rather than interrogating the very *idea* of a "specific" medium, the energy went into valorizing *non-* or *anti-* or *post*-medium-specific art over its supposedly "specific" competitors. Something similar holds for many of the key terms in the Greenbergian lexicon: One need only think of the fate of "optical-ity" to see this pattern played out.[1] Hence, while the normative dimension of modernist aesthetics was frequently inverted, its underlying theoretical framework was just as often taken over.

But I also want to argue—I take it equally noncontroversially—that Greenberg's appeal to Kant was ill founded. This is something that Thi-erry de Duve's work has brought out. If both claims are true, not only did many anti-Greenbergian theorists presuppose a broadly Greenbergian view of aesthetic theory, which is why the latter tended to be equated with "formalism" and dismissed in the face of art after modernism's increasing conceptual complexity, but they also rejected Kant largely on the basis of the damage done in his name by Greenberg.

Indeed, Greenberg's focus on Kant's theory of taste, at the expense of his theory of art, *continues* to overshadow art world receptions of Kant. It is as true, for example, of those broadly sympathetic to Kant, like de Duve, to whom the widespread acceptance of several of the criticisms above may be attributed, and of those broadly unsympathetic, like Danto, who, at least until recently, took his Kant largely at Greenberg's word. Given this, what I do in this paper is straightforward. First, I survey Greenberg's recourse to Kant, pointing out where it is tendentious or con-troversial. I then go on to consider the merits of Danto's and de Duve's claims about Kant and the latter's relevance, if any, for art theory after modernism. I conclude by indicating some resources in Kant's theory of art, as opposed to his theory of taste, for retrieving aesthetics for contem-porary debates about art.

Grounding Modernist Aesthetics: Greenberg's Appeal to Kant

Greenberg famously dubbed Kant the "first real modernist," in "Modernist Painting" (1960), because he used reason to criticize reason and thereby entrenched it more firmly in its "area of competence."[2] But

Greenberg's appeals to Kant are more fundamental than this well-known remark suggests. I shall argue that misreadings of Kant underwrite both Greenberg's modernism and his formalism.

Greenberg's modernism, his characterization of the "best" modern art as a gradual reduction to, and foregrounding of, the "unique and irreducible" features of its medium, was compromised by several assumptions about the individual senses and their relation to individual arts built into his theory from the outset. From "Towards a Newer Laocoon" (1940) onward, Greenberg sought to align specific arts, under the influence of music, with specific senses.[3] But in order to do so he was forced to conceive the intuition of artworks in terms of discrete sensory inputs. Like his psychologizing of Kant, this is essentially a product of Greenberg's deep-seated empiricism. As a result, he conflates judgments of taste, properly so-called, with what Kant would have concurred were aesthetic judgments, albeit of *sense* rather than *reflection*.[4] That is, judgments grounded, like judgments of taste, in feeling, albeit, unlike judgments of taste, in feeling occasioned by objects impacting causally on the sense organs: what Kant would have characterized as judgments rooted in *sensation* rather than in *reflection* upon an object or perceptual configuration's "subjective purposiveness" or "finality" for cognition in general.[5] That is, its suitability for engaging our cognitive faculties in an (optimally) enlivening way. As such, Greenberg's conception of medium-specificity attempts to align a broadly empiricist notion of cognitively uninflected sensation with specific artistic media, as though the sensory impression made by a work of art were a simple correlate of the intrinsic material properties of its medium, from which it could therefore be directly read off.

If this explains *why* Greenberg sought to differentiate the arts in terms of media, the question it provokes is analogous to that provoked by his view of the senses: Namely, *can* the arts be so easily parsed? That this proved feasible historically during the height of Greenberg's authority as a critic clearly does not make this a necessary feature of art's—or even of good art's—identity. Had Greenberg's alleged Kantianism stretched as far as the "Transcendental Aesthetic" of the first *Critique* he could have avoided this impasse. For on Kant's account of space and time as a priori forms of intuition, our perception of artworks, like our perception in general, is grounded in an originary *unity* of sensibility.[6] It is both alien to Kant's epistemology and phenomenologically unpersuasive to construe normal instances of intuition as mere *aggregates* of the senses—the more so when it comes to such culturally and historically freighted entities as artworks.

Greenberg's formalism, his theoretical self-understanding of his activity as a critic in a Kantian mold, is similarly problematic. At the most general level, it suffers from his failure to distinguish between "free" and "dependent" beauty in the third *Critique*. Greenberg applies Kant's account of *pure* aesthetic judgment, a judgment about the aesthetic feeling aroused by free (or conceptually unconstrained) beauty, to artworks—thereby ignoring Kant's more apposite remarks on fine art, genius, and aesthetic ideas, in favor of an account that takes natural beauty and decorative motifs ("designs *à la grecque*, the foliage on borders or on wallpaper") as its paradigm.[7] Above all it is Greenberg's recourse to Kant's account of pure judgments of taste to underwrite a theory of *artistic* value, as though Kant himself had had nothing to say about fine art, that is responsible for the rejection of Kantian aesthetics in subsequent art theory.

As a result, Greenberg misses two conceptual complexities that attach to artworks, even for Kant, and that ought to trouble the widespread perception of Kant as an archformalist in art theory. These are the constraints that the *concept* an artwork is meant to fulfill imposes on artistic beauty and the distinctive cognitive function that conceiving artworks as expressions of aesthetic *ideas* adds to Kant's conception of fine art. Hence, even if Greenberg's primary focus on "all over" abstract painting—with its links to pattern and, arguably, decoration—goes some way to explaining his appeal to Kant's formalism, it does not justify it, since even an abstract work of art would have to be brought under the concept it is meant to fulfill, in submitting its beauty *as art* to aesthetic judgment, at least for Kant.

Moreover, Greenberg routinely empiricizes and psychologizes Kant's theory of aesthetic judgment. Greenberg's belief that he could demonstrate the "objectivity" of taste by appealing to the record of past taste—when induction could not provide the necessity he required to support his argument—is evidence of his empiricization of Kant's account, in this case, of the *claim* to validity over all judging subjects.[8] Relatedly, Greenberg's psychologization of Kant is evidenced by his tendency to conflate the Kantian criterion of "disinterest" as a necessary condition on aesthetic judgment with his own, psychologistic, conception of "aesthetic distance."[9] As a result, Greenberg runs together a transcendental theory that aims to account for how aesthetic judgments are possible with a psychological description of a particular state of mind. Ironically, this robs his theory of what is perhaps most persuasive about it, its attention to the specificity of its artistic object. For if aesthetic experience were really as voluntaristic as this implies, that is, a matter of merely *adopting* a distancing frame of mind toward a given object, the nature of that object itself would fall away as a significant determinant on aesthetic judgment; for one can adopt such an attitude toward anything, at least in principle.[10]

These criticisms show that rejecting Kant's aesthetic theory on the basis of Greenberg's appeal is ill founded. The irony of art world hostility to Greenberg since the 1960s is that art theorists have generally *deferred* to Greenberg's presentation of aesthetics, notably his invocation of Kant, even if they have taken this as a basis for rejecting both aesthetics in general and Kant's aesthetics in particular. But if Greenberg's claims on a Kantian provenance for modernist theory are unwarranted, it follows that rejecting Kant as part and parcel of rejecting modernism results from a distortion. This was most apparent during the high years of anti-aesthetic postmodernism. But rather than make the argument there, I want to focus on two of the most sustained responses to Greenberg's appeal to Kant to date.

"This Is Art" Not "This Is Beautiful": Thierry de Duve's Kant After Greenberg

So far this account has much in common with de Duve's. But I want to add that not only has the art world inherited a *distorted* picture of Kant's aesthetics from Greenberg, as de Duve maintains, it has also inherited an extremely *partial* one. Thus, despite the fact that in art theory Kant's account of aesthetic judgment is routinely dismissed for its formalism, one rarely finds reference to what Kant himself had to say about how his account of aesthetic judgment applies to artworks. And this is as true of sympathetic theorists, such as de Duve, as it has been of Kant's detractors.

De Duve is one of the few art theorists who refuses the standard options of an anti-aesthetic postmodernism *or* a late modernist aestheticism by seeking to do justice to both Greenberg and Duchamp—which, as anyone familiar with how such debates typically break down will be aware, is a highly original undertaking. But despite his desire to make

Kant's aesthetics "actual" (i.e., productive) for a contemporary art audience, de Duve displays his deeper debt to Greenberg by predicating his own position solely on a reformulation of Kant's account of *pure* aesthetic judgment. That this aspect of the "Kant after Duchamp" approach remains central to de Duve's method is apparent from his paper in this volume. Here de Duve brings Kant's reflections on whether the pleasure felt in a judgment of taste precedes the judgment or vice versa to bear on Robert Morris's *Untitled (Three L-Beams)* of 1965, but he does so without thematizing how Kant's own understanding of artworks as vehicles of "aesthetic ideas" or his account of dependent beauty as a conceptually conditioned (and hence "impure") form of aesthetic judgment might complicate this analysis.[11]

And while the focus on pure aesthetic judgment has some prima facie warrant in the case of Greenberg's desire to defend abstract art on purely formal grounds, it is much more of a stretch in the case of de Duve's concern with the historically reflexive, and conceptually complex, art of the "post-Duchamp" tradition. It is thus surprising that de Duve should want to take this route, given his own critique of Greenberg's reading of Kant.

Hence, while de Duve departs from Greenberg in seeing Duchamp as the pivot for a contemporary understanding of aesthetics, he nonetheless follows Greenberg in focusing on pure aesthetic judgment. De Duve's central claim is that bringing Kant "up to date" involves substituting the judgment "this is art" for the judgment "this is beautiful," thereby capturing the transformation in the nature of art embodied in, if not brought about by, Duchamp's readymades. This might look like a category mistake, since the judgment "this is art" is a determinative judgment that subsumes a particular under a concept (namely, the concept art). Hence it is neither a reflective *nor* an aesthetic judgment in Kant's sense. Nonetheless, de Duve maintains that the judgment "this is art" is aesthetic—if only liminally—because it is singular and based on feeling alone.[12] Preserving the fundamental Kantian commitment that aesthetic judgment is noncognitive, because it refers an intuition to the feeling it occasions rather than predicates a concept of an object, de Duve maintains that the judgment "this is art" does not subsume an object under a *concept* ("art") but, rather, confers the *name* "art" on any object judged accordingly.

On de Duve's account, the judgment "this is art" is akin to that original baptism through which a person acquires a proper name. Just as all persons called Tom need have no properties in common in virtue of which they are so called—Tom is not a concept under which persons are subsumed in virtue of possessing the relevant traits—so artworks need have no properties in common in virtue of which they are called art. On the contrary, they need only *sustain comparison* with exemplary works of past art. But this account of what such baptism involves vitiates de Duve's own argument—both that art is a proper name and that the judgment "this is art" remains aesthetic in Kant's sense. De Duve claims that the judgment "this is art" is aesthetic because in making it one holds a candidate work up to previous recipients of that status in one's personal canon to judge whether it is worthy of inclusion by consulting one's faculty of feeling, in this case the feelings past works have occasioned. Like reflective judgment in Kant, this is based on an act of comparison, though what is compared, according to de Duve, is either the works themselves or the feelings they have occasioned. But once the judgment becomes a *comparison between examples*, rather than between a given intuition and the "free play" of the faculties, sensed in feeling, to which it gives rise, it can be neither noncognitive nor aesthetic after all—at least not in Kant's sense.[13] Even taken on its own terms, it is difficult to see by what criteria past feelings, as noncognitive and private, could be reliably reidentified over time for the purpose of such comparison. Moreover, given that what distinguishes proper names from concepts is that they are conferred *without* regard to other bearers of the name, it is hard to see how art can be a proper name when the judgment that confers it is essentially comparative.

The emphasis on proper names aside, de Duve's reading of Kant shares Greenberg's tendency to marginalize the reflective dimension of aesthetic judgment for Kant. That is, de Duve underplays the necessity to reflect critically on the *grounds* of the pleasure in aesthetic judgment and hence on its *warrant* for imputing—even demanding—such pleasure from others. But such reflection is a minimal requirement for laying claim to the agreement of others. By echoing Greenberg's stress on the "immediate" and "involuntary" nature of such judgment, de Duve appears to deprive himself of the most obvious criterion for distinguishing *in principle* between judgments of the beautiful and judgments of the agreeable. Granted, this will always remain a moot point in practice, since one can never know whether one has succeeded in abstracting from every contingent or pathological basis for one's pleasure in an object (i.e., from anything that would render the object of one's judgment merely "agreeable" in Kant's sense). Nonetheless, if aesthetic judgments were really as "automatic" as de Duve claims—by appeal, like Greenberg, to his own experience—what basis could one have for contesting the skeptical rejoinder that claims to universal validity simply mask the subjective preferences of their utterer?

Introspection cannot help us here, as de Duve is clearly aware, because the feelings occasioned by the agreeable and the beautiful need not be distinguishable in experience. But de Duve fails to draw out the full consequences of his own insight, particularly for his view that it is the claim to universality itself that serves as our best indication of a judgment's disinterestedness—and hence of its being a bona fide judgment of taste—and not vice versa.[14] For this appears to beg the question: How can anyone *know* that their claim to universality is warranted and, hence, that their judgment is disinterested? I agree with de Duve that we *do* feel strongly about the apparent "objectivity" of our judgments of taste and it is therefore not a matter of indifference to us whether those whose judgments matter to us concur. In this respect the pleasure we take in the agreeable and the beautiful does appear to be distinct, and the phenomenology of their respective judgments correspondingly different. Nonetheless, the fact that I feel sufficiently passionate or convinced about some of my judgments to declare their universality could just be a psychological fact about me, with any number of contingent causes; hence the fact that I feel moved to demand assent from others concerning *some* feelings of pleasure but not others does nothing to mitigate the fact that *all* claims to universality are equally prone to corruption and, hence, defeasible.

Artistic Versus Natural Beauty: Arthur C. Danto's Greenbergian Kant

In direct contrast to de Duve's account Danto has, until recently, rejected Kantian aesthetics as an adequate basis for the theory of art, often on the basis of Greenberg's appeals to Kant. Danto locates what he calls two "Kantian tenets" underpinning Greenberg's writings.[15] First, just as genius must be unconstrained by rules if it is to produce something original, so too must critical judgment operate in the absence of rules if it is to be adequate to the resultant object. Second, the critic's "practised eye" can tell the good from the bad everywhere, irrespective of whether or not it is informed by knowledge of the tradition to which a given work belongs.

The latter is somewhat uncharitable to Greenberg, who was, unsurprisingly, much better informed about the constraints on the creation of art within a given tradition than Kant. But Danto is right to call the first a Kantian tenet, albeit an inverted one, since for Kant the entailment runs in the opposite direction, from an analysis of aesthetic judgment to the nature of artworks as possible objects of such judgment. Nonetheless, what Danto neglects in this account of Greenberg's debt to Kant is the additional constraint Kant imposes on artistic beauty: Namely that in addition to being beautiful, the beauty of art must be *appropriate* to the concept governing its production as a work. In Kant's example, a beautiful church must not only be beautiful, its beauty must be *fitting* to its purpose as a house of worship: Much that might otherwise please freely in aesthetic judgment would fall foul of this constraint. Thus, the idea of dependent beauty, beauty that is dependent on (or "adherent to") a concept of what the work is meant to be, places a *restriction* on the scope of free beauty rather than negating it altogether. Ironically, this is reminiscent of Danto's own claim that works of art, as "embodied meanings," should be judged for the *appropriateness* or "fit" of their form of presentation to the content thereby presented. Indeed, were this not so, judgments of dependent beauty would fail to conform to the basic requirements of Kant's own account of aesthetic judgment in the "Analytic of the Beautiful." For if artworks fulfilled the concept guiding their production at the *expense* of being freely beautiful, judgments of dependent beauty would reduce to judgments of perfection: They would judge the degree to which a work of art fulfilled the concept guiding its production, hence its perfection as an instance of a kind.[16]

As regards Greenberg's second supposedly "Kantian" tenet, Greenberg's conception of the "practised eye," like Danto's account of it, owes more to David Hume's description of the good judge than to Kant, who never addressed the kinds of disputes that arise when trying to make fine-grained discriminations in taste. Indeed, many of the disputes that Hume recounts (such as that arising from the deleterious effects on taste of a leather-thonged key submerged, unknown to the judges, in a barrel of wine) would not count as differences of taste or instances of reflective aesthetic judgment in Kant's sense.[17] From a Kantian perspective, Hume's account, like Greenberg's, pertains to judgments of *sense* rather than *reflection*. Hence Danto's claim that this is a Kantian tenet is tendentious.

I have already argued that Greenberg fails to recognize the complexity that Kant's distinction between free and dependent beauty and his notion of aesthetic ideas adds to his account of artistic value. Danto however argues from Greenberg's alleged "Kantian tenets" that Kant himself conflates natural and artistic beauty. In support of this claim, Danto cites Kant's remark that "nature is beautiful [*schön*] if it also looks like art; and art can be called fine [*schön*] art only if we are conscious that it is art while yet it looks to us like nature."[18] For Danto this demonstrates the inadequacy of Kant's aesthetics as a basis for the theory of art. But when Kant claims that fine art must "look like" nature, he does not mean what Danto takes him to mean, namely, that fine art must *resemble* nature; he means that it must appear as *unwilled* as nature. Despite being aware that we are judging art rather than nature, Kant holds that "the purposiveness in its form must seem as free from all constraint of chosen rules *as if* it were a product of mere nature."[19] So Kant is not claiming that artworks must be indistinguishable from nature, but that they must appear as free of any laboriousness that would impede their free appreciation. As Kant puts it: "The academic form must not show; there must be no hint that the rule was hovering before the artist's eyes and putting fetters on his mental powers."[20] This lays down no substantive prescriptions on how artworks must look; nor does it entail that the beauty of art must resemble that of nature. *Pace* Danto, art need not look anything like beautiful nature in order to be aesthetically pleasing as art, even for Kant.

To my mind, these criticisms of Greenberg and Kant's aesthetics reflect the thin conception of aesthetics that has underpinned Danto's remarks on the topic to date. I have set out my reservations concerning Danto's way of conceiving "aesthetic" as opposed to "artistic" qualities elsewhere.[21] All I want to note here is that, *despite* broadening his reading of Kant's third *Critique* in *The Abuse of Beauty*, introducing the distinction between "internal" and "external" beauty—that is, between beauty that is (or is not) relevant to a work's appreciation because it is (or is not) mobilized in the service of that work's meaning—and contesting the narrow focus of traditional aesthetics on a limited range of predicates and properties, all of which is to be welcomed, Danto's underlying conception of aesthetics remains remarkably consistent, from *The Transfiguration of the Commonplace* right through to *The Abuse of Beauty*.[22]

Indeed, this is apparent from Danto's chapter in this volume, in which he defines aesthetics as "the way things show themselves, together with the reasons for preferring one way of showing itself to another" and goes on to remark that "as long as there are *visible* differences in how things look, *aesthetics* is inescapable" (my emphasis). Danto's remarks on Duchamp here—according to which "retinal" would function as a synonym for the aesthetic—also suggest little has changed in his understanding of aesthetics since he sought, in *The Transfiguration of the Commonplace*, to uncouple art and aesthetics on the grounds that it cannot explain why Duchamp's urinal is a work of art while all its (notionally) indiscernible counterparts are not. Although Danto may now be prepared to grant aesthetic properties a greater *rhetorical* role than before in "coloring" or "inflecting" our attitude toward the meaning of the work of art, such properties remain as irrelevant, *ontologically*, as ever: They may be a necessary feature of some, but not all, artworks, and so have no place in art's definition. If I remain unconvinced that this conclusion follows from Danto's premises, it is because it appears to entail that there can be artworks that express *no* point of view toward their own content and hence have no recourse to aesthetic properties understood as inflectors of said content.

To see why this ought to be a problem for Danto it is necessary to recall his ontology of art from *The Transfiguration of the Commonplace*. Exhibiting "aboutness" is self-evidently definitional of artworks conceived as "embodied meanings," since for a work to possess meaning requires, minimally, that it is about something or other. Recall also that expressing an attitude, or point of view, *toward* what they are about is what was said to distinguish artworks from "mere representations" (such as maps or diagrams), which are also "about" what they represent, though not art. But if expressing an attitude or point of view toward their own meanings *is* a necessary feature of artworks, as Danto maintains, then aesthetic properties must be so too, given his current understanding of such properties as what *enables* artworks to express an attitude toward the meanings they embody.

Danto recently claimed that *The Abuse of Beauty* considers whether, on a suitably enriched conception of aesthetic qualities as inflectors of meaning, the possession of *some* aesthetic property might prove to be a necessary condition of artworks and so should be added to the two necessary conditions he now claims *The Transfiguration of the Commonplace* adduced, namely, that artworks are about something and embody what they are about, and he concluded that it should not.[23] But this conclusion cannot be warranted, given the interaction between Danto's conception of aesthetics and his definition of artworks. Irrespective of whether he is right that beauty (or any other aesthetic quality) that is "external" to a work's meaning is irrelevant to it as art, it remains that expressing some attitude or point of view toward whatever it is about is supposed to distinguish artworks from "mere representations," according to his own theory; and *that* would seem to require that a work possess some aesthetic qualities to inflect its meaning accordingly. This is a problem that Danto has yet to address.

Retrieving Kant's Aesthetics for Art Theory After Greenberg

So far, the results of this paper have been largely negative. If the argument is sound it brings out various infelicities in Greenberg, Danto, and de Duve's remarks about Kant. Beyond that, it shows that art theory goes astray to the extent that it perceives Kant's aesthetics through the distorting optic of Greenberg's recourse to it, where this leads to a marginalization of Kant's theory of art in favor of an exclusive focus on his theory of aesthetic judgment—regardless of whether this is taken to be essentially isomorphic with art (as in de Duve) or essentially orthogonal to art (as in Danto). Of course, even if one grants both, this still only shows that Kant's aesthetics has been marginalized on the basis of various misreadings; it does not show that the art world may not have been right to reject Kantian aesthetics nonetheless, even if for the wrong reasons. That is, it does not show that Kant's aesthetics *can* be applied to art after modernism. Given this, I want to conclude by pointing out some resources in Kant's theory of art that are underplayed in art theory to this day.

For Kant, artworks are expressions of "aesthetic ideas." Put simply, an aesthetic idea is what is distinctive about either the content of artworks or the way in which they present that content. What is distinctive about the *content* of artworks is either that they present concepts that may be encountered in experience, but with a completeness that experience never affords, or that they communicate ideas that cannot—in principle—be exhibited in experience.[24] What is distinctive about the *way in which* artworks present such content is that they imaginatively "expand" the ideas presented in virtue of the indirect means through which they are forced to embody them in sensible form. For rather than seeking to present the idea itself, which would be impossible—ideas being by definition what cannot be exhibited in experience for Kant—an aesthetic idea presents the "aesthetic attributes" of its object, thereby expressing an idea's "implications" and "kinship with other concepts."[25] In effect, aesthetic ideas indirectly present what cannot be presented directly.

To take one of Kant's own examples: "Jupiter's eagle with the lightning in its claws" expands the idea of God's majesty by presenting it aesthetically. What Kant calls the "logical" attributes of an object, in this case God, would be those in virtue of which it fulfills a concept, in this case majesty. Jupiter's eagle with the lightning in its claws, by contrast, is a metaphorical expression of those same attributes, through which we are encouraged to envisage God's majesty in light of the thoughts provoked by Jupiter's eagle, thereby opening up a rich seam of further possible associations. In this way, artworks are able to indirectly present ideas that would otherwise remain unavailable to intuition and, in doing so, use their aesthetic attributes to provoke "more thought" than a direct conceptual elaboration of the idea could facilitate, thereby "expanding" the idea.[26]

In doing so, aesthetic ideas might be said to achieve the impossible: They allow artworks to present rational ideas in determinate sensuous form. Consider Delacroix's *Liberty Leading the People* (1830) as an example of the sensible embodiment of an idea, in this case freedom, that would have been comprehensible to Kant had he lived to see it. The aesthetic attributes through which freedom is personified in the guise of "Liberty"—shown leading her people to victory (fearlessness, spontaneity, resoluteness, leadership, all attributes of an active self-determining will) while holding a flag, symbol of freedom from oppression, aloft in one hand and clutching a musket in the other—serve to "aesthetically expand" the idea of freedom itself. By presenting freedom in the guise of "Liberty," freedom is depicted concretely as something worth fighting for—indeed, as something requiring courage and fortitude to attain. This is what Kant means when he claims that artworks "quicken" the mind, by freeing imagination from the mechanical task of schematizing concepts of the understanding. No longer constrained to present concepts of the understanding in sensible form, as it is in determinate judgment, aesthetic ideas free the imagination to move swiftly over an array of related thoughts.

By doing so, aesthetic ideas stimulate the mind, albeit in a less structured way than determinate thought, enabling us to think through the ideas presented in a new light.

Now, it might be objected that the forgoing account only works because it takes a representational painting as its object, and that this will be of little use to art in its expanded contemporary context of nontraditional media and forms. To show that this is not the case, I now want to consider a very different example: Art & Language's *Index 01,* also known as *Documenta Index,* after the exhibition in which it was first shown in 1972. My choice of a work by Art & Language is far from innocent, given that their work from this period might be thought to show, as well as any individual artwork might, the *inapplicability* of Kant's aesthetics (as mediated by Greenberg) to art after modernism. Against this perception, I propose that this work be understood as a sensible, though necessarily indirect, embodiment of the *idea* of an exhaustive catalog—necessarily indirect because a truly exhaustive catalog could not be a possible object of experience in Kantian terms.

Documenta Index consists of a cross-referenced index of the group's writings on art to that date and of the relations among them. Though it had various later incarnations, it originally took the form of eight small metal filing cabinets, displayed on four grey plinths, consisting of six tray-like drawers each, containing both published writings and unpublished writings, some of which raised the question of their own status as artworks. These were hinged one on top of the other in a series of nested sequences determined alphabetically and subalphabetically in terms of their order and degree of completion. The cabinets and their contents were displayed together with an index listing their contents in terms of three logical relations (of compatibility, incompatibility, and incomparability) believed to obtain between them.[27] The latter was papered directly onto the walls of the room in which the cabinets were displayed, as if in an attempt to provide an "external" vantage that would render the work's internal relations perspicuous.

At least in terms of its rhetoric of display and address, this work seems to propose an exhaustive catalog not only of the group's writings to that date, which is feasible, being finite, but also, and for my purposes more importantly, it aspires to document a set of logical relations between those writings. But the latter is something that can only exist as an idea, in Kant's sense, given that there are in principle always further relations to be mapped were we acute enough to spot them and had we infinite time and patience at our disposal. Moreover, by embodying the idea of a self-reflexive catalog, the production of the index itself creates a further layer of relations to be mapped, which would then have to be mapped in turn, and so on ad infinitum. Hence, the very undertaking of the work itself makes its goal unrealizable. Nonetheless, by bringing all this together in sensible form, this apparently austere work of art opens up a potentially limitless array of imaginative associations: to lists, taxonomies, and typologies; to attempts at self-documentation, self-reflexivity, and (ultimately) to ideals of complete self-knowledge or transparency; to conversation, collaboration, interaction, study, and learning; and, of course, to various regimes of archiving, cataloging, and the like. As such this work "expands" the idea it embodies in ways consonant with Kant's presentation of aesthetic ideas.

On Kant's account, the expression of ideas in this way gives rise to a feeling of mental vitality—or what he calls a "feeling of life"—in the work's recipient, a feeling of the enhancement, or furtherance, of the subject's cognitive powers. Artworks achieve this, not by giving rise to determinate thought, but because they give rise to a *feeling* of vitality in the free play of the subject's cognitive powers.[28] The little Kant says about what such "free play" might consist in, suggests a kind of freewheeling, associative play in which the imagination moves freely and swiftly from one partial presentation of a concept of the understanding to another; hence his claim that aesthetic ideas encourage the imagination to "spread over an immense realm of kindred presentations that arouse more thought than can be expressed in a concept."[29] It is this imaginative engagement with indirectly presented, sensibly embodied ideas, far removed from the astringent formalism typically attributed to the third *Critique* in art theory and mainstream philosophy of art (outside Kant scholarship), that I want to draw attention to, and thereby retrieve, for contemporary debates about art.

Moreover, although Kant no doubt thought, for historical reasons, of visual art in representational terms, there is nothing in his account of aesthetic ideas that *requires* art be representational, in a narrow sense, as my second example is designed to show. All Kant's account requires is that artworks expand ideas in imaginatively complex ways, and there does not seem to be anything wrong with that thought in the light of more recent art that could not have been envisaged by Kant. Indeed, I have argued elsewhere that many, if not most, artworks typically regarded as anti-aesthetic, according to the formalist conception of aesthetics that the art world inherits from Greenberg, nonetheless engage the mind in ways that may be thought of as aesthetic in Kant's sense: This includes conceptual art, despite the fact that conceptual art is routinely supposed to reveal the shortcomings of aesthetic theory in general, and Kant's aesthetic in particular. What most art regarded as unsuited to, or even incompatible with, aesthetic analysis actually shows, on my account, is not the limit of aesthetic theory per se, nor the limit of Kant's aesthetics in particular, but the limit of formalist aesthetics, as mediated by Greenberg, in coming to terms with the cognitive aspects of art after modernism. That formalism is not coextensive with aesthetic theory should not need saying: That Kant's aesthetics is not narrowly—that is, *restrictively*—formalist is what I hope I have begun to demonstrate here. If I have succeeded, commentators on contemporary art might want to give the third *Critique* a second look.

9

Artistic Creativity
Illusions, Realities, Futures

Paul Crowther

IN LATE MODERN AND postmodern times, art has been redefined as a primarily "managerial" phenomenon, in other words, reduced to its position and use in the art world—something whose meaning is in effect little more than the intersection of those critical, historical, curatorial, and administrative interests that are parasitic upon art practice. The concept of "art" is now determined by professional Western consumers rather than by transcultural productive processes. In this guise, art has no significant future. In this paper, I establish these claims and formulate an appropriate response to them. In particular I propose a rediscovery of the intrinsic value of art and of aesthetic judgments concerning the merit or demerit of particular artworks. In Part One, I outline in more detail the way in which visual art has been colonized by Western managerial interests on the basis of highly problematic art historical and philosophical theories. In Part Two, I analyze the proper understanding of art and the conditions of its creativity and briefly consider its potential postmanagerial future.

Part One

The development of cubism and abstract art of itself seems to make traditional definitions of art problematic. However, as I have argued at great length elsewhere,[1] there is a much greater similarity of meaning between abstract works and conventional pictorial artworks than is commonly realized. In some cases, this kinship extends to such despised attributes as skill as well as to dimensions of semantic and syntactic content. That being said, there are, of course, many developments within the abstract domain that seem much less assimilable on the basis of traditional conceptions of art.

In this respect, of course, one must note especially the significance of Marcel Duchamp and the conceptualist cult that has grown around him since the late 1970s. To explain this latter phenomenon, it is worth remarking upon aspects of Duchamp's "readymades." These are mass-produced objects presented in spaces or formats that are customarily utilized for artistic purposes. The most famous examples of these objects are perhaps *The Bottle Rack* and *Fountain*—the latter being a white porcelain urinal signed "R. Mutt" by the artist. Some of the readymades (the so-called "assisted" ones) involve preexisting artifacts physically modified by Duchamp; but the "unassisted" examples just mentioned involve no significant intervention over and above the act of being presented in art contexts and formats.

Given this, the question arises as to the meaning of these readymades. Are they mere send-ups—acts of mockery aimed at the "highfalutin'" cultural investment that we make in art? Or are they an attempt to extend the boundaries of art by making the artist's idea paramount and the visual object that illustrates it into a mere contingency (i.e., something that does not have to be made by the artist)? It goes without saying, of course, that while, in his writings, Duchamp the provocateur seems to favor the latter he never does so in a highly sustained unambiguous piece of theoretical exposition.

However, the managerial world has few doubts upon the issue. Duchamp is taken to have shown that what is decisive in visual art is the artist's idea rather than his or her making of an artifact. This entails, of course, that we must jettison traditional definitions based on processes of making. Indeed the burden of definition must now fall upon the significance of the artist's ideas. And this means, in turn, that in order to recognize what the idea is, we must examine the specific historical and theoretical context in relation to which the artist linked idea and artifact. In short, information about the work's origins and intentions becomes constitutive of its emergence as art. We require—in the broadest terms— managerial production of one sort or another in order for artistic meaning to be realizable.

This redefinition of art has been sanctified by two major theoretical procedures—one art historical and the other philosophical. The art historical strategy is one adopted from generally fashionable cultural relativism of the genealogical kind. Genealogy in this context seeks to analyze visual art in terms of the gender, race, and class attitudes that it embodies, the audiences to which it was directed, the original circumstances of its execution, the conditions of its subsequent reception, and its relation to preceding models. There is no meaning to the work over and above this nexus of managerial concerns, and to suppose that there is, say, a dimension of aesthetic visual meaning that cannot be reduced to the preceding relational factors, is rejected on the grounds of being "ahistorical" or "essentialist."

Attitudes of this kind are something of a dogma among contemporary art historians and critics of the younger generation. However, a less dogmatic variation on the same theory has also been a dominant tendency in philosophical aesthetics since the late 1970s (at least). This tendency centers on what I call "designation" theories of art. These hold that what makes something a work of art is that an artist designates it thus on the basis of some theoretical standpoint. The most familiar examples of this approach are the institutional definitions of art propounded by Arthur Danto and George Dickie.

Approaches such as these, then, hold that artistic meaning is based on what might be called the external relation model (i.e., meaning is a function, primarily of the relation between an item or items and the artist's use of it in some specific historical and theoretical context). On these terms, as noted earlier, the meaning of art centers on managerial issues.

It cannot be emphasized enough how dramatic the scope of this transformation toward the external relation, or managerial model is. Forget Michelangelo, Duchamp is the real paradigm of artistic creativity, and with this paradigm art appears to be democratized insofar as it escapes from phallocentric questions of skill and can encompass material that reflects the experience of minorities and women. Indeed, it may seem to open up infinite creative possibilities insofar as there is an indefinite number of different objects or states of affairs, which an indefinite number of artists can relate to an indefinite number of theoretical standpoints. All in all, artists are no longer constrained. The future of art is an open one.

However, things are not as they might appear to be. An artwork that is addressed primarily to managerial factors (in the sense already discussed) can aptly be described as "privatized." This is because in being so context-dependent vis-à-vis its meaning, it cannot find intelligibility as a publicly accessible code of communication outside the realm of managerial practices. Indeed, it becomes very difficult to distinguish between artifacts that are used as mere adjuncts to theory and those that stake a claim to genuine artistic status.

And there is an element of contradiction involved here. For while managerially orientated art rarely wishes to be judged as a mere adjunct to theory, neither does it wish to be subjected to aesthetic judgment—and this despite it being obliged to follow the presentational formats of art proper. It also becomes difficult to distinguish between good and bad works, except on the basis of managerial caprice.

Now it might be argued that the breakdown of barriers between art and theory is all to the good and it serves to diminish the pretensions of high art. However, the colonization of art by managerial interests is actually culturally regressive in a significant sense. The continuing legacy of the Thatcher-Reagan years is a consumerist pseudoculture whose striving for novel trivia meets with little critical resistance of a sustained and effective kind. One of the central manifestations of this pseudoculture is what I have called "symbolic arrest."[2] This occurs when vital life practices and institutions are taken over by managerial strategies to such a degree that those strategies become symbolic substitutes for the practices and institutions in question. (So-called quality assurance procedures in education are a good example of this.)

The prevalence of managerially orientated artworks links into this pseudoculture of symbolic arrest quite directly. It answers a need for consumerist change for the sake of it—or rather the appearance of change. I say "appearance" here, for while managerially orientated works seem to offer the possibility of real transformation, this is an illusion.

At issue here is the difference between authentic creativity and mere difference or novelty as such. If something is to be legitimately described as creative, it is surely because it refines or innovates in relation to a practice's established procedures, or establishes an entirely new kind of procedure (factors that I will explore at length in Part Two of this paper).

Now when Duchamp created his readymades, this introduced the possibility of artworks incorporating elements (other than in the sense of mere raw materials) that were not physically made by the artist. And since then, it has become apparent that anything can be designated as art through being related to an appropriate display procedure. One can con-join objects and theory in an indefinite number of ways. One knows this in advance. There is no question, therefore, of managerially orientated art significantly extending the boundaries of art. It has no radical experimen-tal potency. It may be possible to do new things, interesting things even, but nothing of really radical significance.

There is one final decisive critical point in relation to managerially orientated work. The concept of art is a Western construct, but to identify the reason why it has been constructed is to pick out a practice that is transcultural and transhistorical and that underlies many different practi-cal applications. It extends from at least Neolithic times to now and beyond.

This practice centers on the making of images—a practice that has its own intrinsic power and fascination in terms of both creative process and its artifactual outcomes. Indeed it is only on the assumption of such power and fascination that we can explain why so many cultures invest such value in the ritual and worth of the visual image.

Managerially orientated art is an attempt to displace this tradi-tion, to make it seem that what is absolutely central is the "having of ideas about art," rather than the "making of art." It thus privileges a marginal Western idiom that is parasitic upon traditional art practices as though it were the gravitational point of art per se. This is a form of tacit racism.

Against this, it could be argued that managerial art subverts existing white male middle-class patriarchal idioms and thus provides a voice for hitherto repressed or marginalized social groups.

However, this in itself involves a racist assumption, namely that the function of art is to reflect or document experience. Such Western con-sumerist doctrine is radically at odds with patterns of artistic creation in most non-Western cultures. In those cultures, image making and a com-plex interplay of aesthetic and metaphysical meanings are paramount. Art is formative rather than spectatorial; it involves participation rather than the consumption of meaning.

Ironically enough, influential avenues of feminist critique (from the 1980s onward) tend to address art with scarcely any regard for its arti-factual dimensions. They criticize "ocularcentrism" and "scopic regimes" while using a method that fixates and perpetuates the study of art at this Western consumerist level.

I am arguing, then, that the dominance of managerially orientated work is not something that bodes well for the future of art. The question arises, then, of what might constitute a better direction? One direction that will not help at all is that of simply going back to some established idiom such as figuration, abstraction, or whatever, per se. What is needed, rather, is a wholesale reemphasis on art as a process of making rather than as fundamentally an object of managerial or consumer interest. In particular, we need to identify the conditions of artistic creativity and the constraints upon it. It is to this task I now turn.

Part Two

The major constraint upon artistic creativity is in terms of how we define art itself. If such a definition is to have substance, it must answer two basic normative questions: First, why is art intrinsically valuable—in a way that mundane artifacts are not? And second, how is it possible to make judgments of merit and demerit concerning art?

Many useful clues for answering these questions are to be found in Immanuel Kant's critical philosophy. In this respect, we must now consider the link between his much-neglected theory of fine art and his theory of imagination. Consider this statement from Kant, "By an aesthetic idea I mean a presentation of the imagination which prompts much thought, but to which no determinate thought whatsoever . . . can be adequate, so that no language can express it completely and allow us to grasp it."[3]

For Kant, works of fine art present aesthetic ideas, and the images wherein they present them are irreducible to linguistic paraphrase. The reason why is made clear in the following remarks:

A poet ventures to give sensible expression to rational ideas of invisible beings, the realm of the blessed, the realm of hell, eternity, creation, and so on. Or, again, he takes (things) that are indeed exemplified in experience, such as death, energy and all the other vices, as well as love, fame, and so on; but then, by means of an imagination that emulates the example of reason in reaching (for) a maximum, he ventures to give these sensible expression in a way that goes beyond the limits of experience, namely with a completeness for which no example can be found in nature.[4]

This complex passage focuses on the interplay between imagination, and the artist's style in handling a specific medium. Kant defines imagination as the capacity to represent that which is not immediately given in perception.[5] This has two aspects. On the one hand, we can imagine things that happen not to be immediately present in perception but that could become present; and on the other hand, we can imagine things that are not encounterable in perception under any circumstances by virtue of their being wholly fictional.

Kant also holds that imagination is not merely some, as it were, luxury cognitive capacity. It is, in fact, a precondition of any possible experience (insofar as our sense of the present and our mobile occupancy of space are only intelligible insofar as we can project what it is like to occupy times and places other than the one that we are presently occupying). Imagination allows the projection of a phenomenal continuum wherein other cognitive factors such as the acquisition of language and concepts are enabled.

Given this, the fact that art centers on imaging would, in itself, go some way toward explaining its intrinsic value and fascination for us. However, there is another important issue here. For in the last quotation Kant makes much of the fact that the artist's imaging ranges beyond the actuality of experience. We might develop this insight as follows.

Our sense of the real, and our mode of inhabiting it as embodied and social beings, is powerfully shaped and invested with value (or otherwise) through the realm of fantasy, possibility, and impossibility, which we project around it. Of especial importance here is imaginative counterfactuality (i.e. images of things which did not, but which might have, happened if things had been a little different). All these factors are central to both the thematics and expressive effects of the visual arts, literature, and even music.

Such considerations should now be linked to the role of the artist's style in handling his or her medium. The image (in whatever sense it is meant) is an image "of" something, but while being "of" that something, it is, by virtue of being an image, different from that something. Difference here centers on the schematic and fragmentary nature of the image. Despite its central role in our cognitive life, the image is transient and elusive and has its character determined in large part by the imaginative powers (or otherwise) of the person who is projecting the image.

All these factors mean that an image (e.g., a mental image) does not reproduce its object but rather creatively interprets it. And this is even more the case when the power of imagination is exercised in a physical medium such as painting rather than at a mental level. For here the difference between the image and that which it is an image of becomes publicly accessible, stabilized, and varied through the artist's individual relation to the medium and its traditions.

In the case of painting this has some especially remarkable outcomes. As Maurice Merleau-Ponty says vis-à-vis the painter's task:

> Light, lighting, shadow, reflections, color, all the objects of his quest are not altogether real objects, like ghosts, they have only virtual existence. In fact, they exist only at the threshold of profane vision; they are not seen by everyone. The painter's gaze asks them what they do to suddenly cause something to be and to be this thing, what they do to compose this worldly talisman and to make us see the visible.[6]

On these terms, then, the painter captures and interprets the transient and elusive organizational logic of visual appearance itself. In everyday life this logic is largely unnoticed, for if we attended to it in any sustained way we would be simply overwhelmed by visual information. The painter controls this flow by exaggerating some facts and omitting others on the basis of his or her own personal interests in relation to the medium. In this way, what the image represents is more complete than visual reality itself, for it discloses, stabilizes, and celebrates those elusive factors that are involved in a thing or state of affairs becoming visible.

This approach can also be extended to nonfigurative idioms on the basis of the notion of contextual space.[7] For the realm of the visual does not, as it were, exist raw. It is contextualized and given its character by many usually unnoticed visual relations and possibilities over and above those already mentioned. These include visual forms that can be associated with certain kinds of gestural expression, or with possible visual realities in alternative physical and perceptual environments to our usual one, or with scenes arising from unusual perceptual viewpoints on things.

There are a number of other such levels to contextual space, but the decisive factor is that, when dealing with such a work directly and without recourse to documentation concerning the artist's intentions, we do not know which actual level is intended. This gives the work a distinctive enigmatic or allusive power. It plays around—or, better—between the various levels of contextual space.

Now the points that I am developing here all center on what can be called art's metaphysical depth. This means its capacity to go beyond immediate experience by engaging with and interpreting factors that are the basis of our cognitive inherence in the world. But, of course artworks are not theoretical tracts. Their expression of metaphysical depth is inseparable from their identity as this particular sensible object or (in the case of literature) this individual imaginatively intended manifold. One cannot enjoy or appreciate what is at issue in the work without direct engagement with it.

And this means, of course, that we are not just admiring the sensible presentation of an idea but rather the way in which it has been articulated by this specific individual or social ensemble. The image in this context links artist, object, and audience in an extraordinarily complex bond. All parties in the relation have the potential for transformation. This is the explosive realm of the aesthetic idea.

What we get from Kant, then, are directions toward the formative power of art and it is this, and its connection with our fundamental modes of inherence in the word, that explains why art has intrinsic value.

Interestingly, Kant also directs us toward the second normative requirement of the definition of art. This is the question of how distinctions of merit and demerit can be made between modes of representation. Kant argues as follows:

If art merely performs the acts that are required to make a possible object actual, adequate to our cognition of that object, then it is mechanical art; but if what it intends directly is (to arouse) the feeling of pleasure, then it is called aesthetic art. The latter is either agreeable or is that the pleasure should accompany presentations that are mere sensations: It is fine art if the purpose is that the pleasure should accompany presentations that are ways of cognising.[8]

In these decisive observations, Kant makes key normative distinctions. Some representations are made so as to do no more than give simple information or serve definite practical functions. Others are made to do no more than be decorative or to look "nice." Fine art in contrast is made so as to present those modes of formative imaging outlined earlier.

What Kant is, in effect, offering here is a distinction between art with a small *a* and art with a large *A*, on the basis of a difference between mere function and intrinsic significance. He then takes this distinction to an even more important second level. In this respect, we are told that fine art is the product of "genius." There are two especially important aspects to this:

Genius is a talent for producing something for which no determinate rule can be given, not a predisposition consisting of a skill for something that can be learned by following some rule or other; hence the foremost property of genius must be originality. . . . Since nonsense too can be original, the products of genius must be exemplary; hence, though they do not themselves arise through imitation, still they must serve others as this, i.e. as a standard or rule by which to judge.[9]

These two points are of the most far-reaching significance. In relation to the first, for example, while Kant presents originality as bound up with the psychology of creation, it also necessarily has a logical and objective aspect. This is because in order to recognize originality we must be able to compare its products with those of others. Originality emerges only through reference to a horizon of—in the broadest terms—historical difference.

However, Kant shrewdly notes that since there can also be original nonsense, the originality at issue in genius must be of an exemplary character. It must act as a model for producers and interpreters of art.

Interestingly, Kant does not develop the notion of exemplariness in any substantial further terms. But it is possible to do so and to do so, indeed, in surprising depth. The decisive factor here consists of developing the logical scope of specific art media (i.e., the semantic and syntactic codes that are the basis of their formative articulations).

It is important, however, to note one factor that does not satisfy this criterion, namely those acts of artistic designation noted in Part One. It is possible to designate any item or state of affairs as having such and such meaning in relation to art and art theory. But if this meaning can only be generally recognized through reference to some supporting documentary or critical discourse, then it is merely yet another illustration of the Western dogma that the artist can, in principle, designate anything as art. It does not expand the semantic and syntactic scope of the medium in a way that can be exemplary for other artists as artist. In many cases, we have no more than the "original nonsense" noted above.

To see what exemplariness really centers on, we must focus on those factors that are part of the full definition of a specific medium's logical scope. Consider, in this respect the distinction between the linear and painterly emphasis in pictorial style. The former emphasizes outline and clearly defined plastic contours, while the latter blurs edges and is oriented instead toward broad masses and foreshortening achieved by graduated and diffuse effects of tone and shadow.

Now it might be thought that these two tendencies merely describe aspects of how certain Western paintings from the Renaissance onward appear to the viewer. Their significance however, is much deeper—in transhistorical and transcultural terms. This is because they express the two logically basic ways of acting upon a plane surface in order to create a three-dimensional image. One can either incise it, characteristically to delineate contours, or one can place marks upon it, so as to gradually build up an impression of the represented object's plastic substance.

It is of course, also possible to combine these and, in effect, all pictorial creations can be positioned along a notional continuum with incised outline at one extreme and the accumulation of marks upon a surface at the other.

And this is the real significance of the linear-painterly pairing. As stylistic emphases they look back toward these primal alternative possibilities of pictorial formation. This is why, in principle, they can be applied to any historical or cultural context. There is always, accordingly, the chance that a pictorial practice will become orientated to one of these basic formative possibilities and will significantly renew it or innovate in relation to it.

This now enables us to understand the key meaning of exemplariness. An artist can merely copy the basics of another's style because he or she likes it or feels that it discloses something new about the possibilities of the medium. However, in some artists, we will find that the search for a style involves sustained engagement with features that are basic to the semantic and syntactic scope of the medium concerned (as in the case of the linear-painterly pairing just described). I say "scope" rather than "structure" here because many semantic and syntactic factors require a great deal of historical development—in diachronic terms—before they are fully articulated.

These considerations direct us toward the most important criteria of artistic merit. If an artist is original, not just, say in his or her color schemes, but in terms that innovate or refine so as to expand or illuminate the medium's basic logical scope, then the formative power of the medium is also enhanced. Technical transformation and aesthetic achievement are necessarily (though not sufficiently) correlated. It is this correlation (rather than the preferences and interests of dominant power groups) that explains and justifies the notion of a canon.

I have described the many complex categories (in addition to linear and painterly) that define the logical scope of pictorial representation at great length elsewhere.[10] I have also provided them for abstract works in general and even for some cases of conceptual art. The great virtue of this approach is that by emphasizing the semantic and syntactic codes of art, it reorients the analytic standpoint toward the art object and the history of its modes of creation, rather than toward the art consumer and the conditions of reception.

It also enables us to understand the sense in which art has reached its limits. For given that a picture is, by definition, an image of a three-dimensional item or (cognate state of affairs) generated in a two-dimensional plane, then there are, in logical terms, a finite number of possibilities in terms of the general types of reference and syntactic connections that pictorial representation can develop as a communicative code. The exact iconographic meanings of a picture and the uses to which it is put are culturally and historically relative. But such diversity of contexts and uses are functions of a more basic logical structure.

The progression of this structure to its most fully developed form is dependent upon historical transformations, but it does not give rise to the possibility of endless development. In this respect, it is notable that the logical structure of pictorial representation was completely in place by the end of the Renaissance. What has happened since then is systematic stylistic variations that extend or illuminate different aspects of this structure.

With the advent of cubism the limits of the structure were, in effect, acknowledged, and a search was inaugurated for new kinds of semantic and syntactic code upon which art could be based. As I have shown at great length elsewhere,[11] despite the plethora of conflicting artistic manifestoes and radically different visual content, the great abstract and abstracting tendencies are inscribed within a code based on aspects of contextual space. The advent of minimal idioms, such as works by Agnes Gray and Ad Reinhardt's "black" paintings, seem to again suggest that this code has been taken to its logical limits. Similar considerations apply in those cases where conceptual work attains a marginal artistic status.

The question arises, then, of where do we go next? But the answer has already been given. For I have argued that artistic merit is at its highest when an artist discovers or refines factors that are fundamental to the logical structure of an artistic code. If the old codes have been taken as far as they can go in logical terms, then this demands that artists create new ones.

One possibility here is the creation of non-naturalistic codes, which are based on invention rather than some notion of resemblance or visual consistency between the artwork and the realities that it represents. Such non-naturalistic codes would stipulate basic visual axioms or vocabulary that could then be transformed on the basis of invented rules—drawing on conventional or abstract or even conceptual idioms. The challenge would be to find such codes that—despite their artificial basis—were relatively easy to learn and that could generate interesting visual articulations within the respective codes.[12] If this challenge is not met, then the scope and structure of art will continue to be defined exclusively in the dead end terms of Western managerial classes.

A final issue arises. It is quite clear that the problematics of artistic creativity are especially foregrounded by the visual arts. This is because the logical structure and scope of visual media (the negotiation of which is central to artistic creativity) are extremely accessible in phenomenal terms. Such accessibility is due to the fact that the referential basis of such media [resemblance or visual consistency] is easily learned and pertains to the structure of space occupancy itself.

The logical structure of music is also highly accessible, insofar as the tonal system is easily learned and is bound up with fundamental aspects of bodily expression and auditory reality. A similar problem of development has arisen, however. We can already see the canonic effects of music's creative appropriation of techniques for mechanically reproducing sound. However, it is not likely that this admits of much further development. And while serialism and aleatory developments per se have established themselves as alternative musical codes, they have not attained anything like the authority of the tonal system.

Therefore, it may be that music's way forward will be akin to that of visual art and will involve the formulation of artificial expressive auditory codes that might "take" in a way that existing alternatives to tonalism have not. (One possibility is that third world idioms could be of decisive significance in leading the way here.)

In terms of literature and film, the fundamental categories that form the structure and scope of these media and their idioms is not as manifest (at least to the present writer). However, my suspicion is that these too have probably reached the limits of their means of development, over and above constant boundary slippages between their constituent idioms and other art forms.

Now (for reasons indicated throughout this text), through its aesthetic embodiment of metaphysical depth, art will continue to meet—as Hegel would put it—our highest needs. Individuality of vision will always be possible. What will not be possible are the far-reaching structural advances that radically transform the ways in which these needs are met. For this to happen, the invention of new media with their own distinctive structures and scope is required. Work in digital technology and related electronic idioms may well open up this very possibility.

10

Gadamer and the Ambiguity of Appearance

Nicholas Davey

. . . and always *between* the eye's glance.
W. G. Sebald[1]

Aesthetics and Philosophical Hermeneutics

It is a measure of the intellectual stature of philosophical hermeneutics that under the tutelage of Hans-Georg Gadamer, hermeneutics no longer remains a *philosophia secondus*, a method of textual commentary and analysis, but has become a *philosophia prima*, devoted to the conditions appertaining to the *appearance* of meaning in the humanities. The notoriously misunderstood claim of philosophical hermeneutics to universality has little to do with the pursuit of a common mode of understanding.[2] As a *philosophia prima,* hermeneutics attempts to uncover the universal conditions (time, tradition, language, and cultural horizon) that underwrite how meaning *shows* itself. Questions concerning the nature of aesthetic appearance are therefore central to the phenomenological dimensions of philosophical hermeneutics. Philosophical hermeneutics hence accords aesthetics a primary place in its reflections and never characterizes it as a poor relation of the sciences.

Gadamer proclaims the objectivist methodologies of the *Naturwissenschaften* (Natural Sciences) inappropriate for the concerns of *Geisteswissenschaften* (Human Sciences). Whereas the natural sciences require of its observers a methodological distance from the phenomena they study, hermeneutics and other humanist disciplines require the direct phenomenological involvement of interpreters with their subject matters. It is, for Gadamer, philosophically ludicrous if not barbarous to insist that claims to truth that are not or cannot be objectified in the language of demonstrable propositions are subjectively grounded and without objective content. To straightjacket truth claims in such a way ignores how language and the communication of meaning work. Gadamer tirelessly defended his view that both the ability to offer a truth claim in language as well as the always perfectible practice of speaking truthfully depend upon the unsaid and the unspoken, that is, upon those silent reservoirs of culturally embedded meanings that initially inform and guide our utterances.

It is not that such hermeneutical aquifers defy speech but that, like tradition, they can never be fully explicated and made the subject of methodological verification. A text or an artwork can challenge our every-day expectancies and confront us with assumptions we have either taken for granted, overlooked, forgotten, or have not been aware of. Such experiences are genuinely "aesthetic": they allow our lifeworld and that of the other to rise with due clarity within the mind's eye.

Though the full nature of what such experience reveals both about us and to us cannot be objectified, what is "shown" does not lie completely beyond language. To the contrary, what emerges in aesthetic experience requires the delicate precision of careful and sensitive language. Living in a world that recognizes only the palpable and is poorly calibrated to register anything more delicate or surprising, philosophical hermeneutics rallies resistance to the reduction of truth to method alone.[3] For its pursuit of an individual voice that does justice to the particularities and complexities of aesthetic experience and that can allow us to discern the objectivities within subjectivity aesthetic experience, philosophical hermeneutics has an undeniable place within modern aesthetic theory.

The cultural critique implicit within Gadamer's defense of the aesthetic is clear. Philosophical hermeneutics does not dispute or question the achievements of modern science. What, however, it contests are those cultural and political evaluations of the "scientific" that are so enamored of the achievements of technology that they refuse any legitimacy to the individual eye or the subjective voice. What is primarily at issue is the *meaningfulness* of those truths apprehended in the intensity of subjective response that antedate the formal abstractions of scientific objectification. The continued devaluation and marginalization of aesthetic experience as subjective and methodologically arbitrary weakens and desensitizes us to the claims of tradition and shared language horizons; claims that structure our pre-reflective lifeworld and allow us to navigate our way through it.

Gadamer's "Transformation into Structure" Argument

It is astonishing that the importance of philosophical hermeneutics for aesthetics has been so overlooked. For Gadamer, the task of an artwork—its *work* so to speak—is to clear a space (to effect a suspension of disbelief) in which an unseen or overlooked transformative possibility concerning *this* world can appear. Primacy is given to aesthetic appearance as a means of transforming our understanding of the *real*. Gadamer's position is laid out in the section of *Truth and Method* entitled "Transformation into Structure and Total Mediation."[4] In a single and provocative blow, his argument transforms the traditional conceptions of the relation between art and reality. Art imitates neither phenomena nor another unphenomenal world: It has the capacity to bring actuality toward an even greater fulfillment. In effect, art is able to *transform reality into its truth*. It is a transfiguration of the common place (Arthur Danto), which Gadamer identifies as a "transformation" into the true.

The transformation is a transformation into the true. It is not enchantment in the sense of a bewitchment that waits for the redeeming word that will transform things back to what they were, but it is itself redemption and transformation back into true being . . . The world of the work of art . . . is in fact a wholly transformed world. By means of it, everyone recognises that this is how things are. From this viewpoint "reality" is defined as what is untransformed art as the raising up of this reality into its truth.[5]

In a brilliant inversion of the Platonic tradition that is wedded to the idea that an artwork (aesthetic appearance) distracts from, devalues, diminishes, and distances us from the real (the original), Gadamer insists that what appears in an artwork "is an increase in the being of the original."[6] It allows what is presented "to be for the first time what it is"[7] it is "a coming forth of the essence itself"[8] and "belongs so closely to what it is related to that it enriches the being of that as if through a new event of being."[9]

The hermeneutic experience of being addressed, of grasping that there is clearly something true about what is shown to one, involves two things. Firstly one recognizes that the full nature of something familiar was not grasped and secondly one comes to realize its significance perhaps for the first time. In this respect, the hermeneutical dimensions of aesthetic experience are genuinely educational. The recognition of the truth of that which was not initially grasped as true involves a becoming different toward oneself. A phenomenological shift from absentmindedness to mindfulness is involved. However, this shift raises a significant question: What is the character of aesthetic experience that enables us to recognize that this, indeed, is what is occurring?

To answer this Gadamer argues that in unreflective consciousness, "reality" invariably stands for us "in a horizon of the future of observed and feared or, at any rate undecided possibilities . . . (in which) . . . lines of meaning scatter in the void."[10] In stark contrast, however, everything within visual or literary art forms hangs together, forming meaningful wholes. They contain nothing stale or conventional. Unlike the incomplete and undecided possibilities of the everyday, within the artwork "no lines of meaning" disperse.[11] The difference between art and reality in this respect should accord artworks with a certain unreality. The novelty of Gadamer's claim however is that the "unreality" of actuality (its incomplete nature), can be completed by the unreality of art (its ability to create fictional or illusory wholes). The principal claim is that what in actuality remains incomplete and unfulfilled art can complete and fulfill. Gadamer argues,

The being of all play (art) is always realisation, sheer fulfilment, *energeia* which has its *telos* within itself. The world of the work of art, in which play expresses itself fully in the unity of its course, is in fact a wholly transformed world. By means of it everyone recognises that that is how things are . . . *From this viewpoint "reality" is defined as what is untransformed, and art as the raising up of this reality into its truth.*[12]

The "transformation into structure" claims that by means of art and the speculative insights it affords, reality becomes more than what it is. The aesthetic experience of truth has, therefore, more to do with a sense of a truth dawning and recollection, than with reappropriating a fixed truth from a condition of loss. Gadamer argues,

But we do not understand what recognition is in its profoundest nature, if we only see that something that we know already is known again, i.e. that what is familiar is recognised again. The joy of recognition is rather that more becomes known than is already known. In recognition what we know emerges as if through an illumination, from all the chance and variable circumstances that condition it in its essence.[13]

Recollection is not repetition but annunciation. Inverting the standard interpretation of Plato, Gadamer insists that "imitation and representation are not merely a second version or copy but a recognition of the essence . . . they are not merely repetition but a bringing forth."[14] Artistic presentation does not depart from or distort an otherwise independent truth (Plato), but it allows that which is virtual within actuality to be realized, to become such that it can truly speak, and, what is more, speak truly. The reason why the aesthetic apprehension of truth can entail such a shock emerges.

By closing a circle of possible meaning, a visual or literary artwork is able to disclose that circle. The indeterminacy of meaning in actuality implies that there is no knowing in advance how an experiential sequence will develop or resolve. Lacking that insight means that we do not know whether that sequence is a sequence. The brilliance of an artwork's speculative revelation is that it can enable us to perceive a circle of meaning where prior to the insight we saw none. The shock of aesthetic or speculative recognition is suddenly seeing events and experiences that we assumed to be disparate and unconnected as being in fact connected and moving toward a fulfillment of meaning that we had not anticipated. The artistic vision *realizes* (fulfills) what was latent within actuality and thereby allows that actuality to become itself more fully. Insofar as art can brings us to see what we did not initially see in actuality, we are brought to recognize our own blindness: no mean achievement for a *phenomenological* aesthetics!

Three Difficulties with Gadamer's Position

The first difficulty with Gadamer's position concerns the conflict between his accounts of hermeneutical understanding and the transformative nature of aesthetic experience. Why is the experience of aesthetic truth accorded such seminal significance in *Truth and Method* when philosophical hermeneutics *knows* that all meaning is incomplete and open-ended? If experience (*Erfahrung*) remains open and always invites further interpretation, is not any phenomena that presents itself as complete and determinate *inimical* to the expansion of understanding? What "more" can ever be said of the perfect, the whole or complete? Why are we manifestly so shaken by aesthetic truths if we know that any completeness and self-sufficiency of meaning is illusory?[15]

This last question concerns the implications of certain Hegelian undertones within Gadamer's argument. The transformation of structure argument claims that aesthetic experience involves the realization of a certain completeness or wholeness. A successful artwork is credited with the power to found or secure a truth, to make the implicit explicit, to bring a cycle of meaning to full realization. In post-Hegelian aesthetics, this moment marks a return home and the reunion of the self with itself. It redeems disorientation and distanciation. Gadamer's transformation into structure arguments appear to fall within this tradition; however, a philosophy that asserts the impossibility of any final interpretative judgment cannot claim that aesthetic experience brings a circle of meaning to completion.

Secondly, Gadamer's commitment to the "negativity of experience" implies that powerful aesthetic insights can also be *unfounding*. Rather than bringing endorsement and redemption they force an entirely different but nevertheless plausible understanding of the self's position in the world. Given its commitment to the perfectibility of understanding, shouldn't philosophical hermeneutics promote the continual transformation of aesthetic understanding instead of invoking the language of completion? This last question relates to the concept of the *withheld* and how it can be reconciled with the claim that an artwork allows us to understand more fully what something truly is.

Thirdly, although *Truth and Method* insists there is no end to hermeneutic interpretation, the text does not recognize the *enigmatic* nature of art. Gadamer acknowledges that "all encounter with the *language* of art is an encounter with an unfinished event" and that "there is no final exhaustion of what lies in a work of art."[16] Yet these comments refer to the critical assessment of art and not to the direct impact of an artwork's truth claim. In other essays, however, ambiguity is recognized as being central to an encounter with the artwork. Referring to Martin Heidegger, Gadamer remarks that a work of art not only brings something meaningful into experience that was not known before, but that in doing so it brings something new into existence. It is not simply that an artwork lays bare a truth.[17] In speaking to us, it reveals something; it "brings something forth from unconcealedness."[18] An artwork's "truth" is not constituted simply "by laying bare its meaning but rather by the unfathomable depth of its meaning. Thus by its very nature the work of art is a conflict between . . . emergence and sheltering."[19] The artwork's revelation of emergence and sheltering is, furthermore, a disclosure of "the essence of Being itself" for the conflict of revealment and concealment is "the truth of every being."[20] Heidegger does not articulate the conflict of revealment as an enigma but as that "which comes to stand," a "standing-in-itself."[21] What comes to stand in an artwork is a thing or world that is sufficient unto itself. The autonomy of the artwork resides in its ability to reveal the extent to which it also remains concealed within itself. The phrase "coming to stand" invokes a fullness of being where fullness is not a laying bare of its meaning but *a revelation of what has yet to be revealed*. Coming to stand does not indicate a condition of disclosure as opposed to a state of hiddenness but the process whereby a thing—precisely because it partially comes forward into disclosure—also reveals the extent to which it also remains partially undisclosed. Coming to stand does not therefore oppose the intelligible dimensions of a thing against its mysterious aspects. In Heideggerian terms it is precisely because certain aspects of a work are intelligible that the unseen presence of the full mystery of a work can be brought to light. As he remarks in the essay "On the Origin of the Art Work," "the sayable at the same time brings the unsayable into the world."[22] Thus, the disclosed and the withheld are not opposites. The disclosed enables us to discern the presence of the withheld. Without the disclosed, the withheld would be deprived of its promise. It would have no presence as the "as yet to be disclosed." However, the assertions made by the transformation into structure argument about the revelatory powers of an artwork's truth claims are at odds with those about the withheld and enigmatic nature of an artwork.

What has gone wrong? Can these three difficulties be resolved? Gadamer is sometimes not the best advocate for philosophical hermeneutics. The language of *Truth and Method* is overtly formed by Gadamer's acquaintance with the works of Georg Hegel and Wilhelm Dilthey, the style of which is often at odds with the Heideggerian direction of his thinking. Gadamer's later writings on art and aesthetics are more open in their Heideggerian form and content. If the difficulties identified above are reread in the light of Gadamer's later writings, a new way of relating to them can be established. In this context, Gianni Vattimo's remarks about Heidegger's aesthetics are instructive.

In his essay "Art as Oscillation," Vattimo makes a persuasive case for the view that Heidegger's account of aesthetics should also not be read as an apologetics for a Hegelian *Geborgenheit*.[23] Though Heidegger links his aesthetics of disclosure with a process of communal bonding, Vattimo suggests that Heidegger gives *equal* stress to the disruptive (unfounding) element of speculative experience. According to Vattimo's reading, the artwork "is like an encounter with someone whose view of the world is a challenge to our own interpretation." The "art work does not simply slot into the world as it is but purports to shed new light upon the world."[24] Its speculative insight can entail an "experience of estrangement," which then requires recomposition and readjustment. However, the aim of this is not to reach "a final recomposed state . . . but towards keeping this *disorientation* alive."[25] We can accordingly ask of Gadamer's aesthetics whether the unifying function of the transformation into structure argument can be reconciled with the disruptive power of art. Can the centripetal aspect of aesthetic experience (the drive to completion and wholeness) accommodate its centrifugal aspect (the impetus to estrangement and disruption)? Let us first address the question of the relationship between the transformation into structure argument and the question of *Geborgenheit*.

Gadamer's Aesthetics and the Problem of the Withheld

In romantic aesthetics *Geborgenheit* marks an experiential point of reunion. Disorientation and distanciation are redeemed. Because of its references to completing lines of meaning, Gadamer's transformation into structure argument seems to fall within this tradition. The embarrassment to Gadamer's hermeneutic project is obvious. A philosophy that proclaims the finitude of understanding cannot defend the power of aesthetic closure. Gadamer should have been more sensitive to the nuances within his choice of philosophical language. Nevertheless, the transformation into structure argument points to philosophical tools able to overcome this problem.

Gadamer claims that when a hermeneutic subject experiences a completion of meaning they are set at a *distance* from that cycle of meaning, which precludes practical or goal-oriented participation. This distance, or what Gadamer also terms "aesthetic distanciation," is "aesthetic distance in a true sense: it signifies the distance necessary for seeing and understanding."[26] The transformation of structure that allows a subject to see its world differently and to become different to itself also, thereby, sets the hermeneutic subject at a distance from itself. It is appropriate to use a Japanese idiom to describe this setting of a hermeneutic subject at a distance from itself as the *sadness* of understanding, as an expression of understanding's finitude. When philosophical hermeneutics speaks of transformation into structure as the disclosure of meaning within a given cycle of events, it does not necessarily mean that the transformation reveals *the* essential meaning of that cycle but that such a transformation displays a meaning which, in relationship to the interests and concerns of the hermeneutic subject, reveals that cycle to be a cycle in the first place. This is not to say that the *true* meaning of that cycle has been uncovered, only that its elements have been brought together in such a way as to enable the hermeneutic subject to make sense of its place within. In this respect, the hermeneutic subject becomes different to its (former) self. Thus, the very meaningfulness that brings a sense of coherence and unity to a hermeneutic subject can also threaten to disrupt that subject's new-won understanding of itself. The sadness of understanding resides in the fact that the advent of meaning conspires in the conditions of its own dissipation. As soon as something becomes discernible as meaningful, as having a distinct coherence or identity, it becomes something interpretable. Insofar as it becomes interpretable, it is at risk of losing its coherence. In other words, as soon as the hermeneutic subject tries to grasp the meaning that appears to make the disparate parts of its being whole and to see how that meaning is manifest in the particular elements of its being, an ineliminable space opens, dissolving the initial unifying meaning but driving the quest for a new synthesis. As Wolfgang Iser suggests, "the part/whole circle governs all interpretive activity in so far as the whole is understood from its parts, so the parts can be understood only from the whole."[27]

Hence, the sadness of understanding: as soon as the hermeneutic subject attempts to grasp or interpret what has become clear to it in speculative insight, the emergent meaning loses its clarity and the hermeneutic subject is once more set at a distance from itself. Philosophical hermeneutics is, then, quite unlike a philosophy of identity. It does not invoke aesthetics of *Geborgenheit*. What it recognizes within the transformation into structure argument is not the redemptive return of the self to itself but the ever-present possibility of the self losing what it has understood and of becoming different to itself once again. Yet it is this very loss that drives the quest for further hermeneutic translation and transcendence. It is this that in part prevents Gadamer's transformation into structure argument from collapsing into a form of *Geborgenheit*.

Gadamer's conclusion, however, potentially renders the task of hermeneutics more difficult by saying that to understand is to understand that understanding is always in difficulty. If we know that an apparition of the meaningful is one aspect of a subject matter (*Sache*), then it seems that we simultaneously perceive that we stand in a relationship to a *Sache* that is simultaneously *near* and *far*. Perhaps hermeneutical consciousness *knows* that understanding is always in difficulty and that difficulty is inherent in what is being done. Thus the transformation into structure argument and its case for the completion of meaning seems at odds with the *via negativa* of philosophical hermeneutics.

In responding to this last claim we should first note that many of the difficulties under discussion emerge from an opposition that perceives the transformation into structure argument and the *via negativa* spirit of philosophical hermeneutics as being in conflict. However, if the *via negativa* were implicit within the transformation into structure argument and an intimation of meaning were not the opposite of a deconstructive dissipation of meaning but bore the mark of its own dissolution, this conflict would dissipate and the centrifugal and centripetal aspects of the aesthetic experience would be revealed as coinhering. What follows from this is the implication that the "hermeneutic" nature of understanding resides precisely in an awareness of its difficulty. To support this, we need to make brief reference to Hegel, Heidegger, and the closing sections of *Truth and Method*.

For Hegel, "Nothing can be understood in isolation."[28] "A thing" or a meaning "is what it is only in and by reason of its limit. We cannot regard the limit as only external to being which is then and there."[29] Although a perception of meaning might be aesthetically and psychologically immediate, ontologically speaking, it does not stand alone. It always relates to that which "limits" it and to that which is beyond it. Such "transcendent" frameworks of meaning remain inherent within singular perceptions of meaning. A singular perception of meaning is edged with that which it is not (i.e., that virtuality of meaning, which though it surpasses any single perception of meaning, coinheres with it). Such an entailment links directly with Heidegger's conception of the "withheld" (*Bergung/Verbergung*), which as we have seen "brings something forth from unconcealedness." Yet the emergence into light is not the annihilation of concealedness per se but the revelation of a continued sheltering in the dark. There is a clear tension between the emergence and the sheltering that constitutes the *form-niveau* of a work. A work's "truth" is not therefore constituted simply "by laying bare its meaning but rather by the unfathomable depth of its meaning. Thus by its very nature the work of art is a conflict between . . . emergence and sheltering."[30] Coming to stand does not indicate a condition of disclosure as opposed to a state of hiddenness but the process whereby a thing—precisely because it partially comes forward into disclosure—also reveals the extent to which it remains undisclosed. Thus, the disclosed and the withheld are not opposites. The disclosed makes manifest the presence of that which presently remains withheld.

The disclosed enables us to discern the presence of the withheld. Without the disclosed, the withheld would be deprived of its promise. It would have no presence as the "as yet to be disclosed." Referring back to Hegel, we can argue that that which limits or negates a perception of meaning and which transcends it but is not uttered by it (the withheld), is not external to that meaning but is discernible in the very *relatedness* of that meaning. Such relatedness does not concern the relationship between language and what is outside it but between the disclosed and the withheld within perceptions of meaning. This is substantiated by the closing sections of *Truth and Method*.

The closing arguments in *Truth and Method* do not mention Heidegger's conception of the withheld, yet it is implicit within Gadamer's notion of the self-presencing of language or anything that has a language. Being, Gadamer writes, "is self-presentation and all understanding is an event of being."[31] Being "is" the events in which it presents itself. Being "is" its appearances, its images, its interpretations, its language,[32] and, as he asserts elsewhere, "being that can be understood is language."[33] The decisive point is not stated by Gadamer: The event of being that language facilitates involves the bringing forward of the withheld. The essential being of language is self-presentation. Thus, when something is stated in language, something is brought forward (a meaning or a *Sache*), and yet what is brought forward is more than the stated for what is stated can only be stated on the basis of the withheld understood as that incalculably large and complex network of traditional meanings and associations that underlie and enable our deliberations. *Thus, the event of being that language brings forward reveals the presence of the disclosed and the withheld.*

The withheld would have no presence were it not brought forward by the disclosed. The disclosed and the withheld are not opposites but coinhere in one another. There is, in this respect, no openness, on the one hand, and no closedness on the other. To the contrary, a perception of meaning acquires its clarity, resonance, and allure precisely because it intimates the presence of the withheld. It is both vague and distinct, near yet far. Furthermore, it is the intimation of the withheld that allows a perception of meaning to open toward its own depths. Without its ground in the withheld, a perception of meaning could not open to what is both beyond it and more than it. As Heidegger comments, "It is language alone that first provides the possibility of *standing amongst the openness of entities*,"[34] In conclusion, to perceive a meaning as disclosed is to perceive that it is limited by what is withheld and that, as a consequence, the disclosed is always vulnerable to the otherness *within* the withheld. This implies that no matter its aesthetic power, any aesthetic insight will be inconclusive, incomplete, irresolvable, and always renegotiable.

If, however, the disclosed and the withheld are not opposites but mutually coinherent, it can be argued that the *via negativa* of philosophical hermeneutics is indeed implicit within the transformation into structure argument. In other words, there is a clear symmetry between the different elements in Gadamer's reasoning. The conception of something "coming-to-stand" and the processes of "self-presencing" and "event," which are related to our understanding of what an artwork is (or rather "does"), are openly allied to the argument that the withheld is made manifest in the disclosed and would have no presence were it not for the disclosed. The disclosed and the withheld are not opposites.

The argument for coinherence suggests that a hermeneutical awareness of the meaningful is not the opposite of a deconstructive dissipation of meaning. Rather, it is an awareness of that which can potentially dissipate, limit, or negate such meaning as being present within the coming forth of that meaning. It is the hermeneutical equivalent to what William Blake perceives as "the sickness of the rose."[35] To understand that time is (as Heidegger might argue) a condition of beauty's coming forth is to understand that the very time that brings beauty forth is also the time that impels it to fade. For Gadamer it is not Heidegger's conception of time but the instability of language that is at the center of the argument. To understand that the withheld (be it articulated as tradition or as implicitly understood networks of meaning) is the condition of the meaningful coming forth is also to understand that the very fusions of meaning that enable the meaningful to emerge can also generate the conditions of its disappearance. Hermeneutic consciousness knows that understanding is always in difficulty. Yet the *via negativa* of philosophical hermeneutics demands that the central point also be asserted positively. Or, that which makes understanding difficult—the ability of the withheld to disrupt, defer, or dissipate the meaningful—is also that which gives the meaningful its depth, resonance, and weight. This insight allows us to approach the third major problem attached to the transformation into structure argument. How is the transformation into structure argument, which lays claim to an artwork being able to increase the "being" of a subject matter, to be reconciled with the argument that the subject matter of a work can never be given in its fullness since aspects of its content are always withheld?

In his inversion of Platonic aesthetics, Gadamer insists that what appears in an artwork "is an increase in the being of the original"[36] and allows what is presented "to be for the first time what it is."[37] It is "a coming forth of the essence itself" and "belongs so closely to what it is related to that it enriches the being of that as if through a new event of being."[38] However, the argument concerning the withheld seems to speak against these claims. As was argued above, the process of presentation or "coming to stand," which constitutes an artwork, does not indicate a condition of disclosure as opposed to a state of hiddenness but a process whereby something—precisely because it partially comes forward into disclosure— reveals the extent to which it also remains undisclosed. Such an acknowledgement of the withheld implies that an artwork holds something back and that no artwork can bring its content to full realization. It may present its subject matter more fully, but any talk of wholeness and completion would be misplaced. It is hard to avoid the conclusion that there is a direct contradiction between the two aspects of Gadamer's argument. Something cannot be whole yet incomplete.

However, philosophical hermeneutics recognizes that dialogue and criticism are not only driven by opposition and refutation. Dialogue also gains an impetus from the creative effort of attempting to think differently about an issue. Thus, although there is no sense in trying to argue away the formal contradiction between the transformation into structure and the presencing of the withheld arguments, there is a way in which the relationship between the disclosed and the withheld can be rethought.

Conclusion: Transforming the Transformation into Structure Argument

The dispute between the two forms of argument outlined above appears as an opposition between two incommensurable perspectives: Either an artwork completes reality (allows it to become more) or it does not, that is, it reveals the presence within reality of something withheld and absent. The dispute turns on the further supposition that the process of becoming real is a process of becoming realized, a process of fruition, fulfillment, or becoming whole. Conversely, recognition of the withheld implies something not fully realized or incomplete. The dispute is, in other words, marked by the classic opposition between "being" and "not being." This, however, invokes a dualistic way of thinking that is entirely at odds with Gadamer's ontology and its Heideggerian roots. "Being" for Heidegger and Gadamer is "not being" (unchanging substance), nor does it exclude "not being" (absence, negativity, the insubstantial). Being is, clearly, that which is never given completely for its presence in the simultaneity of the disclosed and the withheld. Given this we can look at the transformation argument and its relationship to the problem of the withheld in a different way. Let us briefly recapitulate.

Philosophical hermeneutics accords aesthetic appearance with a positive ontological value. Appearance is what shows itself. Yet what shows itself in art is also appearance in the negative sense. What is revealed is a fiction, for nothing in actuality is whole and complete. Yet this fiction allows us to see reality *as if* it were a work of art, that is, as something whole in which no strands of meaning were left incomplete. Artistic appearance is accorded the power of enabling that which in actuality remains open and unresolved to appear as actualized. Hence the transformation in structure argument claims that aesthetic appearance allows actuality to become more real. This positive affirmation of the ontological status of aesthetic appearance and its accompanying view of the artwork as a vehicle of ontic disclosure assures philosophical hermeneutics of a significant place in the rediscovery of aesthetics.

However, the transformation into structure arguments is problematic. The argument is decidedly vulnerable to the objection that what it presents as coming into appearance within the artwork is indeed illusory and fictional. Wholeness and completeness are not features of actuality. Even worse, this intimation of closure is in contradiction with the hermeneutic insight that incompleteness has a positive valence: In other words, there is always more to be said about and always more to be seen in a work. Finally, the transformation argument as presented in *Truth and Method* is also inconsistent with the Heideggerian concept of art as enigma that Gadamer defends in his later works. Both arguments share the claim that the nature of aesthetic appearance is to bring something forth. But while Gadamer suggests that what comes into appearance is a certain completion of actuality, Heidegger insists that along with what an artwork reveals of a subject matter, it also reveals the presence of the disclosed. Gadamer even remarks that "the closedness and withdrawnness of the work of art is the guarantee of the universal thesis of Heidegger's philosophy, namely, that beings hold themselves back by coming forward into the openness of presence."[39] The consequences of these objections are clear. The artwork as presented within the transformation into structure argument becomes mere appearance once again: Precisely that which marks art from actuality—its completeness and wholeness—reveals art to be truly illusory.

However, my concluding claims are as follows. That there is a certain sense in which the argument for the withheld reverses, once again, the relationship between art and the real that is revealed through aesthetic appearance. Furthermore, the argument for the withheld enables us to think differently about one aspect of the transformation into structure argument. The argument concerning art revealing the withheld transforms things back into their proper reality. And aesthetic appearance becomes once again the medium whereby something does indeed emerge as more real.

In *Truth and Method,* Gadamer occasionally talks of the tyranny of the given and of the dogmatism of the everyday and customary. His notion of hermeneutic horizon makes him profoundly aware of how meaningful objects that are given within our perceptual horizons are not as they appear. The force of the immediately perceived and the power of perceptual expectation blinds us to the fact that such objects are always *more* than they appear, that is, they have complex hermeneutic histories that often hold alternative and different interpretations of their nature.

Gadamer's ontological insight into the hermeneutical constitution of meaningful objects is on a par with his later overtly Heideggerian notion of an artwork. The truth of a perceived object is like the truth of an artwork: "The existing thing does not simply offer us a recognisable and familiar surface contour: it also has an inner depth of self-sufficiency that Heidegger calls its 'standing-in-itself.'"[40] Similarly, the truth of the perceived thing as well as that of the artwork "is not constituted simply by its laying bare its meaning but rather by the unfathomable depth of its meaning."[41] The truth "'that beings hold themselves back by coming forward into the openness of presence'"[42] is one that the easy habits of historical prejudice and the blinding powers of ideology conspire to make difficult to perceive. Instrumentalist reasoning, institutionalized thinking, and social conservatism tend to promote a one-dimensional consciousness that either believes or is led to believe that a thing *is* as it appears, that is, it is without any "inner depth of self-sufficiency."[43] It is at this point that various aspects of the argument concerning the withheld and the transformation into structure argument can be brought together. What releases us from the grip of everyday perception and persuades us that things are indeed as they appear? What frees us from such a one-dimensional perspective? It can be argued that Heidegger's notion of aesthetic perception is able to free us from the superficialities of instrumentalist perception and allows us to discern the presence of the withheld. The artwork with its "unfathomable depth" of meaning reminds us that all objects within the perceived world have "an inner depth of self-sufficiency," a "conflict of revealment and concealment" that is (allegedly) "the truth of *every* being."[44] If so, the argument for the essential "closedness and withdrawnness of the work of art"[45] transforms the transformation into structure argument. The argument for the withheld does not transform the things of actuality into a structure. Nor does it not render them complete or whole, but it allows them (paradoxically) to become "more real" by returning to them their proper (hermeneutic) depth and resonance. In effect, the argument for the withheld suggests that the artwork allows the things it displays to be discerned in the fullness of their being, that is, as beings whose depth, richness, meaningfulness, and allure resides in their holding themselves back while they come forward.[46] Thus from the point of view of Gadamer's phenomenological hermeneutics the artwork as conceived within the argument for the withheld allows for "an increase in the being of the original"[47] by allowing what is presented "to be (seen) for the first time (as) what it is."[48] This is as something that is "standing-in-itself" with an inexhaustible self-sufficiency of meaning that, unlike the completeness and wholeness of the initial transformation into structure argument, is open to constant reinterpretation.

11

Modernisms and Mediations

Peter Osborne

THE RECENT REVIVAL OF aesthetics has displayed a novel openness on the part of English-language philosophy to problems posed by twentieth-century art. At the same time, however, in the very act of this opening, some of the most important aspects of these problems have been foreclosed, by being restricted to the terms of a Kantian aesthetic. This foreclosure is at once conceptual and historical. On the one hand, the critical significance of the concept "art" must be repudiated if the "conceptless judgments" of pure aesthetic experience—free beauty—are to be applicable to its instances, works of art. On the other hand, a historically particular type of art ("aesthetic art") must be treated as exemplary, for art to offer objects appropriate to such aesthetic reflection. That is to say, the relevance of aesthetics to art depends upon the privileging of a certain artistic aestheticism. Aesthetics *hallucinates* this artistic aestheticism as "art." The inherently "conceptual" (i.e., nonaesthetic) aspects of contemporary art are thereby misrecognized in advance as at best only problematically connected to its value as art.[1]

Artistic aestheticism is also, of course, the privileged object of the mainstream of modernist criticism, from Charles Baudelaire to Clement Greenberg. Hence the much-heralded convergence of modernism and aesthetics, the polemical recovery of which motivates much of the current interest in aesthetics. From this point of view, it is with modernism that "art becomes aesthetics," while aesthetics, as a discipline, becomes "the reflective construction of the concepts necessary for the comprehension of the *stakes and meaning of art* in the light of the history of the dominant art of the second half of the 19th century and the first half of the 20th century: modernism."[2] In the 1860s, it seems, European (for which, read "French") art (for which, read "painting") finally caught up with Kant. Aesthetics defers to a certain modernism for the historical content of "art." Aesthetics hallucinates *this modernism* as "art."

But is modernism as straightforward a matter as the proponents of a revived aesthetics presume? Can the aesthetic character of modernism be taken for granted, so as to provide an art historical justification for aesthetics? Is there only one critically and artistically relevant "modernism" here? If more than one, what if any conceptual features does this multiplicity of modernisms share? Is there an overarching, metacritical modernism? What are the critical relations between modernisms? And what are their differing relations to "aesthetic" and to "art," respectively? How, finally, does this multiplicity of modernisms relate to the present, the complex global present of "contemporary art"?

In approaching these questions, I begin by stepping back—both conceptually and historically—to the basic semantic shape of the concept of modernism. For it is only by retrieving the fundamental *thought* of modernism—from both the restricted meaning given to it by a particular hegemonic critical school and its reification into a mere name (the name for "the dominant [Western] art of the second half of the 19th century and the first half of the 20th century")—that we can begin to ascertain its conceptual relations to "art" and to "aesthetic" and, thereby, the scope of its possible critical productivity within current debates. For modernism, on my understanding of the term, is far from over. Indeed, it structures the entire field of contemporary art to the extent to which "art" remains a historically critical practice.[3]

I proceed from the thought of modernism in general to an account of three particular, historically successive, art critical modernisms: aesthetic modernism, medium-specific modernism, and generic modernism, or the modernism associated with a generic concept of art. What consideration of this plurality of artistic modernisms reveals is the central role played in the production of contemporary art by a crisis-ridden array of mediating critical forms. The question of the modernism of contemporary art is primarily the question of the character and the status of these mediating critical forms.

A Step Back: The Double Heritage
of the Modern in Art

The English "modern" (from the Latin *modernus*) means, most simply, "of today." However, this "today" is inscribed within a philosophically
specific temporal form, which seems to have emerged near the beginning
of the fifth century, around the time of the collapse of the Roman Empire, when the cyclical opposition of "old and new" characteristic of antiquity was replaced by a sense of the present as an irreversible break with
the past. As such, the idea of the modern involves the application of a
present-centered phenomenological temporality of present/past/future
(today/yesterday/tomorrow) to a Christian, linear form of historical time.
(Philosophically, one might associate this primacy of the present with
Augustine's notion of the "three-fold" present.) In its basic phenomenological and historical form, the temporality of the modern is thus to be
distinguished from the "objective" chronological time of a quantifiable
succession of homogeneous instants (so-called physical or cosmological
time), to which it is in no way reducible. In particular, the idea of the
modern involves a sense of the present as new (*novus*). More specifically, it
picks out from within the present those things that are new and makes
them constitutive of its historical meaning, or what we might call "the
historical present" itself.[4]

As such, the modern relies upon a certain temporal logic of negation, which, in splitting the present from within, makes "modern" an
inherently subjective, value-laden, *critical* term (whether it be judged
favorably, as it still largely is today, or unfavorably, as it was overwhelm-
ingly prior to the nineteenth century). In the modern, the new within
the present does not merely demand more attention than what is not
new; increasingly, it negates the latter's claim on the definition of the
present itself. As such, "modern" is both an ontological term—a term of
temporal ontology—and a critical term. (Historical ontology is critical
ontology.) This negation is an antiquation, a making old of the not new.
The present becomes divided internally into the new and the old. "Modern" is an agonistic, conflict-generating term; hence the opposition between the Ancients and the Moderns through which the term "modern"
first acquired an epochal, periodizing significance in twelfth-century
Europe. It was not until much later, however, during the eighteenth century, that an intensifying investment in the temporality of the modern as

the new—registered by a break not merely with the old, but with the temporality of tradition itself—gave rise at the end of that century to the term "modernity." The English "modernism" predates the intensified sense of the present as modern associated with the word "modernity," but its application to art in the latter part of the nineteenth century rests upon it.

In its early eighteenth-century applications, the English "modernism," denoting a collective belief in and sympathy for the modern (as an "ism" it is both a collective and an affirmative term) was restricted to linguistic change. "A modernism" was a peculiarity of usage, expression, or style characteristic of recent times—in much the same way that the verb "modernize" was at first also used mainly only of spelling, buildings, and dress. What these contexts share is a clear sense of change needing to be justified.[5] They indicate that, from its beginnings, modernism was a discourse of the legitimation of change. In its most general form, modernism is a collective *affirmation of the modern as such*: an affirmation of temporal negation, an affirmation of the time-determination of the new. In its basic sense, then, modernism in art involves the application of this performative temporal logic of negation to the field of art: The project of the production of the qualitatively new in art or, more precisely, the production of an art appropriate to the qualitative novelty of the historical present itself. In this respect, artistic modernism both leans upon that heightened or intensified sense of the time-consciousness of the modern evoked by the term "modernity" and distinguishes itself from the more strictly future-oriented temporality of the avant-garde.

"Modernity" has a double reference here. It refers first to developments within the periodizing use of the term "modern" that are marked in German by the distinction between *die Moderne* and *Neuzeit* (literally, "new time"). "Modernity" (*Neuzeit*) marks a distinct period within the modern age, not by virtue of any particular social content or historical event, but by virtue of the character of its temporality alone: the self-transcending temporality of an investment in the new that opposes itself to tradition *in general*. Second, it refers directly to the temporal qualities that define modernity as a period. It is this second, more immediately qualitative usage—originating, emblematically, in Baudelaire—that foregrounds the inherently aesthetic aspects of "modernity" as a temporal form and, by retrospective effect, the aesthetic characteristics of "the modern" as well.

In Baudelaire, the temporal aesthetics of "modernity" become the basis of both an artistic (poetic) and an art critical project (painting as "the painting of modern life"). It was out of the reflexivity of this dual application—to art and to art criticism—that what subsequently became canonized as the mainstream of artistic modernism was born. However—and this is the crucial point—there is no necessary connection between the aestheticism of this particular art ("early" modernism, be it visual or literary) and its character *as a modernism*, that is, a result of the ongoing application of the temporal logic of modernism (the affirmation of temporal negation) to the field of art. As a temporal quality of experience, "modernity" is an inherently aesthetic category, but this relation need not necessarily be carried over into the content of modernist art. Rather, the aestheticism of early (late nineteenth-century) modernism was contingent upon the use of "aesthetic" as an autonomizing strategy within the more fundamentally modernist struggle against the received dependencies of artistic tradition.[6] "Aesthetic" functions there as a *symbol* of the modern as negation (negation of art's previous social functions); it is not internally related to the concept of "modern art" as such.

In fact, more generally, in its dynamic sense as a temporal logic of negation, artistic modernism necessarily transcends its own historically inaugural (in this case, "aesthetic") form. Within the ambit of this temporal logic (the historical embeddedness of which is, of course, extra-artistic), there is thus of necessity a *multiplicity* of artistic modernisms, not merely at the level of aesthetic form but at that of the concept of art itself. In particular, as we shall see, historically, there are a multiplicity of modernisms at the level of the most basic relations between "art" and "aesthetic." The differences between them are determined by which aspects of the artistic field the art in question takes as the objects of its practices of negation. Identifying these aspects, we may schematize this generation of a multiplicity of modernisms out of the conceptual logic or basic *operation* of modernism itself. Such schemas provide us with a philosophical framework for a critical history of modernisms. But before I do this, let me return for a moment to Baudelaire, in order to elaborate a little further the senses in which modernity may be said to be "aesthetic" and the way in which the temporal logic of modernism in art nonetheless *disengages* it from its inaugural ("aesthetic") form.

In Baudelaire's famous usage, *modernité* denotes not merely the quality of being modern (being new) but the essential transitoriness that

this quality had by then come to involve, as a result of its intensification and generalization as a lived experience of time. In Baudelaire's
famous formulation, the qualities of *modernité* are "the ephemeral, the
fugitive, the contingent . . . whose metamorphoses are so rapid."[7] This
form of experience had as its condition not merely an extraordinary
acceleration in the rhythm of social change—urbanization, industrial-
ization, revolution—but, more specifically, its condensation into the
metropolitan cultural logic of fashion. Indeed, it was the increasing
importance of fashion to capitalist production—in stimulating both
innovation and consumption—that subsequently led to the identification of modernity as capitalism's paradigmatic cultural form.[8] Baudelaire was concerned with the presence of modernity in art, in distinction
from but not in opposition to modernity in life: as a representation and
heightened form of modernity in life ("the painting of modern life").
His use of the term *modernité* registers both an intensification of temporal experience and an investment in the representation of this temporal intensification as both a philosophical and a cultural value in art.
"Modernity" is aesthetic in a triple sense here, while art is "modern" in
two different ways.

First, "modernity" (like the modern more broadly) is aesthetic in the
technical sense of Immanuel Kant's *Critique of Pure Reason*, where "aesthetic" refers to the doctrine of sensibility (transcendentally, space and
time), since modernity is at root a purely temporal quality. Modernity is
transcendentally aesthetic; it is a historical a priori. Modernity is a *feeling
of time* (although, as a historical *a priori*, it is closer to a schema than a
pure intuition).[9] Second, as an aspect of the beauty of modern life (what
Baudelaire referred to as "the special nature of present-day beauty"), "modernity" is an aesthetic term in the more restricted, famously German
sense of belonging to the critique of taste. Modernity is a *beautiful* feeling
of time. Third, as an attribute of art ("the half of art whose other half is
the eternal and the immutable"), "modernity" is an aesthetic term in the
still more constrained (and in my view confusing) sense in which, at the
beginning of the nineteenth century, "aesthetic" acquired a usage synonymous with "*of art*."[10] Modernity in art, for Baudelaire, is a "distillation"
or "purification" of the beautiful feeling of transitoriness, a distillation
of the beauty of time from life into art, which thereby, paradoxically,
effects its *eternalization*. As Walter Benjamin showed, there is a dialectic
of the transitory and the eternal at work in Baudelaire's thought (they

turn into each other), which extends considerably beyond Baudelaire's self-understanding.[11]

It is the condensation of these three registers of "aesthetic" (of *sensibility*, of *taste*, and of *art*) into the single term "modernity" that makes Baudelaire's text such a pivotal moment in the history of the relationship between aesthetic and art. Baudelaire's is the first historically immanent artistic aestheticism. (Kant—or rather, those who followed him—imposed his philosophical aesthetic onto art, externally.) Baudelaire's exposition of *modernité* is the first successful historical mediation of aesthetic and art. Furthermore, in its affirmation of transitoriness, it is also the first proper (i.e., generalized) modernism. This is the truth of Jay Bernstein's claim, cited above, that "with modernism art becomes aesthetics": With *Baudelaire's* modernism "art becomes aesthetics"—the artistic re-presentation of the aesthetics of modernity. But only for a while . . .

Art may be said to be modernist in two different senses here, corresponding to that mobile empirico-transcendental doublet that characterizes not just Kant's thought of the human but all thought of the historical a priori as well. On the one hand, art may be called "modernist" in the quasi-transcendental sense of gaining its intelligibility from its enactment, within and upon the artistic field, of that performative temporal logic of negation that constitutes the structure of modernism in general. This is modernism as an *operation* or a *generative logic*. On the other hand, art may be called "modernist" in the specific art historical sense of being the modernism of its day: that is, constituted as a *particular* form of negation of a *particular* historically received artistic field. In the first case, modernism is a metacritical term; in the second case, it is a term of an empirical historical criticism. The terminological (and consequently conceptual) difficulty we inherit lies in the fixing of the term "modernism" to a single occurrence of the latter sense, as the *name* of a particular modernism ("the dominant [Western] art of the second half of the 19th century and the first half of the 20th century")—assuming that this century of art exhibits sufficient formal unity to constitute one modernism. But whatever its precise and inevitably disputed borders, this reduction of modernism to an art historical concept effaces its more fundamental transcendental operation as an *ongoing* affirmation of a structure of temporal negation.

If we are to escape the conceptual trap laid by this conventional usage, we must ask: What happens to our understanding of modernism in art when the temporality of the qualitatively new continues to be affirmed, either against the "first" (French) modernism of artistic aestheticism, or in other contexts altogether (e.g., in Japan or China or Brazil or Latvia)? It is at this point that our inquiry intersects with recent debates about modernism and the ontology of the artwork set in motion by Thierry de Duve's *Kant After Duchamp*: specifically, the polemical counterposition of a Greenbergian "specific" modernism to a Duchampian "generic" and nominalistic one. Consideration of this opposition and its relation to the inaugural "aesthetic" modernism of the late nineteenth century will help to clarify the relationship between the quasi-transcendental structure of modernism in general and the (in principle, unlimited) empirical (but nonetheless critically construed) multiplicity of "restricted" historical modernisms.

Artistic Modernisms: "Aesthetic," "Specific," "Generic"

In its fundamental conceptual form, I have suggested, artistic modernism is the ongoing result of an application of the temporal logic of modernism (determinate negation of the old and affirmation of the new) to the field of art. Differences among art critical modernisms will thus depend upon which aspects of this field are the objects, or targets, of particular practices of negation and the mode or manner in which they are negated. It thus becomes possible to produce conceptual schema of the differences among the main Euro-American modernisms in the visual arts, from the latter part of the nineteenth century through to the 1960s. These schemas are at the same time schemas of different ontologies of art, since the practices of negation at issue operate at the fundamental level of the concepts of "art" and "the arts" themselves. As a first approximation, these ontologies may be compared on the basis of the traditional logical division into genera, species, and individuals. On the basis of recent critical debates, three main modernisms in visual art suggest themselves: *aesthetic* modernism, *medium-specific* modernism, and *generically artistic* modernism, or the modernism (which is also a nominalism) of the generic concept of art. Each of these modernisms privileges a different level of the ontological triad of genus/species/individual. (The privileged level is indicated on the diagrams below by the use of an asterisk.)

Aesthetic modernism (Fig. 11.1) negated the system of social dependencies constitutive of the academic art of the first half of the nineteenth

Genus*	Art	Aesthetics of *Techne* (as opposed to of nature)
Species	The Arts	Historically privileged carriers of aesthetic properties
Individuals	Works of Art	Sites of experience of (transcendentally defined) aesthetic singularity

Figure 11.1   Aesthetic modernism (aesthetic ontology): a negation of the received social dependencies of academic art; an affirmation of aesthetic qualities as means of artistic autonomy.
* denotes the ontologically privileged level of logical form

century, on the basis of an affirmation of artistic freedom via the aesthetic concept of art: "free" or "autonomous" aesthetic art. The modernism of art for art's sake (*l'art pour l'art*)—the negation of dependency—was the modernism of aesthetic art. "Aesthetic" was a synecdoche for "freedom" here. To the extent to which *artistic* autonomy was actually an achievement of the market, this freedom is in part illusory. Artistic aestheticism is an *ideology* of autonomy (it misunderstands the autonomy of art). Nonetheless, at a practical and critical level, the bohemian avant-gardes of the second half of the nineteenth century instituted aesthetic art for the first time.[12]

One might think that the proponents of "aesthetic art" could propose certain shared aesthetic qualities that make individual works of art "art." However, being the object of a particular type of (pure aesthetic) judgment cannot provide the unification that is sought at the level of the genus, since such judgments also apply—indeed, they apply paradigmatically—to nature. For the aesthetic tradition, what makes a work of art "art" (*techne*) and what gives it critical value as art (its aesthetic qualities) remain stubbornly disjunctive. Aesthetic criteria must be supplemented by technical criteria in order to define "aesthetic art," but in pure aesthetic judgment these technical criteria must then be forgotten, or disavowed, in order that the object appear purely aesthetic. Nonetheless, the aesthetic primacy of presence as transitoriness in Baudelaire—the temporal aesthetic of the modern itself—does privilege representations of modern life as its metagenre, across the arts.

Despite its occasional critical utilization of a general concept of aesthetic art (inherited from Kant via romanticism), in practice aesthetic modernism—early artistic modernism, artistic aestheticism—was *not* primarily about "art" as such, but about modernity in "the arts." Early modernism inherited from academic art a plurality of historically established discrete arts. The modernity of the arts may be understood as residing in a new emphasis on their autonomously aesthetic qualities, as a result of an emphasis on their "presentness." However, these qualities were nonetheless immanent to the *particular*, historically received, and developing structures of artistic practice that constituted the arts (painting, sculpture, drawing, etc.). These were not merely contingent instantiations of the properties of a generalized quasi-Kantian aesthetic. In this respect, as Greenberg saw, in practice, early modernism involved a retrieval of the aesthetic dimensions of historically received arts, as well as a new emphasis on their exploration and autonomous development—a construction of continuity—in the context of the depiction of modern life. Indeed, only on this basis can the aestheticism of artistic modernism be distinguished from—and valued over—the aestheticism of everyday life, to which it was so intimately related, culturally. It is precisely because aestheticism already contained, in the excess of "aesthetic" over "art," the principle of the movement from "art" to "life" that the historical avant-garde may be considered, in Benjamin's analysis, the secret cargo of aestheticism itself.[13]

In this respect, Greenberg's *medium-specific modernism* (Fig. 11.2) represents a clarification of the artistic logic of aesthetic modernism that highlights the fact that its practices of negation were internal to the received system of the arts (i.e., that they depended upon historically received concepts of painting and sculpture) while neglecting its transformation of subject matter. (Recognition of the latter is T. J. Clark's correction, or—better—*completion* of Greenberg.) From this (by then postimpressionist) standpoint, aesthetic modernism in the arts appeared, critically, as an aesthetic redefinition of artistic mediums. Greenberg's brilliance lay in his mediation of this maintenance of an ontological plurality of arts with the general concept of aesthetic art, through the speculative historical redefinition of "medium" (derived from Lessing),

Genus	Art	1. Common properties of artistic mediums 2. Totality of the arts
Species*	The Arts	Mediums
Individuals	Works of Art	Instances of medium self-definition

Figure 11.2 Medium-specific modernism (ontology of arts as mediums): a negation of non-medium-specific properties; an affirmation of medium specificity.
* denotes the ontologically privileged level of logical form

such that each medium expresses an "irreducible element" of experience.[14] In its speculative completion, the system of the arts was thus implicitly projected to map the totality of the aesthetic. This is the extraordinary, closed structural logic of Greenberg's historical criticism. (Greenberg was essentially a structuralist of mediums.) In the process, Baudelaire's "distillation" or "purification" of transitoriness was generalized from literature across the varying aesthetic properties of the arts (as Baudelaire himself had done in relation to music in his late essay on Wagner), giving rise to the idea of artistic modernism as the ongoing process of the experimental self-purification of artistic mediums. Transformed into medium-specific modernism, aesthetic modernism thereby acquired a certain historicity: the "restricted" historicity internal to the clarification of the structure of mediums.

Yet, ultimately, Greenberg's medium-specific modernism can no more cope with the question of what unifies the concept of art than a generalized aesthetic approach. In fact, perhaps even less so. For medium-specific modernism *ontologizes* the plurality of arts as mediums in such a way, seemingly, as to block the very possibility of attributing significant *critical* meaning to the concept of art in general. From this point of view, the concept of art appears at best aporetic. Writers from both standpoints (general-aesthetic and medium-specific), trading on a fundamental ambiguity of logical form, often use the term "art" as shorthand for the totality of arts and artworks in such a way as to imply that there is some common underlying property, unifying the concept of art and giving meaning to the art-character of each of its instances. Yet in reality there can be no such thing for either position, for the question of artistic mediums (*techne*) remains historically open—open to the development of *new* mediums—in such a way as to undermine the mapping of the transcendental elements of "aesthetic" onto a few discrete, historically established arts (painting and sculpture, in particular). This was, of course, the ground for the historical destruction of Greenberg's critical position and the reason for his increasing (and increasingly incoherent) retreat to a generalized discourse of aesthetic value. The current revival of aesthetics may be seen, in one aspect at least, as an attempt to provide a more adequate philosophical basis for a revived Greenbergianism.

The arbitrariness of restricting aesthetic judgments of art to the terms of a few historically contingent mediums became a critical problem early on in the twentieth century, as soon as appeals to a generic concept of art came to be used strategically within art practices themselves. This not only represented a challenge to the ontological significance of established mediums but, still more fundamentally, to the artistic relevance of "aesthetic" itself. This is the significance of Marcel Duchamp and his criterion of "aesthetic indifference." In Duchamp, the challenge to the ontological significance of a relatively fixed (transcendentally delimited) plurality of arts, mediating between art and individual works of art, and the challenge to the aesthetic substance of works of art go hand in hand. What appeared to others as a process of "purification" of mediums appeared to him, more negatively, as a series of "abandonments." In Duchamp (and others), the serial abandonment of particular aspects of what had been the craft of painting was radicalized into an abandonment of craft (*techne*) in general. This abandonment of craft became the basis of an alternative modernist tradition (an alternative to both aesthetic and medium-specific modernisms): the modernism of a generic concept of art or what we might call a "generic modernism." From the standpoint of the present (post-1960s art), this so-called alternative tradition is, in fact, now the *main* tradition of artistic modernism in the twentieth century, running from Duchamp, Dada, surrealism, and the Russian avant-gardes through to Fluxus, conceptual art, a certain minimalism, and the postconceptual and postminimalist movements of the 1960s, 1970s, and beyond. While critically dominant in the United States in the decade-and-a-half immediately following World War II and currently resurgent in a marginal and modified form, the medium-specific modernism of a plurality of arts is essentially a nineteenth-century tradition.

Critically, what I am calling generic modernism is currently best known through the reconstruction of the generic concept of art as a proper name that emerged in the course of Thierry de Duve's work on Duchamp.[15] Historically, however, it has a far broader scope than the Duchampian and minimalist genealogies with which de Duve is particularly concerned. This raises the question of the adequacy of his theoretically idiosyncratic nominalism to the critical interpretation of the broader tradition.[16] Nonetheless, what de Duve has demonstrated beyond a doubt is: first, that there is more than one philosophical problematic associated with modernism in the visual arts, and, second, that while the initially critically dominant one (medium-specific modernism) is "aesthetic" in origin and orientation, the main competing alternative (generic modernism) is not. I shall refer to de Duve's interpretation of Duchamp's generic concept of art as *generic modernism I* (Fig. 11.3).

What is most striking about this schema is its radical elimination of mediating forms and its resolution of the problem of the relations of individual works to the genus "art," directly, with a nominalism of the proper name "art." The negation of medium here is also negation of ontology, a negation of ontology by naming, or a negative ontology *of* naming. De Duve presents this historically in the form of a repetition: the repetition of the result of Duchamp's dialectical abandonment of painting by Frank Stella and Donald Judd's absolute purification of painting, leaving only its

Genus	Art	1. A proper name 2. Totality of successful claims on the name "art"
Species	[The readymade]	[Vanishing mediator of the destruction of mediums—a negative metamedium]
Individuals*	Works of Art	Instances of claims on the name "art"

Figure 11.3 Generic modernism I (nominalist critique of ontology of "art"): a negation of historically received, craft-based mediums; an affirmation of the enunciative logic of individual claims on the name "art."
* denotes the ontologically privileged level of logical form

object-character behind. Critically, however, de Duve's nominalism is effectively a sophisticated ("enunciative") form of positivism. The modernism of an individual work is dependent on its ability successfully to claim the name "art" in some new way. The critical challenge to those unconvinced by the positivism of de Duve's metacritical artistic nominalism is to theorize the history of post-Duchampian art as the history of a modernist series of *subsequent* determinate negations of the artistic field that derive their intelligibility from the *critical mediations* thereby produced. That is to say, the challenge is to theorize the unity of the generic concept of art conceptually, as the distributive unity of a historical process of determinate negations. The thinker who has attempted to do this most systematically is Theodor Adorno.[17] There is no space to pursue the complex conceptual structure of Adorno's modernist conception of "the preponderance of art" over the individual artwork in any detail here. However, the basic character of its modernism may be schematized as *generic modernism 2* (Fig. 11.4).

Genus	Art	The critical distributional unity of the historical totality of works of art
Species	[Afterlife of the arts within the field of art in general]	A fluid field of critical "isms" and series corresponding to structural negations of aspects of the received artistic field
Individuals	Works of Art	Ontologically distinctive subject-like entities producing the illusion of autonomous meaning production through the mediation of determinate negations

Figure 11.4   Generic modernism 2 (historical ontology of art): a negation of historically received (originally, craft-based) mediums and mediations; an affirmation of new determinate negations of the established artistic field.
* no level of logical form is ontologically privileged on this model of mediations

The critical primacy of the mediations means that no one level in the logical triad is privileged, ontologically. Rather, artistic ontology is distributed across the field of relations between the three levels. It is a broadly—but by no means orthodox—Hegelian model, in which the primacy of negation to the structure of the modern has the logical consequence of a primacy of mediations. Within this structure, however, everything depends on the character of the negations, which is a historically contingent affair. In fact, Adorno acknowledges a growing "nominalism" (in a sense quite different from de Duve's) in contemporary art subsequent to the decline in the regulative authority of mediums. But this nominalism is not a decisive one-off act, it is a tendency—a tendency equivalent to the crisis of modernism itself. For if modernism is all about negation, and therefore mediation, any nominalistic crisis of mediating forms will amount to a crisis of modernism. Contemporary art inhabits the space of this crisis.

This crisis is at once a crisis in the production of a certain kind of art (metacritically modernist art, art that gains its intelligibility from the operational structure of the modern) and a crisis of criticism. By developing mediating critical categories, modernist criticism both recovers the particular modernisms of particular works (thereby completing them as modernist works) and makes such works possible, by functioning as an intellectual form of artistic material. Conceptual confusion about modernism (the reduction of its general economy to a particular, restricted historical instance) thus has determinate *artistic* effects.

12

Aesthetics Beyond Aesthetics

Wolfgang Welsch

STANDARD DEFINITIONS OF AESTHETICS tell us that aesthetics is concerned primarily with art and, in particular, with art's beauty. In what follows, however, I will argue that our understanding of aesthetics can and should be extended beyond art.

The term "aesthetics" already lends itself to a transartistic reading. The Greek root *aisthesis* refers to sensation and perception in general, independent of any reference to art. Everyday use of the word is not restricted to art: We commonly refer to an "aesthetic lifestyle," to "aesthetic qualities" of media presentations, and to the "aestheticization" of entire domains or environments. The philosophical discipline of aesthetics, however, has traditionally focused primarily on art, especially on its conceptual and formalist rather than sensuous aspects.

Alexander Gottlieb Baumgarten's philosophical aesthetics, understood as the "science of sensuous cognition," mentions the arts.[1] However, between Immanuel Kant's *Critique of Judgment* of 1790 and Friedrich Wilhelm Joseph Schelling's *System of Transcendental Idealism* of 1800, the commonly accepted meaning of "aesthetics" changed, so that aesthetics was taken to refer exclusively to the philosophy of art. For a long time this remained the dominant view, shared by philosophers as diverse as Georg Wilhelm Friedrich Hegel and Martin Heidegger, Roman Ingarden, and Theodor W. Adorno.

Exceptions from this view include Schiller's proposal for an "art of life" (*Lebenskunst*), Herbert Marcuse's idea of a new social sensibility, Søren Kierkegaard's description of aesthetic existence, Friedrich Nietzsche's fundamentalization of aesthetic activity, and John Dewey's integration of art into life. However, all these thinkers agreed that art was the principal focus of aesthetics, though not the only one, because they still considered art paradigmatic for the very transartistic aesthetics they advocated. Thus, in philosophy, the restriction of aesthetics to art survives to this day.[2]

The philosophical picture of aesthetics might therefore appear inevitable as a picture that, in Ludwig Wittgenstein's words, has "held us captive" and that we have been unable to abandon because philosophy seems "to repeat it to us inexorably."[3] Nonetheless, I suggest that it is time to abandon the "aesthetics-artistics" equation and, as Wittgenstein put it, "to show the fly the way out of the fly-bottle."[4]

A major motivation for this change is that traditional aesthetics has never been able to fulfill the core task it set itself originally, namely to establish a universal and timeless concept of art—a task with obvious flaws. Schelling possibly expressed the basic conviction of traditional aesthetics most clearly when he said that aesthetics, understood as philosophy of art, should treat only "art as such" and "in no way empirical art,"[5] which was embedded in nature or society.[6] Consequently, a rudimentary knowledge of a few selected artworks was considered sufficient to prompt an intuition of the general concept of art.[7] Important individual artworks and entire historical periods, genres, and so forth were ignored. Paradoxically, perhaps, this meant that the "universal" definitions of aesthetics fell short of capturing the actual history and current practices of art.

Today traditional aesthetics seems inappropriate to many philosophers, as it has been for artists for a very long time. Art practice evidently does not consist in exemplifying a universal concept of art, nor in creating ever new variations of art's essence. Any new work, or any new concept, will tend to have something in common with dominant historical and contemporary art forms but also to differ from them in important aspects. Hence the all important shifts of style and paradigm. It seems more appropriate, then, to see different artistic forms and practices not as coinciding in terms of a universal definition but as overlapping (by "family resemblances" in the Wittgensteinian sense). To state the obvious: There simply is no such thing as an essence of art.

Thus the traditional approach is mistaken in principle, even within the narrow scope of artistics. It misunderstands fundamentally what is involved in the production and appreciation of art. I contend, therefore, that insight into the historical production of different artworks and artistic models, recognition of their family resemblances, and thereby realization of the failures of traditional universalizing aesthetics demand a shift to a new pluralistic approach.

But the reorganization of aesthetics must go beyond the traditional identification of aesthetics with artistics. The internal pluralization of artistics should be complemented by an external pluralization, namely an expansion of aesthetics to transartistic questions.

To establish this, I will argue as follows: First, I will lay out major themes for a new "aesthetics beyond aesthetics." Second, I will clarify the conceptual legitimacy of such aesthetics and make some suggestions for a reorganization of the discipline. In this way I intend to open up aesthetics to issues beyond art and to develop a cross-disciplinary structure for aesthetics. Aesthetics is, then, still about art, but it also encompasses transartistic issues. Third, I will argue that this expansion of aesthetics benefits the analysis of art itself, which can be investigated more adequately through an aesthetics unrestricted to the analysis of art alone.

Principal Themes and the Relevance of an "Aesthetics Beyond Aesthetics"

There are two clusters of reasons supporting the wider view of aesthetics advanced here: One is based on contemporary ways in which reality is designed and fashioned, the other is based on contemporary understandings and interpretations of reality.[8]

Aesthetic Fashioning of Reality—Beautification

We are currently living in a world that is more radically aestheticized than ever before. Wherever we look, beautification and styling (of body, soul, and behavior) seem to have become very important in our lives. In beauty salons and fitness centers we pursue the aesthetic perfection of our bodies; in meditation courses we practice the aestheticizing of our souls; and in etiquette courses we are trained for aesthetically acceptable behavior. What used to be an exchange of goods and products has been taken over by advertising strategists who now sell us entire aesthetic lifestyles. Urban areas too are undergoing face-lifts, and increasingly we redesign the environment in accordance with aesthetic ideals like complexity or natural beauty.[9]

Of course, aesthetic orientation and manipulation have always had effects upon the "real world," or the world outside the art world, however little the discipline of aesthetics may have acknowledged this. But what is new today is the radicality and the global reach of aestheticization. Contemporary aesthetics, then, must recognize and investigate these phenomena, which both extend and, simultaneously, alter the configuration and significance of aesthetics. This means that aestheticians now must attend to aesthetic phenomena in many fields: in the life-world and the world of politics and in the worlds of economy, ecology, ethics, and science.

Some traditional aesthetic programs, for example German idealism, once advocated global aestheticization for the definitive fulfillment of all human tasks and the ultimate happiness of mankind.[10] It appears as if those old aesthetic dreams are being redeemed in the current developments mentioned above—but with results that fall painfully short of the original expectations. We often find not beauty but kitsch; not elation or sublimity but disgust or indifference. Hence something must be wrong with this recent fulfillment of old aesthetic dreams—or with the dreams themselves.

Three critical factors arise. First, its ubiquity deprives beauty of its distinguished character. Hence beauty decays into prettiness or becomes altogether meaningless. (The exceptional cannot become a standard without changing its exceptional quality.) Second, given the importunity of aestheticization, indifference becomes a sensible, almost inevitable attitude. An-aestheticization—our refusal to pay attention to our divinely embellished environment—becomes a survival strategy.[11] Third, a need for nonaesthetics, or unaesthetics, arises—a desire for interruptions and disruptions. Hence a task for contemporary art is *not* to introduce more beauty into the already overly beautified environment but to stop the aestheticization machinery by creating aesthetic deserts and fallow lands in the midst of the hyperaesthetic.[12]

It appears that aestheticians, who are usually keen to praise beauty for moral reasons (as well as for other good ones), have never considered the consequences of an an-aesthetization on the scale experienced today. Nobody could imagine that globalized beautification, for which traditional aesthetics has repeatedly served as rhetorical support, might disfigure the world. It is almost as if the traditional passion for beauty kept us from considering any negative effects of aestheticization, even when these had long since become obvious. In the face of these failures, I will advance a threefold criticism of traditional aesthetics.

First, the wholesale praise of beauty must be challenged. Perhaps we should begin to distinguish mediocre or average beauty from that exceptional phenomenon of greater beauty that instills in us, in Rainer Maria Rilke's words, "the beginning of what's frightening."[13] At any rate, it seems that beauty can be appreciated only in opposition to nonbeauty; it therefore loses its distinctiveness by its very propagation.

Second, traditional aesthetics should be criticized for exclusively or predominantly promoting beauty and thereby for neglecting other aesthetic values. In restricting its subject matter in this way, aesthetics has falsely limited itself; it thus misses the fundamental (aesthetic) point that homogenization systematically counteracts aesthetic qualities and effects.

Third, the efficacy of traditional aesthetics in the economy of our cultural beliefs and desires must be questioned. This involves challenging old aesthetic dogmas in such ways that enable and motivate aesthetics to become self-critical. Consequently, the issues of "aesthetics beyond aesthetics" concern not only those who are already willing to broaden the reach of aesthetics but also those who still adhere to its traditional framework.

Aesthetic Apprehension of Reality

The predominance of aesthetic modes and patterns that mediate our most basic perceptions and interpretations of reality is evident in aesthetic presentations of individual objects or persons and in the highly stylized formats of our daily news. Consider also, for example, the pictorial dominance in advertising, in displays of corporate identity, and in our own visual appearance on Web sites. More importantly, the pictorial demands of visual media in today's world codetermine what might count as news, which means that aesthetic considerations enter into our apprehension of reality. In other words, the "real" has become the "aesthetically presentable." Of central concern here is the ensuing "derealization of reality"—with at least two consequences: a reconfiguration of *aisthesis*, (i.e., of our modes of sense perception) and a revalidation of experiences outside of electronic media.[14]

By "derealization of reality" I mean the ways in which our sense of reality, largely generated by the media, is deeply affected by this increasingly aesthetic mode of mediation.[15] While reality is presented ever more playfully, it has also been subject to constant diminution caused by the peculiarities of media aesthetics, which generally favor free mobility and lightness of bodies and images. Everything is open to possible manipulation. Whatever enters the electronic realm forsakes its stability for an air of transformability. However, not only do we know that everything is potentially manipulable, but we are also aware of actual manipulations. Consider reports from the first Gulf War, replete with technological simulations and the reality of victims and losses erased. It is often unclear whether we are being shown a playback of reality or an aesthetically effective simulation.

Such experiences weaken the difference between (truthful) representation and mere simulation of reality—not only in theory (where this has become commonplace) but also in common experience. We stay tuned because we seem to prefer changing our comprehension of reality to resisting the aesthetic forces at play.

This widespread attitude toward media reality has begun to extend to other domains of everyday reality. The overwhelming persistence of media presentations creates not affliction but its opposite: indifference. In the wake of such mechanisms we tend to treat reality altogether as a simulation. We no longer take it quite so seriously; and amidst this suspension of reality we begin to judge and act differently too. Since these processes are occasioned by the aesthetic peculiarities of the media, any contemporary aesthetic theory must consider them if it intends to analyze the present state of aesthetics and thus to act responsibly.[16]

All of this motivates major philosophical challenges to traditional aesthetic and epistemological paradigms. For example, the primacy of vision, which has shaped occidental culture since the ancient Greeks and which is favored traditionally for its hallmarks of distance, precision, and universality, has been powerfully criticized by authors such as Heidegger and Wittgenstein, as well as Michel Foucault, Jacques Derrida, and Luce Irigaray.[17] But now we have learned also from experience that vision and visual representation no longer provide reliable contact with reality.

This has led to increased attention to the other senses, such as hearing, which provides an interesting alternative model of perception because of its essentially social character and its association with affective elements of perception.[18] Touch has advocates also, because of new developments in media technology[19] and its emphatically corporal nature. In a departure from the traditional hierarchy of the senses, in which vision had priority, the senses are thus given a more equitable assessment where different, purpose-specific hierarchies can be investigated.

A task for a new "aesthetics beyond artistics" could be to analyze these altered states of *aisthesis* and the accompanying changes of cultural patterns in order to provide a clear, reliable account of these transformations.

The New Extension of Aesthetics

Conceptual Clarifications

This project may appear open to the objection that the diversity of (academic and nonacademic) meanings of the term "aesthetic" render the attempt to include all of them in one discipline hopelessly ambiguous and a matter of mere equivocation.

Certainly the expression "aesthetic" is used in various ways. It can refer to art and beauty in particular or to *aisthesis* in general; it may mean a way of life or designate an ontology of virtuality, fictionality, and suspension. In fact, although the problem of the semantic ambiguity of the aesthetic is as old as the discipline itself, no aesthetician has ever given up the term or the discipline.

Wittgenstein indicated a way out of this alleged conceptual difficulty by showing that an expression's coherence need not depend on a unitary essence, but it can occur through emerging "family resemblances." This view has significant consequences for aesthetics. It becomes possible to explain the coherence between very different meanings of "aesthetics." While it is important to differentiate carefully between the different usages, they can still be regarded as interconnected, so that their coincidences and divergences can be investigated. In this way, the full range of aesthetic phenomena becomes the object of aesthetic analysis, and the restriction of aesthetics to artistics is overcome. Any individual researcher may focus, of course, on art in his or her own research, just as another may refer primarily to nonartistic aspects. But, *as a discipline* aesthetics should comprise the full range of interests. The polyvalence of "aesthetics" should be understood as an indication not of the inadequacy of aesthetics but of its richness and profundity. In fact, this is true of many important concepts, like "being"[20] and "logos," whose different meanings are far from implying the impossibility of ontology or logic. We should, therefore, assume the task of an expanded aesthetics and admit the diversity and complexity of aesthetic phenomena, instead of dogmatically narrowing the discipline.

Advantages of Expanding the Discipline

Interdisciplinary and institutional advantages follow from the expansion of aesthetics. Although aesthetics may become more difficult by becoming more complex, it can also facilitate more intensive contact and interchange with other disciplines and thus gain new fields of research. This is advantageous both for the breadth of its issues and for the institutional reality of academic research. A more open and diverse aesthetics may generate greater interest in the full width of its spectrum and for its contributions to contemporary problems. It could also win greater support, including financial support.

The expansion of aesthetics to issues beyond art also benefits analyses of art. Artworks always reach beyond art and refer not only to other artworks but also to transartistic issues and phenomena. This is to say, art already transcends the borders of traditional aesthetics. Thus a thorough analysis of art also requires an "aesthetics beyond aesthetics," namely for the reasons outlined below.

Despite its claim to autonomy, art has always and deliberately reacted to aesthetic phenomena in its surroundings. In a world more aesthetically sparing, it demonstrated the Elysium of beauty. When the modern world tended to repress sensibility, art—heedful of its old bond with the sensuous—understood itself as the harbinger and savior of the sensuous (as with Henri Matisse and Jean Dubuffet). When beautification spread, some art began to counteract it and behaved decidedly demurely (as in arte povera and minimal art). Much contemporary art reacts to the ubiquity of media images in particular. It can oppose their importunity, emulate it, or operate with the frictions between traditional artistic patterns and contemporary media presentations. Such works direct our attention to their references, to other modes of design and perception or to their specific interventions in both artistic and transartistic modes of the aesthetic.

Moreover, the energy of the works can transcend their frames, museum walls, or moments of contemplation. Artworks disclose and generate new perspectives on the world. Upon leaving an exhibition, we can suddenly feel as if we perceive the world with "other eyes," through the optics and dynamics of the artists' works, in the light of the aesthetics they present. Thus we can experience art as something not closed and strictly defined but as opening us up to different ways of viewing the world. In this sense, works of art often serve as tools for extended or intensified perceptions of reality.

Consider further how forms of perception, which today appear natural and self-evident, originated in historical processes mediated by art. Romantic art, for example, had a key role in our view of landscapes. In this way, many of our everyday perceptions are sediments of generations of art experience, as are some behavioral patterns and paradigms of social interaction.[21] Moreover, works of art can also provide models for ways of living. This was a feature of the normative demands of classical art and continues after the dissolution of general norms in the invention of possibilities for individual life planning. Rilke's reflection on the archaic torso of Apollo and his concluding line, "you must change your life," provides an impressive example of this phenomenon.[22]

The border between art and extra-artistic reality should not simply be denied but the entanglements and transitions in between investigated. That is to say, aesthetics of art must consider the dual character of artistic and nonartistic aesthetics. This is why Adorno, who—like perhaps no other—defended the significance of art's autonomy, also opposed the separation of art from reality. He was struck by just "how much these innervations of art are bound up with its position in reality," which "could be viscerally sensed in the bombed German cities of the postwar years. In the face of actual chaos the optical order that the aesthetic sensorium had long ago rejected once again became intensely alluring."[23] Although order had revealed itself as a synonym for purposive rationality, the perception of an order destroyed (by means of a perverted purposive rationality) can still arouse aesthetic yearning for the restoration of order.[24] This implies that aesthetic experience is systematically misunderstood when it is stripped of its references to extra-artistic reality and thus of the contrast that sustains it. This view highlights the complexity of artworks. A brief example will illustrate this.[25]

Francisco de Goya's painting *The Shootings of 3 May 1808* (1814) offers exciting color dynamics and compositional innovations, and it simultaneously provides an interpretation of a historical event. Its aesthetic impulse aims for a certain understanding of the event portrayed and awakens a new attitude toward events of the same type. Several perceptual modes intersect in the perception of the work: the observational manner of the picture and its artistic-aesthetic arrangement, its expressive, dynamic style, the historical significance of the events of May 3, 1808, the narrative of a shocking plot, and the appellative gesture toward future intervention and prohibition. The explosion in the picture aims for the end of such deeds and simultaneously detonates the process of merely aesthetic representation and reception. Clearly, this painting cannot simply be regarded in an aesthetically contemplative manner. Rather it pierces the contemplation cocoon in favor of a multidimensional perception directed toward contexts of communication and life. It thus becomes a warning signal: Events such as this shooting should no longer occur.[26]

A general claim can be derived from this: The perception of a work of art is not a single aesthetic act. Rather, a multitude of different activities from an entire range of aesthetic perceptual modes may enter the perception of a piece. The singular work is thus characterized by a specific selection and combination of aesthetic moments. It stipulates a specific array of perceptual modes, functioning, so to speak, as their point of intersection. A traditionalist aesthetician might object that, of course, several factors are in play in the perception of Goya's picture, but only one of these is the specifically aesthetic one. But this argument comes close to a declaration of bankruptcy, for it implies that aesthetics cannot even consider art, but at best one of art's elements, namely the "aesthetic" one. An aesthetics this narrowly defined has little appeal.

A further important point becomes clear in Édouard Manet's painting *The Execution of Emperor Maximilian* (1867), which obviously uses Goya's work as a model. Here our perception of Manet's painting implicates Goya's work; it is inter-iconic. The failure of recognizing the inter-iconic aspect of the painting would render its appreciation simply deficient; it would miss the complexity of the piece.

Marcel Duchamp's parody of the *Mona Lisa*, *L.H.O.O.Q.* (1919), is a further example of the importance of inter-iconic awareness. In addition, a semantic dimension must also be considered here: The sequence of letters in the title is to be read as *"elle a chaud au cul,"* or "her ass is hot." How ridiculous the retreat to mere aesthetic contemplation would be in this case. In order to understand a work such as this you must not only see but also know, suspect, make inferences. Matters are

not settled by self-referentiality alone. Reflection is here more important than contemplation.

In other words, works of visual art so obviously transcend the merely
contemplative dimension of stereotypical aesthetics. Historical allusions
belong to them, as do semantic and allegorical, societal, everyday, or political dimensions and, of course, emotional and imaginative processes. In
this way, artworks intervene in the economy of our communications and
organize the aesthetic field each in their own way.

This is true not only of visual art but also of music. Adorno highlighted the self-transcending structure of art with reference to Ludwig van
Beethoven: "One is no more equal to a Beethoven symphony without
comprehending its so-called purely musical course than if one is unable to
perceive in it the echo of the French Revolution; how these two aspects are
mediated in the phenomenon belongs to the obstinate and equally un-
avoidable themes of philosophical aesthetics."[27] Adorno's observation that
"aesthetic experience must overstep itself"[28] characterizes *in nuce* my more
general point: The artistic requires the transartistic; and what is singular
about any particular artwork is how it brings together the two.

The foregoing holds not only for all traditional art but also for modern and contemporary art, which in many cases has explicitly committed
itself to a testing, questioning, and altering of its boundaries and conditions. Works of art have shown that they can alter their short- and
long-term conditions, make unaccustomed criteria requisite, or eliminate
perceived artistic boundaries. In this way Duchamp questioned the dic-
tate of visibility, James Joyce the form of the book, Jackson Pollock the
limit of painting, and John Cage the status of music. I would argue that it
was precisely the project of the avant-garde to transcend the confined status of an artistics and to open itself to an "aesthetics beyond aesthetics."
Thus it would be simply anachronistic to ignore or annul these artistic
interventions by means of a theoretical restriction of aesthetics. This is
exemplified in modern and contemporary art practice where extra-artistic
clues become increasingly relevant to an ever-growing variety of artistic
styles and types. One work of art can require the making of connections
that are completely irrelevant for another. Already for some of Kazimir
Malevich's works it is not enough to observe what is factually given,
rather our perception must extend into the cosmic (and Malevich helps us
in this, for instance, through the way he uses black). Similarly, we don't
actually "see" Edvard Munch's painting *The Scream* until we have heard a

scream. With Duchamp, by contrast, the activity of the senses is insufficient altogether; without introducing reflection we would perceive only
banal nonsense. Pollock, on the other hand, can only appropriately be apprehended kinesthetically (but woe betide whoever insists on trying this
with Piet Mondrian). Differently again, Sol LeWitt demands an analytic
construction of vision. Finally, On Kawara can really only be perceived
alongside the horrific vision of the bombing of Hiroshima.

In each instance a specific reconfiguration of the perceptual field
occurs. The palette of conventional aesthetic modes is overturned or re-
configured; traditional hierarchies are overthrown and new ones established. Precisely the perception of something unapparent or unheard—even
of something imperceptible in the traditional sense—can suddenly gain
importance and attain priority. In this way, every work of art intransi-
gently continues to determine and transform the field of perceptual and
associative accomplishments relevant to it.

Thus the perception of art is in principle polyaesthetic. Without
some everyday perceptual competence we would be unable to recognize
the objects depicted in pictures. Some familiarity with art is also an advantage. It cannot hurt to know what a complementary contrast is, or
wherein the artificiality of the seemingly natural central perspective lies.
(It is what lets us see, for example, the measures Masaccio had to take to
produce suspenseful pictures in spite of isocephaly.) In short: We must
know the established codes in order to recognize deviations and new emphases; the *pictor doctus* requires a *receptor doctus*.

If any perception of art involves the probing of various perceptual
modes and clues in the attempt to discover the specific constellation required by the work, then aesthetic experience as a whole is characterized
by a combination of contemplation, imagination, and reflection. And
even contemplation alone is not simply observational but processual and
reflective. It is fundamentally so: Already the mere apprehension of linear
convergence and divergence of color contrasts requires sensible reflection.
What is seen respectively is not a brute fact but the result of a process of
interpretation that is dependent on subsequent viewing. These interpretive
acts, in turn, involve pictorial experience as well as life experience. For
example, it is impossible to grasp the perception that a gesture both
reaches out to, yet shies away from, without a certain maturity and sensitivity on the perceiver's part. References to the life-world thus belong to
the picture process in the same way as inter-iconic allusions.

Furthermore, experiencing art requires a particular openness to the alteration of familiar categories and sectoral divisions. Artists assume the freedom to divide up the world in unaccustomed ways or to disclose unknown correspondences, analogies, or transitions between sectors. Giorgio Morandi's still lifes, for instance, are not straightforward depictions of objects but are also sociograms. Objects are arranged like families. We recognize hierarchies, contacts, fears, self-assertions, evasive maneuvers, dismissals, linkages. One could say that Morandi practices microsociology, just as Mondrian practiced macrosociology. However, Mondrian was also concerned both with pictorial elements and with representing a model for the balancing of life's different aspects as it must be achieved in every individual life and in society as a whole. Hence his silent, seemingly unpretentious works are first fully perceived when their practical dimension is recognized.

Another case in point is art that attempts to transcend the human pale. This was a leitmotif in twentieth-century Western art[29] and has for a long time been characteristic of many strands of non-Western art. In the West, the aim of this recent move toward what I have called a "transhuman stance"[30] is to break open the closed world of human self-reference erected by modernity.[31] In opposition to this deeply rooted anthropocentrism, some artworks attempt to enable us to experience our commonality with a more than human world and with natural and spiritual dimensions irreducible to human making. (In fact, Eastern art has always been committed to articulating this deep connectedness.[32]) Artworks of this type open up unaccustomed features of the relationship between the human and the nonhuman. They transcend the oppositional model in favor of a participatory one. If we are not sensitive to their scope because we merely apply our habitual categories, we cannot make sense of them but may be tempted to reject them as nonsense.

In summary, the field of aesthetic perception is polymorphic. It is distinguished by the fact that neither the range of nor the relationship among perceptual dimensions are permanently fixed, but they are always at stake. Thus, only an attitude that is polyaesthetic as a matter of principle—and as such is attentive to a wide range of different constellations—can do justice to works of art. The inclination toward general aesthetic contemplation or the restriction to formal analysis, by contrast, systematically fails to recognize, and thereby diminishes, their potential to reach beyond.

The comprehensiveness of aesthetics is thus of benefit to art analysis. Since art constantly brings into play a whole palette of perceptions and affords each a certain organization, obviously aesthetics, as the reflexive authority on the aesthetic, should also be in a position to account for diverse kinds of perception, differing constellations, and transartistic entanglements and thus do justice to them.[33]

Incidentally, an "aesthetics beyond aesthetics" is not only fruitful in terms of the purposes of understanding and interpreting art (i.e., for the reception of art) but could be relevant also to the creation of art and thus be interesting to artists. We can open up new perspectives on what art is all about. When an artist (following, say, Schiller's suggestion) discovers art's ability to develop models for the "art of life" (*Lebenskunst*), it might lead to rejection of the traditional search for the perfection of singular works of art—Joseph Beuys is a good example of this. Or when an artist (following, say, Nietzsche) recognizes the constitutive role of aesthetic features in cognition, then they might suddenly think, "Hey, my actual task might consist not in creating art for the sake of art, but rather in developing and exemplifying possible views and ways of perceiving, alternative divergent patterns of perceiving and apprehending." Here Eva Hesse is a good example. In such ways, the transaesthetics proposed here can encourage new paths for art practice and can thus be of interest to artists who for good reasons have been so dissatisfied with traditional aesthetics.

Conclusion: Toward a Transdisciplinary Reorganization of the Discipline

The structure of the discipline of aesthetics will have to be transdisciplinary in the wake of such an expansion. Since aesthetics is a field of research comprising all questions concerning *aisthesis*—with the inclusion of contributions from philosophy, sociology, art history, psychology, anthropology, the neurosciences, biology, and so on[34]—*aisthesis* should provide the framework of the discipline while art, although important, will be only one of its subjects. This means that various studies referring to *aisthesis* could be effective branches of the discipline of aesthetics, which integrates all of them into its institutional structure. Aesthetics, then, would be transdisciplinary and not just display interdisciplinarity when occasioned by meetings with other disciplines. In such an aesthetics, all the branches mentioned ought to be investigated and discussed. Individual aestheticians would be familiar with all of them and research and teach at least some of them—and not just, say, "ontology of art" or the "history of taste."[35] Finally, aesthetics would also become decidedly intercultural. Hitherto the academic discipline has mostly confined itself to a Western perspective. Even when aesthetics was established on other continents, the Western paradigm was adopted. (Japan and other Asian countries are typical examples of this.) Only in recent years have scholars become aware of the inadequacy of this situation.[36]

The history of aesthetics has experienced several significant paradigm shifts. Naturally, such shifts do not happen every day, but they occur and for good reasons. For future generations the transdisciplinary structure of an "aesthetics beyond aesthetics" could appear fairly self-evident. Outside of the discipline of philosophy this already seems to be the case.

13

Intuition and Concrete Particularity in Kant's Transcendental Aesthetic

Adrian Piper

BY "TRANSCENDENTAL AESTHETIC," Immanuel Kant means "the science of all principles of a priori sensibility" (A 21/B 35).[1] Thus the "Transcendental Aesthetics" with which Kant begins the *Critique of Pure Reason* enumerates the necessary presuppositions of, among other things, our ability to make empirical judgments about works of art. These presuppositions are sensible rather than intellectual because, in Kant's view, all intellection that considers objects of any kind, whether abstract or concrete, must at base connect to actual, material objects with which we come into direct contact; and this we can do only through sensibility (A 19/B 33). Here I explore Kant's claims about what must be true of us so that we can make the sorts of aesthetic judgments we make, which, in his view, is not different from what must be true of us so that we can make any other kind of judgment about empirical objects in general.

This last point is worth emphasizing in order to correct an interpretation of Kant's account of aesthetic judgment in the *Critique of Judgment* that wrongly reads Kant as claiming that aesthetic judgments do not have to satisfy the same basic requirements of judgment that hold for any other kind of judgment, such as the synthetic subsumption of such objects under certain necessary and hardwired concepts of understanding, the internal coherence of such judgments with other, nonaesthetic ones of a more abstract and comprehensive character, the unified consciousness within which such judgments are intelligibly made, and so on.[2] Of course Kant recognizes the special character of aesthetic judgments and unpacks it in the third *Critique*. But as we see above, he also states clearly, in the very first paragraph of the first *Critique,* that aesthetic judgment is merely one species of judgment, all of which must satisfy the necessary conditions he enumerates in the subsequent sections of the chronologically prior first *Critique.* Kant does not think it is possible to make judgments of any kind unless these conditions are satisfied. In what follows, I focus on the implications of these conditions for aesthetic judgment specifically, but these implications certainly are not confined to aesthetic judgments alone.

Kant begins the Transcendental Aesthetic with the claim that through intuition we stand in unmediated relation to objects (A 19/B 33). *Intuition* is, for Kant, a precognitive, sensory process through which we situate ourselves spatiotemporally in relation to objects, both internal and external (A 23/B 37). In the case of internal objects, we organize sense-data linearly in time, ensuring that our internal mental representations of objects and the parts of objects we represent proceed in systematic succession. For example, I remember the living room of my old house by calling up successive images of the west wall, the north wall, the east wall, then the south wall; and then the east wall once more, if something of interest there then returns to my memory. In the case of external objects, we also organize sense-data spatially, by projecting and locating the object we construct from them at some particular point outside of ourselves, and thus defining a spatial relation between it and us. Every such external, spatial relationship is also implicitly a temporal one of duration or change, according to the enduring or temporary state of the objects we thus locate; whereas internal relations are only temporal, because we locate them inside rather than outside of our own material and sensory boundaries as subjects. "Unmediated" means, roughly, that there is no intermediary between us and the object with which we are in direct contact. The subject-object relationship is in the intuitive sense direct and unmediated in that we do not interpose any concept or theory or interpretation of the object between ourselves and it; we come into direct contact with it as it is, not as we might identify, interpret, or describe it.

In intuition, the subject and object thus related are both what contemporary philosophers of language would call "concrete particulars," in other words, actual, specific, concrete *things*, rather than examples of concepts or members of classes or subjects of interpretation or theory. They are the metaphysical kind of things we can physically grab—or, in the case of particularly vivid objects of imagination or memory, that can grab us. So the unmediated quality of our sensory relationship to such things is interdependent with their concrete particularity: It is because such things, as intuited, are only themselves and not any further property or conjunction of properties that we might then ascribe to them that no such further concepts, classes, or interpretations interpose themselves as mediators between us and them.

Kant argues that intuition alone is insufficient for knowledge (A 51/ B 75), and even for consciousness (A 99–104). Kant's claim that intuition is insufficient for knowledge follows directly from his definition of knowledge, which requires conceptualization, that is, the ability to ascribe properties to concrete particulars (A 106). In Kant's view, we cannot be said to know something unless we can identify it conceptually in some way. However, Kant also thinks that unless we can conceptualize a concrete particular as being of a certain kind, at least minimally as an object, it cannot enter a subject's unified consciousness at all but instead must remain "nothing but a blind play of representations, that is, less even than a dream" (A 112). Kant's idea here is that in order to be conscious of a concrete particular, we have to be able to recognize it as in some way familiar to us—in shape, color, texture, function, role, or *something* that enables us to connect it with the rest of our conscious experience, not only spatiotemporally, but also at higher cognitive levels.

This thesis is not implausible. It often happens that we can be looking right at something without seeing it, in case we are not primed to see it, and sometimes even if we are. This happens often enough with familiar, pedestrian objects such as keys or pencils. It happens even more frequently with conceptually unfamiliar or anomalous concrete particulars that are foreign to our conceptual scheme. This is the kind of thing such that, in order to visually cognize it at all, we first must be educated to see it, or—literally—to *re-cognize* it. We must be introduced to it, its defining properties must be verbally pointed out to us with considerable fanfare, and we must have its function or significance explained to us, so that the concrete particular that literally did not exist for us before this process of acculturation now becomes recognizable—as a sculpture, scalpel, cloud chamber, or person—minimally deserving of our attention. Once we become familiar enough with the thing to situate it within our preexisting conceptual scheme and extend our preexisting conceptual scheme sufficiently to accommodate it, the presence of this concrete particular then calls forth the relevant concepts, relations, and associations that in turn enable us to register it in consciousness and behave appropriately toward it. From Kant's thesis it would follow that without that familiarizing and acculturating process that enables us to conceptualize the concrete particular in recognizable terms, we cannot be aware of it at all.

Kant's thesis thus implies an interesting trade-off. Through intuition we can have direct and unmediated contact with a concrete particular, as it is, without the interference of any form of conceptual indoctrination—so long as we are prepared to relinquish the ability to theorize about it, to analyze and explain it in such a way as to situate it as an object of knowledge within our conceptual scheme. Alternately, through understanding we can perform all of these discursive functions that enable us intellectually to comprehend the object—so long as we are prepared to relinquish our direct and unmediated contact with it. But we cannot do both at once.

Traditional practices conjoined with such Indian philosophies as Yoga, Samkhya, Vedanta, or Buddhism illustrate how we might do each successively. The ancient philosophy of Samkhya that provides the metaphysical foundation for Yogic meditation offers a particularly rich and rigorous account of how, through the discipline of intensive meditation on a concrete particular at increasingly advanced levels, we gradually learn how to dismantle the rigid conceptual indoctrination that interferes with our direct and unmediated grasp of the reality that lies beyond the boundaries of the individual self.[3] But it rightly cautions that in the process of achieving this brand of insight into the true nature of concrete particulars, we eventually must leave the familiar activities of intellective conceptualization behind; and it warns us not to undertake this advanced practice until we are physically and psychologically ready to do this. Ordinarily this does not occur until we are fully comfortable, at the deepest psychological level, with the reality of our own imminent death. I shall return to this point later.

At the other end of the chronological continuum, we celebrate childhood precisely for its as yet relatively unencumbered access to that reality and to the creative imagination and insight into concrete particulars that as yet porous and inchoate boundaries of the individual self afford. In such fables as "The Emperor's New Clothes," we enshrine the value of an intuitive contact with material reality that is so immediate and uncorrupted by the conceptual indoctrination of culture, politics, and hierarchies of power and control that unvarnished empirical observations that issue from such intuition carry more power and authority than any

attempt at indoctrination could ever achieve. But the price of such innocence is, of course, the ignorance of these more complex social relationships that it precludes. Our natural curiosity to learn more about them,
combined with the more or less automatic forces of acculturation and
maturation, compel us to leave this intuitive immediacy behind as we
develop—rarely if ever suspecting, until it is much too late to retrieve it,
the Faustian bargain into which we have implicitly entered.

For the most discontented and ambitious of truth-seekers, neither
alternative is enough. It is not enough to enjoy intuition and understanding, or understanding and intuition consecutively, in either order of succession. Those of us who work at spinning a theory of everything crave
unmediated intuitive contact with the concrete particulars that will confirm it, and full scholarly respectability for that theory demands some
such empirical verification. Similarly, those of us who work at shedding
our theories of everything in order to achieve that direct and unmediated
contact crave an explanation that will make the resulting experience ratio-
nally intelligible, and full psychological adaptation to that experience requires *this*. These are the two horns of a dilemma: Each end of the
continuum between intuition and understanding impels us toward the
other; and each approach to the other impels us to try to recover what we
have had to sacrifice in order to make the journey. We instinctively want,
and need, both; yet each makes the other impossible in principle. Or so it
seems.

Contemporary artistic practice poses an interesting case against
which to test the soundness of Kant's thesis and the dilemma it appears to
engender. Contemporary artists bear a special relationship to intuition, in
Kant's technical sense, because they have unmediated intuitive access to
the material objects they create. Artists conjure spatiotemporally discrete
concrete particulars in thought and in reality that need not depend on any
specific conceptualizations of them; and that may simply come up in consciousness, present themselves fully developed with respect to detail, with
an urgency that demands their physical realization in advance of any conceptual interpretation that might enable one to explain, even to oneself,
why one feels driven to do so. Or one might conjure such an object through
an entirely spontaneous and unplanned physical process of exploring the
potential of a material or configuration of materials, such that the end result may have the same degree of urgency and importance for its maker,
independent of her ability to verbalize why it does or how she arrived at it.

One way of resolving the dilemma in this case is simply to conclude that, at least according to Kant's technical definition of knowledge, artists do not know what they are doing. They just do it and allot to the critics and art historians the task of figuring out what it means and why they bothered. This comforting interpretation, too, has some plausibility: Many artists do, indeed, find it extremely difficult to theorize about what they are doing while they are doing it. It may take years, if ever, before an artist can put together an intelligible commentary about his work that helps it to make sense to everyone else; and surely this is in part to be explained by precisely that direct, intimate, and unmediated relationship between the artist and the concrete particular he fashions. That particular is too complicated and overwhelming, too cryptic and multifaceted in its connections and associations, to be captured accurately in even the most fine-grained analysis—simplistic textbook descriptions and classifications of it notwithstanding.

Yet the purposeful character of the artistic process belies such a facile resolution and demands, at the very least, Bertrand Russell's distinction between knowing that and knowing how—in other words, between knowledge by description or propositional knowledge on the one hand and practical or applied knowledge by acquaintance on the other. The counterclaim then would be that although artists may not have propositional knowledge about the objects they make (at least not right away), they do have practical, hands-on knowledge of precisely the sort in which the intuitive relation to concrete particulars consists.

However, this distinction will not resolve the dilemma engendered by Kant's thesis, for several reasons. First, Kant rejects the distinction between knowing that and knowing how, and in fact reduces the first to the second. Propositional knowledge of facts, for Kant, is equivalent to the practical ability to do things—specifically, to do things mentally with concepts: to organize sense-data and the representations of objects and properties in a certain way and according to certain rules that ensure their objective status as objects of third person empirical investigation. In fact, concepts for Kant just are rules—or "functions" to use his term—for organizing the representations supplied by intuition systematically (A 68/B 93; A 70/B 95; A 76/B 102; A 80/B 106; A 106).[4]

Second, it is part of Kant's thesis that we cannot even be aware of such bare intuitive processes. Concrete particulars that do not fit the familiar categories by which we make the world and ourselves intelligible have nowhere in consciousness to land, and therefore they float around outside it, unmoored in one's unconscious.

Third, Russell's distinction does not explain the purposive character of artistic production—in other words, that one works long and hard and *deliberately and reflectively* to produce a spatiotemporally discrete concrete particular that has precisely the form it ends up having, independent of its compatibility with prevailing conceptual schemes or theories. This is a matter not merely (and sometimes not at all) of practical skill, but rather of vision—of a kind of knowledge that acquaints one directly with a concrete particular to which one has a form of access that is intuitive without necessarily being either conceptual or practical in any behavioral sense. When one is engaged in the process of bringing a work to material realization, there is something that one knows: not necessarily *that* something is the case, and not necessarily *how* to do something, but rather *when* the work is truly finished, when its final form has been achieved. This involves both knowing that at a particular moment it satisfies one's implicit criteria for completion and also knowing how to edge it to the point at which it does.

I propose that a deeper understanding of Kant's dilemma lies elsewhere in Kant's architectonic—specifically, in a closer look at the conditions Kant enumerates for the unity of the self. This will take us to those parts of the Transcendental Analytic and in particular of the Transcendental Deduction in A and B, in which Kant effectively rethinks the independence of intuition and understanding and finally offers an account in which the two are interdependent. From here I go on to question the extent to which these enumerated conditions of subjective unity can be said to hold—in the process of artistic production on the one hand and in yogic meditation on the other. I conclude that Kant's thesis and its implications are consistent and correct and that neither contemporary artistic practice nor yogic meditation provides a counterexample.

At A 89/B 122 to A 91/B 123, Kant entertains the possibility that concrete particulars might appear in consciousness without being subject to the hardwired categories of understanding that construct the objective empirical world of nature for us. This thought experiment is consistent with his mode of exposition in the Transcendental Aesthetic, for there he has developed an account of space and time as forms of our intuition and an account of the objects we situate therein without any reference to any requirements of conceptualization. It would seem that we could directly and consciously intuit a concrete particular as spatiotemporally discrete, independently of any further cognitive conditions it might have to satisfy in order to register in our awareness and independently of any further judgments we might make about it.

If we could be directly aware of concrete particulars without first having to exercise our capacity of judgment and understanding even in order to register them in conscious awareness, it might then seem possible to subject them, once there, directly to judgments of taste. Such judgments then would have a very unusual character indeed. They would be able to subsume a concrete particular, as it was in itself, directly and disinterestedly under concepts of beauty, form, balance, dimension, and the like, without the intervening necessity of first identifying it with regard to quantity, properties, material status, causal relations, or any more abstract theoretical concepts with which these are interconnected (A 651/B 679). If judgments of taste functioned in this way, not only would they fail to connect the concrete particular object of aesthetic judgment with the empirical and social context of relationships and associations within which the object was identifiable as a plausible candidate of such judgments, that is, as a work of art; but these judgments would also fail even to identify the concrete particular as an object. Judgments of taste of this kind would not only be very peculiar; they would also be incoherent.

Kant's Transcendental Deduction of the Categories is meant to demonstrate why this thought experiment itself is ultimately incoherent: In order for something even to constitute an identifiable empirical object of consciousness of any kind, whether mental or physical, we must understand it as, for example, a certain *quantity* of thing (one, many, everything); it must have certain sensible *qualities* that enable us to fix its type and degree of existence (Kant identifies the existence of the object with the fact that we can intuit sense-data from it at B 138–139); it must stand in certain basic *relations* to other things (its own properties, its causes and effects, its causal interconnections with other bearers of properties); and it must have a specific *modality* (as a possibility, an actuality, or a necessity) (A 80/B 106). No concrete particular that fails to satisfy any of these four requirements is recognizable as an empirical object at all, at least as we understand that notion.

Accordingly, we find Kant in both the A and B Deductions qualifying and revising the account of spatiotemporally discrete objects he offered in the Transcendental Aesthetic (A 99–100; B 136 fn; B 144 fn;

B 150–152; B 154 and fn; B 156; B 160 fn; B 160–162), and it is clear why he must. For even the notion of spatiotemporal discreteness presupposes satisfaction of the category-class of quantity. Even the notion of spatiotemporal location presupposes satisfaction of the category-class of relation. Even the notion of the object as sensible presupposes satisfaction of the category-class of quality. And even the notion of our bearing a direct and unmediated relation to it presupposes satisfaction of the category-class of modality. Hence the forms of intuition—space and time—are not independent of our ability to identify, conceptualize, and theorize about concrete particulars after all; and Kant's claim that we stand in direct and unmediated relation to the objects we intuit has more complex implications.

Of these implications, the most important for present purposes is that our relation to such objects is, indeed, unmediated by contingent, empirical concepts; but it is not unmediated by transcendental ones. The distinction, roughly, is this: *Empirical* concepts are the contingent and socially acculturated concepts by which we identify a particular empirical object, event, or state of affairs relative to the particular local context we ourselves inhabit. Other empirical concepts define that equally contingent and socially acculturated context itself. Empirical concepts must instantiate transcendental ones, because the objects and events they identify must meet the same necessary preconditions for experience. Those "transcendental concepts" or "categories" (Kant uses the terms interchangeably) are the ones enumerated above. These are the innate, hardwired concepts that any concrete particular must instantiate in order to count as an empirical object for us in the first place. By describing these categories as *a priori* and *necessary*, Kant means to call attention to certain basic features of them. They are a priori in the sense that they are hardwired preconditions for having coherent experience of any kind. And they are necessary in two senses: First, they are necessary for coherent experience of empirical objects, and, second, they are logically necessary.

No matter where one stands on the question of the credibility of Kant's table of categories, it would be a mistake to ignore the kernel of Kant's insight that there are certain basic logical principles that any coherent object of empirical experience must satisfy: First, there must be properties that can be ascribed to it, and, second, it cannot both bear and not bear those properties at the same time in the same respect. That is, any such object must satisfy the law of noncontradiction as formulated in predicate logic: $(x) \sim (Fx. \sim Fx).$[5] As Kant expresses it, "The categories . . . are concepts of an object in general, by means of which intuition in regard to the logical functions of judgment is seen as determined. Thus the function of the categorical judgment was the relation of subject to predicate, for example, 'All bodies are divisible'" (B 128). The significance of Kant's claim that the transcendental categories are necessary in this second sense is that it is in this second sense that the connection between the necessity of these concepts and their empirical objectivity is clearest: For good reason, we do, indeed, recognize the objectivity of the law of noncontradiction as valid independent of our wishes, our will, or our existence. Kant's claim of the objectivity of the transcendental categories is based on their fidelity to logical form, and it is this that enables him to propose them as the foundation for Newtonian science, and so for objective judgments about its objects of investigation. Hence there are certain kinds of judgments we are able to make about art objects in particular that have objective status as well.

To then claim that in intuition we stand in direct and unmediated relationship to objects is to say, first, that we stand in direct and unmediated relationship to the empirical objects that intuition (with the help of the categories) has enabled us to construct, and, second, that no contingent, socially acculturated empirical concepts, theories, or interpretations stand between us and them. The objects themselves are the result of the categories' mediation of the sense-data that intuition supplies; but there is no further empirical conceptual intermediary between those resultant objects and us. On this reading, one can have a direct and unmediated relationship to such objects and they can also find a place in consciousness. Intuition provides the direct access to them, and understanding locates them as objects in one's unified awareness. One's relationship to such objects contains elements of both.

With this clarification in hand, let us now reconsider the case of artistic practice. What kind of unmediated access do artists have to the material objects they create? And what is the nature of the intuitive knowledge that allows artists to conjure spatiotemporally discrete objects in advance of any conceptual identification or interpretation of the object that might be invoked to explain, either to themselves or others, the significance of doing so? Both questions have the same answer. For reasons depending on idiosyncrasies of personal development or social and historical circumstance, artists are deficient in socialization in at least one creatively useful way: They are able to see through the contingent empirical concepts by which we are taught to make sense of our social environment, and they choose to specialize in and develop this capacity. These contingent empirical concepts are the ones that are instilled in most of us so deeply that, other things equal, we lose the capacity to recognize the potential of objects, materials, and states of affairs to transcend them. Socialization this deeply rooted leads us to assume unquestioningly that the rules, roles, relationships, and functions of objects we learn in the process of acculturation are necessary ones: that a urinal can have only one function, that a target has only one role, that a skin color can have only one signification. The contingent empirical concepts in accordance with which we assign these unidimensional properties to objects of our experience mediate them not merely by interposing a conceptual scrim between us and them. They also constrain our thinking about every aspect of our surroundings, the familiar, mundane, and conventional.

Contemporary artists are both blessed and also cursed by their willfully insufficient indoctrination in these conventional empirical concepts (perhaps another symptom of the demise of family values). The blessing is to be able to see the anomalous or nonconventional potential of objects, materials, and states of affairs that is hidden to those who are blinded by them. The curse is to be able to see it and indicate or actualize it, without being able to communicate it in familiar terms and concepts one's audience can be expected to understand; to have to stand by, inwardly groaning and writhing, while one's audience first ignores it then flails about wildly, grabbing futilely and erroneously for some such familiar concepts with which to pin it down, and, finally, compresses those erroneous concepts into a twenty-five-words-or-less aphorism with which the work can be catalogued and dismissed. If any such configuration of familiar concepts and principles were in actual fact sufficient to communicate what an artist intuits, he would have no motive for producing the work. Because there is none, the work is destined for misunderstanding so long as his audience relies on them—as they must, in order to communicate with one another about the work. In this conversation, however, the artist is always a reluctant participant at best, having already said what he has to say by other means.

Thus the case of artistic practice does suggest an account of the type of knowledge involved in artistic practice: An artist's knowledge of the empirical object he creates is not propositional but neither is it necessarily practical in any full-blooded sense. Rather, it is intuitive. That means that it is conscious and reflective but nevertheless nonconceptual. It is the kind of knowledge one can have only when one's access to the empirical object is direct and unmediated by culture-bound empirical concepts or theories.

However, this account of artistic knowledge does not resolve the dilemma implied by Kant's thesis, that is, the mutual interconnection and simultaneous incompatibility of intuition and conceptual knowledge. For even if we confine our focus to contingent and culturally specific empirical concepts and theories, it remains true that either we invoke those concepts and theories to explain the concrete particular objects we intuit, in which case we lose the direct and unmediated access to them that intuition affords, or else we divest ourselves of those concepts and theories in order to recover it, in which case we lose the ability to make discursive sense of the resulting contact. This is the way many artists experience the dilemma.

But the dilemma has even more profound dimensions than this. For in order for intuition to bring us into unmediated relation to concrete particulars independent of *any* such conceptual knowledge, that relation itself must reach beyond the transcendental concepts with which even an artist's intuitive knowledge is saturated. That is, it must reach the concrete particulars of which it is true, according to Kant, that although we are in direct and unmediated intuitive contact with them, we nevertheless cannot have even the most minimal knowledge of them as objects: we cannot be consciously aware of them at all. These are the concrete particulars that Kant describes as "noumena," or *things in themselves*. In order to dissect the dilemma at this level, we need to examine more closely Kant's account of in what unified conscious awareness of objects consists.

Kant's conception of the basic structure of a unified consciousness (i.e., the *transcendental unity of apperception*) is grounded in his view of sense-data (i.e., the *transcendental manifold of intuition*) as consisting in singular representations. Were we to provide no systematic organization of the representations we receive in intuition from things in themselves, we would have no awareness of them. For to have awareness of anything, be it mental or physical, is to be able to distinguish the thing we are conscious of from ourselves; that is, the object of consciousness from the conscious subject who is aware of it. But in order to make this distinction, we first have to organize the representations we receive into an object distinct from us; and this, as we have seen above, requires that we arrange those representations according to the rules supplied by the categories of understanding (A 106, A 126). This process of organization Kant calls "transcendental synthesis," and the essence of this notion is that we combine individual representations into a nonarbitrary linear sequence that is given by the categories. So, for example, we situate representation r^1 before r^2, r^3 to follow r^2, r^4 to follow r^3, and so on, thus producing the linear sequence r^1, r^2, r^3, r^4, and so on.

However, this much gives us only a temporal sequence of representations in inner sense. Because this sequence need not meet any requirements of external spatial order, it can be, or seem, arbitrary, in exactly the way that so-called free association often is. In order for this sequence to be nonarbitrary, such that it constructs an external object of outer sense and situates it within the stable spatiotemporal matrix, we must further sort these representations into kinds according to the rules that the categories provide. So, for example, we retain representation r^1 in mind while situating r^2 next in line, and recognize it as *the same as* r^1; we retain r^2 and r^1 in mind while situating r^3 next in line, which we recognize as *the same as* r^2 and r^1; and so on. In so doing, we are using the category of substance (inherence and subsistence) to construct out of these multiple representations a single object that is the same at each moment i.e., that persists through time (A 99–102).

The representations that we thus synthesize into objects of consciousness can have one of two origins: They can originate within us, in sensory reaction to our own mental processes (B 153–155); or they can originate "from elsewhere in intuition" (B 145). Because we can have no unmediated access to things in themselves, including ourselves as we are in ourselves, we can have no way of knowing whether these two origins are mutually exclusive or mutually equivalent—in other words, whether or how many things in themselves there are. But what we can know is that these representations thus combine into identifiable mental content (B 103); that Kant uses the terms "content" and "matter" interchangeably (A 6, A 58/B 83); and that the "transcendental matter of things in themselves" is what corresponds to sensation in the subject (A 143/ B 182). Thus the representations we receive in intuition from those things and organize systematically in understanding, bring us into direct intuitive relation to noumena, or things in themselves, even though, according to Kant, we can have neither awareness nor understanding of them.

Now Kant ascribes consciousness solely to the coherently organized experience of a unified subject, that is, of an individual ego (B 134 fn.). If this assumption is correct, then of course it would follow from the further assumption that this unity is a hardwired *conceptual* unity that such a unified subject can have no direct contact with such things that is unmediated by any such hardwired concepts. However, Samkhyan philosophy disputes the ascription of consciousness to unified subjecthood; and dismantling the conceptual hardwiring that makes such contact impossible is precisely the goal of advanced yogic meditation.

Samkhya contends that consciousness is a function, not of the unified conceptual structure of the individual subject, or ego, but rather of the data that individual subjects may or may not receive in intuition as representations and then subject to that structure. In order to appreciate the Samkhyan thesis, it is useful to compare its form of dualism with Cartesian dualism (Fig. 13.1).

Both Cartesian and Samkhyan dualism make a sharp distinction between body and mind. Both regard the body as inherently insensate and as animated by consciousness. However, whereas Cartesian dualism locates consciousness in the mind, Samkhyan dualism identifies the mind with the same mechanical and insensate matter of which the body is constituted and instead locates consciousness in a state for which there is no analogue in Western philosophy, namely "purusha." The difference between the Cartesian concept of mind and the Samkhyan concept of purusha is that, first, Cartesian dualism regards the mind as nonmaterial and conscious, whereas Samkhyan dualism regards it as material and unconscious; and, second, Cartesian dualism regards consciousness as subjective and personal, whereas Samkhyan dualism regards it as objective and impersonal. It is because consciousness on the Samkhyan view is objective and impersonal, i.e., not a function of the individual subject's ego-unity that Samkhya can dispute Kant's ascription of consciousness to the unified subjecthood of the individual ego. On the Samkhyan view, the individual ego is part of the apparatus of the mind; and the mind, in turn, is not inherently conscious at all. Only its animation by purusha makes it appear to be so.

This is the illusion that advanced yogic meditation attempts to penetrate; and perhaps it is now clear why it is best not to undertake it unless and until one is comfortable with the imminence of one's own death. For the process of penetrating the illusion of individual ego-awareness is the

	Body	Mind	Purusha
	Material	Nonmaterial	
	Nature	Spirit	
	Unconscious	Conscious	
	Casually determined	Free	
Cartesian Dualism	Unintelligent	Intelligent	
	Transient	Enduring	
	Inanimate	Animating	
	Instrument	Agent	
	Personal	Personal	
	Object of consciousness	Subject of consciousness	
	Bhûtas, Tanmâtras:	*Ahamkâra, Buddhi:*	
	Material	Material	Nonmaterial
	Nature	Nature	Spirit
	Unconscious	Unconscious	Conscious
	Causally determined	Causally determined	Free
Samkhyan Dualism	Unintelligent	Unintelligent	Intelligent
	Transient	Transient thoughts + Persisting tendencies	Eternal
	Inanimate	Inanimate	Animating
	Instrument	Instrument	Agent
	Personal	Personal	Impersonal
	Object of consciousness	Object of consciousness	Subject of consciousness

Figure 13.1   Cartesian versus Samkhyan dualism

process of dismantling the conditions that purport to provide its subjective unity: the stable and coherent organization of its experience, the underlying conceptual functions that provide structure and intelligibility both to an external world and also to one's self, and the synthetic unity of the representations that simultaneously constitute both. In order even to undertake such a project, one must take for granted that the dismantling or death of the ego is not equivalent to the death of consciousness and therefore that the individual self and the consciousness that animates it are nonequivalent. One must also take for granted that the meditative practices by which the conceptual structure of the ego is dismantled will, in the end, lay bare precisely that direct and unmediated reality with which intuition connects us, which remains inaccessible to us so long as that conceptual structure remains in place.

In this undertaking Kant's account of synthesis (A 99–102) provides a detailed road map in reverse for both dismantling the conceptual structure of the individual ego and thereby achieving direct and unmediated contact with things in themselves—that is, things as they are in ultimate reality—because the two projects are in fact one and the same. We have seen that in these paragraphs of the Subjective Deduction in A, Kant describes in detail how we construct an enduring object out of intuitional representations that we situate in a nonarbitrary linear order, according to the rules provided by the transcendental conceptual functions. He goes on to state explicitly that the very same rules that provide objective structure to an object of consciousness and situate it in an external world of spatiotemporal and causal relations also provide structure and unity to the subjective consciousness that contemplates it (A 109). This should not be surprising, since all along Kant's account has treated only one set of intuitional representations, not two. It is not as though there were one set of representations that, properly systematized, constituted the subjective unity of the self and a different set that, similarly systematized, constituted the objective and enduring structure of the object. Kant's whole point is that there is only one set of representations that, properly systematized, simultaneously and interdependently constitute both. Tersely put, there are subjects if and only if there are objects of consciousness; dismantle the one and you automatically dismantle the other.

This is why yogic meditation begins at the most elementary level with concentration on a physical object and progresses to more advanced levels *only* once this one has been mastered. It is also why the familiar seven-seconds-per-artwork standard viewing time is so deeply entrenched in the viewing habits of the contemporary art audience. Looking, really looking at any object is hard work, and not just because we have so much else on our minds. It elicits enormous psychological resistance because the more deeply we penetrate into the hidden structure of the object, the more deeply we penetrate into the hidden structure of the self. The more fully and vividly we unpack the complex properties of the object, the more fully and vividly we take apart the complex structuring of the self. And the more intensely we are confronted with the concrete particularity of the object, the more we are brought face-to-face with the boundaries and limitations of an individual ego beyond which we rightly fear to venture. So in the end, no, there is no solution to the dilemma Kant's thesis engenders. The reason we cannot have both direct intuitive contact with and conscious knowledge of the ultimate reality of concrete particulars in themselves is that we would have to sacrifice our concrete particular ego-selves in order to enjoy it. That is a price that most art viewers are unwilling to pay.

Part III   Aesthetics in Artistic and Curatorial Practice

14

Seasonal Fractional Political
Idiosyncratic Aesthetics

Carolee Schneemann

SINCE MY 1991 ESSAY on censorship, cultural dilemmas impinging on my own work register subtle shifts. What lies ahead, lies behind. I am thinking now of *Who Paid the Piper? The CIA and the Cultural Cold War* by Frances Stonor Saunders, her 1999 Granta publication—a comprehensive analysis of the deeply embedded, invisible history by which America's international aesthetic dominance, was facilitated by systems of Cold War cultural support. Any debate on aesthetics is now shadowed by cultural tensions of the U.S. hierarchies: militarism still and again conflated with U.S. aesthetic supremacy. Tony Blair's government and the importance of British artists ride tandem with these couplings: investments, exhibits, production, grants, museum prominence, publications, etc. But considerations of aesthetics and personal censorship become increasingly paradoxical in the face of current U.S. erosions of the constitution—now that dissent is equated with terrorism. Habeas corpus, the core of democratic freedom, has been rescinded: The Patriot Act denies citizens rights to a fair trial, the torture bill can label any citizen whose allegiance is questioned "an enemy combatant," and the integrity of the Geneva convention is no longer viable.

As for censorship of my work, it barely abates. Recent installations and video have been widely exhibited, often accruing critical appreciation and economic rejection. The suppressions continue to be both explicit and obscured. There is always a sticky net of lies to untangle before the bloody-shamed fact. The work is not on the wall. Not in the exhibit. It did not arrive. It was lost. We couldn't find it. We were forced to remove

213

it—this photo grid, this painting/construction, this collage, this film, this video, that essay. And there is never a person to confront. They weren't here. They just left. We don't know what happened. The gallery is closed. It is no longer explicit images of my own physical actions, but the suppression and censorship of my images containing references to war, the disasters of 9/11, Iraq, Lebanon, Palestine.

Issues of race and gender, the retrieval of feminine iconographies that vitalized so much cultural energy of the 1970s, the rediscovery of ancient works, and the inclusion of a history of art created or influenced by women have been integrated as well as vitiated. Popular culture is currently more able to infiltrate and infantilize rigorous cultural principles, whereas up until the postmodern threshold, the most challenging aesthetic principles had some capacity to infiltrate, challenge, and elevate the materials and concepts absorbed by popular culture. Principles of the abject, of appropriation, have codified a welter of aesthetics of cynicism, vacuity, computer tricks, glamour, self-promotion, and grandiose production values.

Now that casual pornography occludes the sensory erotic, when political analysis is cowed and diverted, how can the principles of aesthetic perception, a reimagining, enter postapocalyptic technological visions or disruptive social insights? Where are our more inclusive countermodels? To what immeasurable extent do (or will) contemporary aesthetic issues confront the fascistic erosion of risk, dream, humanistic technologies, agrarian loss (Aphroditian, Arcadian), radicalizing materials? The most subversive and pleasurable aesthetic territory may be interactive art with its dissolution of formal boundaries: tactile, sensuous, often beautiful and didactic in content. Its very dazzling envelopment engages visitors and participants in visionary properties, computer codes, software, projection systems vitalizing space. My earlier installations of kinetic projections are now advanced by computer technologies. This is powerful magic freed from traditional codes, enlarging response and a physicalized dimensionality.

In November 2006 a comprehensive solo exhibit of two seminal works, "Interior Scroll" (photo grids and objects) and "Venus Vectors" (the large sculptural circle of printed Lucite panels with video projection), planned for the Living Art Museum in Reykjavik, Iceland, was cancelled two weeks before the work was to be shipped, after a year of preparation and approval. "Interior Scroll," vilified and valorized endlessly.

In "Devour" (2004), a multichannel video projection, a range of images are edited to contrast evanescent, fragile daily elements with violent,
concussive, speeding fragments. Looped sources of the imagery combine
political disasters, domestic intimacy, and ambiguous menace within enlarged details of gestures—both human and mechanical. Exhibited in
New York at two prestigious galleries, "Devour" received no critical reviews until its subsequent showings in Montreal and Vancouver. ("Devour" was a featured installation in spring 2007 for my solo exhibit at
Toronto's Museum of Contemporary Canadian Art.)

With "Terminal Velocity" (2001), I scanned sequences of newspaper
images from 9/11 to consecrate nine people—among the hundreds—falling
to their inescapable deaths. Computer processes allowed intimate contact
with each figure's isolation in the desolate shifting space. In this communal nightmare, enlarged visual attributes become vivid, unexpectedly captured, made public. These sequences personalize individuals who in their
normal workday were thrown by impact into a gravitational plunge or
chose to escape incineration by leaping into space. The reception to this
memorial work had been violent—outrage—in which signage in the gallery was destroyed and obscenities scrawled in the guest book. Invulnera-
bility and triumph are deeply held as an American certainty. "Terminal
Velocity" has also received passionate critical appreciations. What next?
And what went before!

What follows is a revised version of an essay I wrote in 1991; it presents the (still) underlying patterns of exclusion and censorship.[1]

The Obscene Body Politic

Bullets of projection are aimed into our bodies: Trajectories of phal-
locratic apprehension produce our "wounds." A smoking gun grasped in
that frozen hand. There's a cock/dick tracing this Saturday Night Special
directed at our "privates." Word play / gun play focus sexual frame-up, the
dissolve, deception—the veritable sleight of hand, by which patriarchal
culture constructs its myths, imposes superstitions on the differences between the erotic and the obscene.

In 1964 censorship danced around my Kinetic Theater work, *Meat
Joy*, which I thought of as an erotic rite to *enliven* my guilty culture.
Conceived for the Festival of Free Expression in Paris, organized by
Jean-Jacques Lebel, it was first performed there, at the Centre Culturel

Américain, then in London, and then at Judson Memorial Church in New York, where I had previously choreographed for the Judson Dance Theater and developed other Kinetic Theater works. I had intended the performers to be nude; the moral decency rules in France at that time stipulated that naked male and female performers were subject to arrest *if they moved*; they could remain in the frozen positions of statues without breaking the law. In New York, moving or frozen nudes in public were forbidden. I devised scanty feather-and-fur coverings.

Projection deforms perception of the female body. As bizarrely consecrated in Western creation myths as Athena emerging from Zeus's head; as usurpative of Mother Right as the birth of Dionysus from his father's thigh; as biologically contorted as a Lord Jesus born from the body of a virgin mother. Political and personal violence against women is twined behind/within this stunting defeminization of history. For many of us, the layers of implicit and explicit censorship constructing our social history combine with contemporary contradictions to force our radicalization.

We (women) read, write, research, produce, or lead otherwise creative lives with more public recognition than ever before. These are good times for most of us who will not be torn from our childhood sleep for a brutal clitoral excision, will not endure the probable fifteen pregnancies of our fertile years (forbidden contraception or abortion), and are therefore less likely to die giving birth. We will not be burned as witches or sold into slavery, and even the most transgressive among us may evade being locked up in an asylum. At the same time, however, it is still true that about one out of four of us will be subjected to rape.[2]

Work of women in the arts is fueled by three thousand years of fracture—the "masculinist" enforcement of self-righteous institutionalizations that have dogged our heels. My anger, when I first discovered this subtle and pervasive censorship, this excision, paralleled my later rage and confusion at being denied a feminine pronoun (The artist . . . , *he* . . . Everyone will hand up *his* hat . . . Creative man and his images) and upon discovering that my culture denies females an honorable genital. My sexuality was idealized, fetishized, but the organic experience of my own body was referred to as defiling, stinking, contaminating. Bible study and graffiti under the train trestle shared a common deprecation. *History*, *sexuality*, and *naming* were subsumed, contorted. I would have to be "a spy in the house of art."[3]

Feminist work, in theory, in activism, and in art practices, has been exposing and explicating the ways in which our history had been displaced, lost, and splintered as well as the ways we now integrate our creativity and sexuality. Women artists explore erotic imagery because our bodies exemplify a historic battleground—we are dismantling conventional sexual ideology and its punishing suppressions—and because our experience of our bodies has not corresponded to cultural depiction.

My early work was suppressed and excluded in various confusing ways. First, a nude self-portrait was accepted and then barred from a student exhibition at Bard College. Then, a painting of my companion (boyfriend, James Tenney), naked and asleep, became the object of jokes by faculty and students because of the inclusion of his penis (as an attribute of an actual male person they knew). Next, a gallery invited me to exhibit and subsequently rejected to present a nude photographic sequence titled "Eye Body," made in 1963. At that time the female nude dwelled mainly in girlie magazines, pornographic detective fictions, photographic reports on "primitive natives," classical Western painting, abstract expressionist dismemberments, and the iconic, frontal-spread paper dolls of pop art. I asked myself, "Could there be any other erotic iconography?"

"Eye Body" showed that it was possible. In 1962 I created a loft environment, built of large panels of interlocked, rhythmic color units, broken mirrors and glass, lights, motorized umbrellas. I then wanted to combine my actual body with this work, as an integral material—a further dimension to this construction, a ritualized set of physical transformations. The work that resulted was "Eye Body," which captured images of a shamanic ritual of the sacred erotic.

Covered in paint, grease, chalk, ropes, plastic, I establish my body as visual territory. Not only am I an image-maker, but I explore the image values of flesh as material I choose to work with. The body may remain erotic, sexual, desired, desiring but it is as well votive: marked, written over in a text of stroke and gesture discovered by my creative female will.[4]

Among the thirty-six "transformative actions" of "Eye Body," one photograph of me is a frontal nude with two garden snakes crawling on my torso. Only later, when I further researched early gynocratic cultures, did the affinity of this image to that of the Cretan serpent goddess become apparent. Disturbing and attractive because of its association with an archaic eroticism, its contemporary confrontation with taboos remains to be addressed.

A startling aspect of this image of my naked body is a visible clitoris in *Eye Body—36 Transformative Actions* (1963). Western art history has been obsessed with the female nude, but the image of a contemporary artist as a genitally sexed nude provokes a round of inquisition: What is the meaning of this "obscene" image? Why is it in the art world rather than the "porno" world? Images such as this one from "Eye Body" became classic referents as feminist art historians explored the sacred erotic, the shamanic body, and archetypal linkage to ancient goddess figures, which I had not yet seen in 1963. But the initial reaction of curators and critics I then respected was that these images were narcissistic and lewd. I was told: "If you want to run around naked, don't bother the art world; if you want to paint, go and paint."

A measure of this Western psychosis was clarified when I realized there were only two roles offered for me to fulfill: either that of "pornographer" or that of emissary of Aphrodite. Both elude political and social affect insofar as these roles both function as dumping grounds that cloud constructed for our active group of nine performers.

In both the Paris and New York audiences, informants from the local police stations and from various "moral decency" groups were present. A truncated version of the *Meat Joy* (1964) performance at Vauxhall in London ended abruptly when police entered one door as we performers exited another, covered in blankets, to be hidden on the floors of cars speeding away. During the Paris performance a man from the audience came onstage, pushed me against the wall, and tried to strangle me. I was saved by three older women who had never seen any performance, but were convinced that this assault was not part of it.

"Eye Body" (1963), *Meat Joy* (1964), and my film *Fuses* (1965), form a trio of works whose shameless eroticism emerged from within a culture that has lost and denied its sensory connections to dream, myth, and the female powers. The very fact that these works remain active in the cultural imagination has to do with latent content that the culture is still eager to suppress.

How could a twenty-four-year-old artist insist, *"This* is the truth"? Other artists might have had a sense of affiliation with the power of my images, but from 1963 to 1964 there was no theoretical structure to ground what I was doing, no feminist analysis to redress masculinist tradition, no

overt Jungian connection to a communal unconscious, no semiotic or anthropological scan of archetypes that could link our visual images to what
I called then "primary cultures" (detesting the expression "primitive").

It is also important to remember that there were no funding sources
for "performance art" in the 1960s; the term, the concept, did not exist.
There were wild, crazy Happenings, Fluxus, and Events—all produced
with available trash, found objects, and willing collaborators. If we had
then been applying to government agencies to support us, would forms of
self-censorship have restricted our use of degraded materials or impinged
upon our considered disregard for the comfort of the audience? We came
up out of the shadow world, identified with the suppressed irrational elements of our culture. Our work seized dynamic implications of abstract
expressionism to extend the active visual surface of painting into actual
physical space and time and to dematerialize the frame, the object, the
aesthetic commodity.

There is something female about performance art itself—the way
the body carries form and meaning into ephemeral space and actual
time; the admittance of unconscious, forbidden material, dependent on
self-exposure, self-display. There is a female sense of associative margins
in which artists are a raw material, as nature is, moving freely in realms
of the uncontrollable and suppressed. Performance developed generative
forms without prescriptive mastery: expected (phallic) shaping. Interior-
ity was our nexus, the source of discovery and of our sense of the immediacy of our physicality. Somewhere in the psyche these things
connect with femaleness. Performance art embraced a wide range of
taboos and social issues in a very brief time because it was an open territory. The art world—the art industry (galleries, collectors, magazines,
critics, art departments)—had been wary of performance art. We were
hard to commodify. We sprang out of the canvas and left them holding
the brush, weighted as it was with the expressionistic painters' rending of
private self into public event. I arrived in New York just in time to see my
older painting heroes drunk, fighting, fucking, jumping through win-
dows (sometimes in my loft), crashing their cars enacting heroics that
diverted castration fantasies into symbolic inviolability. Most of the young
guys I followed in initiating Happenings and Fluxus (the root of performance art) soon returned to sculpture and painting; by returning to
objects they stabilized the economic direction of their careers. Claes Old-
enburg, Jim Dine, and Red Grooms stopped performing early on; Al

Hansen, Robert Whitman, and Allan Kaprow at times still presented a performance or event; the Fluxus artists continue to produce both objects and actions. Among the women from my first years in New York—Yoko Ono, Alison Knowles, Charlotte Moorman, Marta Minujin, Yayoi Kusama—we have persisted in making an admixture of objects, installations, and actions.

I began shooting my erotic film, *Fuses*, in 1964. Since my deepest expressive and responsive life core was considered obscene, I wondered if my own visions would displace the pornographic. I had never seen any erotica or pornography that approached what lived sexuality felt like. Teaching myself to make this film with borrowed wind-up Bolexes meant that lovemaking sequences had thirty seconds of film time, thus enforcing my own collage aesthetic.

The need to see, to confront sexual shibboleths was also an underlying motive for my performance *Interior Scroll*, more than ten years later, in 1975. I didn't want to pull a scroll out of my vagina and read it in public, but the culture's terror of my making overt what it wished to suppress fueled the image; it was essential to demonstrate this lived action about "vulvic space" against the abstraction of the female body and its loss of meanings.

I thought of the vagina in many ways—physically, conceptually, as a sculptural form, an architectural referent, the source of sacred knowledge, ecstasy, birth passage, transformation. I saw the vagina as a translucent chamber of which *the serpent was an outward model*. Enlivened by its passage from the visible to the invisible: a spiraled coil ringed with the shape of desire and generative mysteries, with attributes of both female and male sexual powers. This source of interior knowledge could be symbolized as the primary index unifying spirit and flesh in goddess worship. I related womb and vagina to primary knowledge, recorded as earliest history with strokes and cuts on bone and rock. By these marks, I believe, my ancestor measured her menstrual cycles, pregnancies, lunar observations, agricultural notations—the origins of time factoring, of mathematical equivalences—of abstract relations.

Censorship and pornography are blood brothers. We will never find one without the other. If my paintings, photographs, film, and enacted works have been judged obscene, the question arises: Is this because I use the body in its actuality—without contrivance, fetishization, displacement? Is this because my photographic works are usually self-shot, without an external, controlling eye? And are these works obscene because I posit my female body as a locus of autonomy, pleasure, desire and insist that as an artist I can be both image and image maker, merging two aspects of a self deeply fractured in the contemporary imagination? The prohibition of performance works with anti–Vietnam War themes in the 1960s and early 1970s was most extreme. When an audience for my Kinetic Theater piece *Illinois Central* (Chicago, 1968) was prevented by authorities from seeing the performance, the U.S. Information Agency, the fire department, police, local real-estate executives, and the sponsoring staff and trustees of the Museum of Contemporary Art were involved. *Illinois Central* developed from my anti–Vietnam War performance *Snows*. *Snows* had been performed at the Martinique Theater, in Greeley Square in New York, as part of Angry Arts Week, February 1967. A collaboration with Bell Telephone Laboratory engineers permitted the development of an electronic switching system for the performance, by means of which audience reactions could trigger electrical relays to activate 16-mm projectors edging the stage, tape decks with collaged sound, revolving lights, and, in turn, the cues for six performers. Central to *Snows* was my film *Viet-Flakes*, composed from an obsessive collection of Vietnam atrocity images I had clipped from newspapers and foreign magazines over a five-year period. I had taped close-up lenses and magnifying glasses to an 8-mm camera lens to make it physically "travel" within the photographs, producing a rough form of animation. *Snows* was influential in heightening moral outrage at the war. And while this Kinetic Theater work was not censored in any overt way, I believe its reputation led to the disastrous interferences in, and eventual closure of, *Illinois Central.* In Chicago a full complement of permits and city approvals was finally not sufficient to keep the fire department from preventing an audience of two hundred people from entering the abandoned bakery loft we had struggled to prepare, over several weeks, with a 360-degree slide-relay projection of Illinois horizons by Art Sinsabaugh, juxtaposed with my slides of devastated Vietnam landscapes.

 Illinois Central later toured the East Coast, as part of "Inter Media '68,'" produced by John Brockman. At the Brooklyn Academy of Music our performance was disrupted by screaming "plants" (police provocateurs) and provoked a fistfight in the audience. Other forms of sabotage dogged the tour.

 What agency was behind the passing out of hundreds of cups of sangria laced with LSD as I was directing an International Festival in

London, in 1969, in honor of the Chicago Eight? Newsreels, films, performances, musicians, and staff dissolved in acid chaos.

My film *Fuses* has been subject to constant censorship at its showings, despite its special awards in Cannes in 1968 and at the Yale Film Festival in 1972. My art exhibitions have also provoked censorious measures. In 1981 disclaimers were placed at the gallery entrance at Real Art Ways, in Connecticut, for my exhibition "Image/Text"; photo-text works were removed from a group exhibition in Philadelphia in 1976; offending flyers were removed from the Whitney Museum Downtown exhibition "Nothing but Nudes" in 1977. But in some ways implicit censorship is harsher than the overt form: exclusion from exhibitions, denial of grants and teaching positions, the suppression of publicity and controversy itself.

It's interesting that twenty-five years after *Fuses* was made it could be both censored and shown uncensored at the 1989 Moscow Film Festival and could receive its most intensive structural analysis in David James's *Allegories of Cinema*—an analysis in which my motives and methods are fully contextualized (complementing Scott MacDonald's *A Critical Cinema*). *Fuses* was included in a United States–Soviet joint venture program for the Moscow Film Festival, titled "Sexuality in American Films." (The selections from the United States were made by the San Francisco International Film Festival, which has had a long association with the Soviet film agency KINO.) This program presented Philip Kaufman's *Unbearable Lightness of Being* as a feature, *Trash* by Paul Morrissey, *Working Girls* by Lizzy Borden, *She's Gotta Have It* by Spike Lee, *Beyond the Valley of the Dolls* by Russ Meyer, *Desert Hearts* by Donna Deitch, *Sex, Lies, and Videotape* by Stephen Soderbergh, Mark Huestis's program on AIDS, *Heavy Petting* by Obie Benz, and three shorts by James Broughton. Only *Fuses*, after an unscheduled opening-night screening, was canceled from subsequent planned showings (and finally screened unannounced, after pressure from the U.S. organizers). Among all these films, only *Fuses* hit a taboo button in perestroika.

In the United States and the Soviet Union, patriarchal gender constructions systematize the transference and mystification lurking within the idealization of the arts. We are looking at different forms of denial and censorship: One form instigates public outrage, outcry; the other acts as a slow smothering, a constraint. In the former (typically U.S.) instance you may have to fight to protect the immediate fate of your work; in the latter, you have to wait it out, persist, live in the basement.

Censorship breaks your integrity; it is sinister because the work is both physically endangered and engaged in a falsification of motive. In Moscow I struggled against invisible powers and was always the fool because I didn't know where my enemy was. The Russian organizers were cordial, and gracious, and every day they had increasingly unbelievable stories as to why the showing of *Fuses* was postponed or canceled. I was fortunate to have a translator who became a defender, aggressive on behalf of the film. Every time a screening of *Fuses* was diverted he would arrange for TV and print journalists to be present: We would hold interviews about pornography. There seemed to be no context to support a female erotic vision.

One TV interview was conducted under the direction of a small, round woman in her sixties, who arrived at my hotel room with a full crew. She was the head of the sexual education program in the Soviet Union. She introduced the interview: Then Vladimir, my translator, translated her questions and my responses. She smiled approvingly, looking into my eyes as she spoke into the microphone. "What's she saying?" I asked Vladimir. He paused. "She's saying you are a pornographer and a dangerous woman."

Censorship is usually anonymous; you never see its source exactly. Censors are wily and often capricious. Without question, many of my works of the past fifteen years were realized with grants from the National Endowment for the Arts, which supported both production and presentation in sponsoring spaces (themselves supported with National Endowment for the Arts [NEA] funds). These performances, films, and sculptural installations could all be considered erotically or politically objectionable at some level of our society. No other Western industrialized country treats art with our degree of paternalistic suspicion, envy, and greed to possess or uses our system's fitful "allowances" to finance it. (On a radio talk program a man called in and stated: "The whole attack on the NEA is a smoke screen. We don't have any more Commies to distract us from government corruption, so let's go after the artist.")[5]

To what extent does erotic content subvert the formal properties of my work? Can its sexual base penetrate existing aesthetic issues with new meanings?

The disavowal and proscription of essentialism by academic critics has left much of my recent work in suspension. Are there structures of evasion within feminist analysis? How has the female erotic body entered into semiotic discourse? For instance, is the lack of attention to two of my recent works, the 1988 installation, *Venus Vectors*, in which the unraveling of two (menstrual) dream symbols situates a visual morphology of vulvic form, and *Infinity Kisses*, a recent photo series of my cat, Cluny, and me that raises the issue of "inappropriate eroticism" and interspecies communication, an act of censorship?

Censorship is flexible, responsive, motile, adaptive; boundaries of prohibitions are shifted, redefined. Women artists have been censored by exclusion for centuries. But what about the *other* "Others"? What of the artists so socially marginalized, so ignored as to elude acceptable controversy and *its* possible censorship? While a few of us are bathed in (or blinded by) the lights of a concerned media, entire outreach teaching programs, local galleries, and studio and performance spaces in the unglamorous places we call "barrio," "ghetto," "reservation," "inner city," "cultural backwater" have already been cut off from public funding; they no longer exist, much less make trouble.

The NEA as a government institution has been captured and dissolved by rigid, authoritarian elements of the suppressive right. We who are about to be censored (yet again) must reestablish our community to consider the artists among us who, denied overt censorship, are relegated to obscurity even before they have made their mark. Issues of ethnicity, sexuality, radical politics that challenge the grip of an investment ethics, may still be denied a significant place in deepening aesthetic discourse.

WE WHO ARE ADDRESSING THE TABOOS BECOME THE TABOO. THE SUPPRESSORS ARE CONFUSED. THEY CANNOT DISTINGUISH IMAGES FROM THE IMAGE MAKERS.

15

Toward an Ophthalmology of the Aesthetic and an Orthopedics of Seeing

Robert Morris

Speculating beyond the little that is known, we might take the mind/brain to be a complex system with a highly differentiated structure, with separate "faculties," such as the language faculty, those involved in moral and aesthetic judgment.

Noam Chomsky[1]

AESTHETIC AND MORAL FACULTIES—two or one? Chomsky says "those," so maybe he means two. Does it make a difference? One or two, we have here innate capacities to respond to the environment in ways not concerned with truth predications. Charles Sanders Peirce's holism would have cemented the two together at the external level, as well as given the aesthetic more weight to bear, when he said, "aesthetics is the science of ideals, or of that which is objectively admirable without any ulterior reason . . . Ethics, or the science of right and wrong, must appeal to aesthetics for aid in determining the summum bonum. It is the theory of self-controlled, or deliberate, conduct. Logic is the theory of self-controlled, or deliberate, thought; and as such must appeal to ethics for its principles."[2]

Bertrand Russell, while not linking the aesthetic to the moral, might have been more sympathetic to Chomsky's innate notions when he said that "a priori knowledge is knowledge as to ethical value."[3]

Immanuel Kant tied the aesthetics of the sublime to the moral when he said that "in the case of the sublime the link to morality is not, as it is in the case of the beautiful, merely explanatory or interpretive. Here this link justifies the claim of judgments about the sublime to universal validity, on the (legitimate) presupposition that man does in fact have moral feeling."[4] He links the faculty for such a response not to the culture that shapes and conditions it but to the innate when he notes that the response is not "initially produced by the culture and then introduced to society by way of (say) mere convention. Rather, it has its foundation in human nature."[5] The feeling for the sublime in nature is tied to "a mental attunement similar to that for moral feeling."[6]

The early Ludwig Wittgenstein said that "ethics and aesthetics are one and the same."[7]

Do we have a reference yet for the aesthetic? Beyond pointing to its innate nature, do we need anything more precise? Donald Davidson's holism would dispense with reference.[8] Chomsky echoes Davidson when he says that words are used to refer to things and to talk about them, but "it is quite a leap to conclude that the words refer to these things."[9] Certainly complex terms such as "aesthetic" need no precision. Rather they provide "a complex perspective from which to think about, talk about, and refer to things, or what we take to be things."[10]

The aesthetic: an innate faculty, a capacity concerned with affective responses. Leave it at that. What has been endowed in us by what Hume called "the hand of nature" may be beyond introspection and conscious human knowledge.[11] Kant cautioned that the "schematism of our understanding, in its application to appearances and their mere form, is an art concealed in the depths of the human soul, whose modes of activity nature is hardly likely ever to allow us to discover, and have open to our gaze."[12] *So far art has not come through the door. But it hovers in the hall and I can hear its heavy breathing.**

Gottlob Frege ushered in the "linguistic turn" coincident with the turn of the twentieth century by asserting that only in the context of a sentence does a word have meaning. Analytic philosophy is born out of the conviction that only the sentence delivers truth. Frege's analysis of how the sense of a sentence is prior to delivering a posterior reference, which locates its truth value, was problematic but influential. The early Wittgenstein was influenced by Frege, and in the *Tractatus* he tried to establish the priority of sense over reference. In any case meaning and truth are bound together in the Fregean analysis. As Michael Dummett has

---

* This italicized passage, and later ones, function as an "alternative voice" or perspective on the main text.

noted, "Almost anything could be taken as rendering some sentence true: it depends on what the sentence means."[13] The history of analytic philosophy could be written in terms of attempts to define truth and meaning. By assigning meaning to use the later Wittgenstein displaces the concept of truth as central to meaning.[14]

In 1927 Frank Ramsey put forth his "redundancy theory," which argues that assertions of "is true" add nothing to assertions of fact and, pending some difficulties that Ramsey thought could be overcome, could be eliminated from statements. The redundancy theory is the simplest of a class of theories termed "deflationary." In general deflationists see truth as a property of sentences rather than of propositions. Truth is regarded as a not metaphysically deep term. Donald Davidson is perhaps the most well-known recent thinker associated with the deflationary. He regarded truth as a primitive concept, left it undefined, but considered it central to his theory of meaning. Since the mission of philosophy, as generations and generations have seen it, has been to deliver truth, the radicalness of the deflationary stance is striking.

The question is: Can the deflationary be generalized as a strategy that is operative outside the confines of analytical philosophy? Could the deflationary name a strategy that certain earlier philosophers shared? Could it be broadened to other areas of the culture? Is the deflationary as a strategy summed up in Kenneth Surin's remark that it is "the desire to deflate or make transparent our recourses to principles that confer on our thinking this or that manifestation of invariance and stability"?[15] Or is the deflationary much more negative and aggressive than a mere desire for transparency? Could the desire in question be one of Nietzschean negation? Davidson's desire to squeeze truth down to a kind of primitive squeak that carries meaning on its back would seem to go beyond a concern for transparency. And Davidson's infamous remark, "that there is no such thing as a language, not if language is anything like what many philosophers and linguists have supposed,"[16] sounds Nietzschean to me. I think the notion of the deflationary has to be broadened and refocused to include an underlying negativity. Philosophizing with an attitude, a combative, takedown attitude. It could be argued that Socrates' program was mainly negative. If so, he started it all. But deflation is much more than aggressive negation. It involves the dismantling of those boundary presuppositions of implicit limits that are assumed to be necessary for activity in a given field. Paradoxically, the negations of the deflationary have the function of the *Aufhebung* (sublation) and subsequently open up the field for new production. This binding of "removal" and "renewal" suggests the neologism "removal" as a term for this contradictory phenomenon.

There is a commotion in the room next door making it difficult for me to concentrate here. I hear loud arguing, banging on the wall, and sounds of pushing and shoving. It seems that Ace wants to get into the room and take the chair beside Art. Big D, the deflationary, is blocking the door and yelling at the Aesthetic, whom they call Ace. "Get out, bitch!" Big D yells. Art is shoving Big D away from the door. "She just wants to sit down and visit," Art says. "Yeah, yeah, sit in your lap, you mean," Big D says. "I can't stand the two of you making eyes at each other." But Ace has slipped inside and is running around knocking over chairs. Big D's mascot, Little T, is yapping and whimpering at the commotion and pulling at its leash. Real pandemonium next door.

Analytic cubism of 1909–1911 would be the first twentieth-century deflationary manifestation in the arts. And, characteristic of the deflationary, it manifests the dualism of removal. Cubism opens toward a new production while the consequences of its negativity take some time to surface. In cubism the world of light, that world of previous painters, is converted into mud, into black and white and brown. Painting involuntarily impoverishes itself in order to become combative, to go against the world in a way representation never had before. There is great pathos in this assertion by negation. T. J. Clark sees this attitude as one in which the work was done "under the sign of failure."[17] That is, the failure to remake representation. In cubism the image of the body is flattened into a kind of map comprised of irresolvable convex/concave planes that hinge together and multiply across the surface. A shallow spatiality flickers here that speaks of confinement and flatness more than space. Space is negated, or rather what little is allowed suggests its imminent absence. A profound skepticism legislates the airless compression that flickers between figure and ground in these half-burials of the figure beneath shallow planes scattered across the surface like dead leaves. Analytic cubism is a denial of modernism's transcendent and utopian spirit. Of course a profound sense of anxious doubt is already there in those last works of Paul Cézanne, which so inspired Georges Braque and Pablo Picasso. Analytic cubism lasted only a few years. Synthetic cubism set aside the pessimism that saturated the analytic period, and the removal cycle was set in motion.

The anthropologist Colin M. Turnbull studied and lived with the Pygmies of central Africa in the 1950s. The "Molimo" was an object spoken of with both awe and amusement. It was brought out in times of crisis and could be seen only by the men; women would be struck blind, so they said, if they laid eyes on this object of great reverence. Turnbull assumed it was the one great Pygmy art masterpiece. "I had expected an object elaborately carved, decorated with patterns full of ritual significance and symbolism, something sacred, to be revered, the very sight or touch of which might be thought of as dangerous. I felt that I had a right, in the heart of the tropical rain forest, to expect something wonderful and exotic. But now I saw that the instrument . . . was not made of bamboo or wood, and it certainly was not carved or decorated in any way. It was a length of metal drainpipe."[18]

In 1964 I attended a panel discussion at the Museum of Modern Art. The panel members were Marcel Duchamp, William Rubin, and Alfred Barr. Rubin questioned Duchamp in a scholarly, if overly loud way, while Barr nearly whispered in his misty-eyed reverence. The discussion turned to the readymades. Duchamp claimed that he never really understood them, only that he was inherently lazy but felt that from time to time he should nevertheless make some art. He once referred to himself as a defrocked artist. So he, Duchamp, made appointments with himself: on such and such a day, he would just have to make art. When the day arrived, he would choose something just to get it over with, and that would be that. A readymade: not an object he had labored over or crafted, but a mass-produced artifact available to anyone. "But how did you go about this?" Rubin asked. "Well, I would usually find myself in a hardware store on these days. I would look around and choose something. That would be the readymade," Duchamp replied. Ever the academic, Rubin persisted, "But what criteria were employed in the selection of the object?" "Well, I tried to predict which object there I might always remain indifferent toward, and that would be the one I would select," Duchamp said. At this point, Barr piped up and said, "But, oh, Marcel, why do they look so beautiful today?" Duchamp turned toward him and said, "Nobody's perfect."[19]

Thierry de Duve has pointed out that the readymades of Duchamp nominalized the term art, demoting it from a concept to a name.[20] Big-time deflation here. The readymade delivered a blow from which art never really recovered, not to mention the license it extended for the production of mountains of the most egregious art. But the removal cycle makes way for renewed production, which is almost invariably oblivious to the negative insights of the deflationary act. Of course, the possibility exists that Duchamp may not have been telling the truth about his indifference. The bottle rack, the snow shovel, the urinal, the bicycle wheel . . . Was Alfred Barr right, aren't they all "beautiful"? (And weren't they beautiful from the beginning?) Could the aesthetic have been holding Marcel's hand there in the hardware store? After all, Marcel did not object that Barr was wrong. Rather he seemed to be saying that he, Duchamp, had failed. Our perception, being functionally selective, does not allow the experience of chaos. And our choices? We know what we like (a privilege we share with all the lower animals, as Oscar Wilde re-marked), and we know what repels us. Our affective responses have an immense range and the aesthetic response can and has also been elicited by destruction and violence.[21] But doesn't the notion of choice based on nonaffective indifference suggest the oxymoronic? Do we just want to think that the aesthetic can be liposuctioned out of art? If so, don't we have here a misplaced philosophical longing for a testosterone-drenched strategy that could banish the aesthetic? Don't we genderize a masculine philosophy and a feminine art by making such an opposition? If so, how bizarre, given *Rose Sélavy* and all those "ready-maids."

Take a few ordinary kitchen matches, dip them in paint, and, by means of a toy cannon, shoot the matches at a large sheet of glass. Then drill holes in the glass where the paint marks show up. Photograph three squares of gauze ruffled by air currents and use these as patterns. Well, more or less "presto," Duchamp introduced a note of chance into art making in the *Large Glass*. Better, drop three one-meter-long threads from the height of one meter, use these to make templates . . . But do threads really fall into such lovely parabolic curves as displayed in Duchamp's *3 Stoppages-Etalon* (1913–1914)? No matter how gravity behaves or was assisted here, it is what is said about the intention that raises a large sign that reads CHANCE.

The party in the next room is getting loud and there is more banging on the wall. I can hear Big D yelling at Ace, whom he insists on calling "Ms. Ace," in his loud, gravelly voice. The note of contempt is obvious. Ace has grabbed the mascot's leash and is running around the room trying to get Little T to jump over chairs. Art is on a fourth vodka in the corner and looking really out of it.

Given: an aesthetic waterfall and illuminating gas lighting up the readymades. This only lends them the aura Barr saw, an aura they deserve. Barr's judgment was only exercising an innate faculty. True, the dampness and gaseous haze of the aesthetic shrinks their tough, deflationary dimension somewhat. Still, the subtraction of labor and the reduction of art-making to mere choice (whatever the criterion) is deflationary enough. And the accusation that Donatello cast the legs of the Holofernes figure from life instead of modeling them? And the photograph? Such prior examples do not dilute the status of the readymade but stand as precedents for it.

David Hume was, hands down, the greatest deflationary thinker. And Kant, awakening from his "dogmatic slumbers" to plow his vast fields of the systematic, testifies to the inevitability of the cycle of removal. Hume's skepticism about any substantive basis for belief, as well as his deconstruction of induction, probably did keep Kant up nights. But didn't René Descartes found the "Club Déflationnaire?" The membership was quite small then, consisting of Descartes alone, sitting before his fire and perusing his doubt all the way down.

John Cage looked for imperfections in a sheet of paper over which he dropped musical staff lines drawn on acetate. The imperfections became musical notes. Later, following the readymade, Cage admitted all sounds, except those of pain, into the house of music, thereby nominalizing the term music as henceforth the calling of any sound into the pantheon. Even "silence," like the proverbial quantum vacuum, pulses with something. Cage said in effect, "Listen to what is going on because I'm calling it music." Did Cage like the noises he heard sitting motionless at the piano in a tuxedo for four minutes and thirty-three seconds—all that coughing and mumbling and grumbling in the audience? He said he never heard a sound he didn't like (excepting the sound of pain). Get as deflationary as you like, and Cage liked the deflationary, and you just get much more grist for the aesthetic faculty to mill. The aesthetic is not shut out by the deflationary, only extended into new realms. Cage, who admitted to having a "sunny personality," did not need Duchamp's indifference when he had Zen's equivalences. The aesthetic is set free with the readymade and chance.

Jasper Johns, the third member of the twentieth-century Art Club Déflationnaire, squeezed the last breath out of painting at mid-century by flattening it beneath the readymade in his flags, targets, numbers, and alphabets. But he did far more. "Johns rewrote Pollock's pragmatism of material process into one of logical structure. Beginning with his influence on Frank Stella, John's lessons in the paradigm of a structural device that unfolded to complete the work also made minimal art possible."[22] And minimal art demonstrates once again, in its excessive and repetitious productions, the inevitability of the removal cycle.

Someone said that the most dangerous class of people in the world is "young unmarried men between the ages of 18 and 35."[23] Duchamp, Cage, and Johns were young, unmarried men when they assaulted art and left their deflationary cultural scars. But the twentieth-century Art Club Déflationnaire had a fourth member, and she was female. In the early 1960s Simone Forti introduced her "rule games" and the manipulation of objects (including other performers' bodies) into dance. The following of rules, which often required concentration on and responses to clues coded in other performers' actions or by manipulating or traversing objects small and large, generated movement—movement that was often effortful and workmanlike, unselfconscious and clearly devoid of any vestiges of ballet-inspired gesture. Like the other members of the Club, Forti's work admitted the "ordinary" to the arena of art. Her work dealt a heavy blow to the elitist culture of ballet-dependent choreography. And, characteristic of the removal cycle, her work opened the floodgates to new activity in dance. How much the spirit of the late Wittgenstein hovered over the Art Club Déflationnaire is an open question. The readymades came too early. But by the early 1950s, ideas of the "ordinary" had risen from the *Philosophical Investigations*[24] and were in the air.

The deflationary is not initially focused on either the aesthetic or negation as such. It is first of all an inspired adventure of thinking the possible. There is something detached and—the term is not too strong—psychopathic about the space of the deflationary. A Nietzschean imbrication of the creative and destructive has to be posited as well as left unexplained. The deflationary act taps a surge of insight seldom repeated in the individual's career. Nobody shouts "eureka!" more than once. But the question can be asked: Didn't the avant-gardes of modernism follow a deflationary program? There was to be sure a certain regression into the rules of the game in modernism's moves. But such a strategy stopped short of the demolition of premises.

Awfully quiet in the next room. Let's look in. Art is sprawled on the floor passed out. Big D is looking fatigued and slouched in a chair. Little T is licking Big D's hand trying to cheer him up. Big D keeps mumbling to himself . . . "A cross-dresser all along, hmm . . . Ms. Ace was always also Mr. Ace. Hmm . . . Mr. and Ms. He/she . . . her/him . . . Now Ace is gone." Ace has slammed the door on both of them. "Give me some air," Ace says. "I'm out of here and I'm sick of those two creeps. It's the big world for me." Looks like the party is over.

The always feeble theoretical ideology of modernist abstract art was by the mid-twentieth century dead on its feet. But the larger question is, why did visual art production cease bearing cultural weight after the 1970s? The short answer is because of the massive increase in the flood of imagery across a vast array of visual reproduction modalities that had been building in the culture for some time. Besides the expansions of television and advertising imagery, one could point to the "computer-aided design, synthetic holography, flight simulators, computer animation, robotic image recognition, ray tracing, texture mapping, motion control, virtual-environment helmets, magnetic resonance imaging, and multispectral sensors," noted by Jonathan Crary.[25] These modes constitute but a part of the rubric of a "visual culture" so multiple and profuse that it has been called a "pictorial turn" by W.J.T. Mitchell.[26] The engine of such visual multiplicity was of course commodity capitalism, which powered the new visual democracy and destroyed art's elitist aura of the unique and special image. Eric Hobsbawm has noted that shortly after the mid-twentieth century classical high culture was undermined by the "universal triumph of the society of mass consumption. From the 1960s on the images that accompanied human beings in the Western world—and increasingly in the urbanized third world—from birth to death were those advertising or embodying consumption or dedicated to commercial mass entertainment."[27] Language, no less than the visual, was demoted from the high holy books of elitist culture and even came to rest on such places as T-shirts, where, "like magical charms," they lent the wearer "the spiritual merit of the (generally youthful) life-style which those names symbolized and promised."[28] The mass market had replaced modernist dreams of utopia. High art had fled but the aesthetic had not. As Hobsbawm has noted, "Technology had drenched everyday life in private as well as in public with art. Never had it been harder to avoid aesthetic experience. The 'work of art' was lost in the flow of words, of sounds, of images, in the universal environment of what would once have been called art."[29] The culture had become saturated with visual imagery as well as awash in information. Of course this may be too mundane an explanation for the death of high art. Some have proposed a more mythical explanation in which art knelt down to Hegel, heaved a terminal sigh of totalizing, suicidal self-knowledge, and then expired.[30] But naturally art proliferated and expanded in the wake (both senses) of high art's demise. A kind of democratic conceptual folk art rose to take its place toward the end of the 1970s. Anyone could do it. Only the smallest idea was required. And the video camera was cheap. Turn it on and let it run and be kind to your aesthetic faculty.

We have to assume that the aesthetic faculty, always shaped by the existing culture, has been refashioned, remolded, perhaps skewed and broadened by the cultural changes wrought by late-capitalist consumer society with its constant blitz of imagery. Such changes can be highlighted by considering the implosion and irrelevance of Nelson Goodman's differences in "sign-types" articulated in his *Languages of Art.* Here Goodman notes that nonlinguistic signs differ from linguistic systems by virtue of what he calls "density." Echoing Roman Jakobson and Ferdinand de Saussure, Goodman emphasizes the gaps and discontinuities in the linguistic system, which at the simplest level allows for a *p* to be distinguished from a *t* (phonetic differentiation). On the other hand, an image presents no distinctive breaks but is rather a continuous field. It is dense and continuous as compared to the discontinuities of the linguistic. Goodman compares the two systems of signs to the "analog" and the "digital." But he is careful to note that it is history, not an inherent metaphysical character, that determines whether something is read as digital or analog.[31] It is a sign of the changed times that Goodman's distinction between an analog system in which "every difference would make a difference,"[32] and the digital system read through discontinuities, no longer guides our visual processing in an environment flooded with a constant blitz of imagery. It is no accident that the demise of modernism coincides with the ascendancy of a digital system of "reading" images, which has surely also reordered aesthetic responses. Today everything is scanned or "read."[33] There is no time for the contemplation of the continuous, which is associated with previous aesthetic attention to the densities of an image.[34] A post–high art culture is a visual culture in which perception is compressed into the digital mode as a necessary response to the continuous assault of images. The innate aesthetic faculty can only be expected to have shifted with the "pictorial turn." I stop short here of theorizing a new observer, one who is born with a visual attention deficit. But could a post–"baby boomer" stand today in hushed contemplation before, say, Diego Velazquez's *Las Meninas,* noting how every small difference makes a difference in the continuous flow of the image?[35]

Are we freer now that our aesthetic faculty is exercised on the discontinuities of the post–high art general spectacle? Hasn't a democratized visual culture, which returns the possibility of aesthetic reading to everything in sight, fulfilled John Dewey's demand for the merging of art and life?[36] Or has the aesthetic faculty been further dulled by the constant ratcheting up of scale and spectacle, encountered at an ever accelerating pace in the old sites of the museum space as well as outside it? Has the fractious terrain of the perpetual media blitz also honed our aesthetic faculty to triage the incoming barrage and made us quicker on our feet—or with our eyes, as the case may be? As the ophthalmologist asks, replacing one lens with another, "Better or worse?"

I hear a persistent tapping on the wall and feel I should investigate what is going on in the other room, since the party noise has died down. . . . Well, I see Ace has gone, Art is still out cold, Big D is slumped in his chair dozing. Only Little T sits staring at me, motionless, except for a hesitant wag of the tail.

Me: *"You're the only one left, Little T?"*

T: *"I'm always around. And you can drop the diminutive," the mascot replies. I have to admit I'm startled at speech from such a small being.*

Me: *"Well, I heard the tapping and I thought I should . . ."*

T: *"I was doing the tapping and I think it is about time you remembered your Edmund Burke."*

Me: *"But it is the deflationary and the aesthetic I've been worrying about."*

T: *"You are falling into Burke's trap of subliming things."*

Me: *"Me?"*

T: *"Yes, you and your [Art] Club Déflationnaire to begin with. Add to that the murky and mysterious innate aesthetic faculty as that which is forever out of sight. You end up with a few big guys and how they changed history, and all of it shrouded by the murky penumbra of the elusive aesthetic. It's all dark and sublime and Burkean, and . . .*

Me: *"And one gal, don't forget. And I've tried to show how it was the celebration of the ordinary that set the members of the [Art] Club Déflationnaire apart. Implicit in this is a rejection of the sublime as an always reactionary strategy."*[37]

T: *"There is ordinary and there is ordinary. I hung around Davidson long enough to know about the hard ordinary, as opposed to the romantic ordinary."*

Me: *"What about the Wittgensteinian ordinary? He got pretty iconophobic in the Investigations. And you can't have Davidson without the late Wittgenstein."*

T: *"I don't like to keep defending Davidson—after all, look what he did to me. But he wasn't one of the iconophobic philosophers. And his sense of the ordinary was pretty well developed."*

Me: *"You mean his Principle of Charity, that notion that what most people believe is true, that we all seem to believe in things such as it is either raining or it isn't, or that none of us has been far from the surface of the earth, or that . . ."*

T: *"Without our agreement in belief about the mundane ordinary, there could be no meaningful disagreement about the more complex issues. Davidson's ordinary does some heavy lifting."*

Me: *"Well, T, we seem to have lost sight of the metastasized image and all our wayward ways of looking at things, not to mention those unpredictable effects of the aesthetic shade that is always drawn over our seeing. And now that Ace has fled the party for the big world, shouldn't we say a word to remember her by?"*

T: *"Well, we could remind ourselves of Stanley Cavell's remark that 'epistemology is obliged to keep aesthetics under control, as if to guard against the thought that there is something more [and better] seeing can be, or provide, than evidence for claims to know.'"*[38]

Me: *"Perish the thought that there might be pleasure in looking, huh? But I guess that Leonardo's Paragone[39] doesn't go away. Obviously the image is still a threat to some. But you are not so iconophobic, T? Not so puritanical? Wouldn't Jonathan Edwards have cut us more slack than Cavell?"*

T: *"We all peer out into the same bleakness that has descended. Maybe Cavell is right, we can't afford not to know what we are seeing. And*

> *what we can least afford not to see through are the sublimities of*
> *imperialistic war."*

Me: *"So we should constrain our vision, and keep Ace at arm's length?"*

T: *"We know Kant was wrong about a lot of things, one of which was*
his idea of where the sublime led. As for Ace, she can take care of
herself, and she will always be around."

Me: *"But could we practice a way of seeing that allows us to look out onto*
the ordinary world, somehow seeing through the bleakness, to secure
appreciation as well as criticality? Isn't there some therapy for
vision?"

T: *"We never seem to be able to say what we see, or see what we've said.*
And there is always too much to see that can never be said."

Me: *"Don't talk in conundrums."*

T: *"Ace promised to take me for a walk, and I think I hear her calling.*
Enough of this blather. Here, take my leash, and let's go outside and
see what he is pointing at."

16

The Social Turn
Collaboration and Its Discontents

Claire Bishop

The Social Turn

Superflex's internet TV station for elderly residents of a Liverpool housing project (*Tenantspin*, 1999); Annika Eriksson inviting groups and individuals to communicate their ideas and skills at the Frieze Art Fair (*Do You Want an Audience?* 2004); Lincoln Tobier training local residents in Aubervilliers, northeast Paris, to produce half-hour radio programs (*Radio Ld'A*, 2004); Lucy Orta's workshops in Johannesburg (and elsewhere) to teach unemployed people new fashion skills and discuss collective solidarity (*Nexus Architecture*, 1997–); Temporary Services' improvised sculpture environment and neighborhood community in an empty lot in Echo Park, Los Angeles (*Construction Site*, 2005); Jeanne van Heeswijk's project to turn a condemned shopping mall into a cultural center for the residents of Vlaardingen, Rotterdam (*De Strip*, 2001–2004).

The above projects are just a sample of the recent surge of artistic interest in collectivity, collaboration, and direct engagement with "real" people (i.e., those who are not the artist's friends or other artists). Although these practices have had, for the most part, a relatively weak profile in the commercial art world, they nevertheless occupy an increasingly conspicuous presence in the public sector. A number of new institutional frameworks have contributed to this shift. One is the unprecedented expansion of the biennial, another is the rise of "new institutionalism" and the auteur curator with an interest in performative (or self-reflexive) exhibition-making. The art fair as a public-private funded enterprise is one more new forum, and a fourth is the commissioning agency dedicated to the production of temporary projects in the public realm. In her landmark study of site specificity in North America, *One Place After Another* (2002), Miwon Kwon has argued that socially collaborative art takes critiques of "heavy metal" public sculpture as its point of departure to address the site as a *social* rather than formal or phenomenological framework. For Kwon, the removal of Richard Serra's *Tilted Arc* (1981–1987) from Federal Plaza, New York, marked a transition to more discursive models of site specificity, exemplified in the United States by New Genre Public Art: temporary projects that directly engage an audience—particularly groups considered marginalized—as active participants in the production of a process-oriented, politically conscious community event or program. In these projects, intersubjective exchange becomes the focus—and medium—of artistic investigation.

Today's expanded field of engaged practices currently goes under a variety of names: socially engaged art, community based art, experimental communities, dialogic art, littoral art, participatory, interventionist, research-based, or collaborative art. In this respect, the work differs significantly from the type of art discussed by Nicolas Bourriaud in *Relational Aesthetics* (1998), even though these projects appear, theoretically at least, to have much in common. Bourriaud describes as "relational" work that takes as its theoretical horizon "the realm of human interactions and its social context, rather than the assertion of an independent and *private* symbolic space."[1] But despite this emphasis on human relations and their social context, when we look at the artists he supports independently of his arguments, we find that they are less interested in human relations than in the relations between space, temporality, fiction and design, and in rethinking the medium of the exhibition through film and architecture. In contrast to this debate, the projects that form the focus of this paper are less interested in a relational *aesthetic* than in the creative rewards of collaborative activity—whether in the form of working with preexisting communities or establishing one's own interdisciplinary network. Although the objectives and output of these artists and groups vary enormously, all are linked by a belief in the empowering creativity of collective action and shared ideas.

This type of work is part of a historical trajectory of socially oriented practices, from Dada excursions to Situationist *dérives*, that have received relatively little art historical attention. However, a nascent theoretical framework has emerged in recent writing by artists and curators. One of the most frequently cited points of reference is Guy Debord, both for his theorization of collectively produced "situations" and his indictment of the alienating and divisive effects of capitalism in *The Society of the Spectacle* (1967). For the supporters of socially engaged art, the creative energy of participatory practices rehumanize—or at least de-alienate—a society rendered numb and fragmented by the repressive instrumentality of capitalist production.[2] Given the market's near total saturation of our image repertoire, there is a prevalent sense that artistic practice can no longer revolve around the construction of objects to be consumed. "One reason why artists are no longer interested in a passive process of presenter-spectator," writes the Dutch artist Jeanne van Heeswijk, is "the fact that such communication has been entirely appropriated by the commercial world . . . After all, nowadays one could receive an aesthetic experience on every corner."[3] Instead of adding to such fragmented aesthetic experiences, the emphasis is on restoring the social bond, providing a space for creativity and communication otherwise lacking in contemporary society.

Such projects therefore seem to operate with a twofold gesture of opposition and amelioration. Firstly, they work against dominant market imperatives by diffusing single authorship into collaborative activities that, in the words of one critic, transcend "the snares of negation and self-interest."[4] Secondly, they reject object-based contemporary art as elitist and consumerist; instead of supplying the market, art should channel its symbolic capital toward constructive social change. Given these avowed politics, and the commitment that mobilizes this work, it is tempting to argue that socially collaborative art arguably forms what avant-garde we have today: artists using social situations to produce dematerialized, anti-market, politically engaged projects that carry on the historic avant-garde call to blur art and life. But the urgency of this *social* task has led to a situation in which socially collaborative practices are all perceived to be equally important *artistic* gestures of resistance: There can be no failed, unsuccessful, unresolved, or boring works of participatory art, because all are equally essential to the task of strengthening the social bond. While broadly sympathetic to this latter ambition, I would argue that it is also crucial to discuss, analyze, and compare this work critically *as art*.

This task is particularly pressing in Europe. In the United Kingdom, for example, New Labour deploys a rhetoric almost identical to the practitioners of socially engaged art in order to justify public spending on the arts. The question asked by the government is: What can the arts do for society? The answer: increasing employability, minimizing crime, fostering aspiration—anything but the production of culture for its own sake. The production and reception of the arts has thus been reshaped within a political logic, where audience figures, marketing, and demonstrable outcomes are essential to securing public funding.[5] The key word deployed by the government in this context is "social inclusion": The arts must compensate for diminished public services through strategies that are socially *inclusive*. The discourse of social exclusion is not as benign as it sounds, since it represents the primary division in society as one between an *included majority* and an *excluded minority*. Attention is drawn away from inequalities and differences among the included; instead, exclusion appears as a peripheral problem, existing at the boundary of society as an evil to be erased, rather than being understood as one of its structural features. The solution implied by a discourse of social exclusion is simply the goal of transition across the boundary—from excluded to included. Meanwhile, the structural inequalities of society remain uninterrogated.[6]

We can see this elision of positions in the writing of numerous artists and curators on socially collaborative art. For example, the curator Charles Esche has written on the project *Tenantspin*, an Internet-based TV station for the residents of a run-down tower block in Liverpool by the Danish collective Superflex. Although Esche intersperses his article with long quotes from governmental reports about the state of British council housing, his central judgment about this project concerns its effectivity as a "tool" that can "change the image of both the tower block itself and the residents"; in his view, the major achievement of this project is that it has forged a "stronger sense of community in the building."[7] Esche is an innovative and politically engaged curator, but his reluctance— or inability—to discuss the *artistic* value of Superflex's project ultimately renders his value judgments indistinguishable from New Labour arts policy, which is founded on a report by François Matarasso proving the positive impact of social participation upon communities.[8] It lays out fifty benefits of social participation: It reduces isolation by helping people to make friends, develops community networks and sociability, erodes the distinction between consumer and creator, helps offenders and victims address issues of crime, contributes to people's employability, encourages people to accept risk positively, and helps transform the image of public bodies. The latter, I think, are the most insidious: Social participation is viewed positively by the government because it creates submissive citizens who respect authority and accept the "risk" and responsibility of diminished public services. As Paola Merli has pointed out, none of these outcomes will change the structural conditions of people's daily existence, it will only "help" people to accept them.[9]

It should be clear that here I have entered a sociological discourse. What happened to aesthetics? The development of a new artistic terminology by which to discuss and analyze socially engaged practices is now an urgent task—and one that is not assisted by the present-day standoff between the nonbelievers (who reject this work as marginal, misguided, and lacking artistic interest of any kind) and the believers (who reject all aesthetic questions as synonymous with the market and cultural hierarchy). If the former risk condemning us to a world of market-driven painting and sculpture, the latter self-marginalize to the point of artistic and political disempowerment. Both sides of the standoff are too reductive, and a productive rapprochement must take place if we are to create compelling alternatives *both* to the power structures of the art world *and* to a more emancipatory understanding of art's relationship to its viewer. To begin this task, I will more closely examine the criteria by which socially engaged projects are currently articulated.

The Ethical Turn

It is often remarked that socially engaged practices are extremely difficult to discuss within the conventional frameworks of art criticism. Reinaldo Laddaga, for example, has commented in relation to *What's the Time in Vyborg?*, a four-year project by Liisa Roberts undertaken with the assistance of six teenage girls in the city of Vyborg on the Russian-Finnish border:

What's the Time in Vyborg is difficult—perhaps even impossible—to assess as an "art" project in as much as the criteria of its success for those involved could not be described as artistic. The objective of Roberts and the core group of *What's the Time in Vyborg* wasn't simply to offer an aesthetic or intellectual experience to an outside public but to facilitate the creation of a temporary community engaged in the process of solving a series of practical problems. The project aspired to have a real efficacy in the site in which it came to happen. Accordingly, any valuation of it should be at the same time artistic and ethical, practical and political.[10]

Such integrated analyses are rarely to be encountered. Instead we find a recurrent focus on concrete achievements and the fulfillment of social goals. In turn, these are elided into a hazy territory of assumptions that are not so much "practical and political" as ethical or moralistic. This is manifest in a heightened attentiveness as to *how* a given collaboration is undertaken, rather than the meaning of the project as a whole. In other words, artists are judged by their working process—the degree to which they supply good or bad models of collaboration—and criticized for any hint of potential exploitation that fails to fully represent their subjects, as if such a thing were possible. The emphasis is on process over product—or perhaps more accurately, on process *as* product—that is justified on the simple basis of its inversion of capitalism's predilection for the contrary. Consensual collaboration is valued over artistic mastery and individualism.

The writing around the Turkish artists' collective Oda Projesi provides a clear example of the way in which aesthetic judgments are rejected in favor of ethical criteria. Oda Projesi is a group of three artists who, since 1997, have based their activities around a three-room apartment in the Galata district of Istanbul (*Oda Projesi* is Turkish for "room project"). The apartment provides a platform for projects generated by the group in cooperation with their neighbors, such as a children's workshop with the Turkish painter Komet, a community picnic with the sculptor Erik Göngrich, and a parade for children organized by the Tem Yapin theater group.[11] Oda Projesi argue that they wish to open up a context for the possibility of exchange and dialogue, motivated by a desire to integrate with their surroundings. They insist that they are not setting out to improve or heal a situation—one of their project leaflets contains the slogan "exchange not change"—though they evidently see their work as gently oppositional. By working directly with their neighbors to organize workshops and events, they seek to produce a more creative and participatory social fabric. The group talks of creating "blank spaces" and "holes" in the face of an over-organized and bureaucratic society and of being "mediators" between groups of people who normally don't have contact with each other.[12]

Because much of Oda Projesi's work exists on the level of art education and neighborhood events, we can understand the group's members to be dynamic members of the community bringing art to a wider audience. It is important that they are opening up the space for non-object-based practice in Turkey, a country whose art academies and art market are still largely oriented toward painting and sculpture. And one may also be pleased, as I am, that it is three women who have undertaken this task. But their conceptual gesture of reducing authorship to the role of facilitation ultimately leaves little to separate their work from the community arts tradition. Even when transposed to Sweden, Germany, South Korea, and the other countries where Oda Projesi have exhibited, there is little to distinguish their projects from a slew of community-based practices that revolve around a predictable formula: workshops, discussions, meals, film screenings, and walks. Perhaps this is because the question of the aesthetic is not valid for Oda Projesi. When I interviewed the group and asked by what criteria they judge their own work, they replied that it lay in the decisions they make about where and with whom they collaborate: Dynamic and sustained relationships provide their markers of success, rather than aesthetic considerations. Indeed, because their practice is based on collaboration, Oda Projesi considers the aesthetic to be "a dangerous word" that should not be brought into discussion.

Oda Projesi's approach is reiterated by the Swedish curator Maria Lind in a recent essay on their work. Lind is one of the most articulate supporters of political and relational practices, and she undertakes her curatorial work with a trenchant commitment to the social. In her essay on Oda Projesi, she notes that the group is not interested in showing or exhibiting art but in "using art as a means for creating and recreating new relations between people."[13] She goes on to discuss their project in Riem, near Munich, in which the group collaborated with a local Turkish community to organize a tea party, hairdressing and Tupperware parties, guided tours led by the residents, and the installation of a long roll of paper that people wrote and drew on to stimulate conversations. Lind compares this endeavor to Thomas Hirschhorn's *Bataille Monument* (2002), his well-known collaboration with a mainly Turkish community in Kassel for *Documenta 11*. Lind observes that Oda Projesi, contrary to Thomas Hirschhorn, are the better artists because of the equal status they give to their collaborators: "[Hirschhorn's] aim is to create art. For the *Bataille Monument* he had already prepared, and in part also executed, a plan on which he needed help to implement. His participants were paid for their work and their role was that of the 'executor' and not 'co-creator,'" Lind goes on to argue that Hirschhorn's work, by using participants to critique the art genre of the monument, was rightly criticized for "'exhibiting' and making exotic marginalized groups and thereby contributing to a form of a social pornography." By contrast, she writes, Oda Projesi "work[s] with groups of people in their immediate environments and allow[s] them to wield great influence on the project."[14]

It's worth looking closely at Lind's criteria here. Her judgment is based on an ethics of authorial renunciation: The work of Oda Projesi is better than that of Thomas Hirschhorn because it exemplifies a superior model of collaborative practice, one in which individual authorship is suppressed in favor of facilitating others' creativity. The conceptual density and artistic significance of the respective projects are sidelined in favor of a judgment on the artists' relationship with their collaborators. Hirschhorn's (purportedly) exploitative relationship is compared negatively to Oda Projesi's inclusive generosity. In other words, Lind downplays what might be interesting in Oda Projesi's work *as art*—the possible achievement of making dialogue a medium, or the significance of dematerializing a work of art into social process. Instead her criticism is dominated by *ethical* judgments on working procedure and intentionality. Art and the aesthetic are denigrated as merely visual, superfluous, academic—less important than concrete outcomes, or the proposition of a "model" or prototype. In this framework, the artist paradoxically becomes a moral model in return for his or her authorial sacrifice in the name of collaboration.

This value system is particularly marked in curatorial writing, but art theorists also reinforce an ethical disposition. For example, the curator and critic Lucy Lippard concludes her book *The Lure of the Local* (1997), a discussion of site-specific art from an ecological and postcolonial perspective, with an eight-point "ethic of place" for artists who work with communities.[15] Grant Kester's key text on collaborative art, *Conversation Pieces* (2004), while lucidly articulating many of the problems associated with such practices, nevertheless advocates an art of concrete interventions in which the artist does not occupy a position of pedagogical or creative mastery. The Dutch critic Erik Hagoort, in his book *Good Intentions: Judging the Art of Encounter* (2005), argues that we must not shy from making moral judgments on this art: Viewers should weigh up each artist's good intentions.[16] In each of these examples, the status of the artist's intentionality (i.e., a humble lack of authorship) is privileged over a discussion of the work's artistic identity. Paradoxically, this leads to a situation in which not only collectives but individual artists are praised for their conscious authorial renunciation. And this may explain why socially engaged art has become largely exempt from art criticism: Emphasis is continually shifted away from the disruptive *specificity* of a given practice and onto a *generalized* set of ethical precepts.

But if ethical criteria have become the norm for judging this art, we should ask what ethics are being advocated. In *Conversation Pieces*, Grant Kester argues that consultative and "dialogic" art necessitates a shift in our understanding of what art is—away from the visual and sensory (which are individual experiences) and toward "discursive exchange and negotiation." He compares two projects undertaken in East London in the early 1990s: Rachel Whiteread's cast concrete sculpture *House* (1993) and Lorraine Leeson's billboard project *West Meets East* (1992, a collaboration with local Bengali schoolgirls). He argues that neither is the better work of art; they simply make different demands upon the viewer. However, his tone is clearly judgmental. *House* emerged from a studio practice that has little to do with the specific conditions of Bow (a region of East London), while Leeson and her partner Peter Dunn (working under the name The Art of Change) "attempt to learn as much as possible about the cultural and political histories of the people with whom they work, as well as their particular needs and skills. Their artistic identity is based in part upon their capacity to listen, openly and actively."[17] In this type of work, empathetic identification is essential, since only this can facilitate "a reciprocal exchange that allows us to think outside our own lived experience and establish a more compassionate relationship with others."[18]

Kester's emphasis on compassionate identification with the other is typical of the social participation discourse. It represents a familiar summary of the intellectual trends inaugurated by identity politics and elaborated in 1990s theory: respect for the other, recognition of difference, protection of fundamental liberties, and a concern for human rights. The philosopher Peter Dews has recently described this development as an "ethical turn" in which "Questions of conscience and obligation, of recognition and respect, of justice and law, which not so long ago would have been dismissed as the residue of an outdated humanism, have returned to occupy, if not centre stage, then something pretty close to it."[19]

At the center of opposition to this trend have been the philosophers Alain Badiou and Slavoj Žižek who, in different ways, remain skeptical of the jargon of human rights and identity politics.[20] It might seem extreme to compare these philosophical indictments of the ethical turn with the well-meaning advocates of socially collaborative art, but these thinkers provide a poignant lens through which to view the humanist tropes that pervade this artistic discourse. The insistence upon consensual dialogue and sensitivity to difference becomes a new kind of repressive norm—one in which artistic strategies of disruption, intervention, or overidentification are immediately ruled out as "unethical," because all forms of authorship are equated with authority and indicted as total. As Gillian Rose has observed with respect to community architecture, such a denigration of authorship allows simplistic oppositions to remain in place: active versus passive viewer, egotistical versus collaborative artist, privileged versus needy community, aesthetic complexity versus simple expression, cold autonomy versus convivial community.[21]

A resistance to rupturing these categories is found, for example, in Kester's rejection of any art that might offend or trouble its audience—most notably the historical avant-garde, within whose avant-garde lineage he nevertheless wishes to situate social participation as a radical practice. Kester criticizes Dada and Surrealism for seeking to "shock" viewers into being more sensitive and receptive to the world—because for him, this position turns the artist into a privileged bearer of insights, patronizingly informing audiences as to "how things really are."[22] Such an aversion to symbolic disruption potentially signals the end of all courageous thinking and self-censors on the basis of second-guessing how others will think and respond. By contrast, I would argue that shock, discomfort, or frustration—along with absurdity, eccentricity, doubt, or sheer pleasure—are crucial to a work of art's aesthetic and political impact.

The Aesthetic Regime

As I have already indicated, one of the biggest problems in the discussion around socially engaged art is its paradoxical relationship to the aesthetic. By this I do not mean that the work does not fit established notions of the attractive or the beautiful, even though this is often the case. Many social projects photograph very badly, and these images convey very little of the contextual information so crucial to understanding the work. More significant is the tendency for advocates of socially collaborative art to view the aesthetic as (at best) merely visual and (at worst) an elitist realm of unbridled seduction entirely complicit with spectacle. At the same time, these advocates also argue that art is an independent zone, free from the pressures of accountability, institutional bureaucracy, and the rigors of specialization.[23] The upshot is that art is perceived both as *too removed* from the real world *and yet* the only space from which it is possible to experiment: Art must paradoxically remain autonomous *in order to* initiate or achieve a model for social change.[24]

This antinomy has been clearly articulated by the French philosopher Jacques Rancière, whose work since the late 1990s has concerned the relation between aesthetics and politics. Rancière argues that the system of art as we understand it since the Enlightenment—which he calls "the aesthetic regime of art"—is predicated precisely on a tension and confusion between autonomy (the desire for art to be at one remove from means-ends relationships) and heteronomy (that is, the blurring of art and life). For Rancière, the primal scene of this new regime is the moment when, in Schiller's fifteenth letter *On the Aesthetic Education of Man* (1794), he describes a Greek statue known as the Juno Ludovisi as a specimen of "free appearance." Following Kant, Schiller does not judge the work as an accurate depiction of the goddess nor as an idol to be worshipped. Rather, he views it as self-contained, dwelling in itself without purpose or volition, and potentially available to all. As such, the sculpture stands as an example of—and promises—a new community, one that suspends reason and power in a state of equality. The aesthetic regime of art, as inaugurated by Schiller and the romantics, is therefore premised on the paradox that "art is art to the extent that it is something else than art": that it is a sphere *both* at one remove from politics *and* yet always already political because it contains the promise of a better world.[25]

What is significant in Rancière's reworking of the term "aesthetic" is that it concerns *aisthesis*, a mode of sensible perception proper to artistic objects. But rather than considering the *work of art* to be autonomous, it concerns our autonomy of *experience* in relation to art. In this, Rancière reprises Kant's argument that an aesthetic judgment suspends the domination of the faculties by reason (in morality) and understanding (in knowledge). As taken up by Schiller—and Rancière—this freedom or suspension of aesthetic judgment from domination by the faculties suggests the possibility of politics because the undecidability of aesthetic experience brings with it a questioning of how things are organized and therefore the possibility of change (i.e., a redistribution of the sensible world). Aesthetics and politics therefore overlap in their concern for the distribution and sharing out of the sensible world—what Rancière calls *le partage du sensible*. In this framework, it is not possible to conceive of an aesthetic judgment that is not also at the same time a political judgment—a comment on the "distribution of the places and of the capacities or incapacities attached to those places."[26] Both art and politics concern the way in which our world is divided up and shared out.

One of Rancière's key contributions to contemporary debates around art and politics is therefore to reinvent the term "aesthetic" so that it denotes the very linguistic and theoretical domain in which thought about art takes place. In this logic, all claims to be anti-aesthetic or to reject art *still function within the aesthetic regime of art*. Therefore, the aesthetic for Rancière signals an ability to think contradiction: the productive contradiction of art's relationship to social change, which is characterized by the paradox of belief in art's autonomy *and* in it being inextricably bound to the promise of a better world to come.[27] While this antinomy is apparent in many avant-garde practices of the last century, it seems particularly pertinent to analyzing socially engaged art and the terms of its support. When we bring these two discourses together, it becomes evident that the aesthetic doesn't need to be sacrificed at the altar of social change because it always already contains this ameliorative promise.

Directed Reality

However, there are also limitations to Rancière's approach. It would be wrong to deduce that for him *all* art is automatically political; rather, *good* art is necessarily political in its redistribution of sensible forms that have a dissensual relationship both to the autonomous world of art and to the everyday world we inhabit. The translation of this idea into art criticism is less easy, despite the fact that Rancière is unusual among philosophers in paying attention to the art of his own time. He argues against "critical art" that intends to raise our consciousness by inviting us to "see the signs of Capital behind everyday objects"; such didactic art effectively removes the strangeness that bears testimony to the oppressive intolerability of our rationalized world.[28] Even so, Rancière's preferences do incline toward those works that offer a clear message on a political topic—such as Martha Rosler's anti-Vietnam collages *Bringing the War Home* (1967–1972) or Chris Burden's *The Other Vietnam Memorial* (1991).

Rancière's arguments are most persuasive when he describes art that avoids the pitfalls of a didactic critical position in favor of rupture and ambiguity:

Suitable political art would ensure, at one and the same time, the production of a double effect: the readability of a political signification and a sensible or perceptual shock caused, conversely, by the uncanny, by that which resists signification. In fact, this ideal effect is always the object of a negotiation between opposites, between the readability of the message that threatens to destroy the sensible form of art and the radical uncanniness that threatens to destroy all political meaning.[29]

Good art, implies Rancière, must negotiate the tension that, on one hand, pushes art toward "life" and that, on the other hand, separates aesthetic sensoriality from other forms of sensible experience. This friction ideally produces the formation of elements "capable of speaking twice: from their readability and from their unreadability."[30] This shuttling between meanings is possible because artistic forms have no fixed political affiliation. One only has to think of the diverse uses made today of social participation to understand this instability. Audience participation techniques pioneered in the 1960s by companies like The Living Theatre and Théâtre du Soleil have become commonplace conventions in the theatrical mainstream.[31] The most pervasive new trend in the mass media is of course reality television, in which "everyday" people participate both as would-be celebrities and as voters. By failing to take on board these connotations, by rejecting artistic questions as synonymous with the market and cultural hierarchy, and by focusing attention onto the exemplary ethical gesture, socially collaborative art risks ensuring its aesthetic and political irrelevance.[32]

However, there are exceptions to this trend do not sacrifice authorship for the recovery of a fantasmatic social bond. Instead, they play autonomy against heteronomy, sense against nonsense, and are more interested in provocation than in compensatory gestures. Rather than positioning themselves within an activist lineage, in which art is marshaled directly to social change, these artists have a closer relationship to avant-garde theater, performance, or experimental architecture. The success of their work is not dependent upon authorial suppression, but upon the careful deployment of collaboration to produce a multilayered event that resonates across many registers. As such, they think the aesthetic and the political *together*, rather than subordinating both within the exemplary ethical gesture.

Several works by the British artist Jeremy Deller find a place within this tendency. His work forges unexpected encounters between diverse constituencies and often displays a strong interest in class, subculture, and self-organization; these have taken the form both of temporary exhibitions and performance events. *The Battle of Orgreave* (2002) is perhaps his best-known work, a reenactment of a violent clash between miners and policemen in the Yorkshire village of Orgreave in 1984, performed by former miners and local residents together with a number of historical reenactment societies. Although the work seemed to contain a twisted therapeutic element, *The Battle of Orgreave* didn't seem to heal a wound so much as reopen it. Deller's event summoned the experiential potency of political demonstrations but only to expose a wrong seventeen years too late.

The involvement of historical reenactment societies was integral to this shift out of a journalistic register: Their participation symbolically elevated the relatively recent events at Orgreave to the status of English history while also drawing attention to this eccentric leisure activity in which bloody battles are enthusiastically replicated as group entertainment. Although *The Battle of Orgreave* restaged one of the last working-class industrial disputes and served as a corrective to this event's original misrepresentation in the media, this was achieved through a cross section of participants—former miners and the (mainly) middle-class battle reenactors—that dismantled any impression of sentimental class unity. The whole event could be understood as a contemporary form of history painting enacted through the medium of performance.

The Battle of Orgreave's status as a *reenactment* also serves to problematize influential definitions of performance art as founded on the unrepeatable gesture and undermined by documentation.[33] Deller's event formed the pretext for a feature-length film by Mike Figgis, a left-wing filmmaker who explicitly uses the event as a vehicle for his indictment of the Thatcher government. The only video footage that exists of *The Battle of Orgreave* takes the form of short sequences ensconced between Figgis's emotional interviews with former miners, and the clash of tone is disconcerting. Although Deller's event gathered people together to remember and replay a charged and disastrous event, this took place in circumstances more akin to a town fair, with a brass band, hot dog stands, and children running around. As the photographs curiously testify, *The Battle of Orgreave* was constantly on the brink of chaos, but also of family entertainment. As such it harnessed the experiential potency of collective action toward conflicting ends.

The British artist Phil Collins has also used the conventions of social collaboration as a strategy to intervene in dominant codes of political representation and group portraiture. Invited to undertake a residency in Jerusalem in *2004*, he held a disco-dancing marathon for teenagers in Ramallah, which he recorded to produce the two-channel video *They Shoot Horses* (2004). Collins paid nine teenagers to dance continually for eight hours, on two consecutive days, in front of a garish pink wall to an unrelentingly cheesy compilation of pop hits from the past four decades. The teenagers are mesmerizing and irresistible as they move from exuberant dancing to boredom and finally exhaustion. It goes without saying that *They Shoot Horses* is a perverse representation of the site that the artist was invited to respond to: The occupied territories are never shown explicitly but are ever-present *hors-cadre*. They also allow the soundtrack's banal pop lyrics of love and rejection to acquire poignant connotations, in the light of the kids' double endurance of the marathon and of the interminable political crisis in which they are mired. The degree to which Collins's work reconfigures conventional representations of the Middle East become apparent when we consider the puzzled questions regularly overheard when the work is exhibited: How come Palestinians know Beyoncé? How come they're wearing Nike trainers? By voiding the work of direct political narrative, *They Shoot Horses* shows how swiftly this space is filled by fantasies generated by the media's selective production and dissemination of images from the Middle East (in which young Arabs tend to be depicted as either victims or fundamentalists). Collins's choice of backdrop—a bright pink wall with an orange line at head height, a camp spin on police lineups—insinuates that the teenagers (like the conflict they cannot help but embody) are the usual suspects.

Collins takes the title of his work from Sydney Pollack's film *They Shoot Horses, Don't They?* (1969), which follows a handful of characters competing in a dancing marathon held during the Great Depression. The film foreshadows a contemporary culture of reality television, in which the participants' quest for fame and financial success dovetails easily with commercial exploitation. Collins's project inserts itself into this context as much as into the realm of socially and politically engaged art. *They Shoot Horses* plays off the conventions of benevolent socially collaborative practice (it creates a new narrative for its participants and reinforces a social

bond) but combines this with the directorial conventions of reality television. The presentation of the work as a two-screen installation lasting a
full eight-hour working day subverts both genres in its emphatic use of
seduction on the one hand and grueling duration on the other. Collins's
directorial role treads an ambiguous line between ally and taskmaster,
subjecting the teenagers to a relentless onslaught of Western pop.

What interests me in both of these approaches to collaboration is
that they are not undertaken as a corrective to social fragmentation but
instead open onto a sophisticated interrogation of the apparatus of mediation in relation to community and collectivity. Collins and Deller do not
adopt the role of self-suppressing artist-facilitator but are a directorial
force. Here, the authorial role is a trigger for events that would otherwise
have no existence, since their conceptualization is too singular, extravagant, or perverse ever to become the province of socially responsible institutions. As such, their disruptiveness is both political and aesthetic in its
rethinking of dominant representations.

Emancipated Spectators?

At this point there will be an objection: Deller and Collins produce
objects for consumption within a gallery. Not only does their work invite a
passive mode of reception (compared to the active coproductions of "authentic" collaborative art), but it also reinforces the hierarchies of elite culture; despite its engagement with "real people," this art is ultimately
produced for, and consumed by, a middle-class gallery audience and collectors. This argument can be refuted in several ways. Firstly, the idea that
performance documentation is a betrayal of the authentic, unmediated
event has been disproven by a number of theorists in the wake of Peggy
Phelan's *Unmarked: The Politics of Performance* (1993).[34] The binary of "authentic liveness" versus "inauthentic mediation" hovers over any discussion
of participation—be this in art, architecture, or theater—to the point
where it becomes an end in itself. As Ranciere notes, "Even when the dramaturge or the performer does not know what he wants the spectator to
do, he knows at least that the spectator has to do something: switch from
passivity to activity."[35] This injunction to activate is pitched both as a counter to false consciousness and as a realization of the essence of art (or theater) as real life. But the binary of active/passive always ends up in deadlock:
either a disparagement of the spectator because he does nothing while the

performers on stage do something, or the converse claim that those who act are inferior to those who are able to look, contemplate ideas, and have critical distance on the world. As Rancière observes, the two positions can be switched but the structure remains the same: both divide a population into those with capacity on one side and those with incapacity on the other. As such, the binary of active/passive forms an allegory of inequality.

This insight can be extended to the argument that high culture, as found in art galleries, is produced for and on behalf of the ruling classes; by contrast, "the people" (the marginalized, the excluded) can only be emancipated by direct inclusion in the production of a work. This argument—which underpins arts funding agendas influenced by policies of social inclusion—assumes that the poor can only engage physically, while the middle classes have the leisure to think. This argument reinstates the prejudice whereby working-class activity is synonymous with manual labor.[36] It is comparable to sociological critiques of art in which the aesthetic is found to be the preserve of the elite, while the "real people" are found to prefer the popular, the realist, the hands-on. As Rancière argues, in a scathing response to Pierre Bourdieu's *Distinction* (1979), the sociologist-interviewer announces the results in advance and finds out what his questions already presuppose: That things are in their place.[37] So to argue, in the manner of New Labour and the advocates of collaborative art alike, that social participation is particularly suited to the task of social inclusion not only assumes that participants are already in a position of impotence, it actually reinforces this arrangement. Crucially for our argument, Rancière points out that in Bourdieu, the status quo is preserved by never confronting "the aesthetic thing" directly; the gray area of *aisthesis* is excluded: "Questions about music without music, fictitious questions of aesthetics about photographs when they are not perceived as aesthetic, all these produce inevitably what is required by the sociologist: the suppression of intermediaries, of points of meeting and exchange between the people of reproduction and the elite of distinction."[38]

Discussions of participatory art and its documentation proceed with similar exclusions: Without engaging with the "aesthetic thing," the gray areas of slippery meaning are cleaned, contained, and kept in place—subordinated to the statistical affirmation of use-values and direct effects. Without the possibility of blurring and rupture, there is merely a Platonic assignment of bodies to their good "communal" place: an ethical regime of images rather than an aesthetic regime of art.[39]

Some important terms that emerge here are "disruption," "ambiguity," and "pleasure," and the way these converge in psychoanalytic accounts of making art. Rather than obeying a superegoist injunction to make an improving or ameliorative art, Deller and Collins act upon their desire without the incapacitating restrictions of guilt. This fidelity to their desire—rather than to the judgmental eyes of the big "Other"—enables their work to join a tradition of highly authored situations that fuse social reality with carefully calculated artifice (such as the Dada-Season series of artworks and public interventions in April, 1921), in which intersubjective relations are not an end in themselves but serve to unfold a more complex knot of concerns about pleasure, disruption, engagement, and the conventions of social interaction. Instead of extracting art from the "useless" domain of the aesthetic and fusing it with social praxis, the most interesting art of today exists between two vanishing points: "Art becoming mere life or art becoming mere art."[40]

At present, the discursive criteria of participatory, collaborative, and socially engaged art is drawn from a tacit analogy between anticapitalism and the Christian "good soul." In this schema, self-sacrifice is triumphant: The artist should renounce authorial presence in favor of allowing participants to speak through him or her. Some people will consider this a harsh way to express reservations about some of today's most politically ambitious practices, but good intentions should not render this art immune to critical analysis. Art should not have to surrender itself to exemplary gestures, but it can instead use the medium of participation to articulate a contradictory pull between autonomy and social intervention; moreover, it can reflect on this antinomy both in the structure of the work *and* in the conditions of its reception to subsequent audiences. It is to this art—however uncomfortable, exploitative, or confusing it may first appear—that we must turn for an alternative to the well-intentioned homilies that today pass for the critical discourse on social collaboration. These homilies unwittingly push us back toward a platonic regime in which art is valued for its truthfulness and educational efficacy—rather than for inviting us to confront the more uncomfortable considerations of our predicament.

17

The Richter Effect on the Regeneration of Aesthetics

Michael Kelly

I see no point in enumerating the old, lost possibilities of painting. To me, what counts is to say something; what counts is the new possibilities.

Gerhard Richter[1]

AESTHETICS IS AGAIN RECEIVING attention today, after a long period of malign neglect by many artists, art theorists, and philosophers alike. In response to the voice of the anti-aesthetic, which has been dominant for several decades, we now also hear talk of the rediscovery of aesthetics—witness this volume. I welcome this rediscovery, or regeneration,[2] but I think it is important to emphasize that aesthetics must be rediscovered in artistic practices, not just in philosophical theories.[3] Artists are the ones who generate aesthetics in their practices, or not, allowing philosophers and others to discover it there, or not. After all, virtually all iterations of the anti-aesthetic in modernism and postmodernism (e.g., Marcel Duchamp, John Cage, Barnett Newman, Andy Warhol) began within the arts and only later, or simultaneously, received theoretical expression within aesthetics or disciplines that have emerged, in part, to give better expression to the anti-aesthetic. So, while it is possible to develop philosophical critiques of the anti-aesthetic or even to offer compelling theoretical alternatives to it, the only effective response to the anti-aesthetic is going to come, in the end, from the artistic practices of contemporary artists, even if philosophical theories are needed to complement that response. This is especially true today, I think, because theory has reified the anti-aesthetic long after it has played itself out in many of the arts.

Since the way to regenerate aesthetics is to analyze artistic practices, I will discuss one contemporary artist, Gerhard Richter, who explicitly resists anti-aesthetic interpretations of his work, by writing as well as by painting,[4] and who, in doing so, makes the regeneration of aesthetics a viable option that may prove irresistible even to die-hard, anti-aesthetic theorists.[5] In particular, I will analyze Richter's 1988 painting series called *October 18, 1977* (a.k.a. the *Baader-Meinhof* series), first exhibited in February–April 1989 in Haus Ester, a museum designed by Mies van der Rohe in Krefeld, Germany. The paintings collectively serve well as Richter's pictorial statements about whether contemporary painting can assert itself as a living art, whether painting can represent death, whether it is able to critique social-political issues—just to mention several key tasks that anti-aesthetic theorists have designated as beyond the "representational substance" of today's art. Although no one artist can establish new possibilities for art that anti-aesthetic art theorists claim contemporary material conditions do not allow, Richter successfully resists the anti-aesthetic (by accomplishing these tasks), allowing its firm grip on contemporary art to be loosened. At the same time, he allows us to regenerate aesthetics as a theoretical practice needed to explain and support what he has accomplished.

Part One

The Rote Armee Faktion (RAF), also known as the Baader-Meinhof Group, was an urban guerilla or terrorist movement active in West Germany beginning in the late 1960s, although they were formally organized only in 1970. They were first active in the student movement and in Vietnam War protests, and later they were involved in the youth offenders' rights movement and other social causes. The key members—Andreas Baader, Ulrike Meinhof, Gudrun Ensslin, Jean-Karl Raspe, and Thorward Proll—were in jail already by 1972. Baader, Ensslin, and Raspe died in the Stammheim prison (Stuttgart, Germany) on October 18, 1977, allegedly by suicide, while Meinhof died there in May 1976.[6]

Richter's *Baader-Meinhof* series comprise fifteen paintings, depicting mostly the capture and death of the leaders of the first generation of the Baader-Meinhof Group. His paintings are "based" on documentary or source photographs (and videos) of the group taken by the police, media, friends, and a studio photographer (the picture of young Meinhof).

Astrid Proll, a surviving though also imprisoned member of the Baader-Meinhof Group (and the sister of Thorward), published her own book of photographs, *Baader-Meinhof: Pictures on the Run 67-77*, in 1998.[7] In her short introduction she makes a very provocative comment about Richter's paintings that I believe provides great insight into them.

Astrid Proll said she could not bear to look at the 1977 media photographs of her dead comrades until twelve years later when she saw Richter's paintings based on the very same sources—which I call the "Richter Effect." "Thanks to the painter Gerhard Richter, whose *Cycle 18th October 1977* freed these pictures from their mass media context, I was finally able to approach them [*konnte ich mich ihnen annähern*]."[8] What exactly did Richter do in his paintings to deserve Proll's thanks, given the fact that she was trained as a photographer and presumably not a naive viewer? What made it possible for her finally to endure and even draw near to the photographs, many of which she had copies of? Part of her answer is the mass art / high art distinction between the media photographs and Richter's paintings, because she thinks the paintings toned down or even corrected the hype and distortions surrounding the images of the Stammheim events of October 1977, which the media and police largely controlled. Proll objected not only to the content of the images—depictions of her comrades' deaths, which very well could have included her brother or herself—but also to how they were used and abused by the media and police to depict the Baader-Meinhof members as common criminals, or rather as *un*common criminals—in other words, terrorists not deserving of compassion or even basic civil rights. So how come Richter's paintings, based on these identical photographs, did not have the same effect of making Proll turn away from them? On the contrary, she was drawn to the paintings because they made demands on her that she could not ignore. While Richter is clearly separate from the media and police, this separation alone does not fully explain the difference between the respective images. How are Richter's images different and how does this difference make it possible for Proll to "approach" the source photographs only after being drawn to the paintings?

To be sure, some kind of distance is embodied in Richter's paintings, but the twelve years between the first appearance of (many of) the Baader-Meinhof photographs in 1977 and the first exhibition of the paintings in 1989 could have provided distance, too. So there has to be something else involved here besides *temporal* distance, although even Richter acknowledges he needed that time.[9] If Proll had wanted to keep her *psychological* distance from the Baader-Meinhof history by avoiding the photographs, as she had done for years already, she could have maintained that distance by keeping Richter's paintings at bay or by stopping at them instead of going on to look at the photographs. So what attracted her to the paintings, which in turn allowed—even compelled—her to draw near to the photographs? Only if and when this question is answered can we ask the further question: Is the Richter Effect particular to a surviving member of the Baader-Meinhof Group or are others more distant in involvement, time, and place also affected in a similar way?

Richter's paintings *mediate* the experience of the Baader-Meinhof deaths, as well as the experience of the summary events leading up to them insofar as they are embodied in those deaths. So what is this mediation, and how do the paintings achieve it when photographs with apparently equivalent content cannot do so (either at all or only through the paintings)? In general, mediation is tied to a basic function of art, as described by Richter: "Picturing things, taking a view, is what makes us human; art is making sense and giving shape to that sense."[10] Mediation means to engage in art as a way to endure experience as we try to understand the meanings of what experience gives us to endure and, further, as we give shape to those meanings.

Speaking of the difference between the police photographs of the dead terrorists and the paintings of the same, Richter says: "Perhaps I can describe the difference like this: in this particular case, I'd say the photograph provokes *horror* [and *fear*], and the painting—with the same motif—something more like *grief.* That comes very close to what I intended."[11] This does not mean that the paintings provoke grief *instead of* horror and fear; rather, there is a conjunction in the paintings: horror/fear *and* grief, whereas the photographs provoke only horror/fear. So the paintings have added something here, namely, a space for grief. This space is not only metaphorical; it is quite concrete in the sense that the public exhibition of the Baader-Meinhof paintings in a museum (or gallery) is a performative grieving affair, allowing viewers to experience the series as if they were attending a wake or funeral. Even the painting of Meinhof when she was young and innocent is a familiar sight at wakes and funerals because people sometimes want to remember the deceased in their earlier or happier years. Finally, the last painting in the series, *Funeral* (6'6¾" × 10'6"), is large enough that viewers may feel as if they are not only witnessing a

funeral procession but actually participating in it. Insofar as they do witness and participate, they are taking part in Richter's artistic mediation of
the Baader-Meinhof deaths.

When asked about the *object* of the grief, Richter responds that the
grief is not for any "cause" or even for the individual members of the
Baader-Meinhof Group.[12] It is grief for "that is the way it is"—they are
dead.[13] In short, it is grief for the deaths depicted in the paintings. With
this grief comes compassion, as it does in other death settings. Clarifying
now the object of compassion, Richter says that it is not compassion for the
dead terrorists as individuals. Rather, it is compassion for the death that
they had to suffer because of their beliefs, or rather the failure of their beliefs: That is, the compassion is for "the fact that an illusion of being able to
change the world has failed."[14] This failure is not the Baader-Meinhof
Group's alone, but one that others might share if they agree that West German society needed to be changed in certain ways.[15] The grief and compassion are the effects of the way Richter's paintings mediate the experience of
the Baader-Meinhof history, the deaths in Stammheim in particular.

Richter asks that when we talk about the relationship between his
paintings and the Baader-Meinhof deaths depicted in them, we recognize
that we are talking about the mediation of his own relationship to the
deaths: "I can make no statement about reality clearer than my own relationship to reality."[16] That is, the paintings do not embody general statements about the deaths of the Baader-Meinhof Group, which would be
the job of a journalist, historian, or social philosopher. Rather, they are
first, though not only, about a particular individual's relationship to the
experience and meanings of those deaths. The paintings are Richter's way
of mediating those deaths, of making sense of them, and of giving shape
to that sense. Similarly, Astrid Proll decided to publish her book of photographs of the Baader-Meinhof Group as a way to approach or mediate her
own Baader-Meinhof experiences, especially given the way she thinks the
Baader-Meinhof history has been distorted by media-generated myths.
Even though Proll's preferred mode of mediation was photography because of her training, she first needed Richter's paintings to mediate the
source photographs (double mediation instead of double negation). So in
Richter and Proll's cases, despite many differences between them, painting is the primary mode of mediation.

However, Richter is not trying to depict the objective reality of the
Baader-Meinhof deaths. Rather, by depicting the presumed objective real-

ity of the photographs, he is raising the issue of what should count as objective in this case. He is depicting his mediation of the experience of
those deaths, both by showing that they have already been mediated
(when depicted in photographs) and by engaging in his own mediation of
the same deaths in an effort to endure their horror and understand their
meanings. In Richter's words again: "The deaths of the terrorists, and the
related events both before and after, stand for a horror that distressed me
and had haunted me as unfinished business ever since, despite all my efforts to *suppress* it."[17] Elsewhere, he says that his relationship to the
Baader-Meinhof terrorism accounts for this same imprecision of the paintings: "This [his relationship to the experience of the deaths] has a great
deal to do with imprecision, uncertainty, transience, incompleteness, or
whatever."[18] However, this imprecision and the like do not explain the
paintings themselves. Rather, they explain only *why* they were painted:
Richter was trying both to endure—a way to live with[19]—the horror of
the Baader-Meinhof deaths and to understand their meanings. This is
why he describes the act of painting these pictures as a process that made
the content depicted in the photographs more bearable, giving him a voice
about them so that he would no longer be a "mute spectator" in their presence.[20] If horror reduces us to silence, art as mediation allows us to get our
voices back. This is the Richter Effect, as described by Richter himself.

The sense of endurance here—and thus of mediation—is therefore
not that of getting through or over some event but, as Richter explicitly
says, of getting over the suppression of it, getting to the point that one can
handle not being able to endure or understand it—yet. Of course, the
horror of pictures can also induce us to forget what is pictured, if what is
presented (e.g., the brutal reality of death) is too difficult to absorb or process, affectively and intellectually—as it had been for Proll, until she saw
Richter's paintings. By painting these pictures in such a way as to give us
space for grief and compassion, Richter mediates the experience of the
Baader-Meinhof deaths with his art, with what he describes as the daily
practice of painting. What Richter does for himself, he does for Proll;
since any public exhibition of the paintings is a performance of grief and
compassion, the Richter Effect is, in principle, open to the rest of us.

It is important to stress here that the grief—and thus the mediation—
are particular rather than universal. That is, Richter's paintings represent
particular deaths tied to particular events, not some universal sense of
death. To quote John Dewey: "The esthetic portrayal of grief manifests

the grief of a particular individual in connection with a particular event. It is *that* state of sorrow which is depicted, not depression unattached. It has a *local* habitation."[21] The reason particularity is important here is that the themes tied to the Baader-Meinhof Group—death, terrorism, and so on—are too easily universalized because death and now terrorism are everywhere. If understood mainly as universal phenonema (i.e., the themes), however, they no longer have the same effect for Proll or any of the rest of us. While I may be moved by the death of any person or terri-fied by any act of a terrorist, what moves me to the point that I need me-diation to endure the death or act is its particularity. I am moved by *this* person or act *here*. And *I* am the one who is moved. The more I am moved, the more mediation I need, the more I demand art. The particu-larity here is temporal as well as spatial. As Richter says several times, coincidentally in 1977 as the Baader-Meinhof events were unfolding, "I want to picture to myself what is going on *now*. Painting can help with this, and different methods = subjects = themes are different attempts I make in this direction."[22] Richter also says in 1977 that the basic inten-tion in all his work is "to picture to myself what is going on" around him.[23] He even describes his painting as a kind of reporting, suggesting another link to the newspapers that were the source of many of the pho-tographs he worked with. But it is reporting that is not mere repetition; rather, the aim is to create meanings that have the aim of helping him, Proll, and others "to see how it is" in the case of the Baader-Meinhof Group.[24]

Richter's mediation of his relationship to the Baader-Meinhof deaths is not necessarily confined to him, or to Proll, if those of us who view the paintings find that his mediation is successful, that he has truly opened a gray space for compassion and grief (as well as horror and fear) that we, too, can occupy. The public viewing of the paintings as a group is the performative site when the rest of us can see whether we can indeed oc-cupy this space of grief and compassion. That is, while Richter starts with an issue that is of concern to him, his aim is for others to experience his mediation. To do so, however, we first have to understand the aesthetic form(s) of this mediation, the ways that he gives shape to the sense he is able to make of his experience. For this to happen, Richter insists that the paintings have to speak for themselves: "They are there to show them-selves and not me . . . That's why form is so important . . . because with-out form communication stops."[25] So although the mediation starts from a particular and subjective content—a particular artist's relationship to the experience of the Baader-Meinhof deaths—it ends up as something objective: aesthetic form for all to experience.

Part Two

The aesthetic means of mediation in Richter's *Baader-Meinhof* series are the techniques and forms he employs in the process of producing them: composition (cropped or edited versions of photographs), scale (mostly life-size), paint surface (thin), color (all gray), blurring, and so on. Of these, the blurring technique is the most perspicuous and controversial, so it is also most in need of interpretation. To this end, Richter's comments on his blurring technique are quite revealing, although what they reveal is fundamentally different, I think, from how it is typically interpreted by critics.

Richter lists a number of reasons for his blurring technique, which he has utilized almost since the start of his artistic career: "I blur things to make everything equally important and equally unimportant. I blur things so that they do not look artistic or craftsmanlike but technological, smooth and perfect. I blur things to make all the parts a closer fit. Perhaps I also blur out the excess of unimportant information."[26] These statements are sometimes interpreted as if Richter used the blurring technique to erase all aesthetic properties from his paintings (allowing them to embody the anti-aesthetic), as if he were neutralizing any content depicted in them, as if he were destabilizing any meanings of the photographs, or, finally, as if he were doing all the above. For example, Gertrud Koch argues that Richter erases the meaning and intentionality of the source photographs by blurring them and, in so doing, tears them out of time and strips them of any history: "The picture cycle in question puts on display neither the 'beautiful souls of terror' nor the harsh machinery of the state; what they show is blurredness, things out of focus, behind which objects and people disappear."[27] If this were accurate, however, what would account for viewers' engaged, even heated reactions to the Richter paintings?[28] Koch's own answer is that "what is so scandalous about these pictures is not their emotional impact" or cathartic effect "but rather their cold distanciation."[29] Yet if that were true, why would viewers such as Proll react so passionately to cold paintings? Simply because they were cold, and she expected partisan paintings? Or is Koch suggesting that Richter's cold paintings offset the deep, unsettling emotions Proll experienced in the presence of the source photographs (*sie hätten mich zu tief erschüttert*, i.e., "they affected me too deeply")? But the result of such a balancing act would be mere neutrality, a canceling of powerful emotions by the absence of any emotion. How could a series of emotionless paintings enable Proll to approach the photos (*"mich ihnen annähern"*), especially since the German word *Annäherung* suggests a possible reconciliation or rapprochement, not mere neutrality? In short, this type of critical interpretation of the blurring technique is not adequate in the case of the *Baader-Meinhof* paintings because it cannot explain the Richter Effect.

In addition, such an interpretation does not take account of the fact that Richter's blurring technique cannot have the same goal or effect every time he employs it, for that would make the technique independent of the content of the paintings in which it is employed and of the context of their reception. In the particular case of the *Baader-Meinhof* paintings, it is clear that the content of the depictions of death is political because of the views and actions of the Baader-Meinhof Group and the West German government's responses to them. At the same time, the context has remained quite volatile in various venues since the paintings were first exhibited. While Richter insisted that the *October 18, 1977* series be kept together and hoped it would be purchased by a German museum, the Baader-Meinhof political legacy proved too controversial. The series was sold in 1995 to the Museum of Modern Art (MoMA) in New York, where Richter expected that the politics of the paintings would finally not outweigh their aesthetics. However, after being exhibited at MoMA in 1995 and then again in late 2000 / early 2001, the series was part of a Richter retrospective at MoMA in early 2002, roughly six months after the Al-Qaeda attacks in New York on September 11, 2001. These attacks caused some New York viewers (regardless of where they were from) to experience the Richter paintings in a new light because the content of terrorism was no longer largely somebody else's experience. New York viewers were in principle more able to appreciate the need for the type of mediation achieved in Richter's paintings and, moreover, they became more vulnerable to the Richter Effect (and, I would add, better judges of it). Clearly, the *Baader-Meinhof* paintings did not escape the politics of terrorism when they moved to New York—on the contrary. So in using the blurring technique, Richter does not elide the terrorism and political passions of the Baader-Meinhof history and thereby allow us to hide from them, as some critics have claimed; for if that were true, the *Baader-Meinhof* paintings would have been received in New York as if they were history paintings representing a distant past and thus irrelevant to the present.[30] Rather, Richter employs the blurring technique so that we—Proll, New York viewers, and others—can endure and, if possible, understand the politics and pain of terrorism. Thus, the content (Baader-Meinhof legacy) and context (first Germany and now New York) of Richter's paintings ensure that they have a contemporaneity that makes the effect of the blurring technique different from most other uses of it in his work, before or since.[31]

Still, if the blurring technique is different in the *Baader-Meinhof* case, how does it work to generate the Richter Effect? The blurring has a kind of push/pull effect, though not just in the formal way described by Robert Storr, who says that Richter pushes back the photographic images as he pulls the paintings forward.[32] Rather, the paintings *push back the Baader-Meinhof deaths* (because of horror and fear) but in order to allow us to *pull them back* (draw them near for the first time) for purposes of grief and compassion. The push/pull here is affective rather than formal, though it is achieved by the formal means Storr describes. In Richter's words, the paintings have a "blurred look, whereby something has to be shown and simultaneously not shown, in order perhaps to say something else again, a third thing"[33]—third in addition to horror and fear, namely, a space for grief and compassion. The opening up of this space is the effect of the practice—or, again, performance—of painting as the mediation of (the experience of) the Baader-Meinhof deaths.

The issue of the distinctiveness of Richter's use of the blurring technique in the *Baader-Meinhof* series revives the earlier question of how we might best understand the relationship between Richter's paintings and the source photographs. In turn, the revival of this issue raises the question about what the paintings are blurring, that is, what they are a blurring *of.* The source photographs? Richter is emphatic that the paintings not be interpreted as blurred *photographs*, even though he acknowledges that the paintings had their origin, on the level of subject matter, in the photographs. Had he wanted to produce blurred photographs, he could have worked in a darkroom, painted over photographs, or utilized a digital photo-editing program. But that is not what he did—in this case, anyway. Nor are the *Baader-Meinhof* paintings blurred photo-realistic paintings of the source photographs, even though, according to Richter's own description of the painting process for this series, he began with photo-realistic renditions of the photographs.[34] The reason why this second option is not accurate, according to Richter, is the same reason why he refuses to describe his paintings as blurred: Paintings "are never blurred. What we regard as blurring is imprecision, and that means that they are different from the object represented. But, since pictures are not made for purposes of comparison with reality, they cannot be blurred, or imprecise, or different (different from what?). How can, say, paint on canvas be blurred?"[35] In short, whereas photographs can be blurred, as we all have experienced while trying to capture a fleeting moment on camera, paintings cannot be blurred. If they *look* blurred, that is only to say that they are paintings, albeit ones that at the same time have a constitutive relationship to blurred photographs. Paintings offer only the *semblance* of blurring, but a semblance that can have the same aesthetic effect as a blurred photograph, which, if it happens, is to say that it is an effective semblance, as good as a real blur. The important point here, however, is that it is only as paintings, which cannot be blurred, that these works seem to be blurred and thus compared to photographs, which can be blurred. In effect, Richter *engages* the contrast between photography and painting, *adopts* the photographic technique (or accident) of blurring, and *applies* that technique to paintings, all in order to demonstrate the *difference* between the Baader-Meinhof photographs and paintings and, more importantly, to allow the paintings to create the space for grief and compassion that the photographs cannot provide. The photograph-painting difference helps to open up this space.

In seeming to be blurred, Richter's paintings not only announce themselves as paintings rather than as photographs, they also announce that the source photographs are not what they first seemed to be. Photographs are typically thought to offer an *un*mediated (i.e., objective) record of their subject matter because they are said to be causally related to the reality they depict—in the present case, the deaths of the Baader-Meinhof Group. By offering the semblance of blurred versions of these same photographs, the Richter paintings explicitly thematize the mediation involved in this case. That is, by showing that the content of the photographs is subject to mediation, Richter raises the question about when and how mediation enters the picture. Perhaps there is no unmediated causal link between the photographs and their content? Perhaps the difference between the photographs and the paintings is no longer a distinction between unmediated, objective images and mediated, subjective images? The point here, however, is not merely that all images are mediated and thus subjective to some degree, although that would be a point well taken. Rather, the point is that all images are forms of mediation, so mediation alone cannot differentiate one type of image from another.

The way these issues about mediation play out in the *Baader-Meinhof* paintings is something like the following. One main intention of the source photographs, at least those from the media and police, was to achieve closure on the public reception of the Baader-Meinhof Group by announcing, through photography, that the Baader-Meinhof leaders were finally dead. The credibility of the claim of closure rested on the presumed objectivity of the photographs, which in turn rested on the presumption that they were unmediated depictions of the deaths of the Baader-Meinhof leaders. However, in raising the possibility that the photographs are mediations too, Richter's paintings helped to raise doubts about the key presumption and, with it, about the closure that rested on it. In doing so, the paintings render the meanings of the photographs unclear—unclear because now mediated. That is, the photographs that once seemed to provide an *un*mediated record of the deaths of the Baader-Meinhof Group are now possibly mediated and, in any case, no longer as clear as they first seemed to be, so long as there is even any hint of mediation (by those who took the photographs). If the Baader-Meinhof events were thought to achieve closure through the photographs, that closure is now blurred and the events are now open, the deaths are now objects of critical thinking—of aesthetics.

The mediation issues raised by Richter's paintings concern the *meanings* of the Baader-Meinhof deaths, not just their *facticity*, since the basic fact that the key Baader-Meinhof members were dead was presumably established by the photographs (though the "how" of their deaths has long remained a controversy for many people). In the words of Gregg Horowitz, the source photographs render the Baader-Meinhof members as *the dead* (level of facticity) but cannot render *their deadness* (level of meaning), whereas the paintings render their deadness, too, so much so that "the deaths of Baader, Ensslin, and the others were being suffered in the act of painting itself."[36] Richter confirms this point about another performative dimension of his paintings when he says that as he painted the *Baader-Meinhof* series he was "occupied like a gravedigger."[37] In turn, this suffering is sustained by the process of public mourning initiated by the exhibition of the paintings as a funereal performance. Yet, while the important distinction between "the dead" and "their deadness" points again to the difference between the source photographs and the Richter paintings, it does not explain it. The limit of the photographs, their inability to render "their deadness," has to do with their nature as photographs, according to Roland Barthes, because all they can depict is what has been; in doing so, they ratify "what has been" without question, with certainty, thereby providing "a certificate of presence." But, he adds, photographs cannot do the same for meanings because they are contingent and therefore outside meanings.[38] This does not necessarily mean that photographs have no meaning but that their relationship to meaning is a function of their signature relationship to reality. In the gray light of Richter's *Baader-Meinhof* paintings, however, that signature is blurred and photography's claim to provide any "certificate of presence" is called into question since photography is now seen as a form of mediation. This questioning suggests that photography may not even be able to render "the dead," let alone "their deadness," since its claim to do so rested on its being unmediated and it is mediated after all. Moreover, it now seems that "their deadness" (meaning) may very well be the key to "the dead" (facticity), not the other way around. So by being able to render "their deadness," Richter's paintings are also able to render "the dead" in the sense that we do not really know the facts about the deaths of the Baader-Meinhof leaders until we first know the meanings of those facts. By creating public space for "their deadness" through the use of the blurring technique (and other aesthetic tools), Richter has thereby opened up new relations between the meaning and facticity of the Baader-Meinhof deaths, not just new relations between source photographs and a series of paintings.

To clarify what Richter has achieved, we have to ask again: What is the blurring in his paintings a blurring *of,* if it is neither of the photographs nor of the paintings? Should we conclude, as Desa Philippi has, that there "is a futility about asking what these works are about, what their referent might be."[39] Are the paintings really so impenetrable, as Koch also argues? To accept such conclusions is to give up hope that the Richter Effect can be explained. Other critics who have written on the *Baader-Meinhof* series, whether supportively or critically, have drawn a similar conclusion by arguing that the blurring introduces indeterminacy into the Baader-Meinhof history, or at least into our collective memory of it. What is indeterminate, according to this type of interpretation, is not just the deaths of the Baader-Meinhof members who were in the Stamm-heim prison in October 1977, but also the political and violent actions of the group before they were arrested and the actions of the West German government against them, which raised many questions about civil rights for West German citizens as a whole. On this interpretation, the blurred paintings are a pictorial metaphor for the indeterminacy of the Baader-Meinhof history, which means that both "the dead" and "their deadness" are indeterminate.

This kind of interpretation seems to confuse the source photographs and the Richter paintings on the issue of the presence and memory of the Baader-Meinhof Group. While the source photographs of the Baader-Meinhof Group are supposed to assert the causal presence of what they depict and to provide a basis for the memory of the same, they rather have the effect of *denying* the presence of the group and closing off any memory of them, except as criminals. In the words of Rainer Rochlitz, "Richter painted the documents of a historical mess, brought on tragically by the *adjournment* of the work of memory."[40] As we saw, the photographs were intended to achieve closure on a tumultuous chapter of contemporary German history by documenting dead criminals who were to be remembered as such, which is to say they hardly warranted being remembered at all. By contrast, Richter's paintings negate this closure and reestablish a presence for the Baader-Meinhof Group by rekindling people's memory of them, as happened in Proll's case. In effect, Richter returns the Baader-Meinhof members to the realm of the living, where in their deadness they can live among the living. And why would we want them living among us again, given that the period of time marked by the violent actions committed by and against the Baader-Meinhof Group is one few of us would want to relive? The unfortunate answer is that starting from at least the World Trade Center attacks on September 11, 2001, Americans, Europeans, Iraqis, and many other peoples are living in a period marked by terrorist violence, and so long as terrorism is in our midst, we are living with the Baader-Meinhof Group, too. They are part of the contemporaneity of terrorism—sometimes foreign, sometimes domestic, sometimes both—that we need to keep before us if we are ever going to endure its horror and understand its meanings. So something more is going on in Richter's paintings than a metaphor for indeterminacy, something more than the negation of the meanings of the source photographs and the decomposition of the history they depict. According to the very critics who advocate this indeterminacy line of interpretation of

Richter, negation that is not determinate is not acceptable on philosophical grounds. What is negated by Richter's paintings is the media's and police's attempted closures, and what is determinate is the reopening of the Baader-Meinhof case.

Some critics argue, however, that Richter's paintings, precisely because they appear blurred, express moral ambiguity on the topic of terrorism, which allows no room for being on the fence. This is a serious issue. But I think the view that terrorism eliminates moral choice by simplifying all choice to "either for or against" is one that closes off discussion on an important, complex set of social, political, and moral issues. Even if there were any moral certainty and consensus about terrorism among the general public, there still should be room for discussion here. Those who have such certainty should be able to handle discussion, if only to articulate and defend their certainty. Their unwillingness or inability to do so is a symptom of *their un*certainty. So, if Richter's work involves any moral uncertainty, it is not his. Rather, it belongs to those who resist his paintings in the name of a moral certainty that remains elusive.

As I mentioned previously, the Baader-Meinhof Group initially became politically active largely in opposition to the Vietnam War, based on a legitimate critique shared at the time by only some in West Germany and the United States but eventually by most of the general public around the world. That the group eventually adopted violent strategies to express their opposition to the war (and other issues) is likely to be what is remembered more than anything else. Unfortunately, when opposition groups engage in violence, either on their own accord or as a result of government provocation, the effect is that discussion of the legitimacy of their opposition gets shut down. Moreover, as many people such as Jeremy Varon have noted, violence begets repression of many other people besides those perpetrating the violence: "What people remember about the [Baader-Meinhof] era is typically not only the pervasive fear of terrorist violence but also the tremendous constriction of thought and feeling caused by heightened demands for loyalty to the state, enforced, in part, by repression."[41] In response to this constriction and repression, albeit starting twelve years later (and counting), Richter's paintings reopen discussion of the underlying concerns that gave rise to the Baader-Meinhof Group or else of the issues that emerged as a result of the West German government's efforts to suppress it. In Varon's words again: "Critics warned that censorship inhibited precisely the kind of dialogue that would permit the left and West German society as a whole to make sense of the current crisis."[42] It has taken an artist, a painter no less, to reopen this dialogue by creating space for grief and compassion. It is up to the rest of us to take advantage of this opportunity.

Now, even if one were to acknowledge the need for such discussion and agree that Richter helped to generate it, one might ask why he did not paint pictures of the victims of the Baader-Meinhof Group instead of (or in addition to) the terrorists in order to present a more balanced picture of the Baader-Meinhof legacy. After all, he did paint victims in his series of eight paintings of nurses murdered by a serial killer (*Eight Student Nurses*, 1966) and in a painting about the Kennedy assassination, *Woman with Umbrella* (1964), he painted Jacqueline Kennedy in a moment of shock accompanied by grief. Also, in talking once about Warhol's *Thirteen Most Wanted Men* (1964), Richter said he "preferred" to paint victims while Warhol seemed to prefer the criminals.[43] In the Baader-Meinhof case, however, Richter was not interested in photographs of the victims, though there were many of them available. One reason, I think, is that pictures of the victims would not be tied to the full range of issues surrounding the Baader-Meinhof Group and West Germany's reaction to it, and those issues remain controversial and thus need to be discussed. That is, there is no longer any comparable controversy among the general public about the victims, since they did nothing to deserve their fate, even if they were considered guilty in some way (e.g., because of any Nazi past), according to the Baader-Meinhof Group. Although the victims' portraits would still provoke grief and compassion because of their relative innocence, they would not likely open up a broader discussion of the Baader-Meinhof Group. Rather, grief and compassion in that case would only confirm their already largely accepted innocence and their relative separation from the underlying issues.

Of course, Richter could still have painted portraits of the innocent victims as well, again for the sake of balance. Or else he could have painted unsympathetic portraits of the terrorists, which would comple-ment the sympathetic portrayal of the innocent victims. But what would have been the purpose of these additional paintings, given that the inno-cent were already recognized as such and the terrorists were already seen, through the source photographs, in an unsympathetic light? Richter's purpose was presumably something else. He saw a need to express some-thing more than certain innocence and certain guilt, clear victims and clear criminals. It is not that he wanted to blur these distinctions; rather, he wanted to open up discussion of issues that the rush to certainty and closure had shut down. So it is not morally irresponsible that certainty is not the purpose or effect of Richter's paintings (nor the intent of his statements about them). These paintings are indeed tied to uncertainty, for without uncertainty they would have had no raison d'être. But, again, this does not mean that the moral certainty of the criminal/victim framework has been dissolved or that all the basic questions are entirely up for grabs. On the contrary, it means that moral-political nuances, subtleties, and the like can now be introduced. Discussion, deliberation, and debate about the Baader-Meinhof legacy—including the impact on the victims— are opened up by the Richter Effect, by the space for grief and compassion created in Richter's paintings.

In the end, the Baader-Meinhof paintings create a performative space for public grief and compassion that is at the same time an invitation to address a host of questions: What was the Baader-Meinhof trying to achieve and why did they fail? What was the role of violence in their actions and goals? What does it say about West German society that it both generated and suppressed this group? Could somebody feel compassion for the Baader-Meinhof Group (their aspirations as distinct from their persons or actions) as well as for the West German state? Were the civil rights of all West German citizens compromised during the search for the Baader-Meinhof members? How did they really die in Stammheim? While the events of October 18, 1977, were supposed to put an end to the Baader-Meinhof Group, it was the end only of a chapter because successive generations of the group were active until 1998 and also because terrorism has only become more common in the Western world since 1977, as well as elsewhere. Because of the issues and questions, Richter's paintings sustain their contemporaneity since the questions they raise are about the present as well as the past. The nonclosure and thus sustained contemporaneity of the Baader-Meinhof chapter also means we need to be demanding answers of ourselves, and art as mediation is a principal way to do so. Although art can help to demand answers, it cannot provide them; we need more than art for the answers. That is, the Richter paintings do not settle any of the issues they raise, but nor could they be expected to. Rather, their role is to be unsettling, not so much on the question of how the Baader-Meinhof members died, but on the deeper questions of the "why," that is, on the level of meaning(s).

So Richter's paintings open up issues that were once thought to be dead (i.e., closed), and they do so by using a medium thought to be so deficient, especially relative to photography, that it could not achieve the Richter Effect. However, if we agree with Proll that Richter's paintings are indeed adequate representations of death in that they successfully mediate the experience of the Baader-Meinhof deaths, we can also recognize that some paintings are not deficient after all. While no single painting series can by itself overcome a long-standing anti-aesthetic critique of representation (painting especially), it can make us recognize that the anti-aesthetic has its limits, which only artists can enable us to see. Of course, more studies of this kind would be needed to show convincingly that a powerful way to regenerate aesthetics is to challenge the anti-aesthetic by analyzing artworks thought to embody the anti-aesthetic, but one such study is enough to open up this path.

Notes

Introduction

1. The notion of "interdisciplinarity" tends to indicate a prior agreement on the object of research and perhaps on an integrated research method, which is not available for aesthetics. Nonetheless, much of what has been said in favor of interdisciplinarity applies to the notions of cross-disciplinarity and trans-disciplinarity as well. See for example Ivan Gaskell's article on the official Web site of the American Society for Aesthetics, http://www.aesthetics-online.org/articles (accessed May 10, 2008).

2. See Hegel's equation of aesthetics and philosophy of art at the very beginning of his aesthetics lectures, *Hegel's Aesthetics. Lectures on Fine Art*, trans. T. M. Knox (Oxford: Oxford University Press, 1975).

3. Recent defenses of this approach have included Mary Mothersill, *Beauty Restored* (Oxford: Oxford University Press, 1984); Nick Zangwill, *The Metaphysics of Beauty* (Ithaca, NY: Cornell University Press, 2001); and, perhaps surprisingly, Arthur C. Danto, *The Abuse of Beauty* (Chicago: Open Court, 2003).

4. See Pierre Bourdieu, *Distinction: A Social Critique of the Judgment of Taste*, trans. Richard Nice (London: Routledge, 1984); and Terry Eagleton, *The Ideology of the Aesthetic* (Oxford: Blackwell, 1990).

5. This connects with the very beginnings of the discipline. See Alexander Baumgarten, *Aesthetica* (1750/1758), vol. 1, trans. and ed. into German by Dagmar Mirbach in a Latin-German edition (Hamburg: Meiner Verlag, 2007), p. 58. Recently, Carolyn Korsmeyer has asked whether the disgusting might replace concerns with the beautiful and the sublime. See Carolyn Korsmeyer, *Gender and Aesthetics* (London: Routledge, 2004).

6. The recent "Philistine Controversy" is paradigmatic here. See D. Beech, J. Roberts, eds., *The Philistine Controversy* (London: Verso, 2002), p. 13.

7. The idea of *Kunstwissenschaft* (the scientific, rigorous, or systematic study of art) runs through the work of the founding fathers of modern art history: Heinrich Wölfflin and Alois Riegl and the later work of Erwin Panofsky and Ernst Gombrich. For its manifesto

see Hans Sedlmayr, "Toward A Rigorous Study of Art," (1931) in *The Vienna School Reader*, ed. C. Wood (New York: Zone Books, 2000), pp. 131–80.

8. Rosalind E. Krauss, "Using Language to Do Business as Usual," in *Visual Theory: Painting and Interpretation*, ed. N. Bryson, M. A. Holly, K. Moxey (New York: Harper-Collins, 1991), pp. 79–94.

9. See Michael Ann Holly, *Panofsky and the Foundations of Art History* (Ithaca, NY: Cornell University Press, 1984); Michael Podro, *The Critical Historians of Art* (New Haven, CT: Yale University Press, 1984); Eric Fernie, *Art History and Its Methods* (Boston: Phaidon Press, 1995); Donald Preziosi, *The Art of Art History* (Oxford: Oxford University Press, 1998); Paul Crowther, *The Transhistorical Image* (Cambridge: Cambridge University Press, 2002).

10. W.J.T. Mitchell, *What Do Pictures Want?* (Chicago: University of Chicago Press, 2005).

11. "New art history" refers to contextualist approaches (chiefly Marxist, feminist, semiological, structuralist, and psychoanalytic) that, in the 1980s, began to criticize institutional art history (e.g., by uncovering art history's own aesthetic presumptions). See Jonathan Harris, *The New Art History: A Critical Introduction* (London: Routledge, 2001).

12. Following Johann Joachim Winckelmann, Elizabeth Prettejohn speaks of a "kind of collaboration between the viewer and the work," in which aesthetic reflection provides a link between the past and present that emerges only from a direct encounter with aesthetic objects by a perceiving subject. See Elizabeth Prettejohn, *Beauty and Art* (Oxford: Oxford University Press, 2005), p. 22.

13. What Passmore found "dreary" was precisely the tendency of many aestheticians to abstract from the particularities of artworks and the specificities of particular media. John Passmore, "The Dreariness of Aesthetics," *Mind* 60 (1951): 318–35. See also Marx W. Wartowsky, "The Liveliness of Aesthetics," *Journal of Aesthetics and Art Criticism* 46 (1987): 211–18; and Joseph Margolis, "Exorcising the Dreariness of Aesthetics," *Journal of Aesthetics and Art Criticism* 51 (1993): 133–40.

14. Richard Rorty, "Der Roman als Mittel zur Erlösung aus der Selbstbezogenheit," in *Dimensionen ästhetischer Erfahrung*, ed. Joachim Küpper and Christoph Menke (Frankfurt, Germany: Suhrkamp, 2003), pp. 49–66; here, p. 54; quotation trans. from the German by Julia Jansen.

15. Mary Devereaux, "The Philosophical Status of Aesthetics," http://www.aesthetics-online.org/ideas/devereaux.html (accessed September 13, 2006).

16. See note 5.

17. A quick look at recently published collections alone in analytic aesthetics and aesthetics more generally demonstrates the ongoing rediscovery in philosophy. See Alex Neill and Aaron Ridley, eds., *Arguing About Art: Contemporary Philosophical Debates* (London: Routledge, 2001); Peter Lamarque, ed., *Aesthetics and the Philosophy of Art: The Analytic Tradition* (Oxford: Blackwell, 2003); Matthew Kieran, ed., *Contemporary Debates in Aesthetics and the Philosophy of Art* (Oxford: Blackwell, 2003); Jerold Levinson,

ed., *The Oxford Handbook of Aesthetics* (Oxford: Oxford University Press, 2003); Peter Goldie and Elisabeth Schellekens, eds., *Philosophy and Conceptual Art* (Oxford: Clarendon, 2007).

18. Joseph Kosuth, "Art after Philosophy," in *Conceptual Art: A Critical Anthology*, ed. Alexander Alberro and Blake Stimson (Cambridge, MA: MIT Press, 1999), pp. 164–77. Originally published in *Studio International* 178, nos. 915–17 (1969): 134–37, 160–61, 212–13.

19. Anita Silvers, "Aesthetics of Art's Sake, Not for Philosophy's!" *Journal of Aesthetics and Art Criticism* 51 (1993): 141–50; here, 149.

20. Peter Osborne and Andrew Benjamin, *Thinking Art: Beyond Traditional Aesthetics* (London: Institute of Contemporary Art, 1991), p. xi. For a fine example of what can be gained from a sensitive attention to the particularities of artworks, see Peter Osborne, *Conceptual Art* (London: Phaidon, 2002).

21. Mark Wilsher, "Judgment Call," *Art Monthly* 280 (October 2004): 7–10.

22. Hal Foster, ed., *The Anti-Aesthetic: Essays on Postmodern Culture* (New York: New Bay Press, 1998). See also Marcel Duchamp's use of the term "anaesthetic" in "Marcel Duchamp: Apropos of 'Readymades.'" Lecture at the Museum of Modern Art, New York, October 19, 1961. Published in: *Art and Artists* 1, no. 4 (July 1966); and Alan Badiou's recent invocation of "inaesthetics" in *Handbook of Inaesthetics*, trans. Alberto Toscano (Stanford, CA: Stanford University Press, 2005).

23. Major retrospectives of the last few years include Donald Judd (London, Düsseldorf, Basel), Robert Smithson (Los Angeles, Dallas, and New York), Dan Flavin (Washington, Fort Worth, Chicago), Bruce Nauman (Tate Modern, London, which was arguably also a retrospective in audio), and Richard Serra's installation in Bilbao. See also Donna de Salvo, *Open Systems 1970: Rethinking Art C. 1970* (London: Tate, 2005).

24. Lucy Lippard, *Six Years: The Dematerialization of the Art Object from 1966 to 1972* (Berkeley: University of California Press, 1997).

25. Arthur C. Danto, *After the End of Art* (Princeton, NJ: Princeton University Press, 1998).

26. Robert Morris, *Continuous Project Altered Daily: The Writings of Robert Morris* (Cambridge, MA: MIT Press, 1993); Rosalind Krauss, *Passages in Modern Sculpture* (Cambridge, MA: MIT Press, 1977).

27. Nicolas Bourriaud, *Relational Aesthetics* (Dijon, France: Les Presses du Réel, 2002), p. 14.

28. Lippard, *Six Years*.

29. Excellent examples of such work are Isobel Armstrong, *Radical Aesthetics* (Oxford: Blackwell, 2000); and Jonathan Loesberg, *A Return to Aesthetics* (Stanford, CA: Stanford University Press, 2005).

30. Kant's account of the "antinomy of taste" in the *Critique of Judgment* sets a background to this problem; see Kant, *Critique of Judgment*, trans. Werner Pluhar (Indianapolis, IN: Hackett, 1987), especially §§ 56 and 57.

31. Barnett Newman, *Selected Writings and Interviews*, ed. J. P. O'Neill (New York: Knopf, 1990), pp. 242–43, 304.

32. Andrew Bowie, *Aesthetics and Subjectivity* (Manchester, UK: Manchester University Press, 2003), p. 8.

33. It is still important to remember Michel Foucault's warning against the danger of overly facile projections of universal agreement. See Michel Foucault, "What Is an Author?" in *Michel Foucault: Aesthetics, Method, Epistemology (Essential Works by Michel Foucault, vol. 2)*, ed. James D. Faubion, trans. Robert Hurley et al. (New York: New Press, 1998), pp. 205–22.

34. Hal Foster, "Postmodernism: A Preface," in *The Anti-Aesthetic* (Seattle, WA: Bay Press, 1983), p. xv.

35. Paul Mattick, Jr., "Aesthetics and Anti-Aesthetics in the Visual Arts," *Journal of Aesthetics and Art Criticism* 51 (1993): 253–59; here, 258.

36. Clement Greenberg, "Avant-Garde and Kitsch," *Partisan Review* 6 (1939): 34–49. Reprinted in John O'Brian, ed., *The Collected Essays and Criticism*, vol. 1 (Chicago: University of Chicago Press, 1988), pp. 5–22.

37. See Theodor Adorno, "Commitment," in *The Essential Frankfurt School Reader*, ed. Andrew Arato and Eike Gebhardt, trans. F. McDonagh (Oxford: Continuum, 1978), pp. 300–18.

38. Walter Benjamin, "The Author as Producer," in *The Essential Frankfurt School Reader*, ed. Andrew Arato and Eike Gebhardt (Oxford: Continuum, 1978), pp. 254–69, here p. 255. A standard criticism of these practices is that they run the risk of compromising political agendas by aestheticizing them, whilst equally compromising the aesthetic quality of the work by accommodating external, namely political, subject matter. The worry is, in short, that political agendas become no more than further subjects for artistic practice while artistic agendas become no more than further means for political struggle. As a result, the difference between the political and the aesthetic is flattened and the specific significance of either lost. See "No to Beuys" in *Formless*, ed. Rosalind Krauss and Yves-Alain Bois (New York: Zone Books, 1997), pp. 143–46, in which Beuys is criticized for his "drive toward a totalized system in which everything is recuperated by the "social sculpture."

39. Isobel Armstrong, *Radical Aesthetics* (Oxford: Blackwell, 2000), p. 2.

Chapter 1

1. Herbert Read, *Art Now* (1933; repr., London: Faber, 1968), pp. 26–27. Read played a major role in introducing *Kunstwissenschaft* to England (in contrast to Roger Fry who was very much the connoisseur). He also became the first president of the British Society of Aesthetics and promoted Dessoir's ideas through its constitution. The Society in recent years has identified itself with the academic discipline of philosophical aesthetics and has cut itself off from psychological, sociological, and critical approaches to the aesthetic.

2. Available in English as Max Dessoir, *Aesthetics and the Theory of Art: Ästhetik und Allgemeine Kunstwissenschaft* (1923, 2nd ed.; repr., Detroit, MI: Wayne State University Press, 1970).

3. See Robert Fischer, *Über das optische Formgefühl: ein Beitrag zur Ästhetik* (Leipzig: Hermann Credner, 1873); Theodor Lipps, *Ästhetische Faktoren der Raumanschauung. Beitrage zur Psychologie und Physiologie der Sinnesorgane.* (Hamburg: Voss, 1891); and Johannes Volkelt, *Der Symbol-Begriff in der neuesten Ästhetik* (Jena: Hermann Dufft, 1876).

4. See Conrad Fiedler, *Über die Beurteilung von Werken der bildenden Kunst* (Leipzig: S. Hirzel, 1876); and Adolf Hildebrand, *Das Problem der Form in der bildenden Kunst* (Strassburg: J.H.E. Heitz, 1893.)

5. Heinrich Wölfflin, *Classic Art,* trans. Peter and Linda Murray (London: Phaidon, 1952), p. xi.

6. Heinrich Wölfflin, *The Principles of Art History* (New York: Doer, 1950); original published in German in 1915.

7. This is documented so admirably by Elizabeth Gilmore Holt, *The Expanding World of Art 1874–1902* (New Haven, CT: Yale University Press, 1988).

8. Alois Riegl, *Late Roman Art Industry,* trans. Rolf Winkes (Rome: Giorgio Bretschneider, 1985), p. 6.

9. Alois Riegl, *Historical Grammar of the Arts,* trans. Jacqueline E. Jung (New York: Zone Books, 2004), p. 287.

10. Ibid., p. 288.

11. Ibid.

12. Riegl, *Late Roman Art Industry,* p. 9. Thanks to a recent explosion of interest, Riegl's analysis of the history of art is now well-known. See, for example, Richard Woodfield, ed., *Framing Formalism: Riegl's Work* (New York: Routledge, 2001).

13. Julius von Schlosser, "Die Wiener Schule der Kunstgeschichte. Rüblick auf ein Säkulum deutscher Gelehrtenarbeit in Österreich," *Mitteilungen des Österreichischen Instituts für Geschichtsforschung* 13, no. 2 (1934): 64.

14. Julius von Schlosser, "'Stilgeschichte,' und 'Sprachgeschichte' der bildenden Kunst: Ein Rückblick," *Sitzungsberichte der Bayerischen Akademie der Wissenschaften,* Philosophisch-historische Abteilung 1 (1935): 3.

15. Riegl, *Historical Grammar of the Arts,* pp. 292–93.

16. Schlosser, "Stilgeschichte," p. 8.

17. Ibid., p. 10.

18. Ibid.

19. Ibid., p. 12.

20. He quoted Tolstoy in support: "Geniuses are entirely independent of one another. Spare me the attempts to 'explain' Flaubert from Balzac." Ibid., p. 14.

21. Ibid., p. 15.

22. Ibid., p. 16.

23. Ibid., p. 18.

24. Ibid., p. 20.

25. Ibid., p. 21.

26. Now available in translation by Matthew Rampley as "Alois Riegl," in Woodfield, *Framing Formalism,* pp. 33–48; original emphasis.

27. Hans Sedlmayr, "Towards a Rigorous Study of Art," in *The Vienna School Reader*, ed. Christopher Wood (1931; repr., New York: Zone Books, 2000), p. 135.

28. Ibid., p. 139.

29. Ibid., p. 141.

30. Ibid., p. 144; original emphasis.

31. Ibid.

32. Ibid., p. 149; original emphasis.

33. Ibid., pp. 169–70.

34. Ibid., p. 176.

35. Ernst Gombrich, "Wandlungen in der Kunstbetrachtung (Von Winckelmann bis zur Jetzeit)," (1928). This *Hausarbeit* [essay] is cited by courtesy of Sir Ernst.

36. Ibid., pp. 77–78. When I spoke to him about his *Hausarbeit*, Gombrich was still proud of the way in which he had conducted his analysis and still stood by his conclusion. Today one might reexamine it in the light of his essay, "The Logic of Vanity Fair," reprinted in *Ideals and Idols: Essays on Values in History and in Art* (Oxford: Phaidon, 1979).

37. Hans Tietze, *Lebendige Kunstwissenschaft. Zur Krise der Kunst und der Kunstgeschichte* (Vienna: Krystall-Verlag, 1925). Quoted in Gombrich, *Wandlungen*, p. 76.

38. "Art and Scholarship," originally given as an inaugural lecture in 1957, reprinted in E. H. Gombrich, *Meditations on a Hobby Horse* (London: Phaidon, 1963), p. 112.

39. Karl Bühler, *Ausdruckstheorie: Das System an der Geschichte Aufgezeigt* (Jena, Germany: Fischer, 1933).

40. Karl Bühler, *Sprachtheorie: Die Darstellungsfunktion der Sprache* (Jena, Germany: Fischer, 1934). Now available in translation as Karl Bühler, *Theory of Language: The Representational Function of Language*, trans. Donald Fraser Goodwin (Amsterdam: John Benjamins Publishing, 1990).

41. For a good introduction to Bühler's *Organonmodell der Sprache*, see Klaus Lepsky, "Art and Language: Ernst H. Gombrich and Karl Bühler's Theory of Language," in *Gombrich on Art and Psychology*, ed. Richard Woodfield (Manchester, UK: Manchester University Press, 1996), pp. 27–42.

42. E. H. Gombrich, "Raphael's *Stanza della Segnatura* and the Nature of Its Symbolism," *Norm and Form* (1972): 95. Gombrich expanded his accounts of "abstractive relevance" and "mental set" in the preface to the 2000 edition of *Art and Illusion* (Princeton, NJ: Princeton University Press, 2000).

43. E. H. Gombrich, "Art History and Psychology in Vienna Fifty Years Ago," *Art Journal* 44, no. 2 (Summer 1984): 163.

44. This became a theme that ran through Gombrich's publications up to and including his *New York Review of Books* review of John Shearman's *Only Connect . . . Art and the Spectator in the Renaissance* (1993).

45. E. H. Gombrich, "J. Bodonyi, Entstehung und Bedeutung des Goldgrundes in der spätantiken Bildkomposition," *Kritische Berichte zur Kunstgeschichtlichen Literatur* 5

(1935): 65–75 [Gombrich's review of Bodonyi's journal article]; and E. H. Gombrich, "Achievement in Medieval Art," in *Meditations on a Hobby Horse* (London: Phaidon, 1963), pp. 70–77 [originally published in 1937 as "Wertprobleme und mittelalterliche Kunst" in *Kritische Berichte*]. See R. Woodfield, "Gombrich, Formalism and the Description of Works of Art," *British Journal of Aesthetics* 34, no. 2 (1994): 134–45.

46. Karl Bühler, *Die Erscheinungsweisen der Farben* [The Appearances of Colours] (Jena, Germany, 1922).

47. E. H. Gombrich, "Style, Skill and Function in Image Making," (unpublished manuscript, The Trilling Seminar, Columbia University, New York, 1987), pp. 9–10. Cited by courtesy of Sir Ernst.

48. Gombrich, "J. Bodonyi, Entstehung und Bedeutung des Goldgrundes in der Spätantiken Bildkomposition," p. 72.

49. Gombrich, "Achievement in Medieval Art," pp. 75–76.

50. T. S. Eliot, "Tradition and the Individual Talent," in *Selected Essays* (New York: Harcourt Brace, 1950) [originally published in 1919].

51. E. H. Gombrich, *The Story of Art,* 15th ed. (Oxford: Phaidon, 1989), p. 3.

52. Ibid., p. 5.

53. Ibid., p. 13.

54. Ibid., p. 14.

55. The hero of J-K Huysmans, *Against Nature,* trans. Robert Baldick (Harmondsworth: Penguin, 1959).

56. Ibid., p. 98.

57. Bernard Berenson, *The Arch of Constantine* (London: Chapman and Hall, 1954), p. 19.

58. The expression is Gombrich's. See his review, "The Art of the Greeks," in E. H. Gombrich, *Reflections on the History of Art,* ed. Richard Woodfield (Oxford: Phaidon, 1987), p. 12.

59. "Meditations on a Hobby Horse," in Gombrich, *Meditations on a Hobby Horse,* p. 11.

Chapter 2

1. See James Elkins, "Why Don't Art Historians Attend Aesthetics Meetings?" in *Art History versus Aesthetics* (New York: Routledge, 2005).

2. Subrahmanyan Chandrasekhar, *Truth and Beauty: Aesthetics and Motivations in Science* (New York: Viking, 1987).

3. Sidney Perkowitz, "Science and Art Are Closer than You Think," http://webexhibits.org/hockneyoptics/post/perkowitz.html (accessed March 22, 2008).

4. Felice Frankel, "Sightings," *American Scientist* 10 (September–October 2004): 463. This example is pursued in James Elkins, ed., *Visual Practices Across the University.* (Munchen: Wilhelm Fink Verlag, 2007).

5. Leo Steinberg, "Art and Science: Should They Be Yoked?" *Daedalus* 115, no. 1 (1986): 1–16; here, p. 5.

6. T. J. Clark, *Farewell to an Idea: Episodes in a History of Modernism* (New Haven, CT: Yale University Press, 1999).

7. Wesley Trimpi, *Muses of One Mind: The Literary Analysis of Experience and Its Continuity* (Princeton, NJ: Princeton University Press, 1983), discussed in chapter 1 of James Elkins, *The Poetics of Perspective* (Ithaca, NY: Cornell University Press, 1999).

8. Paul Smith, "Seurat, The Natural Scientist?" *Apollo* 132, no. 346 (December 1990): 381–85, especially 382–83.

9. John Gage, "The *Technique* of Seurat: A Reappraisal," *The Art Bulletin* 69, no. 3 (1987): 453.

10. William Innes Homer, *Seurat and the Science of Painting* (Cambridge, MA: MIT Press, 1964), pp. 131–32.

11. Alan Lee, "Seurat and Science," *Art History* 10, no. 2 (1987): 223.

12. Robert L. Herbert, *Georges Seurat 1859–1891* (New York: Metropolitan Museum of Art, 1991), p. 389.

13. Lee, "Seurat and Science," p. 221.

14. Hermann von Helmholtz, "The Relation of Optics to Paintings," in *Selected Writings of Hermann von Helmholtz*, ed. Russell Kahl (Middletown, CT: Wesleyan University Press 1971), p. 317.

15. Martin Kemp, "Science, Non-Science and Nonsense: The Interpretation of Brunelleschi's Perspective," *Art History* 1, no. 2 (1978): 134–61.

16. Gage, "The *Technique* of Seurat," p. 453.

17. Robert L. Herbert, *Neo-Impressionism* (Princeton, NJ: D. Van Nostrand, 1968), p. 20.

18. Recorded by Charles Angrand; see John Rewald, *Post-impressionism: from Van Gogh to Gauguin*, 2nd ed. (New York: Museum of Modern Art, 1962; distributed by Doubleday, Garden City, NY).

19. Herbert, *Neo-Impressionism*, p. 19.

20. Lee, "Seurat and Science," p. 223.

21. Benoit Mandelbrot, *The Fractal Geometry of Nature* (San Francisco: W. H. Freeman, 1982), p. 1.

22. What a contrast between the rococo exuberance of pre- or counter-revolutionary geometry, and the near-total visual bareness of the works of Weierstrass, Cantor, and Peano! In physics, an analogous movement threatened since about 1800, since Laplace's *Celestial Mechanics* avoided all illustration. And it is exemplified by a statement by P.A.M. Dirac (in the preface to his 1930 *Quantum Mechanics*) that nature's "fundamental laws do not govern the world as it appears in our mental picture in any direct way, but instead they control a substratum of which we cannot form a mental picture without introducing irrelevancies."

23. Mandelbrot, *The Fractal Geometry of Nature*, p. 23, citing F. Dyson, "Characterizing Irregularity," *Science* 200, no. 4342 (1978): 677–78.

24. Mandelbrot, *The Fractal Geometry of Nature*, p. 4.

25. For this distinction, which is not the same as Kant's, see James Elkins, "Clarification, Destruction and Negation of Space in the Age of Neoclassicism," *Zeitschrift für Kunstgeschichte* 56, no. 4 (1990): 560–82.

26. These comments do not apply universally; an example of a visually acute researcher is Clifford A. Pickover (IBM Watson Laboratory, Yorktown Heights, NY). On the other hand, the prevalence of "psychedelic" aesthetics is visible in the slides that accompany each issue of the journal *Amygdala*. Some chaotic dynamics remains nonvisual; see "Is Chaos Becoming Conversational?" *Nature* 341 (1989): 17.

27. Slavoj Žižek, *Looking Awry: An Introduction to Jacques Lacan through Popular Culture* (Cambridge, MA: MIT Press, 1991), p. 38.

28. The original reference is E. N. Lorenz, "Deterministic Nonperiodic Flow," *Journal of Atmospheric Science* 20 (1963): 130.

29. For another set of parallels, see A. Senior, "Embracing Wayward Nature: The Influence of Early Chinese Painting and Fractal Geometry on the Work of Contemporary Artists," *Leonardo* 20 (1987): 31–34.

30. Ellen Winner, "Art History Can Trade Insights with the Sciences," *Chronicle Review* [*Chronicle of Higher Education*] 50, no. 43 (2004): B10.

31. David Galenson, *Painting Outside the Lines* (Cambridge, MA: Harvard University Press, 2001).

Chapter 3

1. Adrian Stokes, *The Quattro Cento and Stones of Rimini,* with a foreword by Stephen Bann and introductions by David Carrier and Stephen Kite (1932; repr., University Park, PA: Pennsylvania State University Press, 2002). See my review of this book in *Art Bulletin* LXXXVII, no. 3 (2005), from which a few of these words are taken. Another version of this essay appeared in Stephen Bann, ed., *The Coral Mind: Adrian Stokes's Engagement with Architecture, Art History, Criticism, and Psychoanalysis* (University Park, PA: Pennsylvania State University Press, 2007).

2. Stokes, *The Quattro Cento and Stones of Rimini,* p. 171.

3. See the recent biography of Stokes, especially chapter 8, by Richard Read, *Art and Its Discontents: The Early Life of Adrian Stokes* (University Park, PA: Pennsylvania State University Press, 2002). Also see Stephen Bann, "The Case for Stokes (and Pater)," *Poetry Nation Review* 6, no. 1 (1978): 6–9; Stephen Bann, "Adrian Stokes 1902–1972: A Supplement," *Poetry Nation Review* 1, no. 15 (1980): 30; and Richard Wollheim, "Adrian Stokes, Critic, Painter, Poet," *Times Literary Supplement* 17 (1978): 207–209.

4. David Carrier, "Introduction to *The Quattrocento.*" In the same volume, see Stephen Kite, "Introduction to *The Stones of Rimini,*" who declares that "what connects Stokes to modernism, modernism to Italy, and carving to modernism is the allure of the hieratic stillness of some quattrocento art" (p. 12). See also the sculptures of Henry Moore, Barbara Hepworth, and Ben Nicholson, who emphasize "the *thingness* of the thing" (p. 18).

5. Susan Stewart, *On Longing: Narratives of the Miniature, the Gigantic, the Souvenir, the Collection* (Durham, NC: Duke University Press, 1993), *passim*.

6. Richard Stamelman, *Lost Beyond Telling: Representations of Death and Absence in Modern French Poetry* (Ithaca, NY: Cornell University Press, 1990), p. 7.

7. Michael Ann Holly, "Mourning and Method," *Art Bulletin* LXXXIV, no. 4 (2002): 660–69.

8. Frederick Hartt, *History of Italian Renaissance Art: Painting, Sculpture, Architecture,* 2d ed. (New York: H. N. Abrams, 1979), p. 232. Sam Edgerton told me that Sigismondo was the only man to be "canonized a saint in Hell." A delightful fiction about this episode can be found in Frances Fleetwood, *L'elefante e la rosa. Storia della famiglia Malatesta* [The Elephant and the Rose: Romance of the Malatesta, Family of Rimini] (Imola: Grafiche Galeati, 1970).

9. See Charles Mitchell, "Il Tempio Malatestiano," *Studi Malatestiani: Studi Storici-Fasc.* 110–111 (1978): 71–103.

10. Stokes, *The Quattrocento and Stones of Rimini*, p. 15.

11. Ibid., p. 16.

12. Ibid., p. 18.

13. Ibid., p. 77.

14. Ibid., p. 107.

15. Ibid., p. 77.

16. Ibid., p. 95.

17. Ibid., p. 97.

18. Ibid., p. 158.

19. Ibid., p. 105.

20. Ibid., p. 109.

21. Ibid., pp. 132–33.

22. Ibid., p. 116.

23. Aby Warburg, *The Renewal of Pagan Antiquity: Contributions to the Cultural History of the European Renaissance*, intro. Kurt Forster, trans. David Britt (Los Angeles: Getty Research Institute for the History of Art and the Humanities, 1999).

24. Fernand Braudel, *The Mediterranean and the Mediterranean World in the Age of Philip II,* trans. from French by Sian Reynolds, 1st U.S. ed. (New York: Harper and Row, 1972), p. 16.

25. Stokes, *The Quattrocento and Stones of Rimini*, p. 92.

26. Ibid., p. 87.

27. Ibid., p. 89.

28. Martin Heidegger, "The Origin of a Work of Art," in *Poetry, Language, Thought,* trans. Albert Hofstadter (New York: Harper and Row, 1971), pp. 42–43.

29. John Keats, "Ode on a Grecian Urn," in *Selected Poems*, ed. John Barnard (London: Penguin, 1999). "O Attic shape! Fair attitude! with brede / Of marble men and maidens overwrought, / With forest branches and the trodden weed / Thou, silent form, dost tease us out of thought / As doth eternity" (p. 169).

30. Richard Wollheim, preface to *The Invitation in Art,* by Adrian Stokes (New York: Tavistock Press, 1965), p. xxi.

31. Christopher Bollas, *The Shadow of the Object: Psychoanalysis of the Unthought Known* (New York: Columbia University Press, 1987), p. 16.

32. Sigmund Freud, "Mourning and Melancholia," in *The Standard Edition of the Complete Psychological Works,* ed. James Strachey (London: Hogarth, 1957), vol. 14, pp. 237–58.

33. Melanie Klein, *The Psycho-Analysis of Children,* trans. Alix Strachey, rev. Alix Strachey and H. A. Thorner (1933; repr., London: Hogarth, 1989); the last section on Stokes is "Case Material—Mr. B." See Read, *Art and Its Discontents,* p. 195; Read mentions that there were some attempts to conceal Stokes's identity.

34. Stokes, *The Quattrocento and Stones of Rimini,* pp. 164–65.

35. Maurice Blanchot, *The Station Hill Blanchot Reader: Fiction and Literary Essays,* trans. L. Davis, P. Auster, and R. Lamberton (Barrytown, NY: Station Hill/Barrytown, Ltd., 1998), p. 345.

36. Bollas, *The Shadow of the Object,* p. 40. See D. W. Winnicott, *Playing and Reality* (London: Routledge, 1974). See also Michael Podro, *Depiction* (New Haven, CT: Yale University Press, 1998), pp. 148–49.

37. Stokes, *The Quattrocento and Stones of Rimini,* p. 24.

38. Ibid., p. 158.

39. Adrian Stokes, *The Invitation in Art* (New York: Tavistock Press, 1965), pp. 30, 63; emphasis added.

40. Stamelman, *Lost Beyond Telling,* p. 20.

41. See Stephen Bann's evocation of Barthes's "practice of the text." Stephen Bann, "The Case for Stokes (and Pater)," *Poetry Nation Review* 96, no. 1 (1978); Charles Merewether, "A Lasting Impression," *Trace* (Liverpool, UK: England Biennial catalogue, 1999), p. 168.

42. *Webster's Third New International Dictionary,* 3 volumes (Chicago: Merriam, 1976).

43. Heidegger, "The Origin of a Work of Art," p. 40.

44. Michael Baxandall, *Patterns of Intention: On the Historical Explanation of Pictures* (New Haven, CT: Yale University Press, 1985), pp. 3–4. See Michael Ann Holly, "Patterns in the Shadows: Attention in/to the Writings of Michael Baxandall," *Art History* 21 (December 1998): 46–78.

45. Stokes, *The Quattrocento and Stones of Rimini,* p. 141.

46. Ferdinand de Saussure, *Course in General Linguistics,* ed. Charles Bally and Albert Sechehaye, trans. Wade Baskin (New York: Philosophical Library, 1959).

47. Stokes, *The Quattrocento and Stones of Rimini,* p. 222.

48. Ibid., p. 211.

49. Ibid., p. 223.

50. Ibid., p. 231.

51. Ibid., p. 178.

52. See Erwin Panofsky's essay, "The History of Art as a Humanistic Disciple," in *Meaning in the Visual Arts* (Garden City: Doubleday, 1955), pp. 1–25.

53. John Nobel Wilford, "New Views of a Century of Stars," *International Herald Tribune,* January 18, 2001, p. 10.

54. Stokes, *The Quattrocento and Stones of Rimini,* p. 44.

55. Henri Focillon, *The Life of Forms in Art,* trans. George Kubler (New York: Zone Books, 1992), p. 32.

56. William J. Broad, "In a Lab on Long Island: A Visit to the Big Bang," *New York Times,* January 14, 2003, p. D1.

57. Ibid., p. D4.

58. Ernst Cassirer, *An Essay on Man* (1944; repr., New Haven, CT: Yale University Press, 1978), p. 185.

59. Roland Barthes, *Camera Lucida: Reflections on Photography,* trans. Richard Howard (New York: Hill and Wang, 1981), p. 59.

60. Julia Kristeva, *Black Sun: Depression and Melancholia* (New York: Columbia University Press, 1989), p. 103.

61. George Kubler, *The Shape of Time: Remarks on the History of Things* (New Haven, CT: Yale University Press, 1962), p. 19.

62. Kristeva, *Black Sun,* pp. 8–9.

Chapter 4

I would like to thank audiences at the University College Cork, School of the Art Institute of Chicago, University of Victoria, Society for Literature, Science, and Art, and College Art Association for permitting me to work through these ideas with them. Particular thanks go to Allan Antliff, James Elkins, Anne Goodyear, Adrian Kohn, Mette Gieskes, and the students in my "Krauss" and "Fried" seminars of the last few years. This work is dedicated to Jodi, Levi, and Dox.

1. Michael Fried, "Three American Painters: Kenneth Noland, Jules Olitski, Frank Stella" (1965), in *Art and Objecthood: Essays and Reviews,* ed. Michael Fried (Chicago: University of Chicago Press, 1998), p. 219.

2. Rosalind E. Krauss, *The Optical Unconscious* (Cambridge, MA: MIT Press, 1993), pp. 12–13; see also pp. 23–27.

3. T. J. Clark, "Arguments About Modernism: A Reply to Michael Fried," in *Pollock and After: The Critical Debate,* ed. Francis Frascina (London: Routledge, 2000), p. 103.

4. Compare with William James, "The Will to Believe," in *The Will to Believe and Other Essays in Popular Psychology* (New York: Dover, [1897] 1956), p. 10.

5. Rosalind E. Krauss, *Passages in Modern Sculpture* (1977; repr., Cambridge, MA: MIT Press, 1981), pp. 245 and 266; Krauss, "The Mind/Body Problem: Robert Morris in Series," in *Robert Morris: The Mind/Body Problem* (New York: Guggenheim Museum, 1994), p. 11; and T. J. Clark, *Farewell to an Idea: Episodes from a History of Modernism* (New Haven, CT: Yale University Press, 1999), p. 12.

6. Alexander Alberro, "Beauty Knows No Pain," *Art Journal* 63, no. 2 (2004): 43.

7. James Meyer and Toni Ross, "Aesthetic/Anti-Aesthetic: An Introduction," *Art Journal* 63, no. 2 (2004): 22.

8. Margaret Iverson, "Readymade, Found Object, Photograph," *Art Journal* 63, no. 2 (2004): 57. Two sentences are here combined as one, with the order in which they occur reversed.

9. Mieke Bal and Norman Bryson, "Semiotics and Art History," *Art Bulletin* 73, no. 2 (1991): 174.

10. Hilary Putnam, "Sense, Nonsense, and the Senses: An Inquiry into the Powers of the Human Mind," *Journal of Philosophy* 91, no. 9 (1994): 488–90.

11. Ibid., p. 448. Edwin B. Holt, Walter T. Marvin, William Pepperrell Montague, Ralph Barton Perry, Walter B. Pitkin, and Edward Gleason Spaulding, "Program and First Platform of Six Realists" (1910), in *The New Realism: Cooperative Studies in Philosophy*, ed. Edwin B. Holt. et. al. (New York: MacMillan, 1925), pp. 47–48. Many years after the 1910 manifesto, Ralph Barton Perry, one of the volume's coauthors, asked, "Whatever became of our program of reform?" Herbert W. Schneider, *A History of American Philosophy*, 2nd ed. (New York: Columbia University Press, 1963), p. 512, as cited in Hilary Putnam, *The Threefold Cord: Mind, Body, and World*, The John Dewey Essays in Philosophy, no. 5 (New York: Columbia University Press, 1999), p. 181, n. 25. More than two decades ago, Charles Harrison and Fred Orton also called for realism in engaging art. Charles Harrison and Fred Orton, "Introduction: Modernism, Explanation and Knowledge," in *Modernism, Criticism, Realism: Alternative Contexts for Art*, ed. Charles Harrison and Fred Orton (New York: Harper and Row, 1984), p. xxv.

12. Maurice Merleau-Ponty, quoted in Alex Potts, *The Sculptural Imagination: Figurative, Modernist, Minimalist* (New Haven, CT: Yale University Press, 2000), p. 221; emphasis removed.

13. Clement Greenberg, "Complaints of an Art Critic" (1967), in *Clement Greenberg: The Collected Essays and Criticism*, vol. 4, ed. John O'Brian (Chicago: University of Chicago Press, 1993), p. 269.

14. Michael Fried, "Art and Objecthood" (1967), in *Art and Objecthood: Essays and Reviews*, ed. Michael Fried (Chicago: University of Chicago Press, 1998), p. 165; original emphasis; Rosalind Krauss, "A View of Modernism," *Artforum* 11, no. 1 (1972): 51; and T. J. Clark, "Clement Greenberg's Theory of Art" (1982), in *Pollock and After: The Critical Debate*, ed. Francis Frascina (London: Routledge, 2000), p. 81; original emphasis.

15. Arthur C. Danto, *What Philosophy Is: A Guide to the Elements* (New York: Harper and Row, 1968), p. xi.

16. Clark, "Arguments About Modernism," p. 109.

17. Ibid., p. 106; original emphasis.

18. Putnam, "Sense, Nonsense, and the Senses," 1994, pp. 453 and 488. Compare with Harrison and Orton, "Introduction," p. xix.

19. Michael Fried, "How Modernism Works: A Response to T. J. Clark" in *Pollock and After: The Critical Debate*, ed. Francis Frascina (London: Routledge, 2000), p. 92.

20. Margaret Olin, *Forms of Representation in Alois Riegl's Theory of Art* (University Park: Pennsylvania State University Press, 1992), p. 137.

21. *Jackson Pollock: Tim Clark and Michael Fried in Conversation*, video recording, produced by G. D. Jayalakshmi and Nick Levinson (East Sussex, England: Open University; Ho-Ho-Kus, NJ: Roland Films on Art, 1993).

22. Krauss, *Passages in Modern Sculpture*, p. 287. Harrison and Orton, "Introduction," p. xxi; emphasis removed.

23. Michael Fried, "An Introduction to My Art Criticism," in *Art and Objecthood: Essays and Reviews,* ed. Michael Fried (Chicago: University of Chicago Press, 1998), p. 22; and Fried, "Three American Painters," pp. 224–25.

24. Krauss, *The Optical Unconscious*, p. 293.

25. Clark, *Farewell*, pp. 309–10.

26. Danto, *What Philosophy Is*, p. 148.

27. John R. Searle, *Mind, Language and Society: Philosophy in the Real World* (New York: Basic Books, 1998), p. 17.

28. Terry Eagleton, *After Theory* (New York: Basic Books, 2003), p. 109.

29. Clark, "Arguments About Modernism," p. 109.

30. For more on this point, see David Raskin, "The Shiny Illusionism of Krauss and Judd," *Art Journal* 65, no. 1 (2006): 19–21.

31. Rosalind Krauss, "A View of Modernism," *Artforum* 11, no. 1 (1972): 51.

32. Michael Fried, *Manet's Modernism, or, The Face of Painting in the 1860s* (Chicago: University of Chicago Press, 1996), p. 406.

33. Fried, "An Introduction to My Art Criticism," p. 56, n. 11. In 1965, Fried wrote: "'A man is judged neither by his intention nor by his act,'" Merleau-Ponty has written [Merleau-Ponty's "Indirect Language and the Voices of Silence"], 'but by whether or not he has been able to infuse his deed with values.'" Fried, "Three American Painters," pp. 256 and 263, n. 12. The 1964 English translation, which Fried used in 1998, is Maurice Merleau-Ponty, *Signs*, trans. and intro. Richard C. McCleary (Evanston, IL: Northwestern University Press, 1964), p. 72.

34. Karl R. Popper, "What Is Dialectic?" *Mind* 49, no. 196 (1940): 403–26.

35. Ibid., p. 410; emphasis removed.

36. Karl Popper, *The Poverty of Historicism* (1957; repr., London: Routledge, 2002).

37. Putnam, "Sense, Nonsense, and the Senses," p. 516.

38. Ibid., pp. 446 and 517.

39. William James, "Does 'Consciousness' Exist?" in *Essays in Radical Empiricism*, ed. William James, intro. Ellen Kappy Suckiel, pref. Ralph Barton Perry (1912; repr., Lincoln: University of Nebraska Press, 1996), p. 37.

40. Eagleton, *After Theory*, p. 155.

41. Compare with Mark Bauerlein, *The Pragmatic Mind: Explorations in the Psychology of Belief* (Durham, NC: Duke University Press, 1997), pp. 106–7.

42. Dan Flavin, "Some Remarks . . . Excerpts from a Spleenish Journal," *Artforum* 5, no. 4 (1966), p. 27.

Chapter 5

1. Richard Wollheim, "Response to James I. Porter," in *Erotikon: Essays on Eros, Ancient and Modern,* ed. Shadi Bartsch and Thomas Bartscherer (Chicago: University of Chicago Press, 2005), p. 142.

2. Bridget Riley, "In Conversation with Maurice de Sausmarez" (1967), in *The Eye's Mind: Bridget Riley, Collected Writings 1965–1999,* ed. Robert Kudielka (London: Thames and Hudson, 1999), pp. 58 and 61.

3. Bridget Riley, "According to Sensation: In Conversation with Robert Kudielka" (1990), in *The Eye's Mind: Bridget Riley,* p. 120.

4. Piet Mondrian, quoted in Carl Holty, "Mondrian in New York: A Memoir," *Arts* 31 (1957): 21.

5. Traditional Western art tends to feature modes of production that involve the direct participation of an individual artist-producer. By convention, marks of the hand and similarly idiosyncratic features indicate this personalized process. Accordingly, many viewers hesitate to accept as art any products that lack such signs of personality: photographs, industrially fabricated sculptures like those of Donald Judd, and also paintings like those of Bridget Riley.

6. Riley, "According to Sensation," p. 84.

7. Bridget Riley, "Perception Is the Medium" (1965), in *The Eye's Mind,* pp. 66 and 68.

8. Riley, "According to Sensation," p. 84 (original emphasis). Riley's distinction between the natural wildness of visual sensations and their subjection to a mediated order, either representational or conceptual, has a parallel in Peirce's categories of consciousness. Peircean "Firstness" corresponds to perceptual wildness: "First, feeling, the [mode of] consciousness which can be included with an instant, passive consciousness of quality, without recognition [a factor of representation] or analysis [a factor of conceptualization]." From Charles Sanders Peirce, "A Guess at the Riddle" [c. 1890], in *Collected Papers,* ed. Charles Hartshorne, Paul Weiss, and Arthur W. Burks, 8 vols. (Cambridge, MA: Harvard University Press, 1958–1960), vol. 1, p. 200.

9. Donald Judd, "Barnett Newman" (1964–1970), in *Complete Writings 1959–1975* (Halifax, Canada: Nova Scotia College of Art and Design, 1975), p. 202. Compare Judd's sense that modern painting had developed a problem in "credibility" (his word), having become overly generalized and formulaic, so that artists were working in ways that had little to do with their immediate experience and personal understanding: "The only work you [can] really believe in completely would be your own. After that it shades off in various ways depending upon the time and the period and the people involved so that you believe certain elements in someone else's works and you disbelieve certain elements." From Donald Judd, statement in Barbara Rose, ed., "Is Easel Painting Dead?" symposium, New York University, November 1966 (transcript, Washington, DC: Archives of American Art, Smithsonian Institution), pp. 31–32.

10. Riley, "Perception Is the Medium," pp. 66 and 68.

11. Charles Sanders Peirce, "Telepathy and Perception" (1903), in *Collected Papers,* vol. 7, pp. 369–70.

12. Bridget Riley, statement to author, February 5, 2003.

13. Riley, "According to Sensation," pp. 115–16; original emphasis.

14. Mondrian, quoted in Holty, "Mondrian in New York," p. 21.

15. Riley, "In Conversation with Maurice de Sausmarez," pp. 58 and 61.

16. Richard Serra, "Richard Serra, interviewed by Lynne Cooke, 21 May 1992," in *Richard Serra Drawings* (London: Serpentine Gallery, 1992), p. 13.

17. Serra would coordinate his mark-making with the physicality of his materials: "I no longer wanted to make markings on a piece of paper: I wanted to make the drawing integral to its structure and properties." From Richard Serra, "About Drawing: An Interview" [1977 interview by Lizzie Borden] in *Richard Serra: Writings Interviews* (Chicago: University of Chicago Press, 1994), p. 58.

18. Richard Serra, *Richard Serra Deadweights* (New York: Pace Gallery, 1992), n.p.

19. Serra's own language hovers on the edge of weight as metaphor and weight as felt sensation: "In Cézanne . . . the objects have weight because of the character of their geometries." From Serra, "About Drawing," p. 55.

20. The latter group of properties can be investigated in the absence of external objects, through the movements of the human body: hence Serra's long-standing interest in dance.

21. Richard Serra, "Richard Serra: An Interview by Mark Rosenthal," in *Richard Serra: Drawings and Etchings from Iceland* (New York: Matthew Marks Gallery, 1992), n.p.

22. Richard Serra, "Notes on Drawing" (1987), in *Serra: Writings Interviews*, pp. 178–79.

23. Serra, "About Drawing," p. 51.

24. Compare the related but simpler case of "two black shapes installed on opposite walls [that] foreshorten the width of the room. The enclosure becomes narrower; the compression of the space is haptically registered." From Serra, "Notes on Drawing," p. 178.

25. See Peirce, "Telepathy and Perception," pp. 369–70.

26. Serra, "About Drawing," pp. 51–52; original emphasis.

27. Richard Serra, during interview by Nicholas Serota and David Sylvester, May 27, 1992, from Nicholas Serota, ed., *Richard Serra: Weight and Measure* (London: Tate Gallery, 1992), p. 25. Clement Greenberg responded to Newman similarly: "One reacts to an environment as much as to a picture hung on a wall." From Clement Greenberg, " 'American-Type' Painting" [rev. 1958] in *Art and Culture* (Boston: Beacon Press, 1961), p. 226.

28. Richard Serra, statement (1992) in Barbaralee Diamonstein, *Inside the Artworld* (New York: Rizzoli, 1994), p. 226.

29. Donald Judd, "Some Aspects of Color in General and Red and Black in Particular" (1993) in *Donld Judd*, ed. Nicholas Serota (London: Tate, 2004), p. 147.

30. Maurice Merleau-Ponty, "Eye and Mind" (1961), in *The Primacy of Perception*, ed. James M. Edie, trans. Carleton Dallery (Evanston, IL: Northwestern University Press, 1964), p. 161.

31. Donald Judd, "Jackson Pollock" (1967), in *Complete Writings 1959–1975*, p. 195.

32. In Peircean terms, the feeling is "Firstness," the fact that you feel it is "Secondness," what it is, what you know it *as*, is "Thirdness."

33. Judd, "Some Aspects of Color," pp. 158–59.

34. Donald Judd, "21 February 93," in *Donald Judd: Large-scale Works* (New York: Pace Gallery, 1993), p. 9.

35. William James, "Does Consciousness Exist?" *Journal of Philosophy, Psychology and Scientific Methods* 1 (1 September 1904), p. 491. (I thank David Raskin for alerting me to this text.) For related statements from Peirce, see his letters to William James, September 28, 1904, and October 3, 1904, in *Collected Papers*, vol. 8, pp. 198–206; and "A Guess at the Riddle," vol. 1, pp. 200–201. On breath and the physicality of visual sensation, see Richard Shiff, "Breath of Modernism (Metonymic Drift)," in *In Visible Touch: Modernism and Masculinity*, ed. Terry Smith (Chicago: University of Chicago Press, 1997), pp. 184–213.

36. Donald Judd, "Art and Architecture" (1983), in *Complete Writings 1975–1986*, p. 30; Donald Judd, statement in Angeli Janhsen, ed., "Discussion with Donald Judd," in *Donald Judd* (St. Gall, Switzerland: Kunstverein St. Gallen, 1990), p. 54.

37. Bridget Riley, statement to author, July 25, 2005.

38. Bridget Riley, "The Artist's Eye: Seurat" (1992), in *The Eye's Mind*, p. 180.

39. Riley statement, July 25, 2005.

40. Bridget Riley, statement to author, September 14, 2005.

41. See Richard Shiff, "Whiteout: The Not-Influence Newman Effect," in *Barnett Newman,* ed. Ann Temkin (Philadelphia: Philadelphia Museum of Art, 2002), pp. 77–111.

42. Barnett Newman, interview with David Sylvester [1965], in David Sylvester, "Concerning Barnett Newman," *The Listener* 88 (August 10, 1972): 169–70.

43. Riley, "In Conversation with Maurice de Sausmarez," pp. 58 and 61.

44. As reported by sculptor Herbert Ferber to Kirk Varnedoe in November 1983; see Kirk Varnedoe, "Abstract Expressionism," in *"Primitivism" in 20th Century Art: Affinity of the Tribal and the Modern*, 2 vols., ed. William Rubin (New York: Museum of Modern Art, 1984), vol. 2, p. 635.

45. Barnett Newman, statement in "A Conversation: Barnett Newman and Thomas B. Hess" (1966), in *Barnett Newman: Selected Writings and Interviews*, ed. John P. O'Neill (New York: Knopf, 1990), p. 282.

46. On the historical origins for an aesthetics of anonymity and self-awareness, as a practice of the nineteenth and early twentieth centuries (into the 1940s, Newman's era), see Richard Shiff, "Tangible Datum," in *Estudios de Historia del Arte en Honor de Tomàs Llorens,* ed. Valeriano Bozal (Madrid: Machado, 2007), pp. 509–27.

Chapter 6

1. Immanuel Kant, *Critique of Judgment*, trans. Werner S. Pluhar (Indianapolis, IN: Hackett, 1987), Ak. V 216, p. 61.

2. Ibid., p. 62.

3. Ibid.

4. Ibid., p. 63.

5. Donald Judd, "Specific Objects," *Arts Yearbook VIII* (1965). Reprinted in Donald Judd, *Complete Writings* 1959–1975 (Halifax, Canada: The Press of the Nova Scotia College of Art and Design, 1975), p. 184.

6. Clement Greenberg, "Seminar One," *Arts Magazine* 48 (1973). Reprinted in Clement Greenberg, *Homemade Esthetics* (Oxford: Oxford University Press, 1999), p. 8.

7. Kant, *Critique of Judgment*, Ak. V 219, p. 63.

8. Robert Morris, "Notes on Sculpture, Part I,"*Artforum*, February 1966; repr. in Gregory Battcock, ed. *Minimal Art: A Critical Anthology* (New York: Dutton, 1968), p. 226.

9. Rosalind Krauss, "Death of a Hermeneutic Phantom: Materialization of the Sign in the Work of Peter Eisenman, *a+u*" (1980). Reprinted in Peter Eisenman, *House of Cards* (New York: Oxford University Press, 1987), pp. 166–88.

10. Rosalind Krauss, *Passages in Modern Sculpture* (New York: Viking Press, 1977).

11. Marcia Tucker, *Robert Morris* (New York: Whitney Museum of American Art, 1970), p. 25.

12. I am alluding to the last sentence of Michael Fried's notorious essay, "Art and Objecthood" (1967), where he opposes the mere *presence* of minimal art to the feeling of *presentness* he gets from truly modernist art: "Presentness is grace." Michael Fried, *Artforum* (June 1967). Reprinted in Michael Fried, *Art and Objecthood* (Chicago: University of Chicago Press, 1998), p. 168.

Chapter 7

1. Ludwig Witttgenstein, *Tractatus Logico-Philosophicus,* trans. C. K. Ogden (London: Routledge and Kegan Paul, 1922), 4:003.

2. John Dewey, "The Need for Recovery in Philosophy," [1917] in *The Collected Works of John Dewey*, ed. Jo Ann Boydston (Carbondale: Southern Illinois Press, 1969–1991), vol 10, p. 42.

3. There is no English term. It refers to a mode of organizing knowledge in a given period.

4. All quotations here from Marcel Duchamp. "A propos of 'Readymades.'" A talk delivered at the Museum of Modern Art, New York, October, 19, 1961. Reprinted in Marcel Sanouillet and Elmer Peterson, eds. *Salt Seller: The Writings of Marcel Duchamp (Marchand du Sel)* (New York: Oxford University Press, 1973), pp. 141–42.

5. Pierre Cabanne, *Dialogues with Marcel Duchamp,* trans. Run Padgett (New York: Da Capo Press, 1987), p. 43.

6. Ibid.

7. George Dickie, *Aesthetics: An Introduction* (Waltham, MA: Pegasus Books, 1971), p. 101.

8. Arthur C. Danto, *The Abuse of Beauty: Aesthetics and the Concept of Art* (Chicago: Open Court, 2003).

9. Translated as Hans Belting, *Likeness and Presence: A History of the Image before the Era of Art*, trans. Edmund Jephcott (Chicago: University of Chicago Press, 1994).

10. Charles S. Peirce, *Collected Papers*, ed. Charles Hartshorne and Paul Weiss (Cambridge, MA: Harvard University Press, 1931–58), vol. 8, p. 255.

11. Charles S. Peirce, *Pragmatism as a Principle and Method of Right Thinking: The 1903 Harvard Lectures on Pragmatism*, ed. Patricia Ann Turrisi (Albany: State University of New York Press, 1997), p. 213.

12. Ibid.

13. Martin Heidegger, *Being and Time*, trans. John Macquarrie and Edward Robinson (New York: Harper and Row, 1962), p. 173.

14. Ibid.

15. Immanuel Kant, "Conclusion," in *Critique of Practical Reason and Other Works on the Theory of Ethics*, 5th ed. (London: Longmans, 1898).

16. Heidegger, *Being and Time*, p. 178.

17. "Let us go, children of the fatherland." Opening line of *La Marseillaise*, the French national anthem.

Chapter 8

1. See Rosalind Krauss's relation to Greenberg in Rosalind Krauss, *The Optical Unconscious* (Cambridge, MA: MIT Press, 1993); and Rosalind Krauss and Yve Alain Bois, *Formless: A User's Guide* (Cambridge, MA: MIT Press, 1997). On this, see Diarmuid Costello, "Greenberg's Kant and the Fate of Aesthetics in Contemporary Art Theory," *Journal of Aesthetics and Art Criticism* 65, no. 2, (2007): 217–28.

2. Clement Greenberg, "Modernist Painting," *Collected Essays and Criticism*, Vol. IV, ed. John O'Brian (Chicago: Chicago University Press, 1993), pp. 85–86.

3. Clement Greenberg, "Towards a Newer Laocoon," *Collected Essays and Criticism*, Vol. I, ed. John O'Brian (Chicago: Chicago University Press, 1986).

4. "Agreeable is what the senses like in sensation," A liking for the beautiful must depend on the reflection, regarding an object . . . This dependence on reflection also distinguishes the liking for the beautiful from [that for] the agreeable, which rests entirely on sensation." From Immanuel Kant, *Critique of Judgment*, trans. Werner Pluhar (Indianapolis, IN: Hackett Publishing, 1987), §3, Ak. V 206, p. 47, and §4, Ak. V 207, p. 49.

5. "Pleasure in aesthetic judgment . . . is merely contemplative . . . The very consciousness of a merely formal purposiveness in the play of the subject's cognitive powers, accompanying a presentation . . . is that pleasure." Ibid., §12, Ak. V 222, p. 68.

6. For Kant, space is the form of all outer sensibility, hence a condition of perceiving anything at all in the external world, while time, as the form of inner sensibility is a condition of perceiving anything whatsoever. See Kant, *Critique of Pure Reason*, trans. Norman Kemp Smith (London: MacMillan, 1929), p. 77 (A34/B50).

7. Kant, *Critique of Aesthetic Judgment*, §16, Ak. 229, p.76.

8. See Clement Greenberg, "Can Taste Be Objective?" *Art News* 72, no. 2 (1973): 23. Reprinted in Clement Greenberg, *Homemade Esthetics* (Oxford: Oxford University Press,

1999). For a critique, see Thierry de Duve, "Wavering Reflections," in Thierry de Duve, *Clement Greenberg Between the Lines* (Paris: Dis Voir, 1996), pp. 107–10.

9. Greenberg's conflation of Kantian "disinterestedness" with "aesthetic distance" is often explicit. See Clement Greenberg, "Observations on Esthetic Distance," in Clement Greenberg, *Homemade Esthetics*, p. 74. Greenberg attributes his own psychologistic conception of aesthetic distance to Edward Bullough's account in "Psychical Distance" (1912). Reprinted in Alex Neill and Aaron Ridley, eds., *The Philosophy of Art: Readings Ancient and Modern* (New York: McGraw Hill, 1995), pp. 297–311.

10. Greenberg acknowledges this in Clement Greenberg, "Seminar One," *Arts Magazine* 42, no. 2 (1973): 44. Reprinted as "Intuition and the Esthetic Experience," in Clement Greenberg, *Homemade Esthetics*, pp. 3–9.

11. Kant, *Critique of Judgment*, §9, Ak. V 217–19, pp. 61–64.

12. See Thierry de Duve, *Kant after Duchamp* (Cambridge MA: MIT Press, 1996), chap. 5.

13. "The presentation is referred only to the subject, namely, to his feeling of life, under the name feeling of pleasure or displeasure, and this forms the basis of a very special power of discriminating and judging. This power does not contribute anything to cognition, but *merely compares the given presentation in the subject with the entire presentational power*, of which the mind becomes conscious when it feels its own state." From Kant, *Critique of Judgment*, §1, Ak. V 204, p. 44; my emphasis.

14. Of Kant's claims, "All [this deduction] asserts is that we are justified in presupposing universally in all people the same subjective conditions of the power of judgment that we find in ourselves," de Duve remarks, "I read this passage as the best indication that it is the claim to universality that signals disinterestedness, the free play of the faculties, or purposiveness without purpose, and not vice-versa. This finds confirmation in experience . . . in the fact that we feel strongly about the so-called objectivity—the claim to shareability—of our aesthetic judgments." See Thierry de Duve, "Do Artists Speak on Behalf of All of Us?" in *The Life and Death of Images: Ethics and Aesthetics*, ed. Diarmuid Costello and Dominic Willsdon (London: Tate Publishing, 2008), p. 143.

15. In several recent texts Danto reassesses his relation to Kant. See Arthur C. Danto, *The Abuse of Beauty: Aesthetics and the Concept of Art* (Chicago: Open Court, 2003); and Arthur C. Danto, "Embodied Meanings, Isotypes, and Aesthetical Ideas," *Journal of Aesthetics and Art Criticism* 65, no. 1 (2007): 121–29. Greenberg derived two tenets from his reading of Kant. See Arthur C. Danto, *After the End of Art: Contemporary Art and the Pale of History* (Princeton, NJ: Princeton University Press, 1997), p. 86ff.

16. See Kant, *Critique of Judgment*, §15, Ak. V 228, pp. 74–75.

17. "Where the organs are so fine, as to allow nothing to escape them; and at the same time so exact as to perceive every ingredient in the composition: This we call delicacy of taste." From David Hume, "Of the Standard of Taste," in *The Philosophy of Art*, ed. Alex Neill and Aaron Ridley (New York: McGraw-Hill, 1995), p. 260.

18. Kant, *Critique of Judgment*, §45, Ak. V 307, p. 174.

19. Ibid., §45, Ak. 306, p. 173; my emphasis.

20. Ibid., §45, Ak. 307, p. 174.

21. See Diarmuid Costello, "On Late Style: Arthur Danto's *The Abuse of Beauty*," *British Journal of Aesthetics* 44, no. 4 (2004): 424–39; and Diarmuid Costello, "Whatever Happened to 'Embodiment'?: The Eclipse of Materiality in Danto's Ontology of Art," *Angelaki* 12, no. 2 (2007): 83–94.

22. Arthur C. Danto, *The Transfiguration of the Commonplace* (Cambridge, MA: Harvard University Press, 1981); Arthur C. Danto, *The Abuse of Beauty: Aesthetics and the Concept of Art* (Chicago: Open Court, 2003).

23. See Arthur C. Danto, "Embodied Meanings, Isotypes and Aesthetical Ideas," p. 125.

24. Kant, *Critique of Judgment*, §49, Ak. V 314, pp. 182–83.

25. Ibid., §49, Ak. 315, p. 183.

26. Ibid., §49, Ak. 315, pp. 183–84.

27. On the index itself these relations were symbolized, respectively, by "+" "—" and "T." The latter stood for "transformation," indicating that these documents did not occupy the same logical or ethical space and hence were incomparable. See Charles Harrison, "The Index as Art-work," in Charles Harrison, *Essays on Art & Language* (Cambridge, MA: MIT Press, 2001), p. 65.

28. Kant, *Critique of Judgment*, §1, Ak. V 204, p. 44.

29. Ibid., §49, Ak. 315, pp. 183–84.

Chapter 9

This chapter is based on a paper titled "The Work of Art in the Age of Curatorial Production," which was originally presented as part of a series in the University of Southampton's Golden Jubilee celebrations in 2001. A revised version of the paper was presented at a colloquium on logical progressions in art hosted by the Museum of Modern Art in Antwerp, Belgium, in January, 2004.

1. See Paul Crowther, *The Language of Twentieth-Century Art. A Conceptual History* (New Haven, CT: Yale University Press, 1997).

2. For a detailed discussion of the concept of symbolic arrest see Paul Crowther, *Philosophy After Postmodernism; Civilized Values and the Scope of Knowledge* (New York: Routledge, 2003).

3. Immanuel Kant, *The Critique of Judgment*, trans. Werner Pluhar (Indianapolis, IN: Hackett, 1987), Ak. V 314, p. 182.

4. Ibid., Ak. V 314, p. 183.

5. See Immanuel Kant, *The Critique of Pure of Reason*, trans. N. Kemp-Smith (New York: Macmillan, 1973), p. 111 (B 151).

6. Maurice Merleau-Ponty, "Eye and Mind," in *The Primacy of Perception*, ed. James M. Edie (Evanston, IL: Northwestern University Press, 1964), p. 166.

7. For a sustained discussion of contextual space see chapter 6 of Paul Crowther, *The Transhistorical Image: Philosophizing Art and its History* (Cambridge: Cambridge University Press, 2002).

8. Kant, *Critique of Judgment*, Ak. V, p. 172.

9. Ibid., Ak. 307f., p. 175.

10. For more on these issues see chapter 4 of Crowther, *The Transhistorical Image*.

11. Crowther, *The Transhistorical Image*.

12. See Crowther, *The Language of Twentieth-Century Art*.

Chapter 10

1. W. G. Sebald, *After Nature* (London: Hamish Hamilton, 2002), p. 36; emphasis added.

2. The title of Jürgen Habermas's original critique of *Truth and Method* was "The Hermeneutic Claim to Universality," which appears in Kurt Mueller-Vollmer, *The Hermeneutics Reader* (London: Blackwell, 1988), pp. 294–319.

3. See Sarah Churchill's review of David Guterson's approach to the transcendent in *The Times Literary Supplement*, November 21, 2003, no. 5251.

4. Hans-Georg Gadamer, *Truth and Method* (London: Sheed and Ward, 1989), pp. 110–21. Without wishing to suggest that Gadamer's argument is derivative or borrowed, it is noteworthy that Dilthey uses a conception of *transformation* in a similar context in his essay, "The Imagination of the Poet: Elements for a Poetics" (1887). See Wilhelm Dilthey, *Selected Works*, vol. V, *Poetry and Experience*, ed. R. A. Makkreel and F. Rodi (Princeton, NJ: Princeton University Press, 1985), p. 93. Whereas Dilthey speaks of poetry as a means to the *transformation* of "lived experience" (*Erlebnissen*), Gadamer, consistent in his critique of the latter concept, speaks of art as the transformation of the real.

5. Gadamer, *Truth and Method*, p. 112.

6. Gadamer, *Truth and Method*, p. 140.

7. Gadamer, *Truth and Method*, p. 143.

8. Gadamer, *Truth and Method*, p. 147.

9. Ibid.

10. Gadamer, *Truth and Method*, pp. 112–13.

11. Ibid.

12. Gadamer, *Truth and Method*, p. 62; emphasis added.

13. Gadamer, *Truth and Method*, p. 63.

14. Gadamer, *Truth and Method*, p. 114.

15. See Nicholas Davey, "Of Beauty and Nearness: A Hermeneutic Reflection," *Annales D'Esthetique*, 36 (1996): 115–37. (This journal is published by the Panayotis and Effie Michelis Foundation in Athens, Greece.)

16. Gadamer, *Truth and Method*, pp. 99–100.

17. Hans-Georg Gadamer, *Heidegger's Ways* (Albany: State University Press of New York, 1994), p. 105.

18. Gadamer, *Heidegger's Ways*, p. 107.

19. Ibid.

20. Ibid.

21. Ibid.

22. "The sayable at the same time brings the unsayable into the world" ("Ursprung des Kunstwerkes" ["On the Origin of the Art Work"], pp. 59–60). See Cristina Lafont, *The Linguistic Turn in Hermeneutic Philosophy* (Cambridge, MA: MIT Press, 1999), p. 63.

23. Gianni Vattimo, *The Transparent Society* (London: Polity Press, 1992), pp. 45–61.

24. Ibid., p. 50.

25. Ibid., p. 51.

26. Gadamer, *Truth and Method*, p. 128.

27. Wolfgang Iser, *The Range of Interpretation* (New York: Columbia University Press, 2000), p. 52.

28. Theodor Adorno, *Hegel Three Studies* (Cambridge, MA: MIT Press, 1993), p. 100.

29. Ibid., p. 77.

30. Gadamer, *Heidegger's Ways*, p. 107.

31. Gadamer, *Truth and Method*, p. 474.

32. Joel Weinsheimer, *Philosophical Hermeneutics and Literary Theory* (New Haven, CT: Yale University Press, 1991), p. 123.

33. Gadamer, *Truth and Method*, p. 474.

34. Martin Heidegger, "Hölderlin und das Wesen der Dichtung," in *Erläuterungen zu Hölderlins Dichtung* (Frankfurt, Germany: V. Klostermann, 1944), pp. 33–48;

35. William Blake, "The Sick Rose," in *Songs of Innocence and Experience*, ed. Geoffrey Keynes (Oxford: Oxford University Press, 1970), p. 147.

36. Gadamer, *Truth and Method*, p. 140.

37. Gadamer, *Truth and Method*, p. 143.

38. Gadamer, *Truth and Method*, p. 147.

39. Hans-Georg Gadamer, "Introduction," in *Der Ursprung des Kunstwerkes*, ed. Martin Heidegger (Stuttgart, Germany: Reclam, 1995), p. 108.

40. Ibid., p. 107.

41. Gadamer, *Heidegger's Ways*, p. 107.

42. Gadamer, *Heidegger's Ways*, p. 108.

43. Gadamer, *Heidegger's Way*, p. 107.

44. Ibid.

45. Gadamer, *Heidegger's Way*, p. 108.

46. Gadamer, "Introduction," p. 108.

47. Gadamer, *Truth and Method*, p. 140.

48. Gadamer, *Truth and Method*, p. 143.

Chapter 11

1. "Foreclosure" (the French *forclusion* renders the German *Verwerfung*, which is usually translated into English as "repudiation") is the term used by Lacan to denote "a primordial expulsion of a fundamental signifier from the subject's symbolic universe." Foreclosed signifiers "are not integrated into the subject's unconscious. . . . They do not

return 'from the inside'—they re-emerge, rather, in 'the Real,' particularly through the phenomenon of hallucination." Hence, in this context, we may say: Aesthetics forecloses, and is therefore compelled to hallucinate, "art." From J. Laplanche and J–B. Pontalis, *The Language of Psychoanalysis,* trans. Donald Nicholson-Smith (1973; repr., London: Karnac Books and the Institute of Psycho-Analysis, 1988), p. 166.

2. J. M. Bernstein, "Modernism as Aesthetics and Art History," in *Art History Versus Aesthetics,* ed. James Elkins (New York: Routledge, 2006), pp. 241, 265.

3. Cf. Bernstein, "Modernism as Aesthetics and Art History," p. 266: "the premise that modernism is over is false." The difference between us concerns what, precisely, is meant by "modernism" here; *which* modernism it is that endures. There are many (Arthur Danto, for example) who do not believe that art remains a historically critical practice. For some of them, aesthetics is (re)legitimated on this precise basis, that is, contra modernism. While Bernstein defends modernism as aesthetics (and vice versa) and Danto defends aesthetics after modernism, I defend the metacritical status of modernism *against* its reduction to aesthetics.

4. Peter Osborne, "Modernity: A Different Time," in *The Politics of Time: Modernity and Avant-Garde* (London: Verso, 1995), chap. 1.

5. Raymond Williams, *Keywords: A Vocabulary of Culture and Society* (1976; repr., London: Fontana, 1988), pp. 173–74, 208–9.

6. Pierre Bourdieu, *The Rules of Art: Genesis and Structure of the Literary Field* (1992), trans. Susan Emanuel (Stanford, CA: Stanford University Press, 1995), part I, chaps. 2 and 3, and part III, chap. 3. I abstract here from the fundamental, fascinating, and under-researched issue of the transference of the general concept of "art" from the literary to the visual field, in the course of the nineteenth century.

7. Charles Baudelaire, "The Painter of Modern Life" (1863), in *The Painter of Modern Life and Other Essays,* trans. Jonathan Mayne (London: Phaidon, 1964), p. 13.

8. See Marshall Berman, *All That is Solid Melts into Air: The Experience of Modernity* (New York: Simon and Schuster, 1982).

9. See Peter Osborne, "Modernism as Translation," in *Philosophy in Cultural Theory* (London: Routledge, 2000), p. 58.

10. Baudelaire, "The Painter of Modern Life," p. 13; Peter Osborne, "Art Beyond Aesthetics: Philosophical Criticism, Art History and Contemporary Art," *Art History* 27, no. 4 (2004): 651–70.

11. See Walter Benjamin, *Charles Baudelaire: A Lyric Poet in the Era of High Capitalism,* trans. Harry Zohn (London: Verso, 1983).

12. The concept of an autonomously aesthetic art was prefigured by romanticism, against which academic art was to some extent a reaction, just as romanticism also prefigured the modernist concept of the new. However, neither autonomously aesthetic art nor modernism were actualized in romanticism, where (subsequent to 1800 and the end of Jena romanticism) affirmations of autonomy increasingly took the form of the exaltation of the artist's persona and the absolutization of the artist's point of view. Cf. the section "The Academic Gaze," in Pierre Bourdieu, "Manet and the Institutionalization of Ano-

mie," in *The Field of Cultural Production: Essays on Art and Literature*, ed. Randal Johnson (Cambridge: Polity Press, 1993), pp. 239–50.

13. "'Art for art's sake' was scarcely ever to be taken literally; it was almost always a flag under which sailed a cargo that could not be declared because it still lacked a name." From Walter Benjamin, "Surrealism: The Last Snapshot of the European Intelligentsia" (1929), in *Selected Writings, Volume 2: 1927–1934* (Cambridge, MA: Harvard University Press, 1999), pp. 211–12.

14. Clement Greenberg, "Towards a Newer Laocoon" (1940), in *The Collected Essays and Criticism, Volume 1: Perceptions and Judgments, 1939–1944*, ed. John O'Brian (Chicago: Chicago University Press, 1986), pp. 23–37; Clement Greenberg, "Modernist Painting" (1960), in *The Collected Essays and Criticism, Volume 4: Modernism with a Vengeance, 1957–1969*, ed. John O'Brian (Chicago: Chicago University Press, 1993), pp. 85–93.

15. Thierry de Duve, *Pictorial Nominalism: On Marcel Duchamp's Passage from Painting to the Readymade* (1984), trans. Dana Polan (Minneapolis: University of Minnesota Press, 1991); Thierry de Duve, *Kant After Duchamp* (Cambridge, MA: MIT Press, 1996).

16. For criticism of de Duve's peculiar use of Saul Kripke's philosophy of names, for example, see Jason Gaiger, "Art after Beauty: Retrieving Aesthetic Judgment," *Art History* 20, no. 4 (1997): 611–16.

17. Theodor W. Adorno, *Aesthetic Theory* (1970), trans. Hullot-Kentor (Minneapolis: Minnesota University Press, 1997).

Chapter 12

1. In his *Aesthetica* (part I: 1750; part II: 1758), Baumgarten used examples from the arts, especially poetry, only to illustrate what aesthetic perfection, or the perfection of sensuous knowledge, could be (Repr., New York: Georg Olms, 1979).

2. Interest and support for alternative understandings of aesthetics are easier to find outside the discipline: with theoreticians in other fields and cultural institutions and artists whose work is at odds with established philosophical concepts of aesthetics. See Wolfgang Welsch, ed., *Die Aktualität des Ästhetischen* (Munich: Fink, 1993).

3. Ludwig Wittgenstein makes this point about language. See *Philosophical Investigations*, trans. G.E.M. Anscombe (New York: Macmillan, 1968), p. 48^e [115].

4. Ibid., p. 103^e [309]. This was Wittgenstein's declared "aim of philosophy."

5. Letter to August Wilhelm Schlegel, September 3, 1802 in *Aus Schellings Leben. In Briefen*, vol. 1, ed. G. L. Plitt (Leipzig: Hirzel, 1869), pp. 390–99; here, p. 397.

6. Friedrich Schelling, *Philosophie der Kunst I* (Wissenschaftliche Buchgesellschaft Darmstadt, 1976), pp. 7 and 124, respectively.

7. General problems of traditional aesthetics are discussed in Wolfgang Welsch, "Traditionelle und moderne Ästhetik in ihrem Verhältnis zur Praxis der Kunst," *Zeitschrift für Ästhetik und Allgemeine Kunstwissenschaft* XXVIII (1983): 264–86. For an alternative approach see Wolfgang Welsch, *Ästhetisches Denken* (1990; repr., Stuttgart: Reclam, 1999).

8. By "reality" I mean here the life-world in which we find ourselves as well as the truths and facts that we hold to be valid in it. See Wolfgang Welsch, "Aestheticization Processes: Phenomena, Distinctions, and Prospects," in *Undoing Aesthetics* (London: Sage, 1997), pp. 1–32.

9. For further examples, such as genetic engineering, see Wolfgang Welsch, "Angesichts des Verschwindens von Geist, Kultur und Kunst in der Fun-Gesellschaft," in *Im Spannungsfeld zweier Kulturen. Eine Auseinandersetzung zwischen Geistes-und Naturwissenschaft, Kunst und Technik*, ed. Karen Gloy (Würzburg, Germany: Königshausen and Neumann, 2002), pp. 117–32.

10. See "The 'Oldest System-Programme' of German Idealism," in *Hegel Selections*, ed. M. J. Inwood (London: Macmillan, 1989), pp. 86–87.

11. See Wolfgang "Ästhetik und Anästhetik," in *Ästhetisches Denken*, (1990; repr., Stuttgart: Reclam, 1999), pp. 9–40.

12. Cf. Wolfgang Welsch, "Contemporary Art in Public Space—Feast for the Eyes or Annoyance?" in *Undoing Aesthetics*, pp. 118–22.

13. Rainer Maria Rilke, *Duineser Elegien*, in *Sämtliche Werke*, 6 vols. (Frankfurt am Main, Germany: Insel, 1955–1966), vol. 1, p. 685 (first elegy).

14. See Wolfgang Welsch, "Artificial Paradises? Considering the World of Electronic Media—and Other Worlds," in *Undoing Aesthetics*, pp. 168–90.

15. By "media," I mean mostly electronic media and primarily television, which, although it has become an old-fashioned medium, is still the one everybody knows and uses.

16. In recent years, media theory, not aesthetics, has begun to take on a great part of this task.

17. See Martin Jay's survey *Downcast Eyes: The Denigration of Vision in Twentieth-Century French Thought* (Berkeley: University of California Press, 1994).

18. For more details see Wolfgang Welsch, "On the Way to an Auditive Culture?" in *Undoing Aesthetics*, pp. 150–67.

19. Cf. Derrick de Kerckhove, "Touch versus Vision: Ästhetik neuer Technologien," in *Die Aktualität des Ästhetischen*, ed. Wolfgang Welsch (Munich: Fink, 1993), pp. 137–68.

20. See Aristotle's outline of the many uses of *to on* in Aristotle, *Metaphysics*, vol. 7, ed. W. Jaeger (New York: Oxford University Press, 1957). Aristotle's point here is precisely that such a weak resemblance is completely sufficient for the realization of a science that can refer to all the different senses of being (i.e., metaphysics).

21. George Steiner has shown how much of our amorous behavior and rhetoric has been formed by generations of artistic models. See George Steiner, *Real Presences: Is There Anything in What We Say?* (London: Faber and Faber, 1989).

22. Rainer Maria Rilke, "Archäischer Torso Apollos," in *Sämtliche Werke* 1 (1976): 557.

23. Theodor W. Adorno, *Aesthetic Theory*, trans. Robert Hullor-Kentor (1970; repr., Minneapolis: University of Minnesota Press, 1996), p. 158.

24. Paul Klee had already in 1915 noted a connection of this type in another way: "The more shocking this world (just as today), the more abstract the art, whereas a happy world produces a worldly art." From Paul Klee, *Tagebücher* (Cologne: DuMont, 1957), p. 323.

25. I first presented the following arguments in my essay, "Erweiterungen der Ästhetik—eine Replik," in *Bild und Reflexion*, ed. Birgit Recki and Lambert Wiesing (Munich: Fink, 1997), pp. 39–67.

26. The painting's transgression beyond the museum's threshold was not just metaphorical. In the 1930s, antifascist demonstrators in Paris carried placards that showed Goya's picture.

27. Adorno, *Aesthetic Theory*, p. 349.

28. Ibid.

29. Guillaume Apollinaire declared in 1913: "Above all, artists are people who want to become inhuman. They arduously seek traces of inhumanity." From Guillaume Apollinaire, "Méditations esthétiques. Les Peintres cubists" (1913), in *Œuvres en prose complètes*, II (Paris: Gallimard, 1991), pp. 3–52; here, p. 8 (section "Sur la peinture"). Maurice Merleau-Ponty saw "Cézanne's painting" reveal "the ground of inhuman nature on which the human settles." From Maurice Merleau-Ponty, "Le Doute de Cézanne," in *Sens et non-sens* (1948; repr., Paris: Nagel, 1966), pp. 15–44; here, p. 28. And Adorno famously declared that "art is loyal to humanity only through inhumanity toward it." From Adorno, *Aesthetic Theory*, p. 197.

30. For example, see Wolfgang Welsch, "Art Transcending the Human Pale—Towards a Transhuman Stance," *International Yearbook of Aesthetics*, vol. 5, ed. Ken-ichi Sasaki (2001): 3–23.

31. Remember Denis Diderot's famous claim that "man is the unique concept from which we must start and to which we must refer everything back." From Denis Diderot, "Encyclopédie" (1755), in *Œuvres complètes*, vol. VII: Encyclopédie III (Paris: Hermann, 1976), pp. 174–262; here, p. 212.

32. It is no coincidence that many Western artists interested in these issues were inspired by Eastern art and thinking. John Cage used the Chinese I Ching as an aleatory device (e.g., in his *Music of Changes* from 1951); from 1947 onward he had studied Zen Buddhism with Daisetz T. Suzuki. Morton Feldman liked to compare his long pieces to Asian rugs. Cf. Morton Feldman, "Crippled Symmetry," in *Give My Regards to Eighth Street: Collected Writings of Morton Feldman*, ed. B. H. Friedman (Cambridge, MA: Exact Change, 2000), pp. 134–49.

33. Already in Adorno we read: "Modified aesthetics . . . no longer considers, as did traditional aesthetics, the concept of art to be its obvious correlate. Aesthetic thinking today, in conceiving art, would have to go beyond it." From Theodor W. Adorno, "Funktionalismus heute," in *Gesammelte Schriften*, vol. 10.1 (Frankfurt am Main, Germany: Suhrkamp, 1977), pp. 375–95; here, p. 395.

34. Especially neuroaesthetics and evolutionary aesthetics have lately provided new methods and approaches. See Wolfgang Welsch, "Animal Aesthetics," *Contemporary*

Aesthetics (2004). Available at http://www.contempaesthetics.org/newvolume/pages/article.php?articleID=243 (accessed September 19, 2007).

35. This suggestion of a transdisciplinary structure for aesthetics might seem too radical. However, in my view, almost every discipline today requires such a structure. This has been driven by fundamental changes in our understanding of the structure of rationalities, which legitimately demand alterations in the design of research fields and research objects. It has become obvious that diverse rationalities cannot clearly be delimited because they exhibit in their core entanglements and transitions that undercut traditional departmentalizations. See Wolfgang Welsch, *Vernunft. Die zeitgenössische Vernunftkritik und das Konzept der transversalen Vernunft* (1995; repr., Frankfurt am Main, Germany: Suhrkamp, 2007).

36. Consider, for example, the founding of the Asian Society for Aesthetics in 2001 and the increased number of publications on intercultural aesthetics in the West, such as R. Elberfeld and G. Wohlfart, ed., *Komparative Ästhetik* (Cologne: Edition Chora, 2000); G. Marchianò and R. Milani, ed., *Frontiers of Transculturality in Contemporary Aesthetics* (Turin, Italy: Trauben, 2001); K. Higgins, "Comparative Aesthetics," in *The Oxford Handbook of Aesthetics*, ed. Jerrold Levinson (Oxford: Oxford University Press, 2003), pp. 679–92; Crispin Sartwell, *Six Names of Beauty* (New York: Routledge, 2004). The theme of the 2007 congress of the International Association for Aesthetics in Ankara, Turkey, was "Aesthetics Bridging Cultures."

Chapter 13

1. Immanuel Kant, *Kritik der Reinen Vernunft*, ed. Raymund Schmidt (Hamburg, Germany: Felix Meiner Verlag, 1976). Page citations in the text follow the standard A and B Edition paginations. Translations from the German are mine.

2. Immanuel Kant, *Kritik der Urteilskraft*, ed. Karl Vorländer (Hamburg: Felix Meiner Verlag, 1974).

3. *Samkhya Karika of Isvara Krsna*, trans. Swami Virupakshananda (Madras, India: Sri Ramakrishna Math, 1995). A particularly faithful appropriation into Yoga psychology can be found in *Yoga Philosophy of Patanjali*, trans. [from Sanskrit] Swami Hariharananda Aranya and [into English] P. N. Mukerji (Albany: State University of New York Press, 1983). For a more reader-friendly but less rigorous approach see *Yogasutra of Patanjali with the Commentary of Vyasa*, trans. Bangali Baba (Delhi: Motilal Banarsidass, 1982). Two very friendly popularizations are *How to Know God: The Yoga Aphorisms of Patanjali*, trans. Swami Prabhavananda and Christopher Isherwood (New York: Mentor, 1969); and *Yoga, Discipline of Freedom: The Yoga Sutra Attributed to Patanjali*, trans. Barbara Stoler Miller (Los Angeles: University of California Press, 1995).

4. See my detailed dicussion of Kant's notion of concepts as functions in Adrian Piper, "Kant on the Objectivity of the Moral Law," in *Reclaiming the History of Ethics: Essays for John Rawls*, ed., Andrews Reath, Barbara Herman, and Christine M. Korsgaard (New York: Cambridge University Press, 1997), pp. 240–69. Also see Adrian Piper,

Kant's Metaethics: First Critique Foundations (in process), from which both this chapter and the present discussion are excerpted.

5. I discuss the logical status of Kant's categories and the distinction between transcendental and empirical concepts at greater length in Adrian Piper, "Xenophobia and Kantian Rationalism," *Philosophical Forum XXIV*, 1–3 (1992–1993): 188–232. Reprinted in Robin May Schott, ed., *Feminist Interpretations of Immanuel Kant* (University Park: Pennsylvania State University Press, 1997), pp. 21–73; and in John P. Pittman, ed., *African-American Perspectives and Philosophical Traditions* (New York: Routledge, 1997).

Chapter 14

1. The following section first appeared, in a different form, as "The Obscene Body/Politic" *Art Journal* 50, no. 4 (1991): 28–35.

2. For current statistics check the Web site of the Child and Woman Abuse Study Unit, UK, at http://www.cwasu.org/ and the Web site for the U.S. Department of Justice at http://www.ojp.usdoj.gov/ (both accessed July 10, 2008).

3. Phrase adapted from book title. See Anaïs Nin, *A Spy in the House of Love* (Paris: British Book Centre, 1954).

4. From Carolee Schneemann, *More Than Meat Joy: Complete Performance Works and Selected Writings* (Kingston, NY: McPherson & Co., 1979, 1997).

5. By 2007 this proportion is utterly transformed. Overt sexuality, necrophilia, nudity, animal corpses, and outrageous images provide desired commodifications for glamorous and challenging investment values.

Chapter 15

1. Noam Chomsky, *Language and Thought* (Wakefield, RI: Moyer Bell, 1993), p. 35.

2. Justus Buchler, ed., *Philosophical Writings of Peirce*, ed. Justus Buchler (New York: Dover Publications, 1955), p. 62.

3. Bertrand Russell, *Problems of Philosophy* (Oxford: Oxford University Press, 1959), p. 76.

4. Immanuel Kant, *Critique of Judgment*, trans. Werner S. Pluhar (Indianapolis, IN: Hackett, 1987), p. lxxi.

5. Ibid., Ak. 265, p. 125.

6. Ibid., Ak. 268, p. 128.

7. Ludwig Wittgenstein, *Tractatus Logico-Philosophicus*, trans. D. F. Pears and B. F. McGuinnes (London: Routledge & Kegan Paul, 1961), p. 147.

8. See Donald Davidson, "Reality Without Reference," in *Truth and Interpretation*, ed. Donald Davidson (Oxford: Blackwell, 1984), pp. 215–24.

9. Chomsky, *Language and Thought*, p. 22.

10. Ibid., p. 23.

11. David Hume, *A Treatise of Human Nature*, ed. P.H. Nidditch and L.A. Selby-Bigge (Oxford: Oxford University Press, 1978).

12. Immanuel Kant, *A Critique of Pure Reason,* trans. Norman Kemp Smith (New York: Modern Library, 1958), pp. 110–11 (A 141/B 180f).

13. Michael Dummett, *Origins of Analytic Philosophy* (Cambridge, MA: Harvard University Press, 1994), p. 15.

14. Ludwig Wittgenstein, *Philosophical Investigations* (New York: MacMillan, 1953).

15. Kenneth Surin, "Getting the Picture: Donald Davidson on Robert Morris's Blind Time Drawings IV (Drawing with Davidson)," *South Atlantic Quarterly* 101, no. 1 (2002): 164.

16. Donald Davidson, "A Nice Arrangement of Epitaphs," *Truth and Interpretation,* ed. Ernest LePore (New York: Blackwell, 1986), pp. 433–36.

17. See T. J. Clark's brilliant remarks on cubism in his *Farewell to an Idea* (New Haven, CT: Yale University Press, 1999), p. 187, and throughout chapt. 4.

18. Colin M. Turnbull, *The Forest People* (New York: Simon & Schuster, 1961), p. 75.

19. Dialogue between Marcel Duchamp, William Rubin, and Alfred Barris is cited from memory of a 1964 panel discussion at the Museum of Modern Art in New York City.

20. Thierry de Duve, *Kant After Duchamp* (Cambridge, MA: MIT Press, 1998).

21. One only need recall Filippo Marinetti's and fascism's glorification of war, which, as Walter Benjamin has reminded us, "can experience its own destruction as an aesthetic pleasure of the first order." See Walter Benjamin, "The Work of Art in the Age of Mechanical Reproduction," in *Illuminations,* trans. H. Zohn, intro. Hannah Arendt (New York: Schocken Books, 1969), p. 242.

22. Robert Morris, "From a Chomskian Couch: The Imperialistic Unconscious," *Critical Inquiry* 29 (Summer 2003): 683.

23. I had thought Eric Hobsbawm had made this remark, but my search through his work did not turn up the quote. It is possible that I've imagined he said it.

24. Cf. Wittgenstein, *Philosophical Investigations.*

25. Jonathan Crary, *Techniques of the Observer: On Vision and Modernity in the Nineteenth Century* (Cambridge, MA: The MIT Press, 1990).

26. See W.J.T. Mitchell, "The Pictorial Turn," in *Picture Theory* (Chicago: Chicago University Press, 1994), pp. 11–34.

27. Eric Hobsbawm, *The Age of Extremes* (New York: Vintage, 1994), p. 513.

28. Ibid., p. 513.

29. Ibid., p. 520.

30. See Arthur Danto, "The End of Art," in *The Philosophical Disenfranchisement of Art* (New York: Columbia University Press, 1986), pp. 81–115. Hegel's philosophy of history did of course greatly influence political theory. But most of Hegel's doctrines are patently false. See Bertrand Russell's satirical remarks on Hegel's notions of the "whole" in *A History of Western Philosophy* (New York: Simon & Schuster, 1945), pp. 732–33.

31. See Nelson Goodman, *Languages of Art* (Indianapolis, IN: Hackett, 1976); and W.J.T. Mitchell's incisive analysis of Goodman's thought in W.J.T. Mitchell, *Iconology*

(Chicago: Chicago University Press, 1986), pp. 63–74. I stray from Mitchell's critique of Goodman's formalism in my remarks here.

32. Mitchell, *Iconology*, p. 69.

33. What may never be made clear by cognitive science is how the interface between the visual and verbal operates, not only in terms of the seamless connection that facilitates the interchange between what is seen and said, but the complex and endless conflict between the one and the other. "Reading" is of course the wrong word for this processing of the visual. The fact that it is in play indicates a lag in theorizing the complexities of what Mitchell has called the "pictorial turn."

34. Already Richard Wolin notes how Walter Benjamin (writing "On Some Motifs in Baudelaire" in the late 1930s) "laments the fact that in the modern world the powers of consciousness must be enhanced as a defense against the shocks of everyday life (a problem that is especially acute in the modern metropolis, the locus classicus of shock experience). As a result of this need for constantly vigilant consciousness, our natural and spontaneous capacities for experience are necessarily diminished." Richard Wolin, *Labyrinths* (Amherst: University of Massachusetts Press, 1995), p. 68.

35. See Michel Foucault's remarks on *Las Meninas*, which open his book, *The Order of Things* (New York: Vintage, 1973), pp. 3–6; his remarks unpack the Velazquez by subjecting its surface to an inch by inch analysis. There could be no more relentless pursuit of differences across an image. That its most every difference is a difference in relation to a standard, "classical" space that stands outside the work's representations speaks not only to Velazquez's historical moment before representation had swallowed the world, but to that of Foucault's, when the perception of such densities was still available.

36. See John Dewey, *Art and Experience* (New York: Perigree, 1934).

37. See Morris, "From a Chomskian Couch," for a development of this argument.

38. Stanley Cavell, *In Quest of the Ordinary* (Chicago: University of Chicago, 1998), p. 84.

39. Here da Vinci takes the other side, valorizing the visual over the verbal: "If you, poet, describe the figure of some deities, the writing will not be held in the same veneration as the painted deity, because bows and various prayers will continually be made to the painting. To it will throng many generations from many provinces and from over the eastern seas, and they will demand help from the painting and not from what is written." Leonardo da Vinci, *Treatise on Painting*, trans. A. Philip McMahon, introd. Ludwig H. Heydenreich. (Princeton, NJ: Princeton University Press, 1956), p. 22.

Chapter 16

1. Nicolas Bourriaud, *Relational Aesthetics* (Dijon, France: Presses du Réel, 1998), p. 14.

2. As the art historian Grant Kester observes, art is uniquely placed to counter a world in which "we are reduced to an atomized pseudo-community of consumers, our sensibilities dulled by spectacle and repetition." From Grant Kester, *Conversation Pieces: Community and Communication in Modern Art* (Berkeley: University of California Press,

2004), p. 29. This trope is also found in Bourriaud: "art is the place that produces a spe-cific sociability" because "it *tightens the space of relations*, unlike TV." From Bourriaud, *Relational Aesthetics*, p. 18.

3. Jeanne van Heeswijk, "Fleeting Images of Community," http://www.jeanneworks .net (accessed April 25, 2008).

4. Kester, *Conversation Pieces*, p. 112.

5. See Andrew Brighton, "Consumed by the Political: The Ruination of the Arts Council," *Critical Quarterly* 48, no. 1 (2006): 4.

6. See Ruth Levitas, *The Inclusive Society? Social Exclusion and New Labour* (Basing-stoke, UK: MacMillan, 1998).

7. Charles Esche, "Superhighrise: Community, Technology, Self-Organisation," http://www.superflex.net/text/articles/superhighrise.shtml (accessed April 25, 2008).

8. François Matarasso, *Use or Ornament? The Social Impact of Participation in the Arts* (London: Comedia, 1997).

9. Paola Merli, "Evaluating the Social Impact of Participation in Arts Activities," *International Journal of Cultural Policy* 8, no. 1 (2002): 107–18.

10. Reinaldo Laddaga, "From Forcing to Gathering: On Liisa Robert's 'What's the Time in Vyborg?'" unpublished manuscript, p. 1. *What's the Time in Vyborg?* (2001–2005) comprised a series of workshops, exhibitions, performances, films, and events carried out around the still-ongoing restoration of the city library that Alvar Aalto designed and built in 1939.

11. For a full list of projects, see http://www.odaprojesi.org.

12. Oda Projesi in Claire Bishop, "What We Made Together," *Untitled* 33 (Spring 2005): 22.

13. Maria Lind, "Actualisation of Space," in Claire Doherty, *Contemporary Art: From Studio to Situation* (London: Black Dog, 2004), pp. 109–21.

14. Lind, "Actualisation of Space," pp. 114–15.

15. Lucy Lippard, *The Lure of the Local* (New York: The New Press, 1998), pp. 286–90.

16. Erik Hagoort, *Good Intentions: Judging the Art of Encounter* (Amsterdam: Nether-lands Foundation for Visual Arts, Design and Architecture, 2005), pp. 54–55.

17. Kester, *Conversation Pieces*, p. 24.

18. Ibid., p. 150.

19. Peter Dews, "Uncategorical Imperatives: Adorno, Badiou and the Ethical Turn," *Radical Philosophy* 111 (Jan/Feb 2002): 33.

20. See Alain Badiou, *Ethics: An Essay on the Understanding of Evil* (London: Verso, 2001); Slavoj Žižek, "Multiculturalism, or, the Cultural Logic of Multinational Capital-ism," *New Left Review* (Sept-Oct 1997); and Slavoj Žižek, "Against Human Rights," *New Left Review* 34 (Jul–Aug 2005): 115–31. See also Jacques Rancière, *Hatred of Democracy* (London: Verso, 2006).

21. Gillian Rose, "Social Utopianism—Architectural Illusion," in *The Broken Middle* (Oxford: Blackwell, 1992), p. 306.

22. As a consequence, the participants of collaborative art seem always to be vulnerable creatures, constantly at risk of being misunderstood or exploited.

23. Art has a "relatively autonomous position, which provides a sanctuary where new things can emerge," writes Jeanne van Heeswijk. From Jeanne van Heeswijk, "Fleeting Images of Community," http://www.jeanneworks.net (accessed April 25, 2008). "The world of culture is *the only space left* for me to do what I can do, there's nothing else," says the Chilean artist Alfredo Jaar. From Alfredo Jaar, unpublished interview with the author, May 9, 2005.

24. See Jörg Heiser, "False Alternatives: Critique and Hedonism in the Art of the 1990s," in *Zusammenhänge herstellen/Contextualise* (Hamburger: Kunstverein/Cologne: DuMont, 2003), p. 171.

25. Jacques Rancière, "The Aesthetic Revolution and Its Outcomes," *New Left Review* 14 (March–April 2002): 133–51; and Jacques Rancière, *The Politics of Aesthetics* (London: Continuum, 2004).

26. Jacques Rancière, "The Emancipated Spectator," *Artforum* (March 2007): 271–80.

27. "On the one hand, the futurist and constructivist dream of art's self-suppression in the formation of a new sensible world; on the other hand, the fight to preserve the autonomy of art from all forms of aestheticization of business and power; to preserve it not only as the pure pleasure of art for art's sake but, on the contrary, as an inscription of the unresolved contradiction between the aesthetic promise and the reality of a world of oppression." From Jacques Rancière, *Malaise dans l'Esthétique* (Paris: Editions Galilée, 2004), p. 169; author's translation.

28. Ibid., p. 66.

29. Rancière, *The Politics of Aesthetics,* p. 63.

30. Rancière, *Malaise dans l'Esthétique,* p. 67.

31. See David Callaghan, "Still Signaling Through the Flames: The Living Theatre's Use of Audience Participation in the 1990s," in *Audience Participation: Essays on Inclusion in Performance,* ed. Susan Kattwinkel (Connecticut: Praeger, 2003), pp. 23–36.

32. Rancière suggests that the exemplary ethical gesture is a strategic obfuscation of the political and the aesthetic: "By replacing matters of class conflict by matters of inclusion and exclusion, [contemporary art] puts worries about the 'loss of the social bond,' concerns with 'bare humanity' or tasks of empowering threatened identities in the place of political concerns. Art is summoned thus to put its political potentials at work in reframing a sense of community, mending the social bond, etc. Once more, politics and aesthetics vanish together in Ethics." From Rancière, *The Politics of Aesthetics,* http://theater.kein.org/node/99 (accessed June 21, 2007).

33. This view of performance has been most influentially advanced by Peggy Phelan in *Unmarked: The Politics of Performance* (London: Routledge, 1993).

34. See for example Philip Auslander, *Liveness: Performances in a Mediatised Culture* (London: Routledge, 1999).

35. "The less the dramaturge knows what the spectators must do as a collective, the more he knows that they *must* become a collective, turn their mere agglomeration into

the community that they virtually are." From Rancière, "The Emancipated Spectator," pp. 277–78.

36. See Rancière, interview with François Ewald, "Qu'est-ce que la classe ouvrière?" in *Magazine Littéraire* 175 (Jul–Aug 1981), which is cited in Kristin Ross's introduction to Jacques Rancière, *The Ignorant Schoolmaster: Five Lessons in Intellectual Emancipation* (Stanford, CA: Stanford University Press, 1991), p. xviii.

37. Jacques Rancière, *The Philosopher and His Poor* (Durham, NC: Duke University Press, 2003), p. 188.

38. Rancière, *The Philosopher and His Poor*, p. 189.

39. In Rancière's system, the aesthetic regime of art is preceded by two other regimes. The first is an "ethical regime of images," which is governed by the twofold question of the truth-content of images and the uses to which they are put—in other words, their effects and ends. Central to this regime is Plato's denigration of mimesis. The second is the "representative regime of the arts," a regime of visibility by which the fine arts are classified according to a logic of what can be done and made in each art, a logic that corresponds to the overall hierarchy of social and political occupations. This regime is essentially Aristotelian but stretches to the academy system of the fine arts and its hierarchy of the genres. The aesthetic regime of art, ushered in with the Enlightenment, continues today.

40. Rancière, "The Aesthetic Revolution and Its Outcomes," p. 150.

Chapter 17

I would like to thank Tony O'Connor, Francis Halsall, and Julia Jansen for organizing the 2004 "(Re)Discovering Aesthetics" conference at University College, Cork, Ireland. I would also like to thank the hosts and audiences at the University of Delaware (Art History), Vanderbilt University (Philosophy), and the University of California at Santa Cruz (Art History) where I presented earlier versions of this chapter.

1. Gerhard Richter, *The Daily Practice of Painting: Writings and Interviews 1962–1993*, ed. Hans-Ulrich Obrist, trans. David Britt (London: Anthony d'Offray Gallery308/ Cambridge, MA: MIT Press, 1995), pp. 163, 202.

2. I prefer to speak of a "regeneration" of aesthetics because rediscovery may sound like a restoration of the status quo ante. By contrast, it is crucial to recognize that aesthetics is in need of regeneration because it has been subjected to severe, sometimes justified, modernist and postmodernist critiques motivated by a host of philosophical, political, cultural, and other concerns that have been well documented elsewhere.

3. I also think it is important to emphasize that aesthetics (critical thinking about art, culture, and nature) involves much more than beauty, and that beauty itself is much more than its critics have typically taken it to be. The four-volume *Encyclopedia of Aesthetics,* ed. Michael Kelly (New York: Oxford University Press, 1998) amply documents that the history of aesthetics involves many more issues than beauty. For compelling and varied accounts of the roles and purposes of beauty in modern and contemporary art, see

the recent works of Arthur C. Danto, Umberto Eco, Paul Guyer, Alexander Nehamas, Elizabeth Prettejohn, Elaine Scarry, and Wendy Steiner.

4. Many would discount Richter's (or any artist's) writings about his work on the grounds that they are self-serving or misleading, that the artist's intentions are not to be privileged, or, stronger, that the artist (as author) is dead. By contrast, I think artists' writings are part of a larger body of evidence that we need to consult when we try to understand any art. More than evidence to be taken up by a philosopher or theorist, the artist's words are philosophical. As Gilles Deleuze says about directors who also write about cinema (e.g., Jean-Luc Godard), painters talking about painting "become something else, they become philosophers or theoreticians" and, in that role, they "talk best about what they do," which is why he asserts in his book on Francis Bacon that "we do not listen enough to what painters say." From Gilles Deleuze, *Cinema 2: The Time-Image*, trans. Hugh Tomlinson and Robert Galeta (Minneapolis: University of Minnesota Press, 1989), p. 280; and Constantin V. Boundas, ed., *The Deleuze Reader* (New York: Columbia University Press, 1993), p. 193.

5. For a clear example of an anti-aesthetic interpretation of Richter's work, see Benjamin Buchloh's 1986 interview with Richter, reprinted in Richter, *The Daily Practice of Painting*, pp. 132–65.

6. For images of the Baader-Meinhof series, please search Google images or consult the Robert Storr book cited in footnote 30 below. For a history of the Baader-Meinhof Group, see the video *Germany in Autumn [Deutschland im Herbst]* by Heinrich von Böll et al. (1978; Los Angeles: World Artists Home Video, 1994). See also Jeremy Varon, *Bringing the War Home: The Weather Underground, the Red Army Faction, and Revolutionary Violence in the Sixties and Seventies* (Berkeley: University of California Press, 2004). Later generations of the Baader-Meinhof Group were active as late as 1998, although the last major event was in 1991 at the U.S. Embassy in Bonn during the first Iraq War. According to Varon, forty-three people had been killed in connection with the Baader-Meinhof violence by late 1978: Twenty-eight were victims and fifteen were group members. From Varon, *Bringing the War Home*, p. 198.

7. Astrid Proll left the RAF in 1971; she went to England, where she was captured and extradited in 1978 and imprisoned until 1988.

8. "I was unable to look at [the pictures of dead comrades] for many years." From Astrid Proll, ed., *Baader-Meinhof/Pictures on the Run 67–77* (New York: Scalo, 1998), p. 7.

9. Richter, *The Daily Practice of Painting*, p. 207.

10. Ibid., p. 11.

11. Ibid., p. 189; emphasis added.

12. Ibid., p. 203. Richter does say, however, that when he started the *Baader-Meinhof* series he envisioned something that had more to do with "the subjects' lives." From Ibid., p. 209. His focus and aim changed as he worked on the paintings, for reasons he does not explain.

13. Ibid., p. 200.

14. Ibid., p. 205.

15. Although the Vietnam War was over by 1977, the other issues taken up by the Baader-Meinhof Group, which were more particular to West Germany—such as the Nazi backgrounds of some business and political leaders and questions of social and economic justice—proved to be more intractable.

16. Ibid., p. 74.

17. Ibid., p. 173; emphasis added.

18. Ibid., p. 74.

19. Ibid., pp. 174, 175, 189, 190, 200.

20. Ibid., p. 190; see also p. 200.

21. John Dewey, *Art as Experience* (New York: Penguin Putnam, 1934), p. 91.

22. Richter, *The Daily Practice of Painting*, p. 84; emphasis added.

23. Ibid., p. 92.

24. Ibid., pp. 174, 198, 205.

25. Ibid., pp. 197–98.

26. Ibid., p. 37.

27. Gertrud Koch, "The Richter Scale of Blur," *October* 62 (Fall 1992): 133–42; here, p. 142.

28. This reaction is evident in the comments made by some critics of the *Baader-Meinhof* series. For example, Hilton Kramer accused Richter of making heroes or martyrs out of the terrorists, as if he were promoting the cause of the Baader-Meinhof Group. Hilton Kramer, "Telling Stories, Denying Style: Reflections on MoMA 2000," *New Criterion* 19, no. 5 (January 2001): 4. But I presume these same critics would never say that the *photographs* of the Baader-Meinhof deaths made heroes out of the group. So what explains the alleged celebratory effect of Richter *paintings*, especially given the blurring issue?

29. Koch, "The Richter Scale of Blur," p. 142.

30. Several critics and historians interpret Richter's *Baader-Meinhof* paintings as history paintings. See, for example, Benjamin Buchloh's ; and Robert Storr's *Gerhard Richter: October 18, 1977* (New York: Museum of Modern Art, 2000). But this type of interpretation seems to distance Richter's paintings from the contemporary political experience they are trying to render bearable and intelligible.

31. Evidence of the contemporaneity of the Baader-Meinhof Group is the controversy that erupted in February 2007 when the German court decided to release Brigitte Mohnhaupt, one of the Baader-Meinhof members who has served twenty-four years in prison for her involvement in several murders. (She was imprisoned in the 1970s but released in 1977, only to become the leader for about seven years before returning to prison.)

32. See Storr, *Gerhard Richter: October 18, 1977*.

33. Richter, *The Daily Practice of Painting*, p. 226.

34. Ibid., pp. 189–90.

35. Ibid., p. 74.

36. Gregg Horowitz, *Sustaining Loss: Art and Mournful Life* (Stanford, CA: Stanford University Press, 2001), pp. 141 and 156.

37. Quoted in Storr, *Gerhard Richter: October 18, 1977*, p. 140. For his part, Storr claims that "in photographs we can see death with a nakedness no other medium affords. But photography does not allow us to *contemplate* death." From Storr, p. 242; emphasis added.

38. Roland Barthes, *Camera Lucida: Reflections on Photography*, trans. Richard Howard (New York: Farrar Strauss & Giroux, 1981), pp. 34 and 85.

39. Desa Philippi, "Moments of Interpretation," *October* 62 (Fall 1992): 115–22; here, p. 122.

40. Rainer Rochlitz, " 'Where We Have Got To,' " in Rainer Rochlitz, Benjamin Buchloh, Jean-Francois Chevrier, and Armin Zweite, *Photography and Painting in the Work of Gerhard Richter: Four Essays on Atlas* (Catalan: Museu d'Art Contemporanani de Barcelona, 2000), pp. 103–25; here, p. 120, emphasis added.

41. Varon, *Bringing the War Home*, p. 254.

42. Ibid., p. 263.

43. Quoted in Storr, *Gerhard Richter: Doubt and Belief in Painting* (New York: Museum of Modern Art, 2003), p. 56.

Index

The authorized representative in the EU for product safety and compliance is:
Mare Nostrum Group
B.V Doelen 72
4831 GR Breda
The Netherlands

www.ingramcontent.com/pod-product-compliance
Lightning Source LLC
Chambersburg PA
CBHW020854180526
45163CB00007B/2495

*9 7 8 0 8 0 4 7 5 9 9 1 5 *